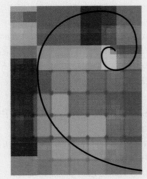

# THE READING-WRITING CONNECTION

## JOHN LANGAN

ATLANTIC CAPE COMMUNITY COLLEGE

*INSTRUCTOR'S EDITION*

**Books in the Townsend Press Reading Series:**

*Groundwork for College Reading with Phonics*
*Groundwork for College Reading*
*Ten Steps to Building College Reading Skills*
*Ten Steps to Improving College Reading Skills*
*Ten Steps to Advancing College Reading Skills*
*Ten Steps to Advanced Reading*

**Books in the Townsend Press Vocabulary Series:**

*Vocabulary Basics*
*Groundwork for a Better Vocabulary*
*Building Vocabulary Skills*
*Building Vocabulary Skills, Short Version*
*Improving Vocabulary Skills*
*Improving Vocabulary Skills, Short Version*
*Advancing Vocabulary Skills*
*Advancing Vocabulary Skills, Short Version*
*Advanced Word Power*

**Supplements Available for Most Books:**

Instructor's Edition
Instructor's Manual and Test Bank
Online Exercises
PowerPoint Slides

Copyright © 2013 by Townsend Press, Inc.
Printed in the United States of America
9  8  7  6  5  4  3  2  1

ISBN (Student Edition): 978-1-59194-301-3
ISBN (Instructor's Edition): 978-1-59194-302-0

**Send book orders and requests for desk copies or supplements to:**
**Townsend Press Book Center**
**439 Kelley Drive**
**West Berlin, New Jersey  08091**

**For even faster service, contact us in any of the following ways:**
**By telephone: 1-800-772-6410**
**By fax: 1-800-225-8894**
**By e-mail: cs@townsendpress.com**
**Through our website: www.townsendpress.com**

# Contents

# Part Two

# Preface: To the Instructor

Have you, as a reading and/or writing instructor, asked yourself these questions:

- Is there a book that will help me teach both essential reading and essential writing skills?

- Is there a book that will clearly explain the connection between effective reading and effective writing?

- Is there a book that will provide selections that students will *want* to read and topics that students will *want* to write about?

If you've asked any of the above questions, *The Reading-Writing Connection* may be the book for you. Suitable for combined reading and writing classes, the book teaches students, in a step-by-step way, the skills needed to think, read, and write with clarity.

In **Part One** of the book, an opening chapter concerns the vocabulary development needed by both readers and writers. Chapters on main ideas and supporting details in reading are then followed by a chapter on main ideas and supporting details in writing. After a chapter describing the steps in the writing process, chapters on relationships in reading are followed by chapters on relationships in writing. A chapter is devoted to inferences in reading and writing, and a final chapter helps students make the transition from reading and writing paragraphs to reading and writing longer selections and essays.

**Part Two** of the book provides fifteen high-appeal selections for extended systematic practice in thinking, reading, and writing.

## Other Features of the Book

**Emphasis on clear thinking.** A basic truth at the heart of both the reading process and the writing process is that any thoughtful communication of ideas has two basic parts: (1) a point is made and (2) that point is supported. As students work their way through this book, they will learn to apply the principle of point and support. They are encouraged when *reading* an essay to look for a central idea as well as for the reasons, examples, and other details that support that idea. They are reminded when *writing* to follow the same basic principle—to make a point and then provide support for that point. And they discover that clear *thinking* involves both recognizing ideas and deciding whether there is solid support for those ideas.

**Frequent practice.** Abundant practice is essential to learning, so this book includes numerous reading and writing activities. Each of the fifteen readings that make up Part Two is accompanied by this sequence of activities:

● **First Impressions.** A freewriting activity titled "First Impressions" helps students think about what they have read. The first question in this activity is always "Did you enjoy reading this selection? Why or why not?" The second and third questions focus on particular issues raised by the essay—issues about which each student should have something to say. Students can respond to one, two, or all three of these questions at the beginning of a class session; or, alternatively, students can record their responses in a "reading journal."

  The "First Impressions" activity provides two added benefits. First, it lays the groundwork for oral participation; many more students can contribute intelligently to classroom discussion after they have collected their thoughts on paper in advance. Second, as an integral step in the writing process, freewriting can supply students with raw material for one or more of the paragraph and essay assignments that follow the selections.

● **Words to Watch and Vocabulary Check.** Challenging words and phrases in each selection are defined in the "Words to Watch" section that precedes each reading. Then a "Vocabulary Check" activity helps students sharpen their skill at deriving meanings from context.

● **Reading Check.** The "Reading Check" is a series of ten comprehension questions that involve four key reading skills: finding the central point and main ideas, recognizing supporting details, making inferences, and understanding the writer's craft. The craft questions include such elements as introduction and conclusion strategies, types of support, patterns of organization, tone, purpose, intended audience, and appropriate titles. As students sharpen these crucial reading skills, they will become better, more insightful readers—and they will be ready to use the same techniques in their own writing.

● **Discussion Questions.** Four discussion questions follow the Reading Check. These questions provide a final chance for students to deepen their understanding of an essay and the issues and values that it presents. They also serve as a helpful intermediate step between reading a selection and writing about it. As noted below, these discussion questions can be used as additional writing topics.

● **Paragraph Assignments and Essay Assignments.** Four writing topics—two paragraph assignments and two essay assignments—conclude the activities for each selection. Half of the assignments involve personal experience topics and an "I" point of view; the other half are "objective" topics that call for a third-person point of view. All the assignments emphasize the basic principle of clear communication: that a student make a clear point and effectively support that point.

**High interest level.** Dull and unvaried exercises, assignments, and readings work against learning. Students need to experience genuine interest in materials that they read and assignments that they write. Everything in the book, including the fifteen readings in Part Two, has been chosen not only for the appropriateness of its reading and writing levels but also for its compelling content.

**Ease of use.** The logical sequence in the chapters—from explanation to example to practice to mastery test—helps make the skills easier to teach.

**Integration of skills.** After learning the connections between reading and writing skills in Part One, students go on to apply the skills to the reading selections and writing assignments in Part Two. Through a great deal of practice in using reading and writing skills, they become effective readers and writers.

**Instructor's edition.** An *Instructor's Edition*—chances are that you are holding it in your hand—is identical to the student book except that it also provides answers to all the practices and tests, as well as comments on most answers.

**Online supplements.** PowerPoint presentations and online exercises are available in the Online Exercise Center at the Townsend Press website: **www.townsendpress.net**.

## Acknowledgments

Many educators have suggested over the years that I develop a book combining reading and writing skills instruction. I thank them for helping to steer me in this direction. And I am grateful as always to my colleagues at Townsend Press who have made the book a team effort: Kathyrn Bernstein, Bill Blauvelt, Denton Cairnes, Beth Johnson, Judith Nadell, Ruth A. Rouff, Barbara Solot, and Hal Taylor have all provided help along the way. I owe particular thanks to Janet M. Goldstein, who, from the time I started Townsend Press many years ago, has brought her extraordinary skills to almost every book the company has published. I have been fortunate to have by my side a colleague inspired by the same goals that have driven me: to help students learn by creating materials that are as clear and as human as possible. Janet, who is a great sports fan, would appreciate this line from Football Hall of Fame coach Vince Lombardi: "Perfection is not attainable, but if we chase perfection, we can catch excellence." Together, Janet and I have spent many years chasing perfection. I am grateful beyond words for her talents.

*John Langan*

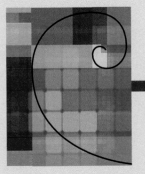

# Introduction

## The Core Reading and Writing Skills: Point and Support

Y ou may sense that reading and writing are vital skills—in school, on the job, and in life. That is in fact the case! And this book will do its best to help you become a better reader and a stronger writer.

To read and write well, you need to understand the difference between **point** and **support**. A **point** is an idea or an opinion. It is also called the **main idea**, and it is usually stated in one sentence. **Support** is the evidence that backs up the idea or opinion—the specific examples, reasons, facts, or other details that help prove the point. Here is a diagram that shows at a glance the two essential skills practiced by good readers and writers:

THE
HEART OF
CLEAR COMMUNICATION

*Good writers and speakers:*

1. Make a point
2. Support the point

*Good readers and listeners:*

1. Recognize the point
2. Recognize the support for the point

Following are three practice exercises that involve cartoons. Working through each exercise will give you a good sense of the difference between point and support.

## PRACTICE 1

Look at the following cartoon:

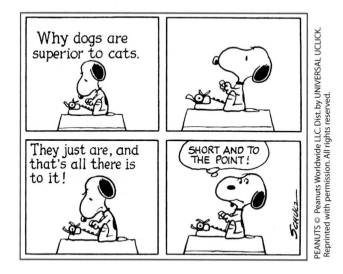

See if you can answer the following questions:

● What is Snoopy's **point** in his paper?

Your answer: His point is that _____

_____ dogs are superior to cats. _____

● What is his **support** for his point?

Your answer: _____ No support is provided. _____

_____

### Explanation

Snoopy's point, of course, is that dogs are superior to cats. But he offers no support whatsoever to back up his point! There are two jokes here. First, he is a dog and so is naturally going to believe that dogs are superior. The other joke is that his evidence ("They just are, and that's all there is to it!") is a lot of empty words. His somewhat guilty look in the last panel suggests that he knows he has not proved his point. To think and write effectively, you must provide **real support** for your points and opinions.

## PRACTICE 2

Here is another cartoon. Answer the questions below it, and then read the explanation.                    *Wording of answers may vary.*

**School was not going well.**

What is the **point** of the cartoon? (It's fairly obvious.) _____
_____
                    School was not going well.

What is the **support** for the point?   The student's grades: C in history,
D in math, F's in biology, English, and Spanish.
_____

The point is that "School was not going well." The support for the point is the specific list of low grades on the student's grade report.

**PRACTICE 3**

Here are three more cartoons. What is the point of each cartoon, and what is the support?

*Wording of answers may vary.*

**Point:** The dog had a really bad day.

**Support:** 1. Ball rolled under sofa

2. Water dish too warm

3. Squeaker in rubber pork chop broke

(Of course, the joke in this cartoon is that the dog's reasons don't seem important enough to cause stress . . . to a human, that is.)

**Point:** The couple's marriage has problems.

**Support:** **1.** He likes to spend money; she likes to save it.

**2.** He's a night person; she's a day person.

**3.** He likes sports; she hates them.

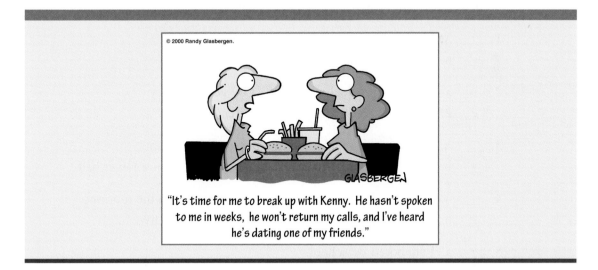

**Point:** It's time for the speaker to break up with Kenny.

**Support:** **1.** He hasn't spoken to her in weeks.

**2.** He won't return her calls.

**3.** He's dating one of her friends.

## More about Point and Support

Look at these two sentences:

_____ My brother's car is a Toyota.

__✓__ My brother's car is a lemon.

*To the Instructor:* For Practice 4, tell students that in each case, the point is the sentence they can ask "Why?" or "For example?" about. If more information is needed, then the sentence is a point that requires support. For example: Why do you think you're getting the flu? What are different ways people deal with conflict?

One of these sentences could be the point, or main idea, of a paragraph, with reasons and details to support the point. The other sentence does not express an idea or opinion. It is just a fact that does not call for any support. Put a check (✓) next to the sentence that is a point. Then read the explanation below.

"My brother's car is a Toyota" is just a fact. It does not need any support. On the other hand, "My brother's car is a lemon" expresses a point or opinion that needs support. As a reader, you should expect to see specific reasons or examples or details showing exactly what is wrong with the car. As a writer, you would be expected to provide the same kind of specific support to explain why you think the car is a lemon.

**Here in a nutshell is what effective reading and writing are about: a point (main idea) followed by solid support for that point.**

## PRACTICE 4

Put a check (✓) in front of the point (it can also be called the *main idea* or *opinion* or *topic sentence*) in each pair of sentences below.

1. _____ A. I have a fever of 102.

    __✓__ B. I must be getting the flu.

2. _____ A. Some people deal with conflict by getting angry.

    __✓__ B. People deal with conflict in different ways.

3. _____ A. Last summer I had a job in a fast-food restaurant.

    __✓__ B. Working in a fast-food restaurant is the worst job I ever had.

4. _____ A. There is often no hot water in the apartment in the morning.

    __✓__ B. The apartment is not a good place in which to live.

5. _____ A. I am bored by school.

    __✓__ B. There are reasons why school bores me.

6. _____ A. People often use their cell phones while driving.

    __✓__ B. Some people have dangerous driving habits.

7. _✓_ A. My sister is an ambitious woman.

_____ B. My sister works two jobs during the day and then goes to school at night.

8. _____ A. It rained every day during our vacation.

_✓_ B. Our vacation turned out to be a disaster.

9. _✓_ A. The monster movie was poorly made.

_____ B. The movie monster was just a spider that had been filmed through a magnifying lens.

10. _✓_ A. There are many problems in our schools.

_____ B. Children who are troublemakers can prevent other students from learning in class.

## Supporting a Point

Look at the following point:

Point: **You should not put your hand into that box.**

This statement hardly stops us from putting our hand in the box. "Why do you say that?" we would probably ask. "Give your reasons." Support is needed so that we can decide for ourselves whether a good point has been made. Suppose the point is followed by these three reasons:

**1** A flesh-eating spider the size of a large crab just crawled into the box.

**2** Inside the box are freshly cut leaves of poison ivy.

**3** A loaded mousetrap is inside, ready to spring.

As you will surely agree, the details do provide solid support for the point. They give us a basis for understanding and agreeing with the point. After seeing these details, we probably won't be putting a hand anywhere near the box.

**PRACTICE 5**

Following are groups of four sentences. In each case, one sentence is the point or main idea, and the other three sentences are details that support and develop this idea. Put a check (✓) in front of the point or idea in each group.

1. ___ A. The burgers are full of gristle.

   ___ B. The roast beef sandwiches have a chemical taste.

   ✓ C. The Beef and Burger Shop is a poor fast-food restaurant.

   ___ D. The french fries are lukewarm and soggy.
   
   Three reasons the Beef and Burger Shop is a poor restaurant are listed.

2. ✓ A. My little brother is really getting into the spirit of Halloween.

   ___ B. Today I found a plastic spider in my soup.

   ___ C. Last night there was a bloody rubber hand on my pillow.

   ___ D. This morning a cardboard tombstone with my name on it appeared in the backyard.   Sentences B, C, and D are three examples of the Halloween spirit.

3. ___ A. Spanking teaches physical violence.

   ✓ B. Spanking is a bad idea.

   ___ C. Spanking often has more to do with the parent's lack of self-discipline than the child.   Sentences A, C, and D are three reasons spanking is a bad idea.

   ___ D. Many studies have shown that spanking does not work.

4. ✓ A. The neighborhood park is not a safe place to play.

   ___ B. Large stray dogs often roam the park.   Sentences B, C, and D are three

   ___ C. Gangs hang out in the park.   reasons the park isn't a safe place to play.

   ___ D. Broken glass litters the ground of the playing fields.

5. ___ A. When you are in a theater, you sometimes have to put up with rude people and crying children.

   ___ B. At home, you can "pause" a movie when you want to leave the room.

   ✓ C. It's more fun to watch movies at home than in a theater.

   ___ D. It's great to watch movies in your pajamas while sitting in your favorite chair.   Three reasons it's more fun to watch movies at home are listed.

6. ✓ A. My family is difficult to cook for.

   ___ B. My father is a vegetarian.

   ___ C. My grandmother, who lives with us, can't digest certain vegetables.

   ___ D. One of my brothers is allergic to milk, wheat, and eggs.
   
   Sentences B, C, and D are three examples of family members it's difficult to cook for.

7.  ___ A. Credit cards have high interest rates.

    ✓ B. People should try not to use credit cards.

    ___ C. Credit cards encourage people to spend more money than they have.

    ___ D. Many credit cards charge yearly fees in addition to monthly interest.

8.  ___ A. Students can type and print out reports on a computer.

    ___ B. The Internet provides an endless supply of information for research papers.

    ✓ C. Computers have made it easier for students to do their work.

    ___ D. A computer can be used to take a class at home.

9.  ✓ A. English was an extremely hard course this year.

    ___ B. I had to do at least three hours of homework for every hour I was in class.

    ___ C. The teacher called on students without warning and deducted points when they didn't know an answer.

    ___ D. I had to write five essays, give three oral reports, and take two major exams.

10. ___ A. Three times a week, I was the last or next-to-last one chosen by team captains.

    ___ B. I was the one who couldn't run a relay race without falling down and throwing up.

    ___ C. I was always the one assigned to stand in right field, where baseballs were seldom hit.

    ✓ D. Physical education class was a nightmare for me, reinforcing the image I had of myself as a klutz.

**Item 7:** Three reasons not to use credit cards are listed.

**Item 8:** Sentences A, B, and D list three ways computers have made students' lives easier.

**Item 9:** Sentences B, C, and D are three reasons English was such a hard course this year.

**Item 10:** Sentences A, B, and C give three reasons physical education was a nightmare for the speaker.

# Other Important Reading and Writing Skills

This book will help you practice and master the two essential reading and writing skills: identifying and providing main ideas and supporting details. The book will also cover other skills that are central to effective reading and writing: developing a good vocabulary, understanding relationships, making inferences, and appreciating the writer's craft.

Here is the sequence of chapters:

**Part One**
Reading and Writing Skills
1 Vocabulary Development for Reading and Writing
2 Main Ideas in Reading
3 Supporting Details in Reading
4 Main Ideas and Supporting Details in Writing
5 Understanding the Writing Process
6 Relationships in Reading
7 Relationships in Writing
8 More Relationships in Reading
9 More Relationships in Writing
10 Inferences in Reading and Writing
11 Longer Selections in Reading and Writing

**Part Two**
Fifteen Selections for Readers and Writers
1 The Yellow Ribbon
2 Adult Children at Home
3 Rowing the Bus
4 All Washed Up?
5 The Scholarship Jacket
6 Taming the Anger Monster
7 All the Good Things
8 Shame
9 "Extra Large, Please"
10 A Change of Attitude
11 Abusive Relationships among the Young
12 A Door Swings Open
13 A Drunken Ride, A Tragic Aftermath
14 Migrant Child to College Woman
15 Students in Shock

# Part One

## Reading and Writing Skills

# 1 Vocabulary Development for Reading and Writing

Improving your vocabulary will make you a better reader and a better writer. It would be nice if there were pills available for this purpose—with each pill automatically adding, say, a hundred words to your vocabulary! But while there is no instant cure for an underdeveloped vocabulary, there are steps you can take to build word power.

Most of all, you need to **read more**. It's a proven fact that the more you read, the more words you will learn. (To choose from over a hundred interesting paperbacks that are available at a non-profit price of $1 per book, visit **www.townsendpress.com** and click on "TP Library & Bluford Series.")

In addition to reading more, you should learn how to understand **vocabulary in context** to figure out the meanings of unfamiliar words. This chapter will show you how to use different kinds of context clues in your reading.

Do you know the meaning of the word *savor*? Look at the following cartoon and see if the sentences underneath (spoken by the older brother) help you choose the correct answer.

GLASBERGEN

© Randy Glasbergen.
www.glasbergen.com

"Eat it slowly so you can SAVOR the taste. If you eat it too fast, you won't fully appreciate the flavor."

___A___ *Savor* (sā′vər) means
A. enjoy.
B. wonder about.
C. forget.

The older brother is advising his younger brother to take enough time to appreciate the taste of the candy. The **context**—the words surrounding the unfamiliar word— tells us that *savor* means "appreciate" or "enjoy." In this chapter, you will learn how to use the context to figure out the meanings of words.

## Understanding Vocabulary in Context

Do you know the meaning of the word *vital*? How about the word *appropriate*? Or the word *passive*?

You may not know the meaning of one or more of these words. However, if you saw these words in sentences, chances are you could come up with fairly accurate definitions. For example, read each sentence below and see if you can understand the meaning of the word in *italics*. In the space provided, write the letter of the meaning you think is correct. Then read the explanation.

Do not use a dictionary for this work. Instead, in each sentence, try the word you think is the answer. For example, put *unimportant* or *necessary* or *surprising* into the sentence in place of *vital* to see which one makes the best sense.

__B__ 1. All animals share the same *vital* needs, such as food, water, and shelter.

    *Vital* (vīt′l) means
    A. unimportant.        B. necessary.        C. surprising.

__A__ 2. In the United States, shaking hands is the *appropriate* way to greet someone; in China, bowing is the right way.

    *Appropriate* (ə-prō′prē-ĭt) means
    A. proper.        B. artificial.        C. insulting.

__B__ 3. Winners in life take an active role in making things happen, instead of being *passive* and waiting for good luck.

    *Passive* (păs′ĭv) means
    A. insincere.        B. inactive.        C. flexible.

In each sentence above, the context surrounding the unfamiliar word provides clues to the word's meaning. You may have guessed from the context that *vital* means "necessary," that *appropriate* means "proper," and that *passive* means "inactive."

Using context clues to understand the meaning of unfamiliar words will help you in three ways:

**1** It will save you time when reading. You will not have to stop to look up words in the dictionary. (Of course, you won't always be able to understand a word from its context, so you should have a dictionary nearby as you read.)

**2** It will improve your "working vocabulary"—words you recognize as you read and will eventually be able to use when you speak and write. You will therefore add to your vocabulary simply by reading thoughtfully.

**3** It will give you a good sense of how a word is actually used, including any shades of meaning it might have.

# Types of Context Clues

There are four common types of context clues:

**1** Examples
**2** Synonyms
**3** Antonyms
**4** General sense of the sentence or passage

In the following sections, you will read about and practice each type. The practices will sharpen your skills in recognizing and using context clues. They will also help you add new words to your vocabulary.

Remember *not* to use a dictionary for these practices. Their purpose is to help you develop the skill of figuring out what words mean *without* using a dictionary. Pronunciations are provided in parentheses for the words, and a guide to pronunciation is on page 30.

## 1   Examples

An unfamiliar word may appear with **examples** that reveal what the word means. For instance, note the examples in this sentence from the previous page: "All animals share the same vital needs, such as food, water, and shelter." The examples—food, water, and shelter—helped you figure out that the word *vital* means "necessary."

Look at the cartoon below and see if the example helps you choose the correct meaning of the word *vague*.

_C_ *Vague* (vāg) means

A. angry.          B. humorous.          C. unclear.

Notice that the example of a vague answer—"Oh, sooner or later"—helps you understand that *vague* means "unclear."

---

## ✓ Check Your Understanding

Now read the items that follow. An *italicized* word in each sentence is followed by examples that serve as context clues for that word. These examples, which are **boldfaced**, will help you figure out the meaning of each word. On each line, write the letter of the answer you think is correct. Then read the explanation that follows.

Note that examples are often introduced with signal words and phrases like *for example, for instance, including,* and *such as.*

_C_  1. In our house, clothes hangers have various odd *functions*. For instance, we use them to **scratch backs** and **hold up plants in the garden.**

*Functions* (fŭngk'shənz) are
A. shapes.          B. problems.          C. uses.

*Hint:* Remember that in the exercises in this chapter, you can insert into each sentence the word you think is the answer. For example, substitute *shapes, problems,* or *uses* in sentence 1 in place of *functions* to see which one fits.

_B_  2. Our baseball team's pitcher has a few *eccentric* habits, such as **throwing exactly thirteen pitches when warming up** and **never wearing socks.**

*Eccentric* (ĭk-sĕn'trĭk) means
A. normal.          B. strange.          C. messy.

_A_  3. Throughout history, humans have built a wide variety of *dwellings*, including **simple mud huts, stone castles,** and **marble mansions.**

*Dwellings* (dwĕl'ĭngs) are
A. homes.          B. stores.          C. churches.

### Explanation

In each sentence, the examples probably helped you to figure out the meanings of the words in italics:

1. The correct answer is C. In sentence 1, the examples of the odd functions of hangers—scratching backs and holding up plants—may have helped you to guess that *functions* means "uses."

2. The correct answer is B. In sentence 2, the examples of strange habits show that *eccentric* means "strange."

3.  The correct answer is A. The examples in sentence 3 indicate that *dwellings* are homes.

Note that the examples in the sentences are introduced by the signal words *for instance*, *such as*, and *including*.

## PRACTICE 1: Examples

Read each item below and then do two things:

1.  Underline the examples that suggest the meaning of the word in italics.
2.  Then write the letter of the word's meaning on the answer line.

Note that the last five sentences have been taken from college textbooks.

___C___  1.  The *debris* in the stadium stands included numerous paper cups, ticket stubs, sandwich wrappings, and cigarette butts. Signal word: *included.*
The examples given are of trash.
*Debris* (də-brē′) means
A. products.          B. papers.          C. trash.

___C___  2.  For his weak stomach, Mario ate a *bland* diet of white bread, rice, and mashed potatoes. The examples given are of mild foods.
*Bland* (blănd) means
A. spicy.            B. varied.          C. mild.

___B___  3.  New York, Boston, and Philadelphia are three of the oldest *urban* areas in the United States. The examples given are of cities.
*Urban* (ûr′bən) means
A. empty.           B. city.            C. country.

___A___  4.  Many people take dietary *supplements*—for example, extra calcium or large doses of vitamin C—in the belief that they will cure or prevent disease. Signal words: *for example*. The examples given are of additions to people's diets.
*Supplements* (sŭp′lə-mənts) means
A. additions.       B. losses.          C. suggestions.

___B___  5.  My uncle often has embarrassing *mishaps*, such as backing his car into the side of his boss's Cadillac and trying to walk through a glass door.
Signal words: *such as*.
*Mishaps* (mĭs′hăps′) means      The examples given are of accidents.
A. clever moves.    B. accidents.       C. projects.

_B_    6. The death of a child and the death of a spouse are two of life's most
       *traumatic* experiences.    The examples given are of painful experiences.

       *Traumatic* (trou-măt′ĭk) means
       A. rare.              B. painful.              C. interesting.

_C_    7. A *transaction*, such as buying or selling a product, is the most basic part
       of an economy.    Signal words: *such as.* The examples
                          given are of business deals.
       *Transaction* (trăn-săk′shən) means
       A. profit.              B. loss.              C. business deal.

_B_    8. Religious *rituals* like baptisms, church weddings, and funeral services
       give many people a sense of peace and comfort.    Signal word: *like.*
                                                          The examples given are of ceremonies.
       *Rituals* (rĭch′oo-əls) means
       A. lessons.              B. ceremonies.              C. prayers.

_A_    9. When discussing the Internet, professionals often use such *jargon* as
       "adware," "clickthrough rate," and "spambot," which others may not
       understand.    Signal words: *such . . . as.* The examples given are
                      words that belong to a special language.
       *Jargon* (jär′gən) means
       A. special language.       B. clear instructions.       C. mean insults.

_B_   10. There are hundreds of different kinds of *retailers*, ranging from car
       dealerships and department stores to frozen-yogurt stands and online
       drugstores.    The examples given are of businesses that sell directly to users.

       *Retailers* (rē′tāl′ərs) means
       A. customers.       B. businesses that sell       C. businesses that
                             directly to users.             make products.

## 2  Synonyms

Context clues are often found in the form of **synonyms**: one or more words that
mean the same or almost the same as the unknown word. Look again at the sentence
on page 16: "In the United States, shaking hands is the *appropriate* way to greet
someone; in China, bowing is the right way." Here the synonym "right" tells you
the meaning of *appropriate*. A synonym may appear anywhere in a sentence as a
restatement of the meaning of the unknown word.

Now look at the cartoon on the following page.

Notice that the synonym for *refrain*—expressed in the dog's words "stop myself"—helps you understand that *refrain* (rĭ-frān′) means "to hold oneself back."

## ✓ *Check Your Understanding*

Each item below includes a word or phrase that is a synonym of the *italicized* word. Underline that synonym in each sentence. Then read the explanation that follows.

1. The cat soon found it <u>useless</u> to smack her paws against the front of the fish tank; her effort to catch a fish was a *futile* (fyo͞ot′l) one.

2. My best friend *squandered* (skwŏn′dərd) all his money; his drinking and gambling <u>wasted</u> his earnings.

3. Because my boss runs the toy store like a *tyrant* (tī′rənt), all of the employees call her "the little <u>dictator</u>."

*Explanation*

In each sentence, the synonym given probably helped you understand the meaning of the word in italics:

1. In the first sentence, the synonym of *futile* is "useless."

2. In sentence 2, the synonym of *squandered* is "wasted."

3. In sentence 3, the synonym of *tyrant* is "dictator."

**PRACTICE 2: Synonyms**

Each item below includes a synonym of the *italicized* word. Write each synonym in the space provided.

Note that the last five items have been taken from college textbooks.

_self-important_    1. Everyone turned to look at the *arrogant* (ăr'ə-gənt) customer who spoke to the manager in a self-important voice.

*Hint:* What does the voice reveal about the customer?

_powerful_    2. The medicine that Nina is taking is very *potent* (pōt'nt). It is so powerful that she must not take it for more than a week. What must the medicine be if Nina has to stop taking it after only one week?

_cloudy_    3. After the heavy rains, the stream became *murky* (mûr'kē); in fact, the water was so cloudy you couldn't see the bottom. What kind of water would you be unable to see through?

_secret_    4. Some overweight people are called *furtive* (fûr'tĭv) eaters because they eat large quantities of food in secret. In what way do these people eat their food?

_believable_    5. A con artist was apparently very believable as he went door to door telling a *plausible* (plô'zə-bəl) story about having his wallet stolen and needing twenty dollars to get home. What kind of story would a con artist have to tell to make people give him money?

_discussion_    6. The first step in reaching a peace agreement was to set up a *dialog* (dī'ə-lŏg') between the two sides. Without discussion, peace was impossible. What would have to be set up in order to reach a peace agreement?

_force_    7. You cannot *coerce* (kō-ûrs') people into learning. If they are not interested, it is impossible to force them. If people aren't interested in learning, what can't be done to them?

_rich_    8. While Ved may not be *affluent* (ăf'lōo-ənt) by American standards, he is rich compared with most people in his homeland of India. Although Ved is rich by Indian standards, what might he not be by American standards?

_prove_    9. Several tests are necessary to *verify* (věr'ə-fī') that a virus is present. One is never enough to prove a virus exists. What will several tests do that one test cannot do?

_variety_    10. The *diversity* (dĭ-vûr'sĭ-tē) of the population of the United States is the result of accepting immigrants from a wide variety of cultures and nations. If the United States accepts people from many different cultures and nations, what would its population have?

Below are some common words that show addition:

**Addition Words**

| one | to begin with | in addition | last |
|---|---|---|---|
| first | another | next | last of all |
| first of all | second | moreover | final |
| for one thing | also | furthermore | finally |

## Examples

The following items contain addition words. Notice how these words introduce ideas that *add to* what has already been said.

- Hippos give birth under water. They *also* nurse their young there.

- One reason people have dogs is for companionship; *another* reason is for protection.

- The human body has six pounds of skin. *Furthermore,* it contains sixty thousand miles of blood vessels.

**PRACTICE 1**

Complete each sentence with a suitable addition word from the box. Try to use each transition once. Then, in the spaces provided, write the letter of the transition you have chosen.

| | | |
|---|---|---|
| **A. also** | **B. another** | **C. for one thing** |
| **D. in addition** | **E. second** | |

*Hint:* Make sure that each addition word or phrase that you choose fits smoothly into the flow of the sentence. Test each choice by reading the sentence aloud.

___B___ 1. One good way to be friendly is to ask people questions about themselves. _____Another_____ way is to listen carefully when they answer.

___A___ 2. Employers today say they want college graduates to have good writing and speaking skills. They _____also_____ want them to be able to think critically and solve problems.

___D___ 3. Almost 80 percent of college students drink alcohol. _____In addition_____, about 40 percent either binge drink or drink to get drunk.

___C___ 4. I find your attitude insulting. _____For one thing_____, you pull out your phone and begin to text-message when I try to talk with you.

___E___ 5. There are different ways to solve problems. One way is simple trial and error. A _____second_____ way to proceed is to break a problem into smaller, more manageable pieces. Each piece is easier to solve than the problem as a whole.

## Words That Show Time

Check (✓) the item that is easier to read and understand:

____ I had blood work done. I went to the doctor.

__✓__ I had blood work done. Then I went to the doctor.

The word *Then* in the second item clarifies the relationship between the sentences. After having blood work done, the speaker goes to the doctor. *Then* and words like it are time words.

## 3    Antonyms

**Antonyms**—words and phrases that mean the opposite of a word—are also useful as context clues. Antonyms are sometimes signaled by words and phrases such as *however, but, yet, on the other hand, instead of,* and *in contrast.*

Look again at the sentence on page 16: "Winners in life take an active role in making things happen, instead of being passive and waiting for good luck." Here the words *instead of* indicate that *passive* must be the opposite of *active.*

Now look at the cartoon below.

"What do you mean 'unreasonable,' Miss Jones? I think this is a perfectly rational way to keep myself organized."

Notice that the antonym "unreasonable" helps you figure out that *rational* (răsh′ə-nəl) must mean "reasonable."

---

✔ ## *Check Your Understanding*

In each of the following sentences, underline the word or phrase that means the opposite of the *italicized* word. Then, on the answer line, write the letter of the meaning of the italicized word. Finally, read the explanation that follows.

_B_    1. The coach takes every opportunity to *reprimand* his players, yet he ignores every chance to praise them.

  *Reprimand* (rĕp′rə-mănd) means

  A. approve of.        B. criticize.        C. choose.

_A_    2. "I am having *acute* pains in my chest now," said the patient, "but an hour ago, all I felt was a <u>dull</u> ache."

*Acute* (ə-kyo͞ot′) means
A. sharp.                B. weak.                C. no.

_B_    3. Some teachers are too *lenient*. I'd rather have <u>strict</u> teachers who take the class seriously.

*Lenient* (lē′nē-ənt) means
A. hard.                B. easygoing.                C. busy.

## Explanation

In each sentence, the antonym given probably helped you understand the meaning of the word in italics:

1. The correct answer is B. *Reprimand* is the opposite of *praise*, so the answer to sentence 1 is *criticize*.

2. The correct answer is A. In sentence 2, the opposite of *acute* is *dull*, so *acute* must mean "sharp."

3. The correct answer is B. In sentence 3, "lenient" teachers are the opposite of "strict" teachers, so *lenient* means "easygoing."

Note that the antonyms of *reprimand* and *acute* are indicated by signal words: *yet* and *but*.

## PRACTICE 3: Antonyms

Each item below includes a word or phrase that is an antonym of the *italicized* word. Underline each of those antonyms. Then, on the line, write the letter of the meaning of the italicized word.

Note that the last five items have been taken from college textbooks.

_A_    1. After his accident, Brad expected an <u>in-depth</u> examination at the hospital. Instead, a doctor gave him a quick, *superficial* checkup and said, "You're fine."

*Hint:* What would be the opposite of an in-depth examination?

*Superficial* (so͞o′pər-fĭsh′əl) means
A. lacking depth.        B. complicated.        C. satisfactory.

_A_ 2. A temporary cough is nothing to worry about, but a *chronic* one can be a sign of a serious illness.  What would be the opposite of a *temporary* cough?

  *Chronic* (krŏn′ĭk) means
  A. continuing.        B. brief.        C. mild.

_C_ 3. When drinking was *prohibited* by the Nineteenth Amendment, alcohol became more popular with some people than it had been when it was allowed.  What would be the opposite of *allowing* alcohol?

  *Prohibited* (prō-hĭb′ĭt-ĭd) means
  A. permitted.        B. defined.        C. forbidden.

_A_ 4. "What we need is an *innovative* idea!" cried the chairman. "All I've heard so far are the same old ones."  What would be the opposite of *old* ideas?

  *Innovative* (ĭn′ə-vā′tĭv) means
  A. new.        B. traditional.        C. loud.

_B_ 5. The class was in *turmoil* when only the substitute teacher was there, but it quickly came to order once the principal entered the room.

  *Turmoil* (tûr′moil′) means      In a classroom, what would be the opposite of *order*?
  A. peace.        B. confusion.        C. attendance.

_B_ 6. In ordinary life, people's facial expressions are *spontaneous*. However, actors must learn to use planned ways of showing emotion.

  *Spontaneous* (spŏn-tā′nē-əs) means      What would be the opposite of *planned*?
  A. varied.        B. unplanned.        C. hidden.

_C_ 7. A computer *novice* is lucky if he or she knows someone who is an expert and is willing to offer advice.  What kind of person would need an expert's help?

  *Novice* (nŏv′ĭs) means
  A. a child.        B. a friend.        C. a beginner.

_C_ 8. Some patients drop out of drug therapy before it is completed. Instead of making progress, they may then *revert* to previous bad habits.

  *Revert* (rĭ-vûrt′) means      What would be the opposite of *making progress*?
  A. say no.        B. improve.        C. go back.

_C_ 9. Our Constitution would be in danger if all Americans were *indifferent to* it. However, history has shown that concerned citizens will always come forward to defend it.  What kind of person would be the opposite of a *concerned* citizen?

  *Indifferent to* (ĭn-dĭf′ər-ənt tōo) means
  A. insulted by.        B. aware of.        C. uninterested in.

_____B_____ 10. In warfare, as in chess, *impulsive* actions will fail. To win in either case, carefully thought-out moves are needed.     *What kind of action is not carefully thought out?*

*Impulsive* (ĭm-pŭl′sĭv) means

   A. fearful.        B. unplanned.        C. strong.

## 4 General Sense of the Sentence or Passage

Often, the context of a new word contains no examples, synonyms, or antonyms. In such cases, you must do a bit more detective work; you'll need to look at any clues provided in the information surrounding the word. Asking yourself questions about the passage may help you make a fairly accurate guess about the meaning of the unfamiliar word.

Look at the cartoon below about a job interview.

© 2005 by Randy Glasbergen.
www.glasbergen.com

"You're exactly what we need—
someone who will be ruthless about cutting costs."

There are no examples, synonyms, or antonyms in the woman's statement. However, the applicant's costume—that of an executioner—and the huge axe he carries suggest that *ruthless* (rooth′lĭs) means "showing no mercy."

## ✔ Check Your Understanding

Each sentence below is followed by a question. Think about each question; then write the letter of the answer you feel is the meaning of the italicized word.

___A___  1. The newlyweds agreed to be very *frugal* in their shopping because they wanted to save enough money to buy a home.

(How would people shop if they wanted to save money?)

*Frugal* (froo′gəl) means
A. thrifty.                    B. wasteful.                    C. interested.

___B___  2. So many customers have complained about the noise in the restaurant that the owners are trying to find ways to *mute* the noise.

(What would the restaurant owners probably want to do about noise?)

*Mute* (myoot) means
A. increase.                    B. quiet.                    C. create.

___C___  3. Friends tried to *dissuade* ninety-year-old Mrs. Kellen from attending her son's trial, but she went anyway, to show her support.

(What would the elderly woman's friends have tried to do to her if they didn't want her to go to her son's trial?)

*Dissuade* (dĭ-swād′) means
A. question.                    B. describe.                    C. discourage.

*Explanation*

In each sentence, your answer to the question should have helped you figure out the meaning of the word in italics:

1. The correct answer is A. The first sentence provides enough evidence for you to guess that *frugal* means "thrifty." The newlyweds had to be thrifty if they wanted to save money.

2. The correct answer is B. *Mute* in the second sentence means "quiet"; a restaurant owner would probably want to reduce the noise.

3. The correct answer is C. *Dissuade* means "discourage"—Mrs. Kellen went to the trial despite her friends' attempts to discourage her.

If you use context clues, you may not get the exact dictionary definition of a word, but you will often be accurate enough to make good sense of what you are reading.

## PRACTICE 4: General Sense of the Sentence or Passage

Figure out the meaning of the word in *italics* by looking at clues in the rest of the sentence. First, try to answer the question in parentheses that follows each item below. Then, on the basis of your answer, write the letter of the meaning you think is correct.

Note that the last five items have been taken from college textbooks.

_C_   1. To reach a *sound* conclusion about an issue, you must carefully consider all the facts involved.

(What kind of conclusion would you reach by carefully considering all the facts?)

*Sound* (sound) means
A. early.      B. obvious.      C. reasonable.

_A_   2. My mother refuses to *divulge* the secret ingredients she uses in her fried chicken recipe.

(What would someone refuse to do with ingredients that are secret?)

*Divulge* (dĭ-vŭlj′) means
A. reveal.      B. hide.      C. invent.

_A_   3. Because the nicotine in cigarettes is harmful, many people favor *stringent* laws against their sale.

(What type of laws would be favored by people concerned about the harm of nicotine?)

*Stringent* (strĭn′jənt) means
A. strict.      B. weak.      C. confusing.

_C_   4. Taking the expression "raining cats and dogs" *literally*, the child looked for little animals on the ground after the storm.

(In what way did the child interpret the phrase "raining cats and dogs"?)

*Literally* (lĭt′ər-ə-lē) means
A. symbolically.      B. musically.      C. as the real facts.

_A_   5. It's too late to *alter* the plans for the party. The restaurant and band have been reserved, and all the invitations have been sent out.

(If the plans have all been made, what is it too late to do to the plans?)

*Alter* (ôl′tər) means
A. change.      B. surprise.      C. repeat.

_B_   6. Organ transplants will not succeed unless the *donor* has the same blood type as the person receiving the organ.

(Who would need to have the same kind of blood as the person receiving the transplant?)

*Donor* (dō'nər) means
A. one who receives.      B. one who gives.      C. one who doubts.

_C_   7. Few American officials in Iraq were *fluent* in the Iraqi language, so all communication had to be in English.

(What would an American have to be in order to communicate in the Iraqi language?)

*Fluent* (floo'ənt) means
A. able to remember.      B. able to teach.      C. able to speak well.

_B_   8. The placing of a huge cable on the floor of the Atlantic Ocean in 1866 made it possible to *transmit* telegraph signals from Europe to North America.

(What did the cable allow us to do with signals between Europe and North America?)

*Transmit* (trăns-mĭt') means
A. check.              B. send.              C. lose.

_A_   9. Over years, the movement of water in a stream will *erode* the surrounding soil and rock. As a result, the stream will be wider and deeper.

(What does water do to soil and rock to enlarge a stream?)

*Erode* (ĭ-rōd') means
A. wear away.          B. escape.          C. build up.

_C_  10. In the 1950s, Americans felt that the Soviet Union was a *menace* threatening their national security. As a result, Senator Joseph McCarthy was able to persuade millions of people that the Soviets had secret agents in the United States government.

(What would a country that threatened our national security be regarded as?)

*Menace* (mĕn'ĭs) means
A. puzzle.             B. friend.             C. danger.

# An Important Point about Textbook Definitions

You don't always have to use context clues or the dictionary to find definitions. Very often, textbook authors provide definitions of important terms. They usually follow a definition with one or more examples to make sure that you understand the word being defined.

Here is a short textbook passage that includes a definition and an example. Note that the term to be defined is set off in **boldface** type, and the definition then follows.

[1]The changing work force has changed lifestyles and needs. [2]No wonder many workers have found **flextime** a desirable choice. [3]Instead of working the standard nine-to-five day, five days a week, they choose their own hours. [4]For instance, they may decide to work four days at ten hours a day rather than five days at eight hours.

Textbook authors, then, often do more than provide context clues: they set off the terms they are defining in *italic* or **boldface** type, as above. When they take the time to define and illustrate a word, you should assume that the material is important enough to learn.

More about textbook definitions and examples appears on pages 190–191 in Chapter 8, "More Relationships in Reading."

## *Pronunciation Guide*

| Long Vowel Sounds | | Other Vowel Sounds | | Consonant Sounds | |
|---|---|---|---|---|---|
| $\bar{a}$ | pay | â | care | j | jump |
| $\bar{e}$ | she | ä | card | k | kiss |
| $\bar{\imath}$ | hi | îr | here | l | let |
| $\bar{o}$ | go | ô | all | m | meet |
| $\overline{oo}$ | cool | oi | oil | n | no |
| $y\overline{oo}$ | use | ou | out | p | put |
| | | ûr | fur | r | red |
| **Short Vowel Sounds** | | ə | ago, item, | s | sell |
| $\breve{a}$ | hat | | easily, | t | top |
| $\breve{e}$ | ten | | gallop, | v | have |
| $\breve{\imath}$ | sit | | circus | w | way |
| $\breve{o}$ | lot | | | y | yes |
| $\breve{oo}$ | look | | | z | zero |
| $\breve{u}$ | up | **Consonant Sounds** | | ch | church |
| $y\breve{oo}$ | cure | b | big | sh | dish |
| | | d | do | *th* | then |
| | | f | fall | th | thick |
| | | g | dog | zh | usual |
| | | h | he | | |

# VOCABULARY DEVELOPMENT FOR READING AND WRITING: Mastery Test 1

**A.** Look at the cartoon below, and then answer the questions that follow.

© 1998 Randy Glasbergen.

"I'm a little apprehensive about the new boss.
His snoopiness makes me uneasy."

_C_ 1. Using the context clues in the cartoon, write the letter of the best meaning of *apprehensive* (ăp′rĭ-hĕn′sĭv) in the space provided.
   A. pleased          B. forgetful          C. worried

_B_ 2. Which kind of context clue helps you understand the meaning of the cartoon?
   A. Examples clue          B. Synonym clue          C. Antonym clue

   **Items 1 and 2:** Synonym clue: *uneasy*.

**B.** For each item below, underline the **examples** that suggest the meaning of the italicized word. Then, on the answer line, write the letter of the meaning of that word.

_A_ 3. Carol survived her freshman year despite various *adverse* (ăd-vûrs′) events. For instance, she missed two weeks of class because of a strep throat and had all her books stolen just before finals.
   A. unfavorable          C. fortunate          Signal words:
   B. evil               D. pleasant           *For instance.*

_D_ 4. The new principal took *drastic* (drăs′tĭk) steps to deal with school funding cuts, including firing teachers and doing away with sports.
   A. funny               C. approving         Signal word:
   B. small               D. extreme           *including.*

*(Continues on next page)*

31

**C.** Each item below includes a word or words that are a **synonym** of the italicized word. Write the synonym of the italicized word in the space provided.

_____show off_____ 5. The old saying "If you've got it, *flaunt* (flônt) it" means that you should show off your good qualities.

The word *means* signals the synonym for *flaunt: show off.*

_____signal_____ 6. The company president made a brief *gesture* (jĕs′chər) with her hand. It was a clear signal that the interview was over.

The second sentence presents the synonym of *gesture: signal.*

**D.** Each item below includes a word or words that are an **antonym** of the italicized word. Underline the antonym of each italicized word. Then, on the answer line, write the letter of the meaning of the italicized word

___D___ 7. The chef hates a <u>dirty</u> kitchen. If the kitchen isn't *immaculate* (ĭ-măk′yə-lĭt) at the end of a day, he insists that somebody stay late to finish cleaning.

The chef hates dirty kitchens. He wants the opposite of *dirty: spotless.*

    A. large           C. crowded
    B. messy          D. spotless

___D___ 8. If parents show *apathy* (ăp′ə-thē) toward their children's education, how can we expect the students to show <u>interest</u>?

If parents show no interest, how can we expect students to show interest?

    A. attention        C. teaching
    B. knowledge      D. lack of interest

**E.** Use the **general sense of each sentence** to figure out the meaning of each italicized word. Then, on the answer line, write the letter of the meaning of the italicized word.

___A___ 9. My aunt is so *obstinate* (ŏb′stə-nĭt) that once she makes up her mind, nothing any member of her family says can change it.

A person who does not change her mind is stubborn.

    A. stubborn        C. easy-going
    B. clever           D. cooperative

___D___ 10. Building the Brooklyn Bridge was a huge struggle involving men, materials, and nature. Numerous *obstacles* (ŏb′stə-kəls) had to be overcome in order to complete the structure in 1883.

    A. buildings        C. places
    B. causes           D. difficulties

A "huge struggle" is likely to involve difficulties.

# VOCABULARY DEVELOPMENT FOR READING AND WRITING: Mastery Test 2

**A.** Look at the cartoon below, and then answer the question that follows.

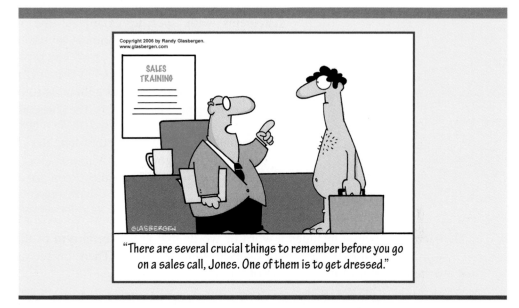

Copyright 2006 by Randy Glasbergen.
www.glasbergen.com

SALES TRAINING

GLASBERGEN

"There are several crucial things to remember before you go on a sales call, Jones. One of them is to get dressed."

___A___  1. Using the context clues in the cartoon, write the letter of the best meaning of *crucial* (krōō′shəl) in the space provided.

    A. very important          B. expensive          C. unusual

    Getting dressed is an example of a very important thing to remember.

**B.** For each item below, underline the **examples** that suggest the meaning of the italicized term. Then, on the answer line, write the letter of the meaning of that word.

___D___  2. The employees showed the *contempt* (kən-tĕmpt′) they felt for their boss by <u>ignoring his memos</u> and <u>making fun of him behind his back.</u>

    A. admiration                C. fear        Examples of insulting

    B. envy                     D. disrespect       acts are given.

___A___  3. The apples were on sale because many of them had *defects* (dē′fĕkts′), such as <u>brown spots</u>, <u>soft places</u>, or <u>small holes in the skin.</u>

    A. imperfections            C. prizes      Examples of imperfections

    B. peelings                D. leaves           are given.

*(Continues on next page)*

**C.** Each item below includes a word or words that are a **synonym** of the italicized word. Write the synonym of the italicized word in the space provided.

_____make clear_____  4. Textbook authors often *clarify* (klăr′ə-fī′) general statements with specific examples; the illustrations make clear what the general point is saying. The second part of the sentence presents a synonym for *clarify: make clear.*

_____never happened before_____  5. The event was *unprecedented* (ŭn-prĕs′ĭ-dĕn′tĭd)—the election of a pig to the student council is something that had never happened before. The phrase after the dash presents a synonym for *unprecedented: never happened before.*

_____die down_____  6. The comedian waited for the laughter to *subside* (səb-sīd′) before going on with his next joke. The audience's reaction did not die down for two whole minutes. The second sentence presents a synonym for *subside: die down.*

**D.** Each item below includes a word or words that are an **antonym** of the italicized word. Underline the antonym of each italicized word. Then, on the answer line, write the letter of the meaning of the italicized word.

___A___ 7. Before the game, the locker room had been cheerful; but now, after losing the game, the players were *morose* (mə-rōs′). *But* signals opposite moods in the locker
   A. sad and gloomy       C. pleased       room: cheerful
   B. tired                D. happy and excited   and morose.

___D___ 8. "It is better to *retreat* (rĭ-trēt′) to safety," said the general, "than to go forward foolishly." *Retreat* is the opposite of *go forward.*
   A. attack               C. look
   B. investigate          D. move back

**E.** Use the **general sense of each sentence** to figure out the meaning of each italicized word. Then, on the answer line, write the letter of the meaning of the italicized word.

___C___ 9. When I couldn't fall asleep last night, I realized I had been *imprudent* (ĭm-prōōd′nt) to drink so much coffee after dinner. If drinking coffee prevents sleep, it is
   A. pleased              C. unwise       unwise to do
   B. clever               D. fortunate    it after dinner.

___D___ 10. How you interpret the *ambiguous* (ăm-bĭg′yōō-əs) sentence "Visiting relatives can be boring" may depend on which you find annoying— relatives who visit or visits to relatives.
   A. long and boring      C. having a clear meaning
   B. difficult to say     D. having more than one meaning
      If a sentence can be interpreted differently, it has more than one meaning.

# VOCABULARY DEVELOPMENT FOR READING AND WRITING: Mastery Test 3

Using context clues for help, write the letter of the best meaning for each italicized word.

_A_ 1. Greg wanted to become *proficient* (prə-fĭsh′ənt) on the saxophone, so he practiced every day for several hours. What would someone
    A. highly skilled    C. dependent    become by practicing
    B. very loud    D. tired    for several hours a day?

_C_ 2. Otis was faced with the *dilemma* (dĭ-lĕm′ə) of putting more money into his ancient Chevy or doing without a car. Example clue:
    A. happy situation    C. unpleasant choice    The sentence
    B. bad mood    D. victory    gives an example of a dilemma.

_D_ 3. Our children are so afraid of snakes that even a toy rubber snake *provokes* (prə-vōks′) panic in them. A toy snake would
    A. amuses    C. prevents    cause panic among
    B. closes    D. causes    kids afraid of snakes.

_B_ 4. Janice often asks *impertinent* (ĭm-pûr′tn-ənt) questions such as "Where did you get that ugly shirt?" or "Did you cut your own hair?"
    A. clever    C. important    Examples of rude
    B. rude    D. friendly    questions are given.

_C_ 5. At the family reunion, the older relatives sat together and *reminisced* (rĕm′ə-nĭst′) for hours about events of fifty years ago.
    A. forgot    C. discussed past events
    B. were irritated    D. argued    What were the older
relatives doing about events of fifty years ago?

_B_ 6. The wolf was *wary* (wâr′ē), circling around the camp until he felt sure that all the hikers were asleep. What does the wolf's
    A. hungry    C. brave    behavior indicate
    B. cautious    D. tired    about him?

_C_ 7. Don't be *naïve* (nä-ēv′) enough to believe commercials and e-mail ads that promise instant riches, effortless weight loss, and valuable free prizes. What kind of person would believe in
    A. dishonest    C. unsuspecting    instant wealth,
    B. absent-minded    D. critical    easy weight loss, and free prizes?

*(Continues on next page)*

_A_ 8. A fight between the two brothers seemed *inevitable* (ĭn-ĕv′ĭ-tə-bəl) that
    rainy Saturday; they had been teasing each other all morning.
    A. unavoidable          C. impossible
    B. welcome              D. unwanted

_C_ 9. The teacher decided that the test results were not *valid* (văl′ĭd) because
    some students had gotten hold of the questions before the test.
    A. high                 C. reliable
    B. interesting          D. unusual

_D_ 10. Because Mac had left out a *vital* (vīt′l) ingredient, the apple cake came
    out looking like a pancake.
    A. bad-tasting          C. small
    B. unnecessary          D. very important

**Item 8:**   A fight becomes unavoidable for two brothers who teased each other all morning.
**Item 9:**   What would the test results *not* be if students had seen the test beforehand?
**Item 10:** Only an important ingredient could change the cake's shape.

# VOCABULARY DEVELOPMENT FOR READING AND WRITING: Mastery Test 4

Using context clues for help, write the letter of the best meaning for each italicized word. Note that all of the sentences have been taken from college textbooks.

___B___ 1. After a baby is born, an older child may become jealous. Wanting the attention the newborn is receiving, the child may *regress* (rĭ-grĕs′) to such behavior as sucking a thumb or crying.

    A. look                         C. talk

    B. go back               D. advance       If an older child begins to suck a thumb or cry, what has the child done?

___D___ 2. Certain marine bacteria contain chemicals that produce light. Passengers sailing at night in the Indian Ocean often pass through "glowing seas" *illuminated* (ĭ-lōō′mə-nāt′ĭd) by countless bacteria.

    A. polluted              C. made dangerous     Synonym-like clues: *produce*

    B. cleaned                D. lit up              *light; glowing.*

___A___ 3. Nobody needs proof to know that conflict is part of life—it is *self-evident* (sĕlf′ ĕv′ĭ-dənt).

    A. obvious               C. unclear     What sorts of things do

    B. possible              D. unlikely    not need to be proved?

___B___ 4. In historical novels, the main events that occur, such as the Civil War, are factual, but many of the characters are *fictitious* (fĭk-tĭsh′əs).

    A. old                      C. unimportant

    B. not real              D. active        *But* signals that *fictitious* means the opposite of *factual.*

___D___ 5. Teenagers are often *gregarious* (grĭ-gâr′ē-əs), finding status and a sense of identity by spending all their leisure time with a particular circle of friends.

    A. quiet and reserved         C. wanting their own way

    B. independent              D. seeking the company of others

                      What kind of people spend so much time with friends?

___B___ 6. It is a *fallacy* (făl′ə-sē) to assume that if one event happens before another, then the first event is the cause of the second one. Actually, the two events may be completely unrelated.

    A. promise               C. good idea

    B. mistake                D. truth

               If the two events may be completely unrelated, it is a mistake to assume one caused the other.

*(Continues on next page)*

_C_    7. Throughout history, governments have attempted to justify their actions through *propaganda* (prŏp′ə-găn′də), including political speeches, books and pamphlets, and media campaigns.
   A. spending money
   B. noise
   C. information spread to support a cause
   D. good behavior    *The examples given are of information spread to support a cause. Signal word: including.*

_D_    8. Patients suffering from tuberculosis used to be placed in *seclusion* (sĭ-klōo′zhən), away from anyone who was in danger of catching the disease.    *Synonym-like clue: away from anyone who was in danger of catching the disease.*
   A. hospitals
   B. bed
   C. groups
   D. away from others

_C_    9. Certain mental disorders can cause *delusions* (dĭ-lōo′zhəns), such as the false belief that one is being spied on by the police.    *The false belief that one is being spied on is an example of a mistaken idea. Signal words: such as.*
   A. sudden actions
   B. good feelings
   C. mistaken ideas
   D. strong objections

_D_   10. The increasing popularity of online social networking sites has led to new legal and ethical problems, such as what should be done about people who use those networks to bully and *harass* (hə-răs′) one another.
   A. support
   B. ignore
   C. agree with
   D. attack
   *Synonym clue: bully.*

# VOCABULARY DEVELOPMENT FOR READING AND WRITING: Mastery Test 5

**A.** Using context clues for help, write the letter of the best meaning for each italicized word.

_D_ 1. The story the former drug addict told was so *engrossing* (ĕn-grō′sĭng) to the students that they didn't move even when the bell rang.

    A. pleasing                  C. confusing     A story that keeps
    B. boring                     D. fascinating   students from leaving must be fascinating.

_B_ 2. Everyone *evacuating* (ĭ-văk′yoō-ā′tĭng) the burning hotel, including those as far up as the twentieth floor, had to use the stairs.

    A. staying in              C. paying for     People use stairs
    B. leaving                  D. arriving at    to leave a building.

_A_ 3. Some members of organizations are good only at thinking up ideas. So although they are able to *initiate* (ĭ-nĭsh′ē-āt′) a project, they need others to complete it.        Antonym clue: *complete.*

    A. start                  C. try out     One group completes
    B. name                 D. work on   a project; the other does the opposite and *initiates*, or begins, the project.

_C_ 4. During high tide, waves advance, covering most or all of the beach, but during low tide, the water *recedes* (rĭ-sēds′), leaving behind seaweed and shells and occasionally leaving fish behind on the sand.

    A. appears             C. goes back  Antonym clue: *advance.*
    B. comes forward       D. becomes dangerous   At low tide, waves advance; at high tide, they do the opposite and *recede*, or go back.

_D_ 5. Colleges have several resources to aid students in determining which *vocations* (vō-kā′shəns) would be best for them. These include preference tests, a job placement center offering information about opportunities in various fields, and the services of career counselors.

    A. classes              C. study skills     Synonym clues:
    B. living arrangements     D. jobs         *job, fields, career.*

*(Continues on next page)*

**B.** Five words are **boldfaced** in the textbook passage below. Write the definition for each boldfaced word, choosing from the definitions in the box. Then write the letter of the definition in the space provided.

Be sure to read the entire passage before making your choices. Note that three definitions will be left over.

| | | |
|---|---|---|
| A. coating | B. drops off | C. enjoyable |
| D. enormous | E. increases | F. lie down |
| G. small | H. step forth | |

¹One of the most unusual bodies of water in the world is the Dead Sea. ²Surrounded by desert, this "sea" is actually 26 percent dissolved minerals, 99 percent of which are salts. ³Over 45 miles long and 11 miles wide, the Dead Sea is so salty that its water actually feels oily and leaves a chalky **residue** on the skin. ⁴Bathers brave enough to **venture** just a few feet into the Dead Sea will discover that the human body floats in the salty mixture. ⁵Because of the **vast** amount of salt in the water, a person can actually **recline** on the surface of the Dead Sea as if it was a giant waterbed. ⁶While clear, the sea's water is so thick that ripples and waves are visible even beneath its surface. ⁷Unfortunately, this natural marvel is shrinking. ⁸Each year, the water level **diminishes** by three feet. ⁹At this rate, the Dead Sea will become a salty desert in a few centuries.

__A__  6. In sentence 3, *residue* (rĕz′ĭ-doo′) means _____coating_____.

__H__  7. In sentence 4, *venture* (vĕn′chər) means _____step forth_____.

__D__  8. In sentence 5, *vast* (văst) means _____enormous_____.

__F__  9. In sentence 5, *recline* (rĭ-klīn′) means _____lie down_____.

__B__ 10. In sentence 8, *diminishes* (dĭ-mĭn′ĭsh-ĭs) means _____drops off_____.

**Item 6:**   What is left on the skin?
**Item 7:**   In order to discover that the human body floats, bathers would have to step forth into the water.
**Item 8:**   Sentences 1–3 discuss the large amount of salt in the Dead Sea.
**Item 9:**   If the surface is like a giant waterbed, people can lie down on it.
**Item 10:** Synonym clue: *is shrinking*.

# VOCABULARY DEVELOPMENT FOR READING AND WRITING: Mastery Test 6

**A.** Using context clues for help, write the letter of the best meaning for each italicized word. Note that all of the sentences have been taken from college textbooks.

_A_ 1. In deciding on a sentence, the judge often considers whether or not the criminal has shown *remorse* (rĭ-môrs'). If there is evidence that the convicted person is sorry for what he or she has done, the punishment tends to be less severe.
Synonym-like clue: *sorry for what he or she has done.*
- A. regret and guilt
- B. evidence
- C. innocence
- D. pleasure and satisfaction

_C_ 2. In the third stage of its life cycle, the caterpillar shuts itself into a cocoon. When it *emerges* (ĭ-mûrj'ĭs) months later, it will be a beautiful butterfly.
Antonym-like clue: *shuts itself into* [a cocoon].
- A. folds up
- B. goes inside
- C. comes out
- D. cries out

_B_ 3. The male woodpecker can be quite *persistent* (pər-sĭs'tənt) in his attempts to attract a female. He is usually not discouraged by her refusal and will continue to court her for several hours.
An animal that continues for hours and is "not discouraged" is steady.
- A. late
- B. steady
- C. afraid
- D. uncaring

_B_ 4. According to research, a majority of U.S. teenagers hold part-time jobs during the school year. Most teens consider their work *tedious* (tē'dē-əs), but some find their jobs to be an enjoyable social experience.
Signal word: *but.* Antonym clue: *enjoyable.*
- A. exciting
- B. boring
- C. helpful
- D. educational

_A_ 5. New employees should be reminded that it is *prudent* (prood'nt) to accept assignments and carry out orders without objecting. Workers who seem unwilling to go along with company policy will probably soon find themselves looking for new jobs.
Accepting assignments and carrying out orders are wise steps for new employees.
- A. wise
- B. friendly
- C. risky
- D. unhelpful

*(Continues on next page)*

**B.** Five words are **boldfaced** in the textbook passage below. Write the definition for each boldfaced word, choosing from the definitions in the box. Then write the letter of the definition in the space provided.

Be sure to read the entire passage before making your choices. Note that three definitions will be left over.

| | | |
|---|---|---|
| A. dangerous | B. discouragement | C. done together |
| D. force | E. get involved | F. imitate |
| G. insincere | H. stand up to | |

¹Studies of school violence suggest that as many as 80 percent of students who witness bullying do nothing to stop it. ²Why? ³According to sociologists, there are four main reasons students refuse to **intervene** and help their peers. ⁴First of all, most bystanders are simply afraid of getting hurt. ⁵Jumping into a fight is **treacherous**—it may lead to injury all too quickly. ⁶A second reason students don't stand up for their peers is that they are afraid bullies will turn on them. ⁷Fear of becoming a new target is such a powerful **deterrent** that most students choose to do nothing—even when their classmates are suffering. ⁸A third reason students don't **compel** bullies to stop is that most bystanders believe their actions can make a situation worse. ⁹In reality, however, doing nothing helps no one and can actually encourage bullies to attack. ¹⁰Last, bystanders do not **confront** bullies because they don't know what to do or how to do it. ¹¹Clearly schools need to teach students how to respond to bullying so that schools—and students—are safer.

___E___   6. In sentence 3, *intervene* (ĭn'tər-vēn') means ___*get involved*___.

___A___   7. In sentence 5, *treacherous* (trĕch'ər-əs) means ___*dangerous*___.

___B___   8. In sentence 7, *deterrent* (dĭ-tûr'ənt) means ___*discouragement*___.

___D___   9. In sentence 8, *compel* (kəm-pĕl') means ___*force*___.

___H___   10. In sentence 10, *confront* (kən-frŭnt') means ___*stand up to*___.

**Item 6:**   Antonym clue: *do nothing to stop it.*
**Item 7:**   Behavior that can lead to injury is dangerous.
**Item 8:**   What would fear of becoming a target do to students?
**Item 9:**   The entire passage is about why bystanders don't force bullies to stop.
**Item 10:** What are bystanders afraid to do to bullies?

# ② Main Ideas in Reading

## What Is the Main Idea?

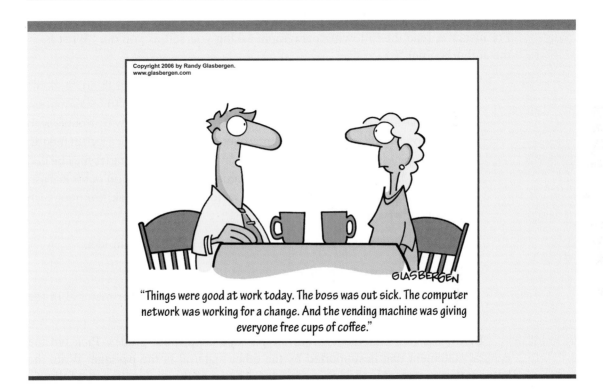

Copyright 2006 by Randy Glasbergen.
www.glasbergen.com

GLASBERGEN

"Things were good at work today. The boss was out sick. The computer network was working for a change. And the vending machine was giving everyone free cups of coffee."

"What's the point?" People ask this question when they want to know what main idea is being presented. Sometimes a main idea is clear right away, as in the cartoon above. What would you say is the speaker's point in the cartoon?

*Explanation*

The main idea is that the speaker had a good day at work. He then supports his point with three specific reasons: the boss was out, the computer network was working, and the vending machine was dispensing free coffee.

When you read, get in the habit of asking, "What is the main point the writer is trying to make?" Recognizing the **main idea**, or point, is the most important key to better reading.

---

✔ ## Check Your Understanding

For instance, read the following paragraph, asking yourself as you do, "What is the author's point?"

> ¹Poor grades in school can have various causes. ²For one thing, students may have financial problems. ³If they need to work long hours to make money, they will have little study time. ⁴Another cause of poor grades may be trouble with relationships. ⁵A student may be unhappy over family problems or a lack of friends. ⁶That unhappiness can harm schoolwork. ⁷A final cause of poor grades may be bad study habits. ⁸Some students have never learned how to take good notes in class, how to manage their time effectively, or how to study a textbook. ⁹Without such study skills, their grades are likely to suffer.

Here is a good two-step way to find an author's point, or main idea:

1  Look for a general statement.

2  Decide if that statement is supported by most of the other material in the paragraph. If it is, you have found the main idea.

Below are four statements from the passage about poor grades. Pick out the general statement that is supported by the other material in the passage. Write the letter of that statement in the space provided. Then read the explanation that follows.

*Four statements from the passage*

    A.  Poor grades in school can have various causes.

    B.  For one thing, students may have financial problems.

    C.  A final cause of poor grades may be bad study habits.

    D.  Some students have never learned how to take good notes in class, how to manage their time effectively, or how to study a textbook.

The general statement that expresses the main idea of the passage is: ___A___

*Explanation*

*Sentence A:*   The phrase "various causes" in sentence A is a general one. It is broad enough to include all of the specific causes mentioned in the other sentences—financial problems, trouble with relationships, and bad study habits. Sentence A, then, is the sentence that expresses the main idea of the passage.

*Sentence B:*   This sentence is about only one type of problem, financial problems. "Financial problems" is not general enough to include the other two listed causes of poor grades: trouble with relationships and bad study habits.

*Sentence C:*   This sentence also mentions only one specific cause: bad study habits. "Bad study habits" is not general enough to include the other two causes presented in the paragraph.

*Sentence D:*   This sentence lists three specific study problems. It does not cover the other material in the paragraph.

## The Main Idea as an "Umbrella" Idea

Think of the main idea as an "umbrella" idea. The main idea is the author's general point. The other material of the paragraph fits under it. That other material is made up of specific supporting details—evidence such as examples, reasons, or facts. The diagram below shows the relationship:

The explanations and activities on the following pages will deepen your understanding of the main idea.

# How Do You Recognize a Main Idea?

To recognize the main idea of a passage, you must **become an active reader**. Active readers *think* as they read. Instead of merely taking in words, an active reader constantly asks, "What's the point?" In addition, active readers use a variety of other strategies to determine an author's main idea. Below are three active reading strategies you can use to help find the main idea in a passage.

**1**  Look for general versus specific ideas.

**2**  Use the topic to lead you to the main idea.

**3**  Use key words to lead you to the main idea.

Each strategy is explained on the following pages.

## 1    Look for General versus Specific Ideas

You saw in the paragraph on the causes of poor grades that the main idea is a *general* idea that is supported by *specific* ideas. To improve your skill at finding main ideas, then, it will be helpful to practice separating general from specific ideas.

## ✔ *Check Your Understanding*

See if you can do the following brief exercises. Then read the explanations that follow.                        *Answers will vary; below are some possibilities.*

1.  You often use general and specific ideas without even realizing it. Consider the following:

    ● *Animal* is a general term. Write the names of three specific animals:

    dog                      raccoon                      bear

    ● *Vegetables* is a general term. Write the names of three specific vegetables:

    carrot                      onion                      celery

    ● *Emotion* is a general term. Write the names of three specific emotions:

    anger                      sadness                      happiness

*Explanation*

In answering the above items, you might have chosen such specific animals as a dog, raccoon, or bear; such specific vegetables as carrots, onions, or celery; such specific emotions as anger, sadness, or happiness.

2. Let's say that a new year is starting, and you decide to make some New Year's resolutions. Your general idea might be as follows:

   *General idea:* Starting in January, I want to make some changes in my life.

   ● Now write three *specific* ideas—three resolutions that you might make:

   Get to bed earlier

   Eat less junk food

   Spend at least a half hour reading each day

## Explanation

Three examples of specific resolutions might be to get to bed earlier, to eat less junk food, and to spend at least a half hour reading each day.

3. In thinking about your teachers, you might decide that one of your high-school English teachers was your best teacher. Your general idea might be as follows:

   *General idea:* _____ Mrs. Hill _____ is the best teacher I ever had.

   ● Now write three *specific* reasons you thought so highly of this teacher:

   She explained ideas clearly.

   She was friendly.

   She spent individual time with each student.

## Explanation

You might, for instance, have liked a given teacher because he or she gave clear explanations of ideas, had a friendly manner, and spent individual time with each student.

4. Finally, suppose you have found a good part-time job. Your general idea might be as follows:

   *General idea:* _____ Working at the diner _____ has been a good part-time job for me.

   ● Now write three *specific* supporting reasons for liking the job:

   Pay of $10.00 per hour

   Convenient work hours after school each day

   Travel time of only fifteen minutes to the job

*Explanation*

Three particular reasons for liking a job might include pay of ten dollars an hour, convenient work hours after school each day, and a short travel time of only fifteen minutes to the job.

---

Now do the practices that follow, which will give you more experience in telling the difference between general and specific ideas.

## PRACTICE 1

Each cluster of words below consists of one general idea and three specific ideas. The general idea includes all the specific ideas. Identify each general idea with a **G** and the specific ideas with an **S**. Look first at the example.

*Example*

_S_  frying

_S_  baking

_G_  cooking

_S_  steaming

*To the Instructor:* You might want to ask questions such as the following:

**Item 1:** Which of the ideas are actual *liquids?*
**Item 2:** Which of the ideas are specific *snacks?*
**Item 3:** Which of the ideas are kinds of *fabrics?*
**Item 4:** Which of the ideas are actual *forms of entertainment?*
Similar questions can be asked for items 5 through 10.

(*Cooking* is the general idea. It includes three specific types of cooking: frying, baking, and steaming.)

1. _S_  soup
   _S_  water
   _G_  liquid
   _S_  coffee

2. _S_  potato chips
   _S_  pretzels
   _S_  salted nuts
   _G_  snacks

3. _S_  cotton
   _G_  fabric
   _S_  silk
   _S_  wool

4. _G_  entertainment
   _S_  movies
   _S_  concerts
   _S_  card games

5. _S_  cans
   _S_  boxes
   _S_  bags
   _G_  containers

6. _S_  rock
   _S_  classical
   _S_  country
   _G_  music

7. _S_ necklace
   _G_ jewelry
   _S_ ring
   _S_ bracelet

8. _G_ fish
   _S_ tuna
   _S_ salmon
   _S_ flounder

9. _S_ coughing
   _S_ sneezing
   _G_ symptom
   _S_ sore throat

10. _S_ speaking
    _S_ listening
    _S_ writing
    _G_ communicating

## PRACTICE 2

In each item below, one idea is general and the others are specific. The general idea includes the specific ideas. In the spaces provided, write two more specific ideas that are covered by the general idea.

**Example**   *General:* school subjects
              *Specific:* biology, Spanish, ___history___, ___math___

(*School subjects* is the general idea; *biology* and *Spanish* are specific subjects, as are *history* and *math*.)

*Answers will vary; below are some possibilities.*

1. *General:* beverages
   *Specific:* iced tea, water, ___milk___, ___coffee___

2. *General:* sport
   *Specific:* baseball, soccer, ___football___, ___basketball___

3. *General:* relatives
   *Specific:* cousin, mother ___father___, ___nephew___

4. *General:* sandwich
   *Specific:* ham, grilled cheese, ___tuna___, ___egg salad___

5. *General:* reading material
   *Specific:* textbook, comic book, ___newspaper___, ___magazine___

6. *General:* seafood
   *Specific:* clams, lobster, ___shrimp___, ___crabmeat___

7. *General:* tone of voice
   *Specific:* excited, surprised, ___angry___, ___pleading___

8. *General:*    negative personal quality
   *Specific:*   greed, cowardice,    _selfishness_ ,    _dishonesty_

9. *General:*    positive personal quality
   *Specific:*   reliability, determination,    _loyalty_ ,    _honesty_

10. *General:*   greeting
    *Specific:*  "How are you," "Hello,"    _"Hi there"_ ,    _"Good morning"_

---

## PRACTICE 3

In the following groups, one statement is the general point (and main idea), and the other statements are specific support for the point. Identify each point with a **P** and each statement of support with an **S.**

1. _S_ A. A mosquito can find you in the dark.
   _S_ B. A mosquito can keep you awake all night.
   _P_ C. Though a mosquito is small, it has a lot of power.
   _S_ D. A mosquito can make you scratch yourself until you bleed.

   Three examples of a mosquito's power are listed.

2. _S_ A. The bread the waiter brought us is stale.
   _S_ B. We've been waiting for our main course for over an hour.
   _S_ C. The people at the next table are awfully loud.
   _P_ D. It is time to speak to the restaurant manager.

   Three reasons to speak to the restaurant manager are listed.

3. _S_ A. The apartment has no closets.
   _S_ B. The kitchen is so small only one person can be there.
   _S_ C. Each morning the apartment fills with exhaust fumes from a nearby bus station.
   _P_ D. The apartment has some real drawbacks.

   Three drawbacks to the apartment are listed.

4. _P_ A. That teacher is very demanding.
   _S_ B. She calls on students who don't make eye contact with her.
   _S_ C. Students must e-mail her if they intend to miss a class.
   _S_ D. A paper handed in late is reduced a whole grade for each day it's late.

   Three ways in which the teacher is demanding are listed.

**PRACTICE 4**

In the following groups—all based on textbook selections—one statement is the general point (and main idea), and the other statements are specific support for the point. Identify each point with a **P** and each statement of support with an **S.**

1. __S__ A. Only one in three adults engages in regular physical activity.

   __S__ B. The percentage of obese adults has more than doubled in the past 40 years.

   __S__ C. About one in five adults still smokes cigarettes.    Statements A, B, and C

   __P__ D. Americans are not as healthy as they should be.    give examples of ways
   Americans are not healthy.

2. __S__ A. Couples committed to each other gain strength from their mutual support.

   __S__ B. Committed couples are financially more successful than singles.

   __P__ C. Committed relationships offer many benefits.

   __S__ D. Happily married adults live longer and have fewer emotional problems.
   Three benefits of committed relationships are listed.

3. __S__ A. Finding safety in numbers, bats live in large colonies numbering from several thousand to a million or more.

   __P__ B. Bats are creatures with a strong instinct to protect their own kind.

   __S__ C. Mother bats, who usually have one offspring per year, leave their young only to get food.

   __S__ D. When colonies containing mother bats are disturbed, the mothers will try to move their young to a safer location.    Three examples of bats'
   protective instinct are listed.

4. __P__ A. In 17th-century Europe, people went through a lot of trouble to wear makeup.

   __S__ B. To wear makeup at that time, men and women had to put an unpleasant mixture of lead, egg whites, and vinegar on their faces.

   __S__ C. Once a person's makeup was applied, he or she had to be careful not to laugh, or the new "face" would crack.

   __S__ D. The lead in the makeup caused scars and blemishes, which had to be covered with patches of cloth.    Statements B, C, and D give examples of
   the trouble people went through to wear makeup.

## 2   Use the Topic to Lead You to the Main Idea

You already know that to find the main idea of a selection, you look first for a general statement. You then check to see if that statement is supported by all or most of the other material in the paragraph. If it is, you've found the main idea. Another approach that can help you find the main idea of a selection is to look for its topic.

The **topic** is the general subject of a selection. It is not a complete sentence, but can be simply expressed in several words. Knowing the topic can help you find a writer's main point about that topic.

Textbook authors use the title of each chapter to state the overall topic of that chapter. They also provide many topics and subtopics in boldface headings within the chapter. For example, here is the title of a section in a psychology textbook:

**Why We Communicate**

And here are the subtopics:

**Physical Needs**

**Identity Needs**

**Social Needs**

**Practical Goals**

If you were studying the above chapter, you could use the topics to help find the main ideas.

But there are many times when you are not given topics—with standardized reading tests, for example, or with individual paragraphs in articles or textbooks. To find the topic of a selection when the topic is not given, ask this simple question:

**Who or what is the selection about?**

For example, look again at the beginning of the paragraph that started this chapter:

Poor grades in school can have various causes.

What, in just a few words, is the above paragraph about? On the line below, write what you think is the topic.

*Topic:* _____ Poor grades in school _____

You probably answered that the topic is "poor grades in school." As you reread the paragraph, you saw that, in fact, every sentence in it is about poor grades.

The next step after finding the topic is to decide what main point the author is making about the topic. Authors often present their main idea in a single sentence. (This sentence is also known as the **main idea sentence** or the **topic sentence**.) As we have already seen, the main point about poor grades is "Poor grades in school can have various causes."

## ✓ *Check Your Understanding*

Let's look now at another paragraph. Read it and then see if you can answer the questions that follow.

> [1]Phobias are continuing fears of things that are not likely to be harmful. [2]For example, some people have a phobia about elevators. [3]They worry that if they enter an elevator, the cable will break and they will fall hundreds of feet to their death. [4]While such an accident can happen, it is extremely rare. [5]Another instance of a phobia is a fear of medical needles. [6]Some people will refuse to receive an injection, even if they are seriously ill. [7]They may faint if given a needle; so great is their fear that they are about to die. [8]Perhaps the most common phobia is fear of public speaking. [9]Some people will not go to school or take jobs if they have to speak before a group. [10]Their fear—that they will embarrass themselves and that people will pity or reject them—has little basis in reality. [11]These and other phobias can usually be overcome, often fairly quickly, with the right direction and treatment.

___B___ 1. Write the letter of the *topic* of the paragraph. To find the topic, ask yourself what the paragraph is about. (It often helps as you read to look for and even circle a word, term, or idea that is repeated in the paragraph.)

    A. dangers
    B. phobias
    C. worry about elevators

___1___ 2. Write the number of the sentence that states the *main idea* of the paragraph. In other words, what point is the author making about the topic? (Remember that the main idea will be supported by the other material in the paragraph.)

### Explanation

As the first sentence of the paragraph suggests, the topic is "phobias." Continuing to read the paragraph, you see that, in fact, everything in it is about phobias. And the main idea is clearly sentence 1: "Phobias are continuing fears of things that are not likely to be harmful." This idea is a general one that sums up what the entire paragraph is about. It is an "umbrella" statement under which all the other material in the paragraph fits. The parts of the paragraph could be shown as follows:

**Topic:** Phobias

**Main idea:** Phobias are continuing fears of things that are not likely to be harmful.

**Supporting details:**

1. Fear that an elevator ride will end in a fall to death.
2. Fear that an injection will cause death.
3. Fear that speaking in public will lead to pity or rejection.

---

The following practices will sharpen your sense of the difference between a topic, the point about the topic (the main idea), and the supporting details.

## PRACTICE 5

Below are groups of four items. In each case, one item is the topic, one is the main idea, and two are details that support and develop the main idea. Label each item with one of the following:

T  — for the **topic** of the paragraph
MI — for the **main idea**
SD — for the **supporting details**

Note that an explanation is provided for the first group; reading it will help you do this practice.

### Group 1

_SD_  A. One pitcher smoothes the dirt on the pitcher's mound before he throws each pitch.

_SD_  B. One infielder sits in the same spot on the dugout bench during every game.

_MI_  C. Some baseball players think that certain superstitious habits help them win games.

_T_  D. Superstitious baseball players.

*Explanation*

All of the statements in Group 1 involve superstitious baseball players, so item D must be the topic. (A topic is expressed in a single word or short phrase and is not a complete sentence.) Statements A and B each describe specific superstitious habits of individual baseball players. Statement C, however, is more general—it states that some players think certain superstitious habits help them win games. Statement C thus gives the main idea, and statements A and B are supporting details that explain that main idea.

**Group 2**

_SD_   A. Houdini learned to pop his shoulder out of its socket in order to escape from straitjackets.

_MI_   B. Harry Houdini, the famous escape artist, worked hard at his career.

_T_   C. Harry Houdini.

_SD_   D. Houdini trained to hold his breath for over five minutes in order to pull off underwater escapes.     All of the statements involve Harry Houdini, so item C is the topic. (Note that C is not a complete sentence.) Statements A and D provide details that show how hard Houdini worked at his career.

**Group 3**

_MI_   A. Some body fat is essential.

_T_   B. Body fat.     All the statements involve body fat, so item B is the topic.

_SD_   C. Body fat insulates against the cold.     (Note that B is not a complete

_SD_   D. Body fat protects organs from injury.     sentence.) Statements C and D explain specific ways in which fat is essential.

**Group 4**

_SD_   A. At dinnertime, instead of cooking, many people simply go to a fast-food restaurant or order take-out.

_SD_   B. More and more families rely on prepared meals from the frozen-foods section or the "deli" counter.

_MI_   C. Home cooking is becoming a lost art.

_T_   D. Home cooking.     Statements A and B provide specific reasons why home cooking (the topic) is becoming a lost art.

## PRACTICE 6

Following are four paragraphs. Read each paragraph and write the letter of the item you think is the topic of the paragraph. Then write the number of the sentence you think states the main idea of the paragraph.

Here is how to proceed:

**1**   Ask yourself, "What seems to be the topic of the paragraph?" (It often helps to look for and even circle a word or idea that is repeated in the paragraph.)

> *Hint*: When looking for the topic, make sure you do not pick one that is either **too broad** (covering a great deal more than is in the selection) or **too narrow** (covering only part of the selection). The topic and the main idea of a selection must include everything in that selection—no more and no less.

**2** Next, ask yourself, "What point is the writer making about this topic?" This will be the main idea. In this practice, it is stated in one of the sentences in the paragraph.

**3** Then test what you think is the main idea by asking, "Is this statement supported by all or most of the other material in the paragraph?"

## Paragraph 1

¹The influence of sports reaches far and wide. ²Most of us have had some experiences with athletics, either as players or as spectators. ³Schools, from kindergarten to college, provide many chances to participate in sports. ⁴Newspapers and the Internet carry more news about sports than about politics, crime, or the economy. ⁵Radio and television newscasts seldom go on the air without a sports report. ⁶Football, basketball, baseball, and other games are often broadcast in full, even in place of regular programming. ⁷Sports have so much influence on our lives that our everyday speech is full of sports expressions: "struck out," "touch base," "ballpark figure," "game plan," "teamwork," "cheap shot," and so on.

_B_ 1. The topic of the paragraph is
    A. athletics.
    B. influence of sports.
    C. sports expressions.

The word *sports* is mentioned six times in the paragraph. Answer A is too broad, and answer C is too narrow.

_1_ 2. Write the number of the sentence that states the main idea of the paragraph. Sentence 1 states that sports' influence reaches far and wide. The remaining sentences provide examples of the influence of sports.

## Paragraph 2

¹The female black widow spider is not as terrible a killer as is generally believed. ²While the creature is certainly poisonous, she is also very shy and will bite humans only when she feels cornered. ³Also, the idea that the black widow always kills the male after mating is untrue. ⁴The male is often spared—if he remembers to tap out a special signal as he ventures onto his mate's web. ⁵The vibrations on the web let her know he is one of her own kind, not an insect to be rushed at and killed.

_A_ 3. The topic of the paragraph is
    A. the female black widow spider.
    B. poisonous spiders.
    C. the unlucky male black widow spider.

Answer B is too broad; answer C is too narrow.

_1_ 4. Write the number of the sentence that states the main idea of the paragraph. Sentence 1 states the female black widow is not as terrible a killer as many believe. Sentences 2–5 provide specific examples to support this idea.

## Paragraph 3

¹Potato chips got their start because of a hard-to-please restaurant customer in 1853. ²In that year, George Crum was working as a chef at an elegant resort in Saratoga Springs, New York. ³He prepared thick-cut French-fried potatoes for diners there. ⁴But one diner kept sending his potatoes back to the kitchen, complaining that they were too thick for his taste. ⁵Crum cut the potatoes thinner and thinner and finally, very annoyed, made a serving of potatoes too thin and crisp to eat with a fork. ⁶To his surprise, the guest loved them. ⁷Other guests demanded a taste. ⁸Soon "Saratoga Chips" were the most popular item on the menu.

_C_ 5. The topic of the paragraph is
   A. a hard-to-please customer.        Answer A is too narrow;
   B. the origins of foods.             answer B is too broad.
   C. potato chips.

_1_ 6. Write the number of the sentence that states the main idea of the
   paragraph.        Sentence 1 states potato chips began with a hard-to-please
   restaurant customer. The remaining sentences provide details to support this idea.

## Paragraph 4

¹People have always loved bike riding. ²Biking, however, can be a dangerous activity. ³One danger is "getting doored"—having a car driver open his or her door directly into the path of an oncoming bike. ⁴Another risk is aggressive drivers who feel they have more right to the roads than bikes do. ⁵Such drivers will scream, honk, or gesture wildly. ⁶They may block off bikers without a signal or a look, giving the biker no time to avoid running off the road or into the car. ⁷An added source of danger for bikers is poor road design, which in many cases allows just enough room for a car on either side of the road, but no extra room for a biker to be on the same road. ⁸Recently, the U.S. Department of Transportation noted that bicycling is now more dangerous than flying in planes or riding in buses, boats, or trains.

_A_ 7. The topic of the paragraph is
   A. biking.
   B. transportation.                   Answer B is too broad;
   C. getting "doored."                 answer C is too narrow.

_2_ 8. Write the number of the sentence that states the main idea of the
   paragraph.        Sentence 1 is introductory material. Sentence 2 states that
   biking can be dangerous. The remaining sentences provide
   specific examples of the dangers of biking.

## 3  Find and Use Key Words to Lead You to the Main Idea

Sometimes authors make it fairly easy to find their main idea. They announce it by using **key words**—words or phrases that are easy to recognize. These key words are clues to the main idea.

One type of key word is a **list word** or words, which tell you a list of items is to follow. For example, the main idea in the paragraph about poor grades was stated like this: *Poor grades in school can have various causes.* The expression *various causes* helps you zero in on the main idea. You realize that the paragraph will be about the causes of poor grades. As you read on and see the series of causes, you know your guess about the main idea was correct.

Below are examples of some common word groups that often announce a main idea. Note that nearly all of them contain a word that ends in **s**—a plural that suggests the supporting details will be a list of items.

*List Words*

| | | |
|---|---|---|
| several kinds of | various causes | a few reasons |
| a number of | a series of | three factors |
| four steps | among the results | several advantages |

When expressions like these appear in a sentence, look carefully to see if that sentence might be the main idea. Chances are a sentence with these words will be followed by a list of major supporting details.

> *Note*  Many other list-word expressions are possible. For example, a writer could begin a paragraph with a sentence containing "four kinds of" or "some advantages of" or "three reasons for." So if you see a sentence with a word group like the ones above, you've probably found the main idea.

---

## ✔ *Check Your Understanding: List Words*

Underline the list words in the following sentences.

> *Hint:*  Remember that list words usually end in *s*.

*Example*   Being a middle child in a large family has several drawbacks.

1. The rising rate of diabetes among young people seems to have three causes.

2. Several symptoms may indicate that a person is having a heart attack.

3. The Pilgrims faced a number of challenges during their first winter in America.

4. Community colleges have some real advantages over four-year colleges.

5. Students offer a variety of excuses for their homework being late.

*Explanation*

In the first sentence, you should have underlined the phrase *three causes*. Those words suggest that a list of the three causes of the rising rate of diabetes among young people may follow. In sentences 2–5, you should have underlined these groups of words: *several symptoms, a number of challenges, some real advantages,* and *a variety of excuses.* Each of those phrases also tells you that a list of supporting details may follow.

There is another type of key word that can alert you to the main idea. This type of key word, called an **addition word**, is generally used right before a supporting detail. Below is a box of words that often introduce major supporting details and help you discover the main idea.

*Addition Words*

| one | to begin with | in addition | last |
|-----|---------------|-------------|------|
| first | another | next | last of all |
| first of all | second | moreover | final |
| for one thing | also | furthermore | finally |

## Check Your Understanding: Addition Words

Reread the paragraph about causes of poor grades and underline the addition words that alert you to supporting details. Also, see if you can circle the list words that suggest the main idea.

> [1]Poor grades in school can have (various causes.) [2]For one thing, students may have financial problems. [3]If they need to work long hours to make money, they will have little study time. [4]Another cause of poor grades may be trouble with relationships. [5]A student may be unhappy over family problems or a lack of friends. [6]That unhappiness can harm schoolwork. [7]A final cause of poor grades may be bad study habits. [8]Some students have never learned how to take good notes in class, how to manage their time effectively, or how to study a textbook. [9]Without such study skills, their grades are likely to suffer.

*Explanation*

The words that introduce each new supporting detail for the main idea are *For one thing, Another*, and *final*. These addition words help you realize that all the details in the paragraph are supporting the idea that poor grades in school can have various causes. You should have underlined these three words.

Since *various causes* are list words, you should have circled them. Even before you saw the addition words, those list words could have suggested to you that the paragraph may list the different causes of poor grades.  As you can see, in this paragraph (as in many others), list words and addition words work hand in hand.

## PRACTICE 7

The chapters that follow will offer a good deal of practice in key words. For now, do the activity below.

**A.** Underline the list words in each of the following sentences.

1. Living alone has a number of advantages.

2. Physical punishment can be harmful to a child in several ways.

3. The Industrial Revolution came about quickly because of three major inventions.

4. A series of mistakes led to the arrest and imprisonment of the wrong person.

5. To memorize materials effectively, there are two important steps to follow.

6. The National Board of Medical Examiners has released some alarming facts about doctors.

**B.** (7–10.) Underline the four addition words or phrases in the following passage.

List words:
*several*
*reasons*

¹Women don't hold more political power in the United States for several reasons. ²First of all, women are still a minority in law and business. ³Those are the fields from which most politicians come. ⁴In addition, political careers usually require a great deal of time spent away from home, and such hours don't tie in well with motherhood. ⁵Also, women are less likely to have a supportive spouse at home, ready to help out with child care, housework, and the like. ⁶Finally, men have not been eager to open up the "boys' club" of political power to women. ⁷They tend to support and encourage upcoming male candidates, not female ones.

## A Note on the Central Point

In selections made up of many paragraphs, the overall main idea is called the **central point**, also known as the **central idea** or **thesis**. You can find a central point in the same way that you find a main idea. First, identify the topic (which is often suggested by the title of the selection). Then look at the supporting material. The paragraphs within the longer reading will provide supporting details for the central point.

# MAIN IDEAS IN READING: Mastery Test 1

**A.** Each cluster of words below consists of one general idea and three specific ideas. The general idea includes all the specific ideas. Underline the general idea in each group.

| | | | |
|---|---|---|---|
| 1. oak | <u>tree</u> | maple | pine |
| 2. iron | tin | <u>metal</u> | aluminum |
| 3. <u>insect</u> | ant | roach | fly |
| 4. basketball | hockey | tennis | <u>sport</u> |

**B.** In each item below, one idea is general, and the other two are specific. The general idea includes the specific ideas. In the spaces provided, write **two** more specific ideas that are covered by the general idea.

*Answers will vary; below are some possibilities.*

5–6. *General:* fruit
*Specific:* orange, pineapple, _____banana_____ , _____grape_____

7–8. *General:* country
*Specific:* Canada, Greece, _____Mexico_____ , _____Egypt_____

9–10. *General:* holiday
*Specific:* Independence Day, Labor Day, _____Thanksgiving_____ , _____Christmas_____

11–12. *General:* criminal
*Specific:* kidnapper, arsonist, _____murderer_____ , _____robber_____

**C.** (13–20.) In each group below, one statement is the general point, and the other statements are specific support for the point. Identify the point with a **P** and each statement of support with an **S**.

## Group 1

___S___ A. Pet owners survive longer after a major illness than people who don't own pets.

___S___ B. Daily time with pets aids relaxation and decreases stress.

___P___ C. Pet ownership has positive effects on people's health.

___S___ D. Petting an animal lowers blood pressure in humans.

List signal: *positive effects.* Statements A, B, and D are three of these effects.

*(Continues on next page)*

## Group 2

_S_ A. Certain harmless snakes eat poisonous ones.

_S_ B. Snakes help control the rodent population by eating mice and rats.

_S_ C. Medicines for humans have been developed from snake venom.

_P_ D. Despite their poor public image, snakes have their good points.

List signal: *good points*.
Statements A, B, and C are three examples of good points about snakes.

# MAIN IDEAS IN READING: Mastery Test 2

**A.** Each cluster of words below consists of one general idea and three specific ideas. The general idea includes all the specific ideas. Underline the general idea in each group.

| | | | |
|---|---|---|---|
| 1. rose | daisy | tulip | <u>flower</u> |
| 2. sofa | <u>furniture</u> | table | chair |
| 3. <u>illness</u> | flu | measles | pneumonia |
| 4. socks | jacket | <u>clothes</u> | shirt |

**B.** In each item below, one idea is general, and the other two are specific. The general idea includes the specific ideas. In the spaces provided, write **two** more specific ideas that are covered by the general idea.

*Answers will vary; below are some possibilities.*

5–6.  *General:*  beverages
      *Specific:*  water, milk, _____coffee_____, _____tea_____

7–8.  *General:*  bird
      *Specific:*  parrot, turkey, _____canary_____, _____pigeon_____

9–10.  *General:*  natural disaster
      *Specific:*  earthquake, hurricane, _____flood_____, _____forest fire_____

11–12.  *General:*  happy event
      *Specific:*  birth of a child,
                 getting an A, _____getting married_____, _____graduation_____

**C.** (13–20.) In each group below, one statement is the general point, and the other statements are specific support for the point. Identify the point with a **P** and each statement of support with an **S**.

**Group 1**

*List signal: several simple steps.*
*Statements A, B, and D are three of these steps.*

_S_ A. Bringing homemade popcorn to the movies is cheaper than buying expensive theater popcorn.

_S_ B. Buying candy at a grocery store, not a theater, cuts candy costs in half.

_P_ C. Moviegoers can take several simple steps to save money at the movie theater.

_S_ D. Going to movies early in the day can reduce ticket prices by several dollars.

*(Continues on next page)*

## Group 2

_S_  A. Naps improve people's moods and alertness.

_S_  B. Taking a nap boosts energy and increases work productivity.

_S_  C. After a nap, it is easier to concentrate and make decisions.

_P_  D. People should take a nap every day.

Statements A, B, and C are specific reasons
people should take a nap every day.

# MAIN IDEAS IN READING: Mastery Test 3

**A.** (1–12.) In each group below, one statement is the general point, and the other statements are specific support for the point. Identify each point with a **P** and each statement of support with an **S**.

## Group 1

_S_ A. Tall buildings in the United States often have twelfth and fourteenth floors—but not a thirteenth floor.

_S_ B. Houses in France are never numbered thirteen.

_P_ C. Throughout the world, the number thirteen is viewed as unlucky.

_S_ D. Many global airlines have removed seat number thirteen from airplane seating charts. *Statements A, B, and D give specific examples that show the number thirteen is viewed as unlucky— the main idea expressed in statement C.*

## Group 2

_P_ A. Restaurant ratings are based on more than just food.

_S_ B. A restaurant's service can be almost as significant as the meal itself.

_S_ C. For many restaurant critics, the comfort of the surroundings will be a part of their evaluation.

_S_ D. Menu prices are always taken into consideration. *Statements B, C, and D give examples of things other than food that determine a restaurant's ratings.*

## Group 3

_S_ A. The average American child is exposed to 12,000 violent acts—including rape and murder—on TV each year.

_S_ B. Adults who watch TV two hours a day increase their chances of obesity by 25 percent and diabetes by 14 percent.

_S_ C. Toddlers who watch TV for an hour each day increase their risk of having attention problems by 10 percent.

_P_ D. TV watching can be an unhealthy activity. *Statements A, B, and C give specific reasons why watching TV is unhealthy.*

*(Continues on next page)*

**B.** (13–20.) Each group of four items includes one topic, one main idea, and two supporting ideas. In the space provided, label each item with one of the following:

    T  — for the **topic** of the paragraph
    MI — for the **main idea**
    SD — for the **supporting details**

## Group 1

_SD_  A. Researchers believe one quarter of "mysterious" fires in dwellings in the United States are caused by rats.

_T_  B. Problems caused by rats.

_SD_  C. Studies show that rats are to blame for 26 percent of electrical cable failures in houses and apartments.

_MI_  D. Rats cause serious problems to homeowners and apartment dwellers.

Item B is the topic (a phrase). Items A and C present specific problems caused by rats, the main idea expressed in item D.

## Group 2

_SD_  A. Young Americans are more likely to eat fast food, avoid exercise, be obese, and smoke cigarettes.

_SD_  B. Many do not have health insurance or get regular physical or dental exams and do not receive health care when they need it.

_MI_  C. Young Americans moving into adulthood face significant health risks.

_T_  D. Health risks for young Americans.

Item D is the topic (a phrase). Items A and B name specific reasons young Americans face health risks, the main idea expressed in item C.

# MAIN IDEAS IN READING: Mastery Test 4

**A.** (1–12.) In each group below, one statement is the general point, and the other statements are specific support for the point. Identify each point with a **P** and each statement of support with an **S**.

## Group 1

_P_   A. Some people find it difficult to live without technology.

_S_   B. You never see them sitting quietly reading a book.

_S_   C. When they are out during the day, they do a lot of text-messaging or talking on their cell phones.

_S_   D. At home they watch TV, read e-mail, and spend time on Facebook and other social networks.    Statements B, C, and D describe activities that illustrate how involved some people are with technology. These support the main idea in statement A—that some people find it difficult to live without technology.

## Group 2

_S_   A. Most teens who work do so to develop responsibility and gain independence from their parents.

_S_   B. Almost all teens who work are motivated by a desire to earn spending money.

_S_   C. For a majority of teens, work offers an opportunity to spend time with peers.

_P_   D. Teenagers choose to work during the school year for a variety of reasons.

      Statement D has a list clue: *a variety of reasons.* Statements A, B, and C give specific reasons teenagers work during the school year.

## Group 3

_S_   A. Panic disorder, a type of anxiety in which people experience feelings of panic, affects eight out of every thousand people.

_P_   B. Anxiety is a widespread disorder that many people deal with each day.

_S_   C. Five to 10 percent of Americans suffer from phobias, a type of anxiety in which people experience intense fear of things such as spiders, dogs, or bridges.

_S_   D. About 12 million Americans experience strong fear in social situations— social anxiety—each year.

      Statements A, C, and D present statistics that support the idea that anxiety is a widespread disorder, the main point expressed in answer B.

*(Continues on next page)*

**B.** (13–20.) Each group of four items includes one topic, one main idea, and two supporting ideas. In the space provided, label each item with one of the following:

T   — for the **topic** of the paragraph
MI  — for the **main idea**
SD  — for the **supporting details**

## Group 1

_SD_  A. Women have 15–20 percent more "gray matter" in their brains than men.

_SD_  B. A man's brain is larger and has more "white matter" than a woman's.

_MI_  C. When it comes to their brains, men and women are not equal.

_T_  D. Men's and women's brains.    Item D is the topic (a phrase). Items A and B provide specific examples of how men's and women's brains are not equal, the main idea expressed in item C.

## Group 2

_MI_  A. Crocodiles have shown a remarkable ability to survive.

_SD_  B. Crocodile-like creatures have existed for around 200 million years.

_T_  C. The survival of crocodiles.

_SD_  D. Crocodiles have been known to survive an entire year without food.    Item C is the topic (a phrase). Items B and D provide specific details that show crocodiles have remarkable survival ability, the main idea expressed in item A.

# MAIN IDEAS IN READING: Mastery Test 5

**A.** (1–4.) In the group below, one statement is the general point, and the other statements are specific support for the point. Identify the point with a **P** and each statement of support with an **S**.

_S_  A. On each square inch of your skin, there are millions of live bacteria.

_S_  B. Your mouth is home to the "tooth amoeba," a tiny organism that feeds on food and dead cells. *Statements A, B, and D provide examples of organisms that live on the human body.*

_P_  C. Your body, like those of all humans, is home to many organisms.

_S_  D. Tiny mites live in the roots of your eyelashes and feed on dead tissue.

**B.** (5–12.) Each group of four items includes one topic, one main idea, and two supporting details. In the space provided, label each item with one of the following:

**T**  — for the **topic** of the paragraph
**MI** — for the **main idea**
**SD** — for the **supporting details**

## Group 1

_SD_  A. One or two cups of coffee a day relieve drowsiness and can increase concentration.

_SD_  B. Drinking a cup of coffee before a workout boosts strength and fights muscle fatigue.

_T_  C. The effects of drinking coffee.

_MI_  D. Coffee, when consumed in reasonable amounts, can produce positive effects on the body. *Item C is the topic (a phrase). Item D contains list words (positive effects) to suggest the main idea. Items A and B list those effects.*

## Group 2

_SD_  A. Sunglasses that block harmful ultraviolet light were first developed by the space program.

_MI_  B. Surprisingly, the U.S. space program has led to some useful items in everyday life.

_SD_  C. The material in football helmets and protective padding was first made to protect astronauts in space.

_T_  D. Some unexpected benefits of the U.S. space program. *Item D is the topic (a phrase). Item B contains list words (some useful items) to suggest the main idea. Items A and C present examples of those useful items.*

*(Continues on next page)*

**C.** In the space provided, write the letter of the list words in each sentence. (List words are a clue to what supporting details to look for in a paragraph.)

**Items 13–16:**
See page 58. The words *a number of, several key factors, effects,* and *reasons* often signal main ideas.

___A___ 13. People who do not vote in national elections give a number of excuses.
    A. *a number of excuses*        C. *people who do not vote*
    B. *national elections*

___C___ 14. To decide whether or not to take a job, consider several key factors.
    A. *To decide*      B. *whether or not*      C. *several key factors*

___C___ 15. One study after another has found that cigarette smoking has long-term effects on the body.
    A. *One study after another*      C. *long-term effects*
    B. *cigarette smoking*

___C___ 16. Advertising should not be permitted on children's television shows for a variety of reasons.
    A. *Advertising should not be permitted*      C. *a variety of reasons*
    B. *children's television shows*

**D.** Read the following passage. Then, in the space provided, write the letter of the addition words that introduce each supporting detail.

**Items 17–20:**
See page 59. Addition words such as *For one thing, In addition, Another,* and *Finally* are commonly used to signal details that support the main idea.

¹Illiterate people face great problems in our society. ²For one thing, people who cannot read or write are limited in a world full of print. ³They can't read stories in the newspaper or the menu in a restaurant. ⁴In a supermarket, they must depend on packages with familiar pictures and colors. ⁵In addition, illiterate people do not vote. ⁶As a result, they are "half-citizens" who cannot exercise their democratic rights. ⁷Another problem is in pursuing an education. ⁸Illiterate people find it difficult to take courses that might help them advance in their job or get a better job. ⁹Finally, they have trouble helping their children learn. ¹⁰They are not able to help with homework and often do not visit a school for fear of embarrassing their child or themselves.

___B___ 17. The addition words that signal the first problem of illiterate people are
    A. *limited in a world full of print.*
    B. *For one thing.*
    C. *familiar pictures and colors.*

___C___ 18. The addition words that signal the second problem of illiterate people are
    A. *"half-citizens."*    B. *democratic rights.*    C. *In addition.*

___A___ 19. The addition word that signals the third problem of illiterate people is
    A. *Another.*    B. *education.*    C. *courses.*

___C___ 20. The addition word that signals the fourth problem of illiterate people is
    A. *trouble.*    B. *embarrassing.*    C. *Finally.*

# MAIN IDEAS IN READING: Mastery Test 6

**A.** (1–4.) In the group below, one statement is the general point, and the other statements are specific support for the point. Identify the point with a **P** and each statement of support with an **S.**

_S_ A. Hungry fans can buy anything from hot dogs to barbecued sandwiches to vegetarian food.

_S_ B. The restrooms are large, plentiful, and well maintained.

_S_ C. No matter where you sit, you always have a good view of the action.

_P_ D. The new stadium is a great place to enjoy a game.    Statements A, B, and C are specific examples of why the new stadium is a great place to enjoy a game.

**B.** (5–12.) Each group of four items includes one topic, one main idea, and two supporting details. In the space provided, label each item with one of the following:

  T — for the **topic** of the paragraph
  MI — for the **main idea**
  SD — for the **supporting details**

## Group 1

_SD_ A. Those exposed to secondhand smoke for 30 years or more are 23 percent more likely to get lung cancer.

_MI_ B. Exposure to secondhand smoke presents a number of serious health hazards to nonsmokers.

_T_ C. Exposure to secondhand smoke.

_SD_ D. Nonsmokers exposed to secondhand smoke at home have a 15 percent higher death rate than those exposed to clean air.

Item C is the topic (a phrase). Item B contains list words (*a number of serious health hazards*) to suggest the main idea. Items A and D list those hazards.

## Group 2

_T_ A. Advances in computer technology.

_SD_ B. E-mail is now used to steal people's identification and credit card information.

_SD_ C. High-speed Internet connections are used to send harmful viruses around the world.

_MI_ D. Advances in computer technology have created new tools for criminals.    Item A is the topic (a phrase). Item D, the main idea, states that computer technology has given criminals new tools. Items B and C are examples of those tools.

*(Continues on next page)*

**C.** In the space provided, write the letter of the list words in each sentence.

Items 13–16: See page 58. The words *for several reasons, a number of,* and *some* often signal main ideas.

_C_ 13. Most mothers cradle their babies in their left arms for several reasons.
    A. *Most mothers*         C. *for several reasons*
    B. *cradle their babies*

_B_ 14. Marriage has undergone a number of changes in recent years.
    A. *Marriage*         C. *in recent years*
    B. *a number of changes*

_C_ 15. The original versions of famous fairy tales have some shocking outcomes.
    A. *original versions*         C. *some shocking outcomes*
    B. *famous fairy tales*

_C_ 16. Although most celebrities would probably not choose different lives, they would agree that fame has some real drawbacks.
    A. *most celebrities*         C. *some real drawbacks*
    B. *different lives*

**D.** Read the following passage. Then, in the space provided, write the letter of the addition words that introduce each supporting detail.

Items 17–20: See page 59. Addition words such as *first, also, next,* and *final* are commonly used to signal details that support the main idea.

[1]There are several parenting styles. [2]The <u>first</u> is the authoritarian style. [3]Authoritarian parents give orders and punish their children if those orders are not quickly obeyed. [4]There is <u>also</u> the authoritative style. [5]Authoritative parents make it clear they are in charge, but they are open to seeing their children's point of view. [6]The <u>next</u> style is that of permissive parents, who avoid ever saying "no" and give the children a good deal of power. [7]The <u>final</u> parenting style is uninvolved. [8]An uninvolved parent does not ask much of children, and does not give much attention either. [9]Most child-raising experts feel that children's needs are best met by authoritative parents.

_B_ 17. The addition word that signals the first parenting style is
    A. *several.*       B. *first.*       C. *punish.*

_A_ 18. The addition word that signals the second parenting style is
    A. *also.*       B. *but.*       C. *point.*

_C_ 19. The addition word that signals the third parenting style is
    A. *permissive.*       B. *avoid.*       C. *next.*

_B_ 20. The addition word that signals the fourth parenting style is
    A. *uninvolved.*       B. *final.*       C. *best.*

# ③ Supporting Details in Reading

$L$ook at the cartoon below and see if you can answer the questions that follow.

© Randy Glasbergen.
www.glasbergen.com

GLASBERGEN

"No thanks, I don't need any insurance. I don't live in a house. I don't drive a car. I don't own anything. And I don't get sick."

● What is the frog's *main idea*, or point?

● What is his *support* for his point?

*Explanation*

The frog's main idea, or point, is that he does not need any insurance. He supports his point by providing four reasons he doesn't need health insurance: no house, no car, no possessions, no health worries.

Chapter 2 introduced you to the most important reading skill—the ability to find the main idea. A closely related reading skill is the ability to locate supporting details. Supporting details provide the added information that is needed for you to make sense of a main idea.

# What Are Supporting Details?

**Supporting details** are reasons, examples, steps, or other kinds of evidence that explain a main idea, or point.

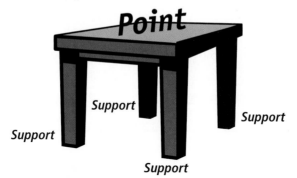

In the model paragraph in Chapter 2, the supporting details appear as a series of reasons:

> [1]Poor grades in school can have various causes. [2]For one thing, students may have financial problems. [3]If they need to work long hours to make money, they will have little study time. [4]Another cause of poor grades may be trouble with relationships. [5]A student may be unhappy over family problems or a lack of friends. [6]That unhappiness can harm schoolwork. [7]A final cause of poor grades may be bad study habits. [8]Some students have never learned how to take good notes in class, how to manage their time effectively, or how to study a textbook. [9]Without such study skills, their grades are likely to suffer.

---

## ✔ Check Your Understanding

See if you can complete the basic outline below that shows the three reasons that support the main idea. The first one has been added for you. Then read the explanation that follows.

**Main idea:  Poor grades in school can have various causes.**

Supporting detail 1:  Financial problems

Supporting detail 2: _Trouble with relationships_

Supporting detail 3: _Bad study habits_

*Explanation*

You should have added "Trouble with relationships" and "Bad study habits" as the two other supporting details. Notice that the supporting details provide the added information—the specific causes of poor grades—that is needed for you to fully understand the main idea. To read effectively, then, you must recognize both main ideas and the details that support those ideas.

In the paragraph on the previous page, about poor grades, the supporting details are *reasons*. Now look at the paragraph below, in which the main idea is explained by *examples*. In the outline provided, write in the main idea and the words that serve as examples.

[1]Some everyday words are actually based on people's names. [2]For example, the word *sandwich* originated when the Earl of Sandwich, a British nobleman who loved to play cards, became hungry during a game in 1762. [3]Not wanting to stop playing, he asked a servant to bring him some roast beef between two pieces of toasted bread. [4]The quick portable snack was soon called a *sandwich*. [5]Another person whose name became a word is a Frenchman named Dr. Guillotin. [6]During the French Revolution, he pleaded for a quicker, kinder way than hanging to execute criminals. [7]The result was the *guillotine*, a machine with a heavy blade used to behead people. [8]A third example comes from a 19th-century Irish landlord named Mr. Boycott. [9]When he refused to lower the high rents he was charging, his tenants stopped speaking to him. [10]Today, to *boycott* means to refuse to do business with a person or company.

**Main idea:** _Some everyday words are actually based on people's names._

　　Supporting detail 1: _Sandwich_

　　Supporting detail 2: _Guillotine_

　　Supporting detail 3: _Boycott_

*Explanation*

The main idea is the first sentence of the paragraph, and the supporting details are the three examples given: *sandwich, guillotine,* and *boycott*.

# Outlining

Preparing an outline of a passage will help you see clearly the relationship between a main idea and its supporting details. Notice how the outlines on this page and the next page help you see and understand material at a glance.

**Outlines** are lists that show the important parts of a piece of writing. They begin with a main idea, with supporting details placed, in order, underneath the main idea. There may be two levels of supporting details—major and minor. The **major details** explain and develop the main idea. In turn, the **minor details** under them help fill out and make clear the major details.

Once you know how to outline, you can use the skill to prepare very useful study notes. Instead of studying fact after fact in sentence after sentence, you can organize the material into outlines. Good outlines clearly tie ideas together, making them easier to understand and remember.

Below is a more detailed outline of the paragraph on poor grades. This outline shows both major and minor details:

**Main idea:  Poor grades in school can have various causes.**

| | |
|---|---|
| **Major detail:** | 1.  Financial problems |
| Minor details: | a.  Need to work long hours after school |
| | b.  No time left to study |
| **Major detail:** | 2.  Trouble with relationships |
| Minor details: | a.  Unhappiness over family problems |
| | b.  Unhappiness over a lack of friends |
| **Major detail:** | 3.  Bad study habits |
| Minor details: | a.  No skill in taking class notes |
| | b.  No skill in time management |
| | c.  No skill in studying a textbook |

The main idea is supported and explained by the major details, and in turn the major details are supported and explained by the minor details. For example, the major detail of "bad study habits" is supported by three details: no skill in notetaking, time management, or textbook studying.

## ✔ Check Your Understanding

See if you can fill in the missing major and minor supporting details in the outline of the following paragraph.

> [1]To motivate workers, managers should practice several methods of building self-esteem. [2]One way to build self-esteem is to show a genuine interest in what workers have to say. [3]Ask for their opinions, and really listen to their responses. [4]A second method of improving self-esteem is to practice good conversational habits. [5]Do so in three ways: by looking a worker in the eye, by smiling frequently, and by calling workers by their first name—the most important word in the language to every person. [6]Last of all, managers can build esteem by admitting mistakes. [7]Doing so, they show that it is simply human to do the wrong thing at times.

**Main idea:** **To motivate workers, managers should practice several methods of building self-esteem.**

1. Show genuine interest in what workers have to say.
   a. Ask for their opinions.
   b. Really listen to their responses.
2. Practice good conversational habits. _____.
   a. Look a worker in the eye. _____
   b. Smile frequently. _____
   c. Call workers by first name. _____
3. Admit mistakes. _____

*Wording of answers may vary.*

### Explanation

You should have added two major details: (2) practice good conversational habits; (3) admit mistakes. And below the second major supporting detail, you should have added three minor details: (a) look a worker in the eye; (b) smile frequently; (c) call workers by first name.

Notice that just as the main idea is more general than its supporting details, major details are more general than minor ones. For instance, the major detail "to practice good conversational habits" is more general than the three minor supporting details: looking a worker in the eye, smiling, and using first names.

## Outlining Tips

The following tips will help you prepare outlines:

 **TIP 1    Look for words that tell you a list of details is coming.** List words were introduced in Chapter 2 on page 58. Here are some common list words:

*List Words*

| | | |
|---|---|---|
| several kinds of | various causes | a few reasons |
| a number of | a series of | three factors |
| four steps | among the results | several advantages |

For example, look again at the main ideas in two of the paragraphs already discussed, and circle the list words:

- Poor grades in school can have (various causes.)
- To motivate workers, managers should practice (several methods) of building self-esteem.

*Explanation*

In the main ideas above, the words *various causes* and *several methods* tell us that a list of major details is coming. You will not always be given such helpful signals that a list of details will follow. However, be ready to take advantage of them when they are present. Such list words can help you understand quickly the basic organization of a passage.

 **TIP 2    Look for words that signal major details.** Such words are called **addition words**, and they were also introduced in Chapter 2 on pages 59–60. Here are some common addition words:

*Addition Words*

| | | | |
|---|---|---|---|
| one | to begin with | in addition | last |
| first | another | next | last of all |
| first of all | second | moreover | final |
| for one thing | also | furthermore | finally |

## ✔ Check Your Understanding

Now look again at the selection on poor grades, shown below, and answer the questions that follow.

> ¹Poor grades in school can have various causes. ²For one thing, students may have financial problems. ³If they need to work long hours to make money, they will have little study time. ⁴Another cause of poor grades may be trouble with relationships. ⁵A student may be unhappy over family problems or a lack of friends. ⁶That unhappiness can harm schoolwork. ⁷A final cause of poor grades may be bad study habits. ⁸Some students have never learned how to take good notes in class, how to manage their time effectively, or how to study a textbook. ⁹Without such study skills, their grades are likely to suffer.

- Which words signal the first major detail? _____ For one thing _____
- Which word signals the second major detail? _____ Another _____
- Which word signals the third major detail? _____ final _____

Look also at the selection on motivating workers, shown below, and answer the questions that follow.

> ¹To motivate workers, managers should practice several methods of building self-esteem. ²One way to build self-esteem is to show a genuine interest in what workers have to say. ³Ask for their opinions and really listen to their responses. ⁴A second method of improving self-esteem is to practice good conversational habits. ⁵Do so in three ways: by looking a worker in the eye, by smiling frequently, and by calling workers by their first name—the most important word in the language to every person. ⁶Last of all, managers can build esteem by admitting mistakes. ⁷Doing so, they show that it is simply human to do the wrong thing at times.

- Which word signals the first major detail? _____ One _____
- Which word signals the second major detail? _____ second _____
- Which words signal the third major detail? _____ Last of all _____

### Explanation
In the first selection, on poor grades, the addition word signals are *For one thing,* *Another,* and *final.* In the second selection, on motivating workers, the word signals are *One, second,* and *Last of all.*

**TIP 3    In your outline, put all supporting details of equal importance at the same distance from the margin.** In the outline of the paragraph on poor grades (page 76), the three major supporting details all begin at the margin. Likewise, the minor supporting details are all indented at the same distance from the margin. You can therefore see at a glance the main idea, the major details, and the minor details.

---

## ✔ *Check Your Understanding*

Put appropriate numbers *(1, 2, 3)* and letters *(a, b, c)* in front of the major and minor details in the following outline.

    **Main idea**

      <u>1</u>  **Major detail**

        <u>a</u>  Minor detail

        <u>b</u>  Minor detail

      <u>2</u>  **Major detail**

        <u>a</u>  Minor detail

        <u>b</u>  Minor detail

      <u>3</u>  **Major detail**

*Explanation*

You should have put a *1, 2,* and *3* in front of the major details and an *a* and *b* in front of the minor details. Note that an outline proceeds from the most general to the most specific, from main idea to major details to minor details.

---

The practice that follows will give you experience in finding major details, in separating major details from minor details, and in preparing outlines.

> *Hint:*   As you read each passage in this practice and those that follow, circle the list words and underline the addition words. Another helpful technique is to number the major details in each passage *1, 2, 3,* etc.

## PRACTICE 1

Read each passage. Then complete the outline that follows by filling in the missing major and minor details. (Some details have been added for you.) Finally, answer the questions that follow each outline.

*To the Instructor:*  You may want to remind students to circle list words, underline addition words, and put numbers before major details. These markings have been inserted for you in the practices in this *Instructor's Edition*.

## Passage 1

List words
*(signs of
addiction to
shopping)*
suggest the
main idea in
sentence 2.
Addition words
*(One . . .
second . . .
Another . . .
Last of all)*
signal the major
supporting
details.

[1]We all enjoy buying a new shirt or book or DVD. [2]According to experts, though, some people show signs of addiction to shopping. [3]One such sign is that a shopper develops[1] serious money problems. [4]Checks are bounced, or credit card debt becomes so great that the minimal payment cannot be made each month. [5]A second sign of a shopping addict is a[2] distinct mood pattern. [6]Before shopping, tension builds up in the addict as he or she looks forward to a "fix." [7]After shopping, there is a pleasant release from that tension, and for a time the shopper will feel happy and at rest. [8]Another sign of a shopping addict is[3] shoplifting, especially if this has not been a behavior of the person in the past. [9]Last of all, a shopping addict often suffers from[4] other addictive behaviors, such as overeating, overdrinking, or frequent gambling.

**Main idea: Some people show signs of addiction to shopping.**

*Wording of answers may vary.*

1. Serious money problems
   a. Checks that bounce
   b. Minimal monthly payment on credit card cannot be made

2. Distinct mood pattern
   a. Tension before shopping
   b. After shopping, a pleasant release from tension

3. Shoplifting

4. Other addictive behaviors

## Questions about the passage

- Which words in the main idea tell you that a list is coming?
  signs of addiction to shopping

- Which word signals the first major detail? One

- Which word signals the second major detail? second

- Which word signals the third major detail? Another

- Which words signal the fourth major detail? Last of all

## Passage 2

List words *(several advantages)* suggest the main idea in sentence 1. Addition words *(One . . . Moreover . . . Finally)* signal the major supporting details.

[1]There are (several advantages) to watching a football game or other sports event on television instead of going to the game itself. [2]One advantage is that it's [1]cheaper to watch a game at home. [3]Going to a sports event can cost at least $50 for parking and an admission ticket. [4]Then it's all too easy to spend an added $30 for drinks and snacks. [5]Moreover, it's [2]more comfortable at home. [6]There is no bumper-to-bumper traffic to and from a sports arena or stadium. [7]There are no noisy, pushy crowds of people to deal with while trying to get to one's seat, which is made out of uncomfortably hard plastic or wood. [8]Finally, watching a game on television is [3]more informative. [9]Camera coverage is so good that every play is seen close up, and many plays are shown on instant replay. [10]At the same time, the game is explained in great detail by very informed commentators. [11]The fan at home always enjoys an insider's view about what is happening in the game at every minute.

**Main idea:** There are several advantages to watching a football game or other sports event on television instead of going to the game itself.

1. <u>Cheaper</u>.

   a. $50 for parking and admission to event

   b. <u>Additional $30 for drinks and snacks</u>

2. <u>More comfortable</u>.

   a. <u>No bumper-to-bumper traffic</u>

   b. No noisy, pushy crowds or hard seats

3. <u>More informative</u>.

   a. <u>Close-ups and instant replays</u>

   b. <u>Detailed explanations by commentators</u>

### Questions about the passage

● Which words in the main idea tell you that a list of details is coming?
   <u>several advantages</u>

● Which word signals the first major detail?    <u>One</u>

● Which word signals the second major detail?    <u>Moreover</u>

● Which word signals the third major detail?    <u>Finally</u>

# Preparing Maps

Students sometimes find it helpful to use maps rather than outlines. **Maps**, or diagrams, are highly visual outlines in which circles, boxes, or other shapes show the relationship between main ideas and supporting details. Each major detail is connected to the main idea. If minor details are included, each is connected to the major detail it explains.

## ✔ *Check Your Understanding*

Read the following passage, and then see if you can complete the map and answer the questions that follow.

¹People daydream for a variety of reasons. ²One cause of daydreaming is ¹boredom, at school or on the job. ³To make life more interesting, people imagine being somewhere else. ⁴For example, a student might dream of lying on the beach and flirting with an attractive person on a nearby blanket. ⁵A production worker might dream about winning the lottery or becoming the big boss at the company. ⁶Another cause of daydreaming is ²a lack of something. ⁷For instance, a starving person might dream about food, or a poor person might dream about owning a house or a car. ⁸A third cause of daydreaming is ³angry feelings. ⁹An angry student might dream about getting a hated math instructor fired.

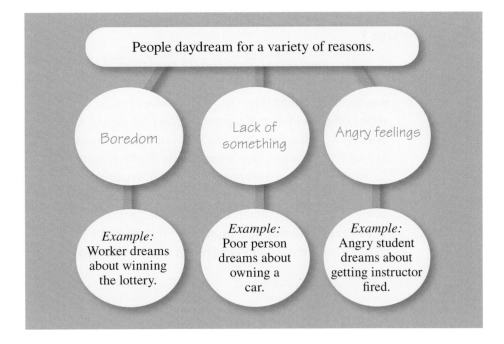

*Questions about the passage*

● Which words in the main idea tell you that a list of details is coming?

_____ *a variety of reasons* _____

● Which word signals the first major detail?  _____ *One* _____

● Which word signals the second major detail? _____ *Another* _____

● Which word signals the third major detail? _____ *third* _____

*Explanation*

In the main idea above, the words *a variety of reasons* tell us that a list of major details is coming.

The word signals for the three major reasons are *One, Another,* and *third*. The map also includes minor details in the form of examples.

*To the Instructor:* Again, you may want to remind students to circle list words, underline addition words, and put numbers before major details.

## PRACTICE 2

Read each passage. Then complete the map that follows by filling in the missing major details. Finally, answer the questions that follow each map.

*Wording of answers in the maps may vary.*

### Passage 1

¹To complain to people and still keep them as friends, follow ⟨several sensible⟩ ⟨guidelines⟩ for criticism. ²First, be specific. Don't say, "Your behavior at the dinner was awful!" ³Instead, say, "You embarrassed me by getting drunk and loud and telling off-color jokes to my parents." ⁴Second, stick to the present. ⁵Hauling up old offenses from last month or last year just takes away attention from the problem at hand. ⁶In addition, don't use insults. ⁷Calling someone names like "idiot" or "animal" will only create anger and hurt any chance of getting the person to listen to you. ⁸The last guideline is to complain privately. ⁹Never criticize a person in front of friends, parents, children, or anyone else, for that matter. ¹⁰Criticizing in front of others has the same effect as insults. ¹¹It shames the person being criticized and makes it likely that he or she will want to put you down rather than listen to you.

List words *(several sensible guidelines)* suggest the main idea in sentence 1.
Addition words *(First . . . Second . . . In addition . . . last)* signal the major supporting details.

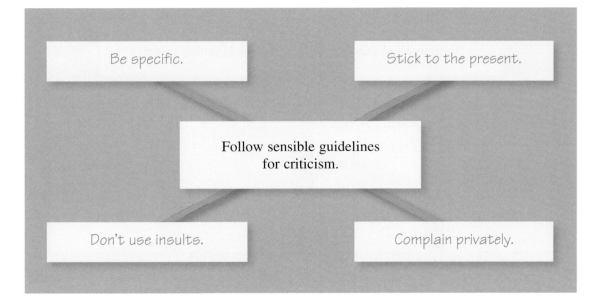

### Questions about the passage

- Which words in the main idea tell you that a list of details is coming?

  *several sensible guidelines*

- Which word signals the first major detail? *First*
- Which word signals the second major detail? *Second*
- Which words signal the third major detail? *In addition*
- Which word signals the fourth major detail? *last*

## Passage 2

¹Some heart attacks are sudden and intense—like ones we might see in a movie—where no one doubts what's happening. ²But most heart attacks start slowly, with mild pain or discomfort. ³Often people affected aren't sure what's wrong and wait too long before getting help. ⁴Here are various signs that can mean a heart attack is taking place. ⁵For one thing, you may have chest discomfort. ⁶Most heart attacks involve discomfort in the center of the chest that lasts more than a few minutes, or that goes away but then comes back. ⁷It can feel like uncomfortable pressure, squeezing, fullness or pain. ⁸Next, you may have pain or discomfort in other areas of the upper body, including one or both arms, the back, neck, jaw, or stomach. ⁹Also, you may have shortness of breath. ¹⁰This feeling often comes with chest discomfort, but it can occur without it. ¹¹Finally, you may experience lightheadedness, nausea, or a cold sweat.

List words (*various signs*) suggest the main idea in sentence 4.
Addition words (*For one thing . . . Next . . . Also . . . Finally*) signal the major supporting details.

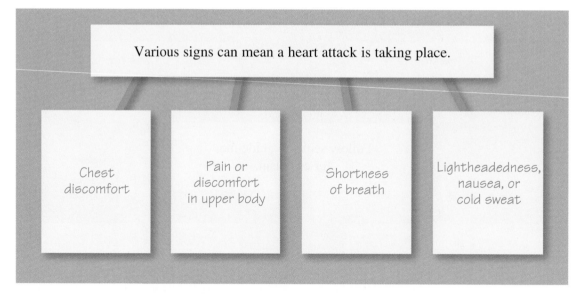

*Various signs can mean a heart attack is taking place.*

| Chest discomfort | Pain or discomfort in upper body | Shortness of breath | Lightheadedness, nausea, or cold sweat |

### *Questions about the passage*

- Which words in the main idea tell you that a list of details is coming?

  _____ various signs _____

- Which words signal the first major detail? _____ For one thing

- Which word signals the second major detail? _____ Next _____

- Which word signals the third major detail? _____ Also _____

- Which word signals the final major details? _____ Finally _____

## A Final Note

This chapter has centered on supporting details as they appear in well-organized paragraphs. But keep in mind that supporting details are part of readings of any length, including selections that may not have an easy-to-follow list of one major detail after another. The readings in Part Two of this book will give you practice in answering all kinds of questions about key supporting details. These questions will develop your ability to pay close, careful attention to what you are reading.

# SUPPORTING DETAILS IN READING: Mastery Test 1

**A.** (1–6.) Complete the outline below by filling in the missing major details. Then answer the questions that follow the outline. *Wording of details may vary.*

> [1]If you are like most people, you feel that writing is not one of your talents, and there's nothing you can do about it. [2]The truth is that some common-sense tips can help you become a better writer. [3]<u>First of all</u>, write often. [4]Like other crafts, writing improves with practice. [5]<u>Also</u>, organize your material with an outline. [6]An outline will provide you with a good guideline without limiting you, as you can change it at any time. [7]<u>Next</u>, write in a plain style. [8]Don't try to use overly fancy language. [9]Instead, just say what you mean simply and clearly. [10]<u>Finally</u>, tighten your writing. [11]Nothing improves writing more than eliminating unnecessary words.

**Main idea: Some common-sense tips can help you become a better writer.**

1. <u>Write often.</u>

2. <u>Organize your material with an outline.</u>

3. <u>Write in a plain style.</u>

4. <u>Tighten your writing.</u>

*Questions about the passage*

5. Which addition words introduce the first major detail?

   _____ First of all _____

6. Which addition word introduces the second major detail?

   _____ Also _____

List words (*some common-sense tips*) suggest the main idea in sentence 2. Addition words (*First of all, Also, Next, Finally*) signal the major supporting details.

*To the Instructor:*
The addition words in the test passages are underlined in this *Instructor's Edition*.

*(Continues on next page)*

**B.** (7–10.) Fill in the major details needed to complete the map below.

> ¹The 14th-century Italian poet Dante is probably best known for a work called *The Inferno*. ²In it, he writes of visiting the nine circles of Hell. ³As he goes down from each level to an even deeper one, he sees the worst of all evildoers. ⁴Here are candidates for the people Dante might put in the lowest levels of Hell if he were writing today. ⁵I think that child molesters would be suitable for the seventh circle of Hell. ⁶Any person who would coldly rob a child of his or her innocence, trust, and physical and emotional well-being deserves no better. ⁷Next, to the eighth circle, I would send selfish politicians who sit in comfortable offices and make decisions that send young men and women off to die in needless wars. ⁸Politicians must be willing to fight those wars themselves—and send their own sons and daughters into battle—before they declare war. ⁹Last, in the lowest circle of Hell, I would place terrorists of every nationality, faith, or cause. ¹⁰There is no moral justification for spreading fear, death, and suffering as the bodies of the innocent are blown apart. ¹¹The lowest circle of Hell is the only place fit for terrorists.

*Wording of details may vary.*

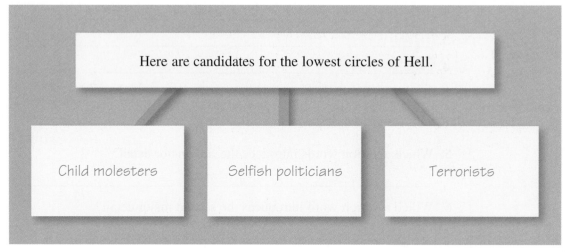

10. Which two addition words introduce the people in the eighth and ninth circles?

    _____ Next _____          _____ Last _____

    Sentences 1–3 provide introductory details.
    Sentence 4 uses key words to signal the main idea: *Here are candidates.*

# SUPPORTING DETAILS IN READING: Mastery Test 2

**A.** (1–6.) Complete the outline below by filling in the missing major details.

¹There are a number of ways to tell if a person has a drug problem. ²First, a drug abuser cannot stop using or drinking. ³Secondly, the person turns into a "different" person when she or he is using the drug, acting in unusual ways. ⁴Another signal is that the user makes excuses for using drugs. ⁵He or she will say that it was an especially bad day at school or work, or that a relationship has become very stressful. ⁶Fourth, an abuser will try to cover up drug use, or will pretend that it "isn't that bad." ⁷Yet another signal is that the abuser will forget things that happen while he or she is high or drunk. ⁸Finally, the abuser will be the last to recognize that he or she has a problem.

*Wording of answers may vary.*

**Main idea: There are ways to tell if a person has a drug problem.**

1. Drug abuser cannot stop using or drinking.
   _____

2. Drug abuser turns into a different person when using.
   _____

3. User makes excuses for using drugs.
   _____

4. User will try to cover up drug use or will pretend it isn't that bad.
   _____

5. User will forget what happens while he or she is high or drunk.
   _____

6. Abuser will be the last to recognize he or she has a problem.
   _____

List words: *a number of ways.*
Addition words (underlined) signal the major supporting details.

*(Continues on next page)*

**B.** (7–10.) Fill in the major details needed to complete the map below. Then answer the question that follows the map.        *Wording of details may vary.*

¹Experts have several theories to explain why people yawn. ²One explanation is that yawns help boost oxygen levels in the blood. ³By forcing the body to breathe deeply, yawns increase airflow to the lungs and rush oxygen to the bloodstream. ⁴A second theory is that yawns help the body change its level of alertness. ⁵It is for this reason yawns happen whether a person is waking up or getting sleepy. ⁶Yet another explanation is that yawns, like stretches, give the body exercise. ⁷When a person yawns, blood pressure and heart rate gently increase and muscles flex. ⁸No matter what the cause for yawning, one thing is clear. ⁹Fifty-five percent of the people who read this paragraph will yawn in less than five minutes.

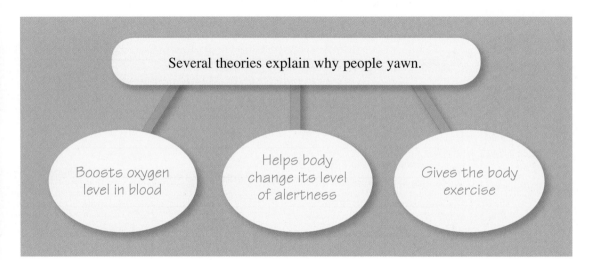

Several theories explain why people yawn.

Boosts oxygen level in blood

Helps body change its level of alertness

Gives the body exercise

10. What are **two** of the addition words used to set off the major details in the passage?

*Any two of the following: One, second, another*

List words: *several theories.*
Addition words (underlined) signal the major supporting details.

## SUPPORTING DETAILS IN READING: Mastery Test 3

**A.** (1–6.) Complete the outline below by filling in the missing major and minor details. Some details have been added for you. *Wording of answers may vary.*

¹There are several guidelines you can follow to avoid being bitten by a dog. ²First of all, don't trust appearances. ³A dog with a wagging tail isn't always friendly. ⁴Even small dogs that look harmless can deliver a painful bite. ⁵Secondly, be cautious. ⁶Allow a dog to see and sniff you before you pet it. ⁷Be especially careful around a dog when it's eating, sleeping, or caring for puppies. ⁸Next, watch for warning signs. ⁹Dogs that stare at you with their heads lowered are probably unfriendly. ¹⁰Likewise, a dog that growls or shows its teeth should be avoided. ¹¹Fourth, learn defensive strategies to prevent a dog from biting you. ¹²For example, stand still with arms at your sides if you find yourself facing an angry dog. ¹³Also avoid eye contact with the dangerous animal so that it knows you are not challenging it.

**Main idea: There are several guidelines you can follow to avoid being bitten by a dog.**

1. Don't trust appearances.

   a. A dog wagging its tail isn't always friendly.

   b. Small harmless-looking dogs can deliver a painful bite.

2. Be cautious.

   a. Let a dog see and sniff you before petting it.

   b. Be especially careful around a dog that's eating, sleeping, or caring for puppies.

3. Watch for warning signs.

   a. Dogs that stare with lowered heads are probably not friendly.

   b. Dogs that growl or show their teeth should be avoided.

4. Learn defensive strategies.

   a. Stand still with arms at your sides if you face an angry dog.

   b. Avoid eye contact with a dangerous dog.

List words: *several guidelines.*
Addition words (underlined) signal the major supporting details.

*(Continues on next page)*

91

**B.** (7–10.) Fill in the major details needed to complete the map below. Then answer the question that follows the map.

¹Practically everyone needs to complain at times about a product or service that has been unsatisfactory. ²It is helpful, then, to keep in mind some steps for effective written complaints. ³<u>First</u>, always address your complaint to a person in charge, such as a manager or the head of the company. ⁴You can get the person's name by calling the company's switchboard. ⁵<u>Next</u>, write your complaint in a clear and matter-of-fact way. ⁶You will be taken less seriously if you sound emotional or threatening. ⁷<u>Finally</u>, explain exactly what action you want taken. ⁸If, for example, you want a company to replace a defective microwave, say, "Please give me the go-ahead to return this microwave. ⁹Then arrange for a new one to be sent to me." ¹⁰Don't leave it up to the company to figure out what you would consider a satisfactory response.

*Wording of details may vary.*

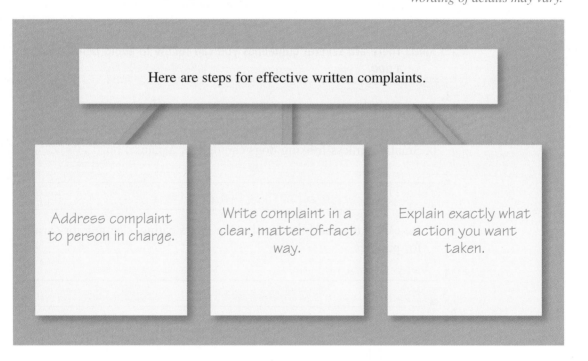

Here are steps for effective written complaints.

| Address complaint to person in charge. | Write complaint in a clear, matter-of-fact way. | Explain exactly what action you want taken. |

10.  What are the **three** addition words used to set off the major details in the passage?

        First                    Next                    Finally

List words: *steps for effective written complaints.*
Addition words (underlined) announce the major supporting details.

# SUPPORTING DETAILS IN READING:  Mastery Test 4

**A.** (1–6.) Complete the outline below by filling in the missing major and minor details. Some details have been added for you. *Wording of answers may vary.*

¹High schools should require all students to wear uniforms. ²One reason for doing so is that uniforms would save money for parents and children. ³Families could simply buy two or three inexpensive uniforms. ⁴They would not have to constantly put out money for designer jeans, fancy sneakers, and other high-priced clothing. ⁵A second advantage of uniforms is that students would not have to spend time worrying about clothes. ⁶They could get up every day knowing what they were wearing to school. ⁷Their attention, then, could be focused on schoolwork and learning and not on making a fashion statement. ⁸Last, uniforms would help all students get along better. ⁹Well-off students would not be able to act superior by wearing expensive clothes, and students from modest backgrounds would not have to feel inferior because of lower-cost wardrobes.

**Main idea: High schools should require all students to wear uniforms.**

1. Uniforms would save money for parents and children. _____

    a. Families could just buy two or three inexpensive uniforms.

    b. They wouldn't have to buy designer jeans, fancy sneakers, and other high-priced clothing.

2. Students would not have to spend time worrying about clothes. _____

    a. Students would know what they were going to wear every day.

    b. They could concentrate on schoolwork and learning, not on making a fashion statement.

3. Uniforms would help all students get along better. _____

    a. Well-off students would not be able to act superior.

    b. Students from modest backgrounds would not have to feel inferior because of lower-cost clothes.

Implied list words: *several reasons.*
A "should" statement usually suggests that details will explain "why."
Addition words (underlined) announce the major supporting details.

*(Continues on next page)*

**B.** (7–10.) Fill in the major details and the one minor detail needed to complete the map below.

*Wording of answers may vary.*

¹A number of factors influence the pace at which people age. ²<u>First of all</u>, genes—traits inherited from parents—play a major role in how people age. ³Genes play a role in how much hair loss we have or how much weight we gain. ⁴Genes also help explain why some people at 75 years old look 60, while others who are 60 appear to be 75. ⁵A <u>second</u> factor that influences aging is a person's lifestyle. ⁶Older-looking skin and wrinkles can be caused by too much sun exposure in youth—part of an outdoor, active lifestyle. ⁷On the other hand, a person who does not exercise is more likely to look and feel older than one who is physically active. ⁸Social forces are a <u>third</u> factor that influence aging. ⁹Older people who feel isolated or lonely often age faster than those who don't report having those feelings. ¹⁰But older people who are involved with others—their families, religious groups, or peer groups—age more slowly and live longer than those who don't.

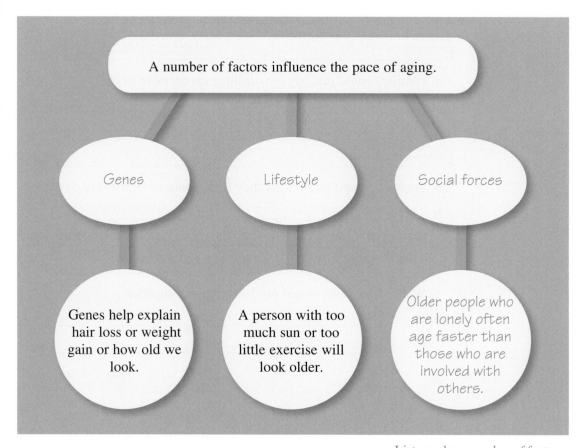

List words: *a number of factors.*
Addition words (underlined) signal the three major supporting details.

# SUPPORTING DETAILS IN READING: Mastery Test 5

**A.** (1–6.) Complete the outline below by filling in the missing major and minor details. Some details have been added for you. *Wording of answers may vary.*

¹Certain physical conditions affect how well people perform their work. ²Temperature is <u>one</u> factor that has been shown to greatly influence workers. ³If a workspace is too warm, people become cranky and uncomfortable. ⁴On the other hand, workers who are cold are more likely to pursue nonwork activities, such as chatting or making warm drinks. ⁵Color is <u>another</u> factor that affects worker performance. ⁶A workspace that has lots of red tends to stimulate and excite workers. ⁷Blue, on the other hand, usually soothes workers, making them feel relaxed and comfortable. ⁸<u>Finally</u>, lighting has a powerful effect on employees. ⁹Bright, direct light encourages good listening, close concentration, and comfortable reading. ¹⁰Low light, however, promotes relaxation and personal conversation—rather than getting work done.

**Main idea: Physical conditions affect work performance.**

1. Temperature
   a. If a workspace is too warm, workers become cranky and uncomfortable.
   b. Cold workers are more likely to pursue nonwork activities.

2. Color
   a. Reds tend to stimulate and excite workers.
   b. Blue soothes workers.

3. Lighting
   a. Bright, direct light encourages good listening, close concentration, and comfortable reading.
   b. Low light promotes relaxation and personal conversation.

List words: *Certain physical conditions.*
Addition words (underlined) signal the major supporting details.

*(Continues on next page)*

**B.** (7–10.) Fill in the major details and one minor detail needed to complete the map below.

*Wording of answers may vary.*

¹Nearly every family has members who don't get along. ²But for some, these disagreements grow into painful feuds that can last for years. ³Fortunately, there are certain strategies that can help heal even the most difficult family feuds. ⁴The <u>first</u> step is to get people to share the blame for their disagreement. ⁵Family rifts are rarely caused by a single person. ⁶For healing to take place, then, everyone involved must accept responsibility for his or her part in the conflict. ⁷The <u>second</u> step is to increase the communication between family members. ⁸Writing a note, making a phone call, or attending a family event allows people to express their feelings to each other. ⁹Such actions show care and help rebuild damaged relationships. ¹⁰A <u>third</u> step is to set realistic goals. ¹¹A family feud that has lasted for thirty years will not be solved by a single talk. ¹²However, that talk may lead to a truce and help build a foundation for healing.

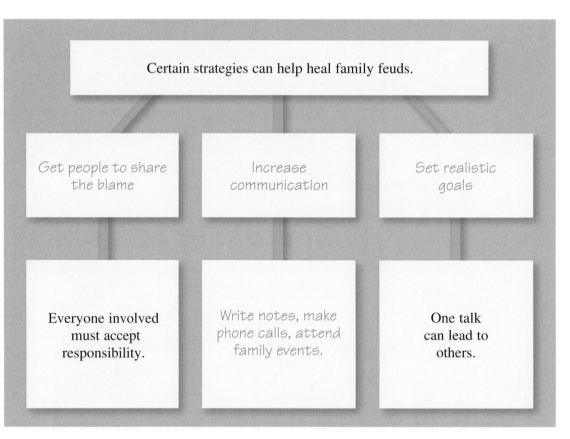

The first two sentences are introductory details.
List words: *certain strategies*.
Addition words (underlined) introduce the major supporting details.

# SUPPORTING DETAILS IN READING: Mastery Test 6

**A.** (1–6.) Complete the outline below by filling in the missing major and minor details. Some details have been added for you. *Wording of answers may vary.*

> ¹People sometimes express their thoughts not by speaking, but by using their bodies in various ways. ²<u>One</u> way people use the body to communicate is through the eyes. ³By glaring, people can send the message that they are angry without saying a word. ⁴Likewise, people can show interest in what another person is saying by just looking at the person, using direct eye contact to send the message. ⁵<u>Another</u> way that people use their bodies to communicate is through facial expressions. ⁶Studies show that people all over the world use the same facial expressions to show emotions. ⁷Just by looking at a face, it is possible to tell if a person is sad, happy, afraid, or surprised. ⁸Body posture is a <u>third</u> way that people send messages to each other without speaking. ⁹For example, sitting upright or leaning forward shows great interest and attention. ¹⁰On the other hand, if a person has arms crossed at the chest, it is a sign that he or she dislikes or disagrees with the speaker.

**Main idea: People can communicate by using their bodies.**

1.  Through the eyes
    a.  By glaring, people can show they are angry without saying a word.
    b.  People can show interest in a speaker through direct eye contact.
2.  Through facial expressions
    a.  All over the world, people use the same facial expressions to show emotions.
    b.  By looking at a face, one can tell if a person is sad, happy, afraid, or surprised.
3.  Through body posture
    a.  A person who is sitting upright or leaning forward shows great interest and attention.
    b.  A person with arms crossed dislikes or disagrees with the speaker.

List words: *various ways.*
Addition words (underlined) signal the major supporting details.

*(Continues on next page)*

**B.** (7–10.) Fill in the major details and one minor detail needed to complete the map below.    *Wording of answers may vary.*

¹Mysteries are questions in life without satisfying answers. ²One mystery is why there is so much hatred on the planet. ³We are all mortal and here on Earth for only a little while. ⁴Yet instead of being kind to one another, we continue to start wars—the main effect of which is to kill each other. ⁵A <u>second</u> mystery is how good and evil can exist together in the same person. ⁶For example, we have all heard of a person who is liked and even admired in the community. ⁷We then learn that the person has been abusing his wife or children. ⁸A <u>third</u> mystery is why some wealthy Christians do little to help the poor. ⁹They go to church on Sunday but act as if the lives of the poor are none of their concern. ¹⁰Yet the Bible says that it's easier for a rich man to pass through the eye of a needle than to enter the kingdom of Heaven.

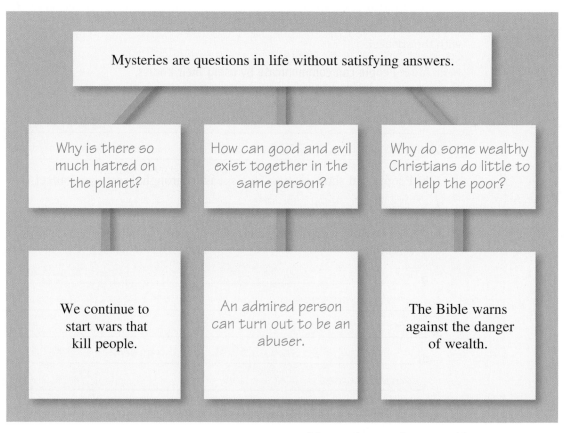

Mysteries are questions in life without satisfying answers.

| Why is there so much hatred on the planet? | How can good and evil exist together in the same person? | Why do some wealthy Christians do little to help the poor? |
| --- | --- | --- |
| We continue to start wars that kill people. | An admired person can turn out to be an abuser. | The Bible warns against the danger of wealth. |

List words: *questions . . . without . . . answers.*
Addition words (underlined) signal the major details.

# 4 Main Ideas and Supporting Details in Writing

**A** **paragraph** is a series of sentences that support a main idea, or point. A paragraph typically starts with the main idea or point (also called the **topic sentence**), and the rest of the paragraph provides specific details to support and develop the point. The illustration below shows the relationship between point and support.

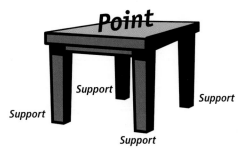

## Outlining

An outline is a helpful way to plan a paper or to analyze it. An **outline** shows at a glance the point of a paper and a numbered list of the items that support the point. Here is an example of a paragraph and an outline of the paragraph.

¹People in my family love our dog Punch. ²However, I have several reasons for wanting to get rid of Punch. ³First of all, he knows I don't like him. ⁴Sometimes he gives me an evil look and curls his top lip back to show me his teeth. ⁵The message is clearly, "Someday I'm going to bite you." ⁶Another reason to get rid of Punch is he sheds everywhere. ⁷Every surface in our house is covered with Punch hair. ⁸I spend more time brushing it off my clothes than I do mowing the lawn. ⁹Last of all, Punch is an early riser, while (on weekends) I am not. ¹⁰He will start barking and whining to go outside at 7 a.m., and it's my job to take care of him. ¹¹When I told my family that I had a list of good reasons for getting rid of Punch, they said they would make up a list of reasons to get rid of me.

**Point: I have several reasons for wanting to get rid of Punch.**

**Supporting detail: 1.** He knows I don't like him.

**Supporting detail: 2.** Punch sheds everywhere.

**Supporting detail: 3.** Punch is an early riser.

**PRACTICE 1**

Look at each of the following five paragraphs and then complete the outline for each paragraph. Notice that words such as *first, also, another,* and *finally* often signal each new item of support.                    *Wording of answers may vary.*

1. ¹Being a celebrity is often difficult. ²First of all, celebrities have to look almost perfect all the time. ³There's always a photographer ready to take an unflattering picture of a famous person looking dumpy in old clothes. ⁴Celebrities <u>also</u> sacrifice their private lives. ⁵Their personal struggles, divorces, or family tragedies all end up as front-page news. ⁶<u>Last</u>, and most frightening of all, celebrities are in constant danger of the wrong kind of attention. ⁷Threatening letters and even physical attacks from crazy fans are things a celebrity must contend with.

*The three difficulties are introduced with the transitions* First of all, also, *and* last.

**Point:** Being a celebrity is often difficult.

**Supporting detail: 1.** Celebrities have to look almost perfect all the time.

**Supporting detail: 2.** Celebrities sacrifice their private lives.

**Supporting detail: 3.** Celebrities are in constant danger of the wrong kind of attention.

2. ¹People lie for different reasons. ²<u>One</u> common reason is to avoid hurting someone's feelings. ³For example, a friend might ask, "Do you like my new haircut?" ⁴If you think it's ugly, you might still answer, "Yes." ⁵<u>Another</u> common reason for lying is to avoid a fight. ⁶Say a friend angers you and then asks, "Are you upset with me?" ⁷You might answer, "No," to avoid an argument. ⁸People <u>also</u> lie so that they'll fit in, as when you listen to a boring person and politely say, "That's interesting." ⁹<u>In addition</u>, people lie to avoid spending more time with someone. ¹⁰For instance, you might lie, "I have to go now."

*The four reasons for lying are introduced with the transitions* One, Another, also, *and* In addition.

**Point:** People lie for different reasons.

**Supporting detail: 1.** To avoid hurting someone's feelings

**Supporting detail: 2.** To avoid a fight

**Supporting detail: 3.** To fit in

**Supporting detail: 4.** To avoid spending more time with someone

3. ¹You don't have to scare your family with statistics about heart attacks. ²There are several positive ways to encourage your family to exercise more often. ³<u>To begin with</u>, get them to exercise more often by emphasizing how good they'll feel and how much better they'll look if they work out on a regular basis. ⁴A <u>second</u> method you can use is to set an example. ⁵If they see you walking to stores rather than driving, they might be encouraged

The three positive ways to encourage family members to exercise are introduced with the transitions *To begin with, second,* and *finally.*

to do likewise. **⁶Finally,** make exercise a family activity. **⁷**Suggest that the whole family go hiking or camping together, take up early morning jogging, or join the Y at the group rate.

**Point:** _There are several positive ways to encourage your family to exercise more often._

**Supporting detail: 1.** _Emphasize how good they'll feel and look if they work out regularly._
**Supporting detail: 2.** _Set an example._
**Supporting detail: 3.** _Make exercise a family activity._

The four warning signs of depression are introduced with the following transitions: *One, In addition, third,* and *last of all.*

4. **¹**Serious depression, as opposed to the fleeting kind we all feel at times, has definite warning signs. **²One** symptom of depression is a change in sleep patterns—either sleeplessness or sleeping too much. **³In addition,** abnormal eating patterns may develop, either eating too much or loss of appetite. **⁴**A <u>third</u> sign is trouble in thinking or concentrating—even to the point of finding it difficult to read a magazine or newspaper. **⁵**And <u>last of all</u>, a general feeling of hopelessness may signal depression. **⁶**People feel indifferent to their families and jobs and may begin to think that life is not worth living.

**Point:** _Serious depression has definite warning signs._

**Supporting detail: 1.** _A change in sleep patterns_
**Supporting detail: 2.** _Abnormal eating patterns_
**Supporting detail: 3.** _Trouble in thinking or concentrating_
**Supporting detail: 4.** _A general feeling of hopelessness_

Four factors that can interfere with memory are introduced with the following transitions: *For one thing, Also, another,* and *In addition.*

5. **¹**Several factors can interfere with having a good memory. **²For one thing,** there can be a lack of motivation. **³**Without a real desire to learn or remember something, you probably won't. **⁴Also** a factor is a lack of practice. **⁵**To stay sharp, memory skills, like any other skill, must be used on a regular basis. **⁶**Yet <u>another</u> factor that can hurt memory is self-doubt. **⁷**If you're convinced you won't remember something, you probably won't. **⁸In addition,** distraction can interfere with memory. **⁹**If you're distracted by a television or by conversation nearby, try to find a quiet environment before trying to commit something to memory.

**Point:** _Several factors can interfere with having a good memory._

**Supporting detail: 1.** _Lack of motivation_
**Supporting detail: 2.** _Lack of practice_
**Supporting detail: 3.** _Self-doubt_
**Supporting detail: 4.** _Distraction_

## A Note on Topics

As you learned in Chapter 2, the **topic** is a general subject. A good reader looks for the topic of a selection and then the idea that is expressed about that topic. A good writer starts with a topic and then decides what idea to advance about that topic. In the outlines you have just considered, it is easy to identify the topics and the ideas about the topics:

| Topic | Topic sentence (main idea) |
|---|---|
| My dog Punch | I have several reasons for wanting to get rid of Punch. |
| Celebrities | Being a celebrity is often difficult. |
| Why people lie | People lie for different reasons. |
| Exercise | There are several possible ways to encourage your family to exercise more often. |
| Depression | Serious depression has definite warning signs. |
| Memory | Several factors can interfere with having a good memory. |

**PRACTICE 2**

Here are fifteen topics. See if you can write main ideas about any five of them. Put your topic sentences in the spaces provided.

*Examples*

| Teacher | My senior business teacher, Mrs. Catherine, was the best teacher I ever had. |
|---|---|
| Fast-food restaurants | Given a choice, I prefer a fast-food restaurant to a diner. |
| My dog | Rusty, my golden retriever, has some odd habits. |

| | | |
|---|---|---|
| Living at home | College classes | Night person |
| TV commercials | Boss | My dog (or cat) |
| Fast-food restaurant | Exercise | Texting |
| Teacher | Landlord | Alcohol |
| Drivers | Sleep | Bad habits |

**1.** _____ *Answers will vary.* _____

_____

**2.** _____

_____

**3.** _____

_____

**4.** _____

_____

**5.** _____

_____

# Staying on Point

One common mistake in writing a paper is to go off point. Think of your point as the bull's-eye in a target. Every sentence and detail in a paper should be **relevant**, meaning that it hits the bull's-eye—it supports your point. Otherwise, your paper will not be convincing. Instead of hitting the target and proving your point, your "support" will be **irrelevant**. In other words, it will miss the point completely.

Let's say you decide your point is going to be that your family car is a lemon. If you then provide details about the car's good features, you are going off point. Or perhaps your point is that your aunt is a generous person. If you provide details about her sense of humor or odd habits, you are going off point. Or your point could be that your apartment is not a good place to live. If you provide details about the convenient location of the apartment, you're missing the target.

Look at the following outline of a paragraph. The point is followed by six facts, only three of which are on target in supporting the point. The other facts are irrelevant to the point. See if you can check the three **relevant** statements of support—the ones that hit the bull's-eye.

**Point:  My dog Otis is not very bright.**

✓ 1. He's five years old and doesn't respond to his name yet.

___ 2. He cries when I leave for work every day.

___ 3. He always gets excited when visitors arrive.

✓ 4. He often attacks the backyard hedge as if it's a hostile animal.

___ 5. He gets along very well with my neighbor's cat.

✓ 6. I often have to put food in front of him because he can't find it by himself.

Now read the following comments on the six items to see which ones you should have checked and why.

*Explanation*

1. Most dogs know their names. Otis's unfamiliarity with his own name reveals a weak memory, and memory is one aspect of intelligence. You should have checked this item.

2. Even an intelligent dog might be sad when its companions leave the house.

3. Both bright and not-so-bright dogs are happy to see old and new human friends.

4. The inability to distinguish between a bush and an animal—friendly or hostile— suggests a lack of analytical skills. You should have checked this item.

5. Dogs of all degrees of intelligence have been known to be friendly with cats.

6. Most dogs recognize food much more often than their owners would like them to. Otis's inability to find food clearly indicates poor problem-solving skills. You should also have checked this item.

As illustrated on the previous page, you want all the details you provide in a paper to be on target and hit the bull's-eye in support of your point.

**PRACTICE 3**

Each point is followed by three statements that provide relevant, on-target support and three that do not. In the spaces, write the letters of the three **relevant** statements of support.

1. **Point:  I'm a perfect example of someone who has "math anxiety."**

   A. I feel dread every time I sit down to take our Friday math quiz.
   B. Fear of math is almost as widespread as fear of public speaking.
   C. During my last math test, I "froze" and didn't even try to answer most of the questions.
   D. I also have a great deal of anxiety when I sit down to write a paper.
   E. I turned down a summer job as a salesclerk because I would have had to figure out how much change customers should get back.
   F. I used to be afraid to raise my hand in class, but now it's easier for me to answer questions.

   *Items that logically support the point:* ____A____   ____C____   ____E____

   Answer B is about how common math anxiety is, not about the writer's own anxiety. Answer D is about a different kind of anxiety. Answer F is evidence that the writer now is *less* anxious about something.

2. **Point:  Elephants are very intelligent animals.**

   A. For years, hunters shot elephants to obtain the ivory from their tusks.
   B. Like chimps, elephants can recognize their reflections in mirrors.
   C. Elephants tear off branches of trees to use as fly swatters.
   D. Elephants have been seen keeping vigil over their dead companions.
   E. An elephant can live as long as sixty-five years.
   F. Elephants should not be forced to perform in circuses.

   *Items that logically support the point:* ____B____   ____C____   ____D____

   Answer A is about elephants as hunters' prey. Answer E is about an elephant's life span. Answer F is a judgment about what elephants should not be forced to do; it has nothing to do with the animals' intelligence.

3. **Point:  Drinking coffee can be bad for people.**

   A. Some people don't like the taste of decaffeinated coffees.
   B. Coffee in the evening can interfere with sleep at night.
   C. As addictions go, coffee is less dangerous than tobacco.
   D. Too much coffee can cause the hands to shake.
   E. Drinking too much coffee can lead to a faster heartbeat and light-headedness.
   F. Most coffees cost under five dollars a pound.

   *Items that logically support the point:* ____B____   ____D____   ____E____

   Answer A is about taste. Answer C is about coffee being less dangerous than tobacco. Answer F is about cost.

4. **Point:  If you think school is difficult, it's even harder for older students.**

Answer A only mentions adults going to school, not how hard it might be. Answer E is not related to difficulty. Answer F is a positive concept related to an older student's potential contribution.

A. Studies show that more and more adults are returning to school.

B. It takes a lot of work to re-learn study habits.

C. Many older students have family and job responsibilities in addition to classes.

D. Some older students are afraid of not "fitting in."

E. It is never too late to gain new knowledge.

F. Older students can contribute to class discussions by talking about their "real-world" experiences.

*Items that logically support the point:* ___B___   ___C___   ___D___

5. **Point:  Workers in early American factories led difficult lives.**

Answer C is about females working, not about their difficult lives. Answer D only mentions the period when early factories were built. Answer F relates to how unions improved conditions for workers.

A. The average work day was twelve hours long.

B. Early factory workers were paid pennies an hour.

C. Female factory workers often worked in textile mills.

D. The first American factories were built in the late 1700s.

E. All workers on power machines risked accidents that could maim or kill.

F. Labor unions have greatly improved conditions in today's factories.

*Items that logically support the point:* ___A___   ___B___   ___E___

6. **Point:  Schools should eliminate the summer vacation.**

Answer B relates to students' energy, which is unrelated to "summer vacation." Answer D relates to comfort in the classroom. Answer F supports keeping the summer vacation, not eliminating it.

A. It costs too much money for school buildings to remain empty in the summer months.

B. Students have more energy than adults.

C. Year-round school can better prepare students for year-round work in the adult world.

D. During summer classes, schools should be air-conditioned.

E. Students will learn more and forget less if they attend school twelve months a year.

F. Students won't be able to take summer jobs that would provide money for college.

*Items that logically support the point:* ___A___   ___C___   ___E___

7. **Point:  Some people have very poor telephone manners.**

Answer B mentions cordless phones, which are unrelated to telephone manners. Answer C has nothing to do with manners. Answer E states some people don't like to talk on the phone, but doesn't say what they do if they get a phone call.

A. They never identify themselves, but just begin the conversation.

B. They often make their calls on cordless phones.

C. They have an unlisted telephone number.

D. They conduct conversations with people around them at the same time they're talking on the phone.

E. Some people don't like to talk on the phone.

F. They often call around 6 p.m., which is most people's dinner hour.

*Items that logically support the point:* _____A_____ _____D_____ _____F_____

8. **Point:  My father's boss is an unpleasant man to work for.**

Answer B is about his wife, not the boss. Answer C mentions office decoration, and has no bearing on the unpleasantness of the boss. Answer F discusses parking tickets, which are not related to the boss's unpleasantness.

A. He barks orders and never asks for an employee's opinion.

B. His fashion-plate wife is said to be even nastier than he is.

C. His office is decorated in dull browns and grays.

D. Even when he invites employees out to lunch, he expects them to pick up their own checks.

E. He changes his mind so often that an employee who pleased him on Friday can be in the doghouse by Monday.

F. He once accumulated so many parking tickets that the police actually came to his home to arrest him.

*Items that logically support the point:* _____A_____ _____D_____ _____E_____

9. **Point:  There are some simple ways to save money at the supermarket.**

Answer C is about how a shopping list can be organized, not about saving money. Answer E is about saving time, not money. Answer F concerns which fruits and veggies are better for you; it does not mention money.

A. Avoid products which charge extra for packaging, such as cheese wrapped individually by slice.

B. Buy store brands of basic items instead of expensive name-brand products.

C. Some people organize a shopping list alphabetically; others group items by categories.

D. Shop when you are not hungry, so that you won't be tempted to buy pricey treats.

E. Go to the store at odd hours or on weekdays to reduce the time you spend in lines.

F. Buy locally grown fruits and vegetables, which are often better for you than canned or frozen ones.

*Items that logically support the point:* _____A_____ _____B_____ _____D_____

10. **Point: Nobody in this neighborhood will miss the Martins when they move.**

A. Both the Martins are retired now and rarely leave their home.

Answer A does not mention the Martins moving. Answer C is about tree removal, not the Martins' bad behavior. Answer E makes an excuse for Mr. Martin's behavior.

B. They keep their poor dog chained to a tree 24 hours a day, and it howls for much of that time.

C. They recently had a tree removed from their front yard because its roots were growing into the sewer line.

D. Over the past few years, the outside of their house has begun to look shabbier and shabbier.

E. Mr. Martin has been sick for years, so you can understand his being short-tempered.

F. When the neighborhood kids play ball anywhere near their house, Mr. Martin yells at them, "Keep your ball game off my property!"

*Items that logically support the point:* ___B___    ___D___    ___F___

## PRACTICE 4

Here is another activity that will sharpen your ability to decide whether evidence truly supports a point. Each point below is followed by three items of information. Put a check (✓) next to the **one** item that **logically** supports the point.

1. **Point: That child is very curious.**

_____ A. [1]He was reciting the alphabet when he was only three years old. [2]By age seven, he was doing math at a fourth-grade level. [3]He skipped third and fifth grades.

_____ B. [1]His favorite word is "NO!" [2]He doesn't start picking up his toys until the fifth or sixth time he is told. [3]Mealtime is a battle to get him to eat properly.

___✓___ C. [1]He has taken apart all the clocks in the house to see how they work. [2]He borrowed his father's hammer to break rocks because he "wanted to see what they looked like inside." [3]He is forever asking questions that start with "How" and "Why."

Item A supports the point "That child is very intelligent."
Item B supports the point "That child is stubborn."

2. **Point: Aunt Isabel is my least favorite relative.**

_✓_    A.    ¹When we meet, she always has something critical to say, such as "What have you done with your hair?" or "You look terrible in that color." ²She calls my sister "the smart sister" and me "the dumb one." ³On my birthday, she said, "I didn't think you wanted a present."

Item B supports the point "Aunt Isabel is someone I admire." Item C is about Isabel's physical appearance, not about why the speaker does not like her.

_____    B.    ¹She works as a billing clerk at a hospital. ²She dropped out of high school, but earned her GED and then attended community college. ³She's held the job for more than 15 years and has been the hospital's "Employee of the Month" a number of times.

_____    C.    ¹Isabel is about five foot seven and is a little on the heavy side. ²She wears her hair very short and always has on long dangly earrings. ³She's almost 50 but looks younger. ⁴She wears very little makeup—just some mascara and sometimes lip gloss.

3. **Point: Our biology teacher is lazy.**

_✓_    A.    ¹He has his top students present the lessons to the class so he doesn't have to do anything. ²If someone is having trouble in class, he tells him or her to get help from one of the other students. ³So he doesn't have to grade papers, he allows us to grade each other's homework and test papers, even midterm and final exams.

Item B supports the point "Our biology teacher is tough." Item C supports the point "Our biology teacher is organized, professional, and prompt."

_____    B.    ¹His favorite saying is, "There is no such thing as partial credit. ²Either the answer is right or it isn't." ³We can expect at least two hours of biology homework every night, and more on weekends and holidays. ⁴Even the best students in class have trouble finishing his tests before the end of the period, and the average grade for his class is a C.

_____    C.    ¹He always arrives exactly on time for class; you could set your watch by him. ²He predictably begins with two or three questions, then lectures for most of the period, and with five minutes to go, writes on the board exactly what he wants us to read before the next class.

4. **Point: Margo is a very rude worker.**

_____ A. ¹She can barely stay awake while at work. ²Almost every day, she arrives at the store a few minutes late, having slept till the last minute. ³She works in slow motion, and it takes her so long to do any one thing that people never ask for her help. ⁴If she didn't spend the day pumping herself full of caffeine, she probably would not be able to move at all.

Item A supports the point "Margo is slow and unreliable."
Item C supports the point "Margo is a very good worker."

__✓__ B. ¹She keeps customers waiting while she talks with a coworker. ²When someone asks her about a sale item, she snaps, "If it isn't on the shelf, we don't have it!" ³When her boss isn't watching her, she answers the telephone by saying, "Yeah, what do you want?"

_____ C. ¹She can answer the phone, ring up a customer's purchases, and count large amounts of money all at the same time. ²She often volunteers to help customers bring their bags to their cars. ³She does not mind taking time to answer a customer's question or help someone stock a shelf.

5. **Point: That roller coaster is dangerous.**

_____ A. ¹It is slower than any other roller coaster in the state. ²The curves of its track are so wide and the hills are so shallow that a ride on this roller coaster seems like a drive in the country. ³People don't scream when they ride it. ⁴Instead, they enjoy the view from above the park.

Item A supports the point "The roller coaster isn't scary."
Item B supports the point "The roller coaster is impressive."

_____ B. ¹It is known as one of the best roller coasters in the country. ²People will wait in lines for hours just to try it. ³At certain points it reaches the same speeds as cars do on highways. ⁴The track is so tall and long that you can see it miles away.

__✓__ C. ¹Last year, it broke down several times, leaving people stranded in their cars sixty feet off the ground. ²In most cars, the seatbelts are torn and don't always buckle properly. ³One area of the track shakes and makes a strange grinding sound whenever a car passes over it.

6. **Point: Greg is irresponsible.**

_____ A. ¹He gives up his bus seat to elderly commuters. ²When he sees people carrying heavy packages or struggling with squirming children, he rushes to open doors to help them out.

_____ B. ¹No matter how much trouble I'm having with my English assignment, he refuses to do any of it for me. ²He says that between his own homework and his job, he doesn't have time. ³But he always gets B's, and I have trouble getting C's. ⁴Furthermore, when I need someone to cover for me at work so that I can see my girlfriend, he's always too busy with something else to help me out.

_____✓_____ C.   ¹He never pays his bills on time. ²When he borrows things, he returns them damaged, or not at all. ³He is usually late for appointments, if he even remembers them at all.   Item C supports the point that Greg is irresponsible. Item A suggests Greg is considerate. Item B suggests Greg is busy with his own life.

7.  **Point: The meal I cooked for my girlfriend was horrible.**

_____ A.   ¹The chicken took an hour to prepare and two hours to cook. ²I had to travel for twenty miles to find a produce store that sold the vegetables I wanted. ³In order to make all this food, I had to buy a whole new set of pots and pans. ⁴Afterward, it took me hours to clean the kitchen and wash the dishes.

Item C supports the point that the meal was horrible.
Item A suggests the meal was lots of work.
Item B does not discuss the meal.

_____ B.   ¹My girlfriend's car would not start when she wanted to come over. ²By the time she arrived, she was two hours late and very angry. ³As we sat down to eat, all she could talk about was how much it would cost to have her car fixed. ⁴When I tried to change the subject, she said I never listen to her, so I apologized. ⁵Then she accused me of apologizing too much. ⁶We both got so mad that we hardly touched dinner.

_____✓_____ C.   ¹The chicken came out so tough and dry that I could barely cut it with a steak knife. ²I overcooked the fresh vegetables so much that they changed from a bright green color to the color of an army jeep. ³The cake I tried to bake collapsed into itself, turning into a shapeless chewy mass that resembled a giant cookie.

8.  **Point: High-school proms should be banned.**

_____✓_____ A.   ¹Proms pressure students to spend a ridiculous amount of money on gowns, tuxes, flowers, and even limos. ²Prom preparations distract students for many weeks from the real business of school, which is education. ³In addition, the social pressure to get a date for the prom makes many people miserable.

Items B and C present matter-of-fact details about proms, not reasons proms should be banned.

_____ B.   ¹Proms usually feature a theme, and the room the prom is held in is decorated according to that theme. ²Often a photographer is hired to take pictures of the couples as they arrive. ³Some proms even have thrones set up for the prom king and queen.

_____ C.   ¹At most schools, proms are chaperoned by teachers and administrators. ²Of course, the students would prefer that no adults were in the room, especially adults who should stay in the classroom or office where they belong. ³What they don't realize is that the chaperones are often as ill at ease as the students they are watching.

9. **Point: Neil is a hypocrite—he usually does the opposite of what he says.**

_✓_ A.   [1]He spent a half hour talking and laughing with someone yesterday, then later confided to me, "I can't stand that man!" [2]He lectures his daughters about the dangers of drug addiction, but he is a heavy drinker and smoker.

_____ B.   [1]He waits until December to put in winter storm windows, and his Christmas tree is often still up in March. [2]He usually pays his bills a few days after they are due, and he never gets around to dental or medical checkups until real problems develop.

_____ C.   [1]After thirty-seven years of marriage, he still writes love letters to his wife. [2]He took early retirement so he could stay home and care for her when an illness left her bedridden. [3]He never leaves the house without bringing her back something special.

   Item B supports the point "Neil is lazy." Item C supports the point "Neil is a loving, caring husband."

10. **Point: My boss is considerate.**

_____ A.   [1]She greets employees and customers alike with a warm smile and a hearty, "Hi! How are you today?" [2]She is forever telling us, "A stranger is just a friend you haven't met yet."

_✓_ B.   [1]Instead of giving us orders, she asks us to do things. [2]She always thanks an employee for completing a task. [3]She often helps out when she sees that things are getting stressful.

_____ C.   [1]Getting a raise out of her is impossible—even for long-term employees. [2]Her secretary is still using an old typewriter because the boss won't buy anything new. [3]We had to have the retirement party for the office manager during our lunch hour, and the boss was waiting by the time clock when we got back—to make sure we weren't a minute late.

   Item A supports the point "My boss is very friendly." Item C supports the point "My boss is stingy."

# Providing Enough Support

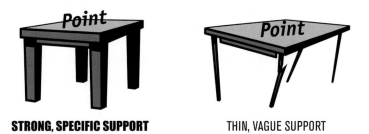

**STRONG, SPECIFIC SUPPORT**          THIN, VAGUE SUPPORT

Another common mistake in writing a paper is not providing enough *specific* details. Truly specific details excite the reader's interest; they *show* what the writer means. They are the opposite of dull, wordy writing that provides thin support for a point.

**Specific details**, as shown in the illustration above, provide solid support for a point. Thin and vague details do not. Lazy writers are content to produce undersupported paragraphs, but good writers are willing to take the time needed to think carefully about and to build a solid paper.

## PRACTICE 5

Each of the ten points below is followed by two items of support. Put a check (✓) next to the item that is specific and clearly shows us the writer's point. By contrast, the other item will be vague, dull, or wordy and lack sharp details.

1. **I could tell I was coming down with the flu.**

    _____ A. ¹I began feeling lousy while I was at school. ²By the time I got home, it was even worse. ³The symptoms kept developing, one after another. ⁴I went to bed feeling horrible, and there was no doubt that I was really in for it. ⁵I could tell I was going to feel awful for days. ⁶Getting the flu is such a miserable experience that I really would not wish it on anyone.

    Item B provides specific details: types of symptoms (cough, blurred vision, headache, fever of 102°, shivering, aching).

    ✓ B. ¹I know exactly when the flu hit. ²I was at my desk when I felt a tickle in my throat. ³I began to cough, and the cough refused to go away. ⁴A few minutes later, the words on my computer screen began to swim. ⁵I could feel a deep headache developing behind my eyes. ⁶By the time I got home later that afternoon, I had a fever of 102. ⁷I crawled into bed shivering, even with three blankets. ⁸And I was aching so badly I felt as though I'd been hit by a truck.

2. **My brother is accident-prone.**

Item A lists specific details: the "funny but . . . dangerous result" of trying to open the Krazy-Glue (lips sealed shut, trip to emergency room).

  ✓   A. ¹Once he tried to open a tube of Krazy Glue with his teeth. ²When the cap came loose, glue squirted out and sealed his lips shut. ³They had to be pried open in a hospital ER.

_____ B. ¹Even when he does simple jobs, he seems to get into trouble. ²This can lead to funny but sometimes dangerous results. ³Things never seem to go right for him, and he often needs the help of others to get out of one problem or another.

3. **When money gets tight, our family finds ways to economize.**

_____ A. ¹There are a lot of corners we can cut when we need to. ²If you think about it, there are plenty of unnecessary expenses every day that people can cut out when necessary. ³Food and entertainment are two categories that eat up a lot of money needlessly. ⁴Those expenses may not seem like a lot individually, but they can add up to quite a bit. ⁵My family has gotten good at being aware of such small ways to save.

Answer B lists specific ways to economize: simple breakfast, packing lunches, buying economy-sized items, cutting back on impulse purchases, renting a DVD instead of going to the movies.

  ✓   B. ¹We have a simple breakfast like oatmeal rather than bacon and eggs. ²We pack lunches rather than eat in the school cafeteria or restaurants. ³We plan ahead for those lunches, buying economy sizes of peanut butter, lunch meat, and fruit. ⁴We cut back on buying impulse items like candy, chips, and coffee or soda drinks. ⁵Rather than going out to the movies at eight dollars a head, we rent a DVD and make popcorn at home.

4. **Our old car is ready for the junk pile.**

_____ A. ¹If the car's problems were just cosmetic, we might be able to live with them, but it's worse than that. ²Our car has major mechanical problems that would cost more to fix than would be worth it. ³Even if we did fix them, that would leave a lot of smaller problems to deal with. ⁴Those problems not only affect its appearance but definitely make the car unsafe. ⁵It's time to say goodbye to the old heap.

Answer B lists specific problems with the car: transmission repair, engine burns oil, air conditioner and heater are shot, upholstery, interior and window problems.

  ✓   B. ¹The transmission slips, and our mechanic told us it would cost $2,000 to get it repaired. ²That's more than the car is worth. ³Because the engine burns oil, we have to add a quart a week. ⁴In addition, the air conditioner and heater are shot, the upholstery is stained or torn, the cover has fallen off the glove box, the rear-view mirror is loose, and the driver's window sticks much of the time in the "down" position.

### 5.  **The little boy was in a stubborn mood.**

The little boy's facial expression and his emphatic "NO!" are specific references to someone being stubborn.

_____ A.  ¹When I asked him to do something, he gave me nothing but trouble. ²He seemed determined to make things difficult for me, for he had made his mind up.

___✓___ B.  ¹When I asked him to stop playing in the yard and come indoors, he looked me squarely in the eye and shouted "NO!" and then spelled it out: "N…O!"

### 6.  **The food in the cafeteria is terrible some days.**

The cafeteria's veggies are "limp and salty," the macaroni is "gluey and tasteless," the pizza is "spongy and cold," the beef needs "diamond-tipped teeth," and the hamburgers taste like rubber."

_____ A.  ¹They serve canned vegetables, which are not as good as fresh ones. ²The macaroni and cheese does not do anything for your appetite, and the pizza is not as good as the kind you can get at a pizzeria. ³Some of the meat is virtually inedible. ⁴Lots of luck if you want something good to drink.

___✓___ B.  ¹The string beans and other canned vegetables are limp and salty, and the macaroni and cheese is gluey and tasteless. ²The pizza is usually spongy and cold and does not have much cheese on it. ³You'd need diamond-tipped teeth to be able to chew the beef in the stew. ⁴The hamburgers taste like rubber.

### 7.  **Our new kitten causes us lots of trouble.**

"Shredded the curtains," "nearly drowned in the washing machine," and "scratches and bites" are specific examples of causing problems.

___✓___ A.  ¹He has shredded the curtains in my bedroom with his claws. ²He nearly drowned when he crawled into the washing machine. ³And my hands look like raw hamburger from his playful scratches and bites.

_____ B.  ¹He seems to destroy everything he touches. ²He's always getting into places where he doesn't belong. ³Sometimes he plays too roughly, and that can be painful.

### 8.  **Speaking before a group is a problem for many people.**

Pretending to be ill, stage fright, stammering, and blushing are specific examples of how speaking before a group is a problem that people want to avoid.

_____ A.  ¹Many people will go to almost any length to avoid speaking to a group. ²If they are forced to do it, they can feel so anxious that they actually develop physical symptoms. ³If asked, people will often prefer that anything happen to them as an alternative to having to speak in public.

___✓___ B.  ¹Some people will pretend to be ill to avoid speaking publicly. ²Stage fright, stammering, and blushing are frequent reactions. ³When asked to rank their worst fears, people often list public speaking as even worse than death.

9. **My uncle knew very little about cooking when he got his first apartment.**

_____ A. ¹He had to live on whatever he had in the freezer for a while. ²He was not any good in the kitchen and went through a trial-and-error process of learning how to prepare things to eat. ³More often than not with his meals, he would make mistakes first, and someone who knows what to do in preparing food would probably not believe some of the things that he did.

Item B lists frozen dinners, exploding an egg in the microwave, and putting slices of cheese and bread in a toaster as specific examples of "knew very little about cooking."

___✓___ B. ¹The only dinners he ate for the first three weeks were frozen turkey or chicken dinners. ²When he got tired of Cheerios for breakfast, he tried to cook an egg by putting a whole egg in the microwave, where it exploded. ³Then for lunch one day, instead of a bologna sandwich, he attempted to make a grilled cheese sandwich by putting slices of cheese and bread in a toaster.

10. **My family has real problems.**

___✓___ A. ¹My mom was diagnosed with type 2 diabetes and hypertension, but we cannot afford the medications she should now be taking. ²Since my dad lost his job as an insurance agent, we've started to fall behind on our mortgage payments. ³Then my sister was caught shoplifting cosmetics from our local drug store.

Item A gives clear examples of a family's real problems: Mom's health situation, Dad's unemployment, major financial difficulties, and sister "acting out."

_____ B. ¹My mom has some serious health problems, and it is really going to be a challenge for us to try to deal with them. ²My dad is not employed at the present, and so there is no money coming in. ³As a result, we're having to deal with major financial difficulties. ⁴Then my sister has been acting out because of all the stress in the family.

# MAIN IDEAS AND SUPPORTING DETAILS IN WRITING: Mastery Test 1

In the groups of sentences that follow, one sentence is the point or idea, and the other sentences are details that support and develop this idea. Put a check (✓) in front of the point or main idea in each group.

1. _✓_ A. A traffic light is needed at the intersection.

   ___ B. A number of accidents have occurred at that intersection.

   ___ C. Drivers sometimes ignore the stop sign at that intersection.
   > Statements B and C are reasons "a traffic light is needed."

2. ___ A. A television is always blaring in one corner of the lounge.

   _✓_ B. The student lounge is not a place for quiet study.

   ___ C. There are always people in the lounge laughing and talking loudly to each other.
   > Statement A and C support the idea that "the student lounge is not a place for quiet study."

3. _✓_ A. High schools need to teach personal finance skills.

   ___ B. Many young people do not know how to budget their money.

   ___ C. More and more people are getting into serious credit-card debt.
   > Statement B and C explain why we need to teach personal finance skills.

4. ___ A. Cats refuse to learn silly tricks just to amuse people.

   _✓_ B. Cats are more sensible than dogs.

   ___ C. Dogs will accept cruel mistreatment, but if a cat is mistreated, it will run away.
   > Statement A and C support the idea that "cats are more sensible than dogs."

5. ___ A. Fewer companies are offering health plans and retirement benefits.

   _✓_ B. Conditions in the workplace are tougher than they used to be.

   ___ C. In many industries, workers have had to take pay cuts.
   > Statements A and C provide specific ways in which "conditions . . . are tougher."

6. ___ A. Chemicals in dark chocolate help protect arteries from heart disease.

   ___ B. Dark chocolate contains ingredients that fight depression.

   _✓_ C. Dark chocolate can be good for the human body.
   > Statements A and B are reasons that "dark chocolate can be good for the human body."

7. ___ A. The stimulant effects of a daily cup of coffee have been proved to reduce suicide rates.

   ___ B. Coffee flushes from the bloodstream the excess fat that clogs arteries.

   ___ C. Coffee supplies a large dose of antioxidants, chemicals which prevent the formation of tumors.

   _✓_ D. Even though coffee can make you jittery and interfere with sleep, there are real health benefits to drinking coffee.
   > Statements A, B, and C state three health benefits of drinking coffee.

*(Continues on next page)*

8. ___ A. Teaching is a great way to learn because one needs to know the material well enough to explain it.

   ✓ B. All students should be required to teach a class for a day.

   ___ C. By teaching a class, students will better appreciate their teachers' efforts.

   ___ D. Some students may pay more attention when another student teaches, out of curiosity if nothing else.    Statements A, C, and D are reasons that "students should be required to teach a class for a day."

9. ___ A. A common dream involves taking a test you haven't prepared for.

   ___ B. Many people dream about being in public only half dressed.

   ✓ C. Certain themes appear in many people's dreams.

   ___ D. Many people dream of falling from a great height and trying to wake up before they hit the ground.
        Statements A, B, and D describe specific themes that appear in dreams.

10. ✓ A. People should cut down on drinking soda.

   ___ B. Most cans of regular soda contain 10 teaspoons of sugar.

   ___ C. Caffeinated sodas make hyperactive kids even more hyper.

   ___ D. Soda has no nutritional value.
        Statement B, C, and D are specific reasons why "people should cut down on drinking soda."

# MAIN IDEAS AND SUPPORTING DETAILS IN WRITING: Mastery Test 2

Look at each of the following five paragraphs and then complete the outline for each paragraph. Words such as *first, also, another,* and *finally* often signal each new item of support. Note that some paragraphs begin with an introductory sentence or two before the main idea appears.               *Wording of answers may vary.*

1.  ¹Spanking is a bad idea. ²<u>First of all</u>, think about the lesson that a child learns when he is spanked. ³He learns that physical violence is a way to deal with a problem. ⁴Spanking tells him that bigger, stronger people are allowed to hit smaller, weaker people. ⁵<u>In addition</u>, a spanking often has more to do with a parent's emotions than the child's behavior. ⁶Parents under stress may spank a child to ease their own problems and frustrations. ⁷And <u>finally</u>, spanking is just not effective discipline. ⁸Children should be taught through careful and consistent explanations to behave in a certain way. ⁹They will develop better self-control than children who behave only to avoid getting hit.

*The reasons spanking is a bad idea are introduced with the transitions First of all, In addition,* and *finally.*

**Point:** _Spanking is a bad idea._

**Supporting detail: 1.** _Spanking teaches physical violence._

**Supporting detail: 2.** _Spanking often has more to do with the parent than the child._

**Supporting detail: 3.** _Spanking is not effective discipline._

2.  ¹Clapping and applause serve a number of purposes. ²<u>First of all</u>, sometimes people clap to show encouragement. ³Think of a child nervously walking onto a stage to perform a magic trick for an audience. ⁴Often, audience members will clap to show their support before the child even begins to perform. ⁵<u>Another</u> reason people clap is out of joy or excitement. ⁶This can be seen at concerts when people begin to suddenly clap in time with the music. ⁷Another reason for applause is as a sign of respect. ⁸Famous and admired people usually receive big rounds of applause simply for being introduced. ⁹<u>Last of all</u>, people clap to show appreciation. ¹⁰After a speaker has delivered a talk or a performer has sung or played, people will applaud to show their gratitude.

*The purposes of clapping are introduced by the transitions First of all, Another,* and *Last of all.*

**Point:** _Clapping and applause serve a number of purposes._

**Supporting detail: 1.** _To show encouragement_

**Supporting detail: 2.** _Out of joy or excitement_

**Supporting detail: 3.** _As a sign of respect_

**Supporting detail: 4.** _To show appreciation_

3.  ¹When you die, what will happen to your body? ²Most people end up underground in a metal coffin. ³But this final resting place is expensive and takes up valuable land. ⁴Fortunately, there are less costly ways to dispose of your remains. ⁵<u>One</u> popular option is cremation. ⁶This low-priced option involves burning your body until it is reduced to a pile of ash. ⁷Your ash can be kept by loved ones or sprinkled in a special spot. ⁸A <u>second</u> option is natural burial. ⁹In this case, your body is buried in a cardboard box or cloth blanket that decays rapidly in soil, leaving no metals or chemicals in the ground. ¹⁰A <u>final</u> option is to

*(Continues on next page)*

Less costly alternatives to traditional burial are introduced by the transitions *One, second,* and *final.*

donate your body to science. [11]This option is free and allows you to contribute to medical science and to the welfare of humankind long after your death.

**Point:** _There are less costly ways than a traditional burial to dispose of_ _your remains._

**Supporting detail: 1.** _Cremation_

**Supporting detail: 2.** _Natural burial_

**Supporting detail: 3.** _Donate your body to science_

4. [1]Self-disclosure is a special type of conversation in which we share intimate information and feelings with another person. [2]There are many reasons why we disclose personal information. [3]One is simply to express our feelings—to "get them off our chest." [4]After a hard day at work, we may eagerly tell a friend just how angry we are at our boss and how unappreciated we feel. [5]A second reason for self-disclosure is to gain greater understanding and self-awareness. [6]Talking to a friend about a problem can help us to clarify our thoughts about the situation. [7]Social approval is also a reason for disclosing information. [8]By seeing how a listener reacts to what we say, we get information about the appropriateness of our views. [9]People may reassure us that our reactions are "perfectly normal" or suggest that we're "blowing things out of proportion." [10]Yet another common reason for self-disclosure is relationship development. [11]The sharing of personal information is an important way to begin a relationship and to move toward increasing levels of intimacy.

The reasons we disclose personal information are introduced by the transitions *One, second, also,* and *another.*

**Point:** _There are many reasons why we disclose personal information._

**Supporting detail: 1.** _Express our feelings_

**Supporting detail: 2.** _Greater understanding and self-awareness_

**Supporting detail: 3.** _Social approval_

**Supporting detail: 4.** _Relationship development_

5. [1]Storytelling can be a good way to calm down a restless child. [2]Here are some tips on how to involve your child in a story you are telling. [3]First, grab their interest from the start. [4]If the story is imaginary, you might start with "Once upon a time, . . . ." [5]If the story is true, you might begin with "Many years ago, . . . " or "Before you were born, . . . " [6]Next, have a setting for your story. [7]For a fictional story, a phrase such as "in the forest" gives children a useful frame of reference. [8]For a nonfiction story, even something like "at a campground outside of town" gives children a frame of reference. [9]Third, appeal to the senses. [10]Describe how things look. [11]For instance, you might mention colors that characters are wearing. [12]Or imitate the sounds of parts of your story—for instance, a train whistle or a birdcall. [13]When appropriate, also include descriptions of how things smelled and felt.

Some tips on involving your child in a story you are telling are introduced by the transitions *First, Next,* and *Third.*

**Point:** _Here are some tips on how to involve your child in a story you are telling._

**Supporting detail: 1.** _Grab the child's interest from the start._

**Supporting detail: 2.** _Have a setting for your story._

**Supporting detail: 3.** _Appeal to the senses._

# MAIN IDEAS AND SUPPORTING DETAILS IN WRITING: Mastery Test 3

**A.** (1–3.) Each point is followed by three statements that provide relevant, on-target support and three that do not. In the spaces, write the letters of the three **relevant** statements of support.

*Items A, B, and C each show that the writer needs a larger apartment: the kitchen is too small, the living room is too small, and there is no storage space. Items D and E— Neither the friend's huge apartment nor the higher rents in this part of town supports the point that the writer needs a larger apartment.*

1. **Point:  I need a bigger apartment.**

   A. There's barely enough room in the kitchen to turn around.

   B. My living room is the size of a closet.

   C. Because there's no storage space, boxes are piled on the floor.

   D. My best friend has a huge apartment.

   E. Rents are higher on this side of town.

   *Items that logically support the point:* ____A____   ____B____   ____C____

*Items A, B, and E each point out a reason to abolish grades: students would learn for the sake of learning; teachers would have more planning time; grades do not measure knowledge. Item C is a reason to keep grades, not to abolish them. Item D is about the history of grades.*

2. **Point:  The use of grades in school should be abolished.**

   A. Students would learn for the sake of learning—not for the sake of grades.

   B. Teachers would have more time to spend on lesson planning.

   C. Some students may not be motivated without grades.

   D. The use of grades dates back to the 1500s.

   E. Grades don't always accurately measure a student's knowledge.

   *Items that logically support the point:* ____A____   ____B____   ____E____

*Items A, D, and E each point out a reason not to take the car: it stalls, it makes a strange grinding sound, and it has a lot of miles on it. Items B and C suggest reasons to take the car: air conditioning, power windows, and a new muffler.*

3. **Point:  I don't think we should take my car on a long trip.**

   A. It stalls out in rainy weather.

   B. It has air conditioning and power windows.

   C. I recently had the muffler replaced.

   D. Whenever I shift gears, I hear a strange grinding sound.

   E. The odometer reads 174,286 miles.

   *Items that logically support the point:* ____A____   ____D____   ____E____

*(Continues on next page)*

**B.** (4–5.) Each point below is followed by three items of information. Put a check (✓) next to the **one** item that **logically** supports the point.

4. **Point:** Pursuing a dream is important.

Item A explains why it is important to pursue a dream: it helps people learn about themselves, it gives people confidence and focus, and it prevents regretting not pursuing the dream.
Item B supports the idea that it is bad to pursue a dream.
Item C supports the idea that people's dreams change as people age.

___✓___ A. ¹Most people learn a lot about themselves when they go after what they really want. ²Even if their dreams don't come true, the experience will give them confidence and a better idea of what they want to do in life. ³People often regret not pursuing a dream.

_____ B. ¹Dreams are usually unrealistic. ²It is hard for some people to face the fact that their dream of becoming a famous inventor, writer, or musician will never come true. ³It is better to be realistic than disappointed.

_____ C. ¹As people get older, they are often unwilling to take the chances they might have taken when they were younger. ²Dreams of fame, fortune, and success begin to fade. ³Often, dreams are let go in favor of security and comfort.

5. **Point:** Nelson is unfriendly.

Item A explains why Nelson has few friends, not that he is unfriendly.
Item B describes actions that demonstrate Nelson's unfriendliness: he shows no interest in relationships, he does not go to parties, and he never smiles or starts conversations.
Item C shows that Nelson cares about animals, not that he is unfriendly.

_____ A. ¹His family moved a lot as he was growing up. ²He went to four different schools during high school. ³As soon as he made new friends, he often had to leave them behind.

___✓___ B. ¹He shows no interest in relationships. ²Even though he gets invited to parties and other get-togethers, he rarely shows up. ³He never smiles or makes an effort to start a conversation with anyone.

_____ C. ¹He volunteers at the local pet shelter and cares for abandoned cats and dogs. ²He has adopted several of the animals he's cared for. ³Some of his best friends are stray animals.

# MAIN IDEAS AND SUPPORTING DETAILS IN WRITING: Mastery Test 4

Each of the five points below is followed by two items of support. Put a check (✓) next to the item that is specific and clearly shows us the writer's point. By contrast, the other item will be vague, dull, or wordy and lack sharp details.

1. **My son spends too much time on the Internet.**

Item A is vague: "constantly," "never," "given up all," "without a break," "people he knows," and "an obsession." These descriptions are not as clear and specific as those in Item B: "eight hours a day," "at least five [computer] windows open," "eats . . . in front of the computer," and "quit playing . . . or hanging out . . . in favor of being online."

_____ A. ¹He's on it constantly. ²I honestly never see him without his laptop. ³He's given up all his other interests in favor of staring at the computer screen. ⁴He goes from website to website without a break. ⁵His "friends" are all people that he talks to online, rather than people he knows in real life. ⁶Being online has truly become an obsession for him.

___✓___ B. ¹When my son isn't at school, he is on the Internet. ²I estimate he's staring at a computer screen for eight hours a day. ³He'll have at least five windows open at all times, including Facebook, several IM conversations, and a role-playing game called World of Warcraft. ⁴He eats his breakfast and dinner in front of the computer. ⁵He's quit playing basketball or hanging out with his friends in favor of being online.

2. **The new stock person is not working out.**

Item A is clear and specific about the new stock person's problems: He "put [signs] in the wrong place." He was caught "talking on his cell phone" when he should have been working. He dropped ketchup bottles. Item B lacks those sharp details. He "doesn't pay attention," "puts things in the wrong place," was "caught . . . goofing off," is "clumsy," and has a "poor attitude."

___✓___ A. ¹When I told him to put up the ad signs in the dairy aisle, he put some of them in the wrong place, so we had to sell those items at a reduced price. ²The other evening, I caught him in the stockroom talking on his cell phone when he should have been mopping the floors. ³When he stocked the condiment section, he dropped two ketchup bottles, causing a big mess that he was very slow about cleaning up. ⁴If his job performance doesn't improve, I will have to fire him.

_____ B. ¹He doesn't pay attention to what he's doing and tends to put things in the wrong place. ²That confuses customers and costs us money. ³In addition, I've caught him goofing off in the stockroom when he should be working out on the floor. ⁴He's clumsy, and has accidentally ruined some food items. I really expected he'd be a better employee than this. ⁵He seems to have a poor attitude, too. Unless he improves, he will soon be an ex-employee.

3. **My blind date with Kathy was a disaster.**

_____ A. ¹My friend Deb's cousin Kathy was pretty and nice, but I made a terrible first impression on her. ²I know she'll never go out with me again. ³Everything that could go wrong did. ⁴I was so nervous that I was clumsy and made a mess in the restaurant where we went for dinner. ⁵That made me more nervous than ever, and I said all the wrong things. ⁶My jokes fell flat, and even my attempts to compliment

*(Continues on next page)*

123

Item A is vague: "terrible first impression," "was clumsy and made a mess," "said all the wrong things," "my jokes fell flat," "said stupid things and acted stupid." Item B gives specific examples of the writer's clumsiness and awkwardness: he dropped a forkful of spaghetti, joked that the hospital doesn't let him out often, and suggested that Deb had described Kathy in unflattering terms.

her went badly. [7]I said stupid things and acted stupid. [8]I'm sure she was relieved when the evening was over.

___✓___ B. [1]My friend Deb set me up with her cousin Kathy. [2]Kathy was really attractive and I wanted to impress her, so that made me nervous. [3]At the restaurant I ordered spaghetti and promptly dropped a forkful of it, getting tomato sauce all over my shirt and the tablecloth. [4]I tried to make a joke, saying, "This is why the hospital doesn't let me out very often," but she just looked at me blankly. [5]Later I said, "From what Deb said, I had no idea you'd be so pretty." [6]She looked unhappy and I realized I'd just gotten Deb in trouble. [7]I don't think Kathy will go out with me again.

4. **The movie was terrible.**

Item A describes the movie specifically, giving examples of "unbelievable coincidences," "awful script," and silly casting. Item B is vague, describing the plot as "stupid," dialog as "ridiculous," and casting as "terrible" with no specific examples.

___✓___ A. [1]The plot was full of unbelievable coincidences, like when the two main characters meet in China and find out they are brothers. [2]Then there was the awful script. [3]One of the men actually said, "Wow, it's really cool to unexpectedly meet the brother I never knew existed." [4]The casting was silly as well. [5]One of the "brothers" was short, heavy, and had blond hair, and the other was very tall and thin and was dark-haired. [6]They didn't look like they could be related.

___ B. [1]The plot was really stupid and the acting was even worse. [2]Some of the dialog was so ridiculous it made me laugh out loud, even though it was supposed to be serious. [3]Even the casting was terrible—the actors were not at all convincing as their characters. [4]Overall, the movie was simply unbelievable. [5]I spent most of my time in the theater thinking, "This could never be true. [6]None of this is believable."

5. **My grandparents are old-fashioned.**

Item A is specific about how grandparents are old-fashioned, citing examples such as they don't have cable TV; they don't own a computer, DVR, or cell phone; Grandma wears a muumuu and Grandpa wears wire-rim glasses; they watch reruns of the old *Lawrence Welk Show*. Item B is vague, referring to out-of-date technology, old reruns, and old people's hobbies.

___✓___ A. [1]They still use an antenna on their TV rather than get cable or satellite service. [2]They don't own a computer, DVR, or cell phone. [3]My grandmother wears those baggy house dresses with flowers on them—I think you call them muumuus. [4]I told my grandfather he looks like Ben Franklin with his wire-rim glasses. [5]My grandmother still bakes her own cakes and pies, while my grandfather collects stamps. [6]Whenever I go over there, it seems like they're always got the TV turned to reruns of the old *Lawrence Welk Show*.

___ B. [1]Even though they could easily afford the latest gadgets, they insist on sticking with technology that was out-of-date twenty years ago. [2]I offered to buy them a new flat-screen TV, but they told me to save my money. [3]Maybe it doesn't matter, since they would probably only use it to watch reruns of old shows. [4]Style-wise, they're still living in the past. [5]And their hobbies are exactly the type of things you'd expect old people to enjoy doing. [6]Whenever I visit them, it's like traveling back in time to a simpler era .

# 5 Understanding the Writing Process

Now that you know the two basic goals in effective writing—to make a point and support that point—it's time to write some simple paragraphs and to experience the writing process. Even professional writers do not sit down and write a paper in a single draft. Instead, they work on it a step at a time. Writing a paper is a process that can be divided into the following steps:

Step 1  Getting Started through Prewriting
Step 2  Preparing a Scratch Outline
Step 3  Writing the First Draft
Step 4  Revising and Editing
Step 5  Reading the Paper Aloud

With each of the three paragraph assignments that follow, you will learn a different prewriting strategy that will help you generate supporting details. The three strategies are freewriting, questioning, and list making.

## PRACTICE 1: Using Freewriting to Develop a Paragraph

Write a paragraph that supports the following main idea:

**Main idea: There are three people I'd like to send to a desert island.**

### How to Proceed

**1. Freewrite**. Your purpose in the paragraph is to provide specific support for your main idea or point. To help think about and develop your support, spend some time freewriting. **Freewriting** is just sitting down and writing whatever comes into your mind about your point. Do this for ten minutes or so. Write without stopping and without worrying in the slightest about spelling, grammar, and the like. None of that matters at this early draft stage while you are thinking on paper. Simply get down all the information that occurs to you about your point.

*To the Instructor:* There are no correct answers to the practice exercises in this chapter. Instead, students' paragraphs should be evaluated according to the following:
• Is there a clearly expressed main idea?
• Are there enough details to support the main idea? Are the details *relevant?*
• Are transitions used to move from one detail to the next?
• Does the final sentence tie the details together and bring the paragraph to a close?

125

Look at some of the freewriting done by a student named Victor:

> For sure my landlord is one person I want to say good ridance. only time I hear from him is my check is late if you call him about a problem all you get is his voice saying he will call back ha! forget about hearing from him. I'm on the grond floor and at night started hearin all these sounds at nite they was in a storage room next to my bedrum I looked in that spot one day and their were big dropings everywhere it must have been RATS and lots of luck with my landlord doing anything I had to buy some poison bate myself and put it there

Notice that there are mistakes with spelling, grammar, and punctuation in Victor's freewriting. He is not concerned about such matters—*nor should he be*—at this stage. He is just concentrating on getting thoughts and details down on paper, and he knows that writing things down at random can help him think about his topic.

You should take the same approach when freewriting: explore your topic without worrying at all about writing "correctly." In this early stage of the writing process, you are just trying to figure out what you want to say.

**2. Prepare a Scratch Outline.** Your freewriting will eventually help you figure out which three people you want to write about. Your goal is to have three supporting items for your paragraph. Write down the three people and number them 1, 2, and 3.

Here are the three people that Victor decided to focus on in a scratch outline:

> There are three people I'd like to send to a desert island.
> 1. landlord
> 2. upstairs neighbor
> 3. brother's girlfriend

**3. Write the First Draft.** The first draft is just that—a rough first draft as you put at least some of your details down and get an overall sense of the shape of your paper. You still do not have to worry about spelling or punctuation at this stage of the writing process. You want to create the foundation of your paper—its main point and its supporting details. In later drafts, you can build on what you have in the first draft.

Here is Victor's first draft:

> I've got three people for a desert island. First, my landlord. I call him about problem and I never hear from him. Nothing but a waste of my time calling him. I'm not going to chase after him, I have my own life to live. I notice one day my smoke alarm is broken. I put in a new battery and tryed to test it, it still didn't work. He needs to replace it or something. Every once in a while the tolet leaks a bit and there is water around the base of the toilet. That I then have to wipe up. Lots of luck getting him to respond. I've call and never any answer. But the biggest thing was hearing rats in the shed next my bedroom. Number 2, I want to send my neigbor upstairs to the island. Why would anyone make noise at 2 in the morning? Just because he's awake he thinks he has the right to keep others up. Then there is the number 3 the girlfriend that my brother goes with. She talks on and on and is so rude. Your trying to say something and she cuts you off.  Get her to the island.

**4. Revise and Edit.** Ideally, put your paper aside for a while before doing later drafts. When you revise, try to do all of the following:

- Omit any details that do not truly support the topic sentence.
- Add more details as needed, making sure you have enough specific details for each of your supporting items.
- Add addition words such as *first, another, second, also,* or *finally* to signal to the reader you are moving from one person to another.
- Include a final "caboose" sentence that rounds off the paper, bringing it to a close.

On the next page is the paragraph that Victor eventually produced after revising and editing it. Underline the addition words in his paper that show he is moving from one person to the next.

There are three people I'd like to send to a desert island. The <u>first</u> would be my landlord. As far as I can tell, my landlord believes that his only responsibility is to collect his tenants' rent. If we contact him about any concern—the toilet leaks, rats in the building, the smoke alarm is broken—his response is not to respond. I'd be glad to send him to the desert island forever. The <u>second</u> person I would send is my upstairs neighbor. Now, I understand that the guy works second shift and doesn't get home until midnight. What I don't understand is why he doesn't show a little consideration to people who work normal hours. It's not unusual for him to start moving furniture or hammering nails in the walls or playing loud music at 2 a.m. I'd gladly put him on a one-way trip to that island. And the <u>final</u> person I'd like to say goodbye to is my brother's girlfriend. It's bad enough that this girl doesn't have a job and doesn't have any interests. She also doesn't have anything to talk about other than what celebrities are getting divorced or having too much plastic surgery. On top of that, she cuts people off when they're talking to her. She can join my landlord and neighbor on that island forever.

**5. Read the Paper Aloud.** Always proofread a paper by reading it out loud. Make sure you read exactly what is on the page. Hearing how your writing sounds is an excellent way to pick up grammar and punctuation problems in your writing. Chances are that you'll find sentence mistakes at every spot where your paper does not read smoothly and clearly. This point is so important that it bears repeating: *To help find mistakes in your paper, read it out loud!*

By consulting a grammar and punctuation handbook as needed, you'll learn to identify and correct mistakes that you may be making.

*A Final Note:* When writing your "desert island" paragraph, you should, of course, use people and supporting details other than the ones in Victor's paper. Your goal is to prove to your reader through convincing details just why the three people you describe should go to a desert island. Imagine you're presenting your evidence to a jury. Your goal is to provide such strong specific evidence that the jury—your readers—will find them all "guilty as charged."

## PRACTICE 2: Using Questions to Develop a Paragraph

Write a paragraph that supports the following point:

**Main idea:** Today was a good [or bad] day in my life.

## How to Proceed

**1. Ask Questions.** Your purpose in the paragraph is to provide specific support for your point. To help think about and develop your support, spend some time asking yourself questions. As you do, write down answers to those questions. Your questions can start with words like *what, when, where, why*, and *how*.

Here are some questions that a student named Ellen asked while developing her paper:

> When did the good parts of the day occur?
> Where was I during the good parts?
> Why did they make me feel good?
> How did I react?

**2. Prepare a Scratch Outline.** Your questioning will eventually help you develop the specific details about why the day was a good one. Your goal is to have at least several supporting items for your paragraph. Write down those details and number them 1, 2, and 3. Here are the details that Ellen decided to focus on.

> 1. beautiful morning
> 2. did well on math quiz
> 3. nice conversation at lunch
> 4. good exercise walking home
> 5. pizza for dinner

**3–4. Write a First Draft, Revise, and Edit.** On the next page is the paragraph that Ellen eventually produced. Underline the addition words that indicate each of Ellen's reasons for calling it a good day.

> Today was a good day in my life. <u>First of all</u>, the weather was simply beautiful. It was one of those warm early spring days when the sun was shining and the birds were singing and the earth smelled of growing things. I felt like the planet was a good place to be. <u>Secondly</u>, there was a surprise quiz in my math class that I totally aced. I've been working hard in that class, and it was satisfying to know that I'd been prepared and done well. <u>Next</u>, at lunchtime, I sat out on the lawn watching some kids playing Frisbee in the sunshine. Everyone seemed very relaxed, and there was a lot of good-natured talking and laughter. A guy from my history class stopped to talk for a few minutes. I don't expect to ever date him or anything, but it's always nice to spend time with a friendly guy. <u>Also</u>, after my afternoon class was over, I decided to walk home, rather than take the bus. It's a two-mile trip, and it actually was enjoyable to use my body and get a bit of exercise. <u>Finally</u>, my mother decided that the weather was too nice to cook a meal that night, and so we ordered pizza, my favorite meal. I know I'll go to sleep tonight with a smile on my face.

**5. Read the Paper Aloud.** Always proofread a paper by reading it out loud. Make sure you read exactly what is on the page. Hearing how your writing sounds is an excellent way to pick up grammar and punctuation problems in your writing. Chances are that you'll find sentence mistakes at every spot where your paper does not read smoothly and clearly. This point is so important that it bears repeating: *To help find mistakes in your paper, read it out loud!*

By consulting a grammar and punctuation handbook as needed, you'll learn to identify and correct mistakes that you may be making.

## PRACTICE 3: Using a List to Develop a Paragraph

Write a paragraph that supports the following point:

**Main idea:** If I could eat anything I wanted one day, without worrying about cost or calories, here is what I'd eat.

### How to Proceed

**1. Make a List.** In **list making** (also known as **brainstorming**), you make a list of ideas and details that could go into your paper. Simply pile these items up, one after another, without worrying about putting them in any special order. Try to think of as many details as possible and to make them as specific as possible. Here are the initial items on the list of a student named Casey.

> orange juice—freshly squeezed
> oatmeal with brown sugar and cinnamon
> toasted English muffin with butter
> four slices of lightly crisp bacon
> . . . .

Expand your list with one detail after another—taking yourself through breakfast, lunch, and dinner, and adding in snacks, desserts, and drinks as well. Don't worry about putting your items in order at this point—just get down a list of as many items as you can think of. You can easily delete or add more items and put them into the right sequence later. At this prewriting stage, you're just accumulating raw material and thinking about your topic by putting a long list of details on paper.

**2. Prepare a Scratch Outline.** Once you have your list, prepare a scratch outline of your paragraph. It will serve as a guide to just how to proceed in writing your paragraph. Here is Casey's scratch outline:

> 1. Breakfast
> 2. Mid-morning drink and snack
> 3. Lunch
> 4. Dinner
> 5. After-dinner drinks and desserts

**3–4. Write a First Draft, Revise, and Edit.** Here is just the first part of a long paragraph that Casey wrote. Notice that words such as *then* and *after* signal to the reader the student is moving from one part of the fantasy dining day to the next.

> If I could eat anything I wanted one day, without worrying about cost or calories, here is what I would eat. I'd start off with a small glass of orange juice—the kind that has a lot of pulp in it, so you feel like you're drinking a freshly-squeezed orange. Then, I'd have a small bowl of oatmeal with cream and brown sugar and cinnamon on it. After that, I'd go on to have about four pieces of very crisp bacon along with two eggs that would be prepared once over lightly. . . .

*Note:* If you really detail your ideal food and drink day, you might end up writing a fairly long paragraph—it might even be several paragraphs, covering the morning, afternoon, and evening. That is perfectly fine to do for this exercise. The more words you get down and the more specifics you offer, the more practice you are getting at providing details to support your opening point.

**5. Read the Paper Aloud.** Always proofread a paper by reading it out loud. Make sure you read exactly what is on the page. Hearing how your writing sounds is an excellent way to pick up grammar and punctuation problems in your writing. Chances are that you'll find sentence mistakes at every spot where your paper does not read smoothly and clearly. This point is so important that it bears repeating: *To help find mistakes in your paper, read it out loud!*

By consulting a grammar and punctuation handbook as needed, you'll learn to identify and correct mistakes that you may be making.

## A Final Thought

To master the two basic goals in effective writing—making and supporting a point—and to learn to use the prewriting techniques of freewriting, asking questions, and list making, you need to practice. Do so by writing paragraphs on each of the three assignments in Mastery Tests 2, 3, and 4.

# UNDERSTANDING THE WRITING PROCESS: Mastery Test 1

Each item below is an example of one stage in the writing process for the following assignment:

**Assignment:** Write a paragraph in which you describe a cruel person you have known. In it, be sure to provide specific details that illustrate the person's cruelty.

Identify each item by labeling it with one of the following:

> **A. Freewriting**       **B. List making**       **C. Questioning**
> **D. Scratch outline**   **E. First draft**

_B_

cruel neighbor
named Irene or Elaine—I forget
cold eyes
kids were scared of her
wouldn't let Joanie come out and play because she was bad
wouldn't let kids come to birthday party
lived in red brick house with yellow shutters
never yelled—really scary
moved away soon afterward

A list of specific details, in no particular order

_E_

[1]When I think of the word "cruel," I remember a woman who lived in my neighborhood many years ago. [2]Her name was Irene or Elaine or something like that. [3]She lived in a red-brick house with yellow shutters on the windows. [4]She had a lot of kids. [5]Thin little kids who always had cuts and bruises all over them. [6]When I invited them to come over, they would just say, "She wouldn't like it." [7]One creepy thing I remember is that when their mother wanted them to come in, she didn't call them. [8]She would just stand in the doorway, looking at them, she had the coldest eyes I've ever seen. [9]When they saw her watching them, the kids would hurry into the house. [10]Once, I remember Joanie didn't come out to play for what seemed like weeks. [11]When I finally saw her, I asked where she had been. [12]She looked at the ground and whispered, "I couldn't play because I was bad." [13]I never heard their mother yell at them, and that was the scariest thing of all about her. [14]Ordinary mothers yell sometimes, but not her. [15]The only time I remember hearing her voice was when I invited the kids to my 9th birthday party. [16]I walked up to her and asked if they could come. [17]I remember the kids looking at the ground as I asked. [18]She smiled in a nasty way and said, "I don't think so." [19]On the day of the party I remember seeing Joanie looking out the window. [20]Soon after that they moved away.

A paragraph containing a clear main point and specific details

*(Continues on next page)*

<u>C</u>    *Who was cruel?* My neighbor Irene (or Elaine)

*Where was she?* Down the street from me

*When did I meet her?* I was almost 9 years old

*What made her seem cruel?* Never yelled, just looked at kids (scary), cold eyes, nasty smile

*How was she cruel?* She wouldn't let her kids play or visit, kept Joanie indoors because she was bad

A list of questions; the answers are specific details

<u>A</u>    [1]Cruel sounds like a wicked stepmother in a fairy tale. [2]do I know anybody cruel. [3]You can be bad but not cruel—cruel is when they can't fight back. [4]Cruel = hurting things like babies or little kids. [5]A creepy woman used to live on our street with all the kids. [6]Name was Elaine Irene something like that? [7]Whoa that's been a long time ago. [8]something was really bad about her. [9]they were scared of her. [10]Me too. [11]Didn't want to be near that house. [12]Cold cold eyes. [13]Did she ever smile? [14]So quiet but not nice quiet. [15]Scary quiet. [16]Kids always had bruises and cuts on them. [17]Did she do that? [18]They were home sick a lot. [19]I saw them look out of the windows. [20]They always seemed scared.

Writing whatever about the topic comes into the mind, without worrying about spelling or grammar

<u>D</u>    When I think of the word "cruel," I remember a woman who lived in my neighborhood many years ago.

1.  Lived in red-brick house with lots of kids
2.  Didn't call them—just stood in doorway and looked at them with cold eyes
3.  Kept Joanie in house because she was bad
4.  Never yelled—scary
5.  Wouldn't let kids come to my 9th birthday party

A mini-outline containing a clear main point and a list of specific details to include in the paper

# UNDERSTANDING THE WRITING PROCESS: Mastery Test 2 (Freewriting)

Use the prewriting technique of freewriting to help you do a paragraph on the following assignment.

**Hometown or Neighborhood.** If a friend asked whether your hometown or your neighborhood would be a good place for him or her to move to, what would be your response? Write a letter to your friend explaining the advantages or disadvantages of living there.

Your main idea can simply be a sentence like, "There would be several advantages (*or* disadvantages) to living in my hometown (*or* neighborhood)." For example:

● I would recommend several reasons for moving to Cape May, New Jersey.

● There are some real drawbacks to living in the Alden Park neighborhood where I grew up in Chicago.

## How to Proceed

*To the Instructor:*
A student's score on this test should be based on your evaluation of whether he or she has written an A, B, C, D, or F paper.

Suggested equivalents:

A = 90 to 100
B = 80 to 89
C = 70 to 79
D = 60 to 69
F = 59 and below

**1. Freewrite.** Before you actually write the first draft, spend ten or fifteen minutes freewriting. Just sit down and write whatever comes into your mind about your hometown or neighborhood. You might write, "I'm going to think of things I really liked about my hometown" and then write them down as they occur to you. Write without stopping and without worrying at all about spelling, grammar, and the like. After you've written for a while about things you liked, you may want to write "Now I'm going to try to think of things that I didn't like" and just put them down as they occur to you. In general, think on paper and try to get down as much positive and negative information as you can. You are using the freewriting process to try to figure out what you want to say. When you are done, you'll probably have a sense of whether you want your paragraph to be a thumbs-up or a thumbs-down account of your hometown or neighborhood.

**2. Ask questions and/or make a list.** You may then find it helps to also use other prewriting techniques. Perhaps ask yourself questions about what was good and what was bad about your hometown or neighborhood. Or see if you can make up a list of good things and bad things about your hometown or neighborhood. The goal of your prewriting techniques is to help you determine what direction your paper will take and what kinds of support you can provide for your point of view. You'll then be ready to do a scratch outline.

**3. Prepare a scratch outline.** Write out your main idea and briefly list your supporting items.

> **Main Idea**
> > **Supporting reason 1**
> > **Supporting reason 2**
> > **Supporting reason 3**

*(Continues on next page)*

**4. Write and revise.** Write a first draft of your paper, and then go on to revise it in one or more additional drafts. Remember that your goal is to advance a point and then do a solid job of supporting that point. Use addition words such as *first, second,* and *finally* to signal to the reader that you are moving from one advantage or drawback to another.

Here, as a model, is one student's response to the assignment. Notice that his paragraph begins with two sentences of introduction before stating its topic sentence.

> After living in my current apartment for three years, I have gotten to know my neighborhood well. It's not the most upscale area by any means, and a newcomer might not think it's all that attractive. But over time, I've found three real advantages to the area. First of all, most people who live here have been here for years. There aren't a lot of people moving in and out. That gives the neighborhood a real sense of community. People noticed, for example, when Miss Henderson stopped taking her mail in. Neighbors checked on her, found out she wasn't well, and got her the help she needed. For another example, when Nina next door had twins, the neighbors organized to deliver meals for the first week she was home with the babies. A second advantage to my neighborhood is that it is within walking distance of several good food markets. There's a meat market, a fruit and vegetable store, and a bakery. I like being able to shop in my own neighborhood and get to know the people I'm buying from. The merchants begin to feel like friends, not just salespeople. The final advantage of my neighborhood is that it is very close to a subway stop. As you know, if you live in a city, that is an important feature. I have to walk only two blocks to get the subway, and then for the price of a token I'm quickly on my way anywhere I want to go. If I ever have to leave my neighborhood, I will definitely miss these three good points.

**5. Read your paper aloud.** After you have edited and proofread your paper, be sure to *read it out loud.* Hearing how your writing sounds is an excellent way to pick up grammar and punctuation problems in your writing. Chances are that you'll find sentence mistakes at spots where your paper does not read smoothly and clearly. Use a grammar handbook, if necessary, to see what corrections are needed. Make the required corrections to remove the trouble spots.

# UNDERSTANDING THE WRITING PROCESS: Mastery Test 3 (Asking Questions)

Use the prewriting technique of asking questions to write a paragraph on the following assignment.

**Giving Advice.** Write a paragraph in which you give advice to three people you know, either personally or from a distance. Perhaps one of the people is in your family; perhaps another is a friend; perhaps another is a movie star or a politician or other public figure. In any case, imagine that you have been given an opportunity to tell them what—in your opinion—they are doing wrong and what they should do to correct the error of their ways.

Your main idea can be something like, "Even though they would say it is none of my business, here is my personal advice to three people I know."

## How to Proceed

**1. Ask questions.** Here are some questions you might ask in thinking about how to do this assignment.

1. *Who are some of the people I'd most like to give advice to?*
2. *What have they done that makes them need my advice?*
3. *What and where were the occasions where they made the wrong decisions or behaved in the wrong ways?*
4. *Why will they benefit from my advice?*
5. *How will their lives be better if they follow my advice?*

As you ask questions and think of answers, write out your thoughts and responses as they occur to you. Remember not to worry about spelling, grammar, and the like. You just want to do some thinking on paper as you gradually figure out which people you want to focus on and what advice you think will serve them well.

**2. Freewrite and/or make a list.** You may then find it helps to also use other prewriting techniques. Perhaps freewrite about one or more of the people you have in mind. Or see if you can make up a list of mistakes you feel they have made and a list of the actions they need to take to get back in the good graces of others. You'll eventually be ready to do a scratch outline.

**3. Prepare a scratch outline.** Write out your main idea and briefly list your supporting items.

### Main Idea
1. **First person**
2. **Second person**
3. **Third person**

*(Continues on next page)*

**4. Write and revise.** Write a first draft of your paper, and then go on to revise it in one or more additional drafts. Remember that your goal is to advance a point and then do a solid job of supporting that point. Use addition words such as *one, another*, and *last* to signal to the reader that you are moving from one person to another.

Here, as a model, is one student's response to the assignment. Notice that her paragraph begins with two sentences of introduction before stating its topic sentence.

I try to only give advice when someone asks me for it. But I often find myself giving people advice silently, in my own mind. Right now, there are three people I'd really like to give out-loud advice to. The first is my cousin Luisa. Luisa is married to a nice man named Carlos. When we're together, she constantly nags and criticizes and corrects him about things that don't matter at all. He'll be telling a story, and she'll interrupt over and over to say things like, "No, Carlos; it didn't happen on Tuesday! And it couldn't have been in the morning, because I remember we'd already had lunch." By the time she's done correcting him, no one can remember what the story was about, and everyone is embarrassed and irritated. So my advice to Luisa is, stop and think before you criticize Carlos. It isn't good for your marriage! The second person I'd like to give advice to is a certain television personality I won't name here, but she hosts a talk show. My advice to her is, girl, stop with the cosmetic surgery!! Every time I see her, her forehead is tighter and shinier, her lips are puffier, and her eyes are so wide open I don't believe she can blink them. Her entire face is beginning to look like a Halloween mask, with an expression that never changes. I'd tell her it's better to have a few wrinkles and still look like a human being. The final person I'd like to give advice to is my friend Josh. Josh is a good-looking guy who has no trouble attracting girls. But he's always in an unhappy relationship. He's constantly announcing that he has a new girlfriend and that <u>this</u> one is so much better than his previous one. But after a few months, or even weeks, he's telling everyone that the new girl is clingy, or possessive, or insecure, or too independent, or not independent enough . . . you get the idea. The point is that Josh always thinks the problem is with the girl, never with him. I'd like to advise Josh to spend some time looking inside to figure out why his relationships keep failing, rather than always blaming the other person.

**5. Read your paper aloud.** After you have edited and proofread your paper, be sure to *read it out loud*. Hearing how your writing sounds is an excellent way to pick up grammar and punctuation problems in your writing. Chances are that you'll find sentence mistakes at spots where your paper does not read smoothly and clearly. Use a grammar handbook, if necessary, to see what corrections are needed. Make the required corrections to remove the trouble spots.

## UNDERSTANDING THE WRITING PROCESS: Mastery Test 4 (List Making)

Use the prewriting technique of list making to help you do a paragraph on the following assignment.

**Directions to a Place**. Write a set of specific directions on how to get from your classroom to your house. Imagine you are giving these directions to a stranger who has just come into the room and who wants to deliver a million dollars to your home. Because the stranger does not know your neighborhood, you'll want to give exact directions, including various landmarks. You don't want the million dollars to get lost!

Your main idea can simply be, "Here is how to get from this classroom to my house."

### How to Proceed

**1. Make a list.** Before you actually write the first draft of the paper, make up a list of all the directions involved. For example, here is one student's list:

*To the Instructor:*
A student's score on this test should be based on your evaluation of whether he or she has written an A, B, C, D, or F paper.

Suggested equivalents:

A = 90 to 100
B = 80 to 89
C = 70 to 79
D = 60 to 69
F = 59 and below

Leave this building through the main entrance.

Turn to your left and follow the curving brick walkway about 500 feet to where it ends on Academy Road.

Turn left on Academy Road and go four blocks to the intersection with Route 73.

At the intersection, you'll see an Exxon gas station and a Pizza Hut restaurant.

Turn right and go 3 blocks down Route 73.

After the first block, the street signs will say "Maple Avenue" instead of Route 73.

Maple Avenue/Route 73 will come to a five-point intersection.

Imagine the intersection is like a clock; you want to turn on the road that is at 2:00. It is called Lamont Street.

You'll see a wooden building with a bunch of doctors' offices in it between it and the next road (at about 4:00).

Travel 2.4 miles on Lamont Street.

Slow down when you see the big Catholic church on your right. Just after the church, take a right on Meredith Avenue.

My house is the 9th one on the right. The address is 256 Meredith Avenue.

The house is made of red brick, and there is a blue bicycle chained to the porch.

*(Continues on next page)*

**2. Prepare a scratch outline.** Write out your main idea and the list of directions needed. When the student who did the above list put together all his directions, he had a total of five turns that need to be taken to get to his house.

**3. Write and revise.** Write a first draft of your paper, and then go on to revise it in one or more additional drafts. Remember that your goal is to advance a point and then do a solid job of supporting that point. Use addition words such as *to begin with, next, then,* and *after* to signal to the reader that you are moving from one direction to the next.

**4. Read your paper aloud.** After you have edited and proofread your paper, be sure to *read it out loud*. Hearing how your writing sounds is an excellent way to pick up grammar and punctuation problems in your writing. Chances are that you'll find sentence mistakes at spots where your paper does not read smoothly and clearly. Use a grammar handbook, if necessary, to see what corrections are needed. Make the required corrections to remove the trouble spots.

# 6 Relationships in Reading

**G**ood readers and writers understand the relationships between ideas. This chapter explains the basic relationships you should recognize as a reader.

Ideas in a reading selection are almost always connected to each other. Learning to recognize these connections, or **relationships**, will help you become a better reader.

As you will see, authors use two common methods to show relationships and make their ideas clear. These two methods—**transitions** and **patterns of organization**—are explained in turn in this chapter.

# Transitions

Look at the following two items. Then check (✓) the one that is easier to read and understand:

\_\_\_\_ Paperback books cost less than hardback books. They are easier to carry.

✓ Paperback books cost less than hardback books. Also, they are easier to carry.

You probably found the second item a bit easier to read and follow. The word *also* makes it clear that the writer is discussing the advantages of paperback books. One advantage is that the books are less expensive. An *additional* advantage is that they are easier to carry.

**Transitions** are words or phrases (such as *also*) that show the relationship between ideas. They are "bridge" words, carrying the reader across from one idea to the next.

Paperback books cost less than hardback books.  , they are easier to carry.

Two major types of transitions are described in this chapter: words that show addition and words that show time.

## Words That Show Addition

Once again, put a check (✓) beside the item that is easier to read and understand:

\_\_\_\_ Climbing stairs is good exercise for your muscles. It burns a lot of calories.

✓ Climbing stairs is good exercise for your muscles. In addition, it burns a lot of calories.

The words *In addition* in the second item helps make the relationship between the two sentences clear. The author is listing the benefits of climbing stairs. The first benefit is good exercise for the muscles. In addition, climbing stairs burns a lot of calories. *In addition* and words like it are known as addition words.

**Addition words** signal added ideas. These words tell you a writer is presenting one or more ideas that continue along the same line of thought as a previous idea. Like all transitions, addition words help writers organize their information and present it clearly to readers. In the cartoon on the next page, the words *To begin with* introduce a list, and the words *Second* and *Also* add to the list of reasons why the dog should be hired.

**Time words** indicate a time relationship. These transitions tell us *when* something happened in relation to when something else happened. They help writers organize and make clear the order of events, stages, and steps in a process. In the cartoon below, the words *First, Then,* and *Finally* mark different stages in "growing up."

"Growing up isn't easy. First, in preschool, you have to learn to tie your shoes. Then in kindergarten, it's the alphabet. Finally, in first grade, they hit you with addition and subtraction."

Here are some common time words:

*Time Words*

| | | | |
|---|---|---|---|
| before | next | while | later |
| previously | soon | during | after |
| first | often | until | eventually |
| second | as | now | finally |
| third | when | then | last |

*Note:* Additional ways of showing time are dates ("In 1850 . . ."; "Throughout the 20th century . . ."; "By 2018 . . .") and other time references ("Within a week . . ."; "by the end of the month . . ."; "in two years . . .").

### Examples

The following items contain time words. Notice how these words show us *when* something takes place.

● *After* our kids take their morning showers, there is usually no hot water left.

● It used to take me thirty-five minutes to get to school. *Now*, because of road construction, that time has nearly tripled.

● I begin my "Things To Do" list by writing down everything I need to do the next day. *Then* I label each item A (very important), B (important), or C (not important).

## Helpful Tips about Transitions

Here are two points to keep in mind about transitions:

 **TIP 1** **Some transition words have the same meaning.** For example, *also, moreover*, and *furthermore* all mean "in addition." Authors typically use a variety of transitions to avoid repetition.

 **TIP 2** **Certain words can serve as two different types of transitions, depending on how they are used.** For example, the word *first* may be used as an addition word to show that the author is presenting a series of points, as in the following sentences:

● My mother has some strange kitchen habits. *First*, she loves to cook with the television on full blast. *Moreover*, she . . .

*First* may also be used to signal a time sequence, as in this sentence:

● The paramedics raced to the man who had collapsed on the sidewalk. *First*, they checked his pulse and breathing. *Then* . . .

**PRACTICE 2**

Complete each sentence with a suitable time word from the box. Try to use each transition once. Then, in the spaces provided, write the letter of the transition you have chosen.                                     *Answers may vary.*

| | | |
|---|---|---|
| **A.** after | **B.** before | **C.** during |
| **D.** then | **E.** when | |

> *Hint:* Make sure that each time word that you choose fits smoothly into the flow of the sentence. Test each choice by reading the sentence aloud.

___A___  1. _____After_____ playing outside most of the day, the children fell asleep quickly that night.

___E___  2. _____When_____ I was in the shower, a hairy spider crept out of the drain.

___D___  3. First, my uncle studies the food ads to see which stores have the best specials. _____Then_____ he clips all the cents-off coupons.

___B___  4. _____Before_____ the school lays off any teachers, it should reduce the size of its office staff.

___C___  5. Some people rudely talk with each other and use their cell phones _____during_____ a movie.

# Patterns of Organization

You have learned that transitions show the relationships between ideas in sentences. In the same way, **patterns of organization** show the relationships between supporting details in paragraphs, essays, and chapters. It helps to recognize the patterns in which authors arrange information. You will then be better able to understand and remember what you read.

The rest of this chapter discusses two major patterns of organization:

● The **list of items pattern**
  (Addition words are often used in this pattern of organization.)

● The **time order pattern**
  (Time words are often used in this pattern of organization.)

Noticing the transitions in a passage often can help you become aware of its pattern of organization. Transitions can also help you find the major supporting details.

# 1    The List of Items Pattern

| List of Items |
|:---:|
| Item 1 |
| Item 2 |
| Item 3 |

To understand the list of items pattern, try to arrange the following group of sentences in an order that makes sense. Put a *1* in front of the sentence that should come first, a *2* in front of the sentence that comes next, a *3* in front of the third sentence, and a *4* in front of the sentence that should come last. The result will be a short paragraph. Use the addition words as a guide.

___3___ Also, when you're on foot, you are more likely to meet neighbors and make new friends.

___4___ Finally, a brisk walk is an excellent and inexpensive form of exercise.

___1___ Walking can be a rewarding experience.

___2___ For one thing, walking lets you see firsthand what's going on in your neighborhood.

This paragraph should begin with the main idea: "Walking can be a rewarding experience." The next three sentences go on to list three reasons, resulting in the pattern of organization known as a list of items. The transitions *For one thing, Also,* and *Finally* introduce the points being listed and indicate their order. The sentences should read as follows:

> [1]Walking can be a rewarding experience. [2]For one thing, walking lets you see firsthand what's going on in your neighborhood. [3]Also, when you're on foot, you are more likely to meet neighbors and make new friends. [4]Finally, a brisk walk is an excellent and inexpensive form of exercise.

A **list of items** is a series of reasons, examples, or other points that support an idea. The items are listed in the order the author prefers. Addition words are often used in a list of items to tell us that another supporting point is being added to one or more points already mentioned. Textbook authors frequently organize material into lists of items, such as a list of tips for becoming a better writer, the results of stress, or the reasons why some people never vote.

*Addition Words Used in the List of Items Pattern*

| | | | |
|---|---|---|---|
| one | to begin with | in addition | last |
| first | another | next | last of all |
| first of all | second | moreover | final |
| for one thing | also | furthermore | finally |

## ✔ *Check Your Understanding*

The paragraph below is organized as a list of items. Complete the outline of the paragraph by adding the three major details listed in the paragraph. Then read the explanation that follows.

To help you find the major details, do two things to the paragraph:

- Underline the addition words that introduce the major details in the list;
- Number (*1, 2, . . .* ) each item in the list.

¹A number of different theories attempt to explain crime. ²<u>One</u> theory says that crime is caused by ¹biology. ³This explanation says that people inherit the tendency to commit crime much as they inherit eye color. ⁴<u>Another</u> theory suggests that crime is caused by ²psychological factors. ⁵According to this view, anger caused in childhood—by such painful events as abuse and neglect—drives people to commit crimes. ⁶A <u>third</u>, more recent view is that crime is caused by ³social forces. ⁷According to this theory, economic, social, and political inequalities create an environment in which crime is likely to happen.

**Main idea:  A number of different theories attempt to explain crime.**

*Wording of answers may vary.*

1. _____ Biology _____
2. _____ Psychological factors _____
3. _____ Social forces _____

### *Explanation*

The main idea is that a number of different theories attempt to explain crime. Note the list words: "a number of different theories." (At times you may also express the main idea in a short heading that describes what's being listed; the heading here could be "Theories to Explain Crime.") Following are the three theories you should have added to the outline:

1. Crime is caused by biology. (This item is signaled by the addition word *One*.)
2. Crime is caused by psychological factors. (This item is signaled by the addition word *Another*.)
3. Crime is caused by social forces. (This item is signaled by the addition word *third*.)

**PRACTICE 3**

**A.** The following passage uses a listing pattern. Outline the passage by filling in the major details.

> *Hint:* Underline the addition words that introduce the items in the list, and number the items.

The phrase *three different types of kindness* suggests a list of items.
**Item 1:** Natural kindness (introduced with the addition words *First of all*).
**Item 2:** Rule-guided kindness (introduced with the addition word *second*).

[1]Research has revealed three different types of kindness. [2]<u>First of all</u>, there is [1]natural kindness, based on our ability to identify with others and sense what they're feeling. [3]This kindness shows up at a very early age. [4]A grade-school child who says that a caged gorilla looks sad or who gets upset when another child is bullied has this natural kindness. [5]The <u>second</u> type of kindness is [2]rule-guided. [6]Rule-guided people have learned "It's wrong to do that." [7]For example, rule-guided children do not hit other children because they have been taught that hitting is wrong. [8]The <u>last</u> type of kindness is [3]imitative. [9]We imitate the behavior of people we admire. [10]For instance, imitative children who admire their parents will avoid behavior that their parents disapprove of—because they want to be like their parents.

**Main idea:** **Research has revealed three different types of kindness.**

1.  Natural _____     *Wording of answers may vary.*

2.  Rule-guided _____

3.  Imitative _____

**Item 3:** Imitative kindness (introduced with the addition word *last*).

**B.** The following passage uses a listing pattern. Complete the map of the passage by filling in the missing major details.

[1]Opossums use a few defense methods to cope with danger. [2]The best-known defense is [1]"playing dead." [3]An opossum using this defense goes into a coma. [4]In that state, it appears dead and can be dropped, kicked, or even cut without responding. [5]This may seem to be a foolish method of defense, for it leaves the animal open to attack. [6]But many predators will not eat what they haven't killed, and others won't attack something that doesn't run away from them. [7]However, most opossums—over 90 percent—never use this method. [8]Instead, their defense is simply to [2]run away from danger immediately. [9]<u>Finally</u>, others use the method of trying to [3]scare off enemies—they hiss, salivate, bare their teeth, excrete wastes, or release a terrible odor.

**To the Instructor:**
In this *Instructor's Edition*, throughout this chapter and the tests that follow, transitions relevant to the patterns of organization are underlined.

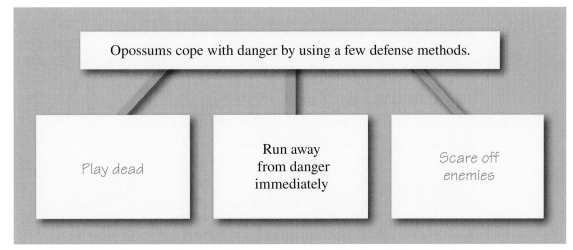

Sentence 2 presents the first defense method: "playing dead." Sentence 8 presents the second method: "run away." Sentence 9 presents the third method: "scare off enemies."

## 2   The Time Order Pattern

To understand the time order pattern, try to arrange the following group of sentences in an order that makes sense. Put a *1* in front of the sentence that should come first, a *2* in front of the sentence that comes next, a *3* in front of the third sentence, and a *4* in front of the sentence that should come last. The result will be a short paragraph. Use the time words as a guide.

   3   After the dish had been brought to Germany, a German cook decided to broil the meat, calling it Hamburg steak.

   4   Finally, German immigrants took the dish to the United States, where it became known as "hamburger."

   1   For centuries, a dish made of raw ground beef was eaten by the Tartars, a group living in central Asia.

   2   Then a merchant from Germany discovered the Tartars' recipe for ground beef and took it to his hometown, Hamburg.

Authors usually present events in the order in which they happen, resulting in a pattern of organization known as **time order**. Clues to the pattern of the above sentences are time words (*Then, After, Finally*). The sentences should read as follows:

[1]For centuries, a dish made of raw ground beef was eaten by the Tartars, a group living in central Asia. [2]Then a merchant from Germany discovered the Tartars' recipe for ground beef and took it to his hometown, Hamburg. [3]After the dish had been brought to Germany, a German cook decided to broil the meat, calling it Hamburg steak. [4]Finally, German immigrants took the dish to the United States, where it became known as "hamburger."

*Time Words Used in the Time Order Pattern*

| | | | |
|---|---|---|---|
| before | next | while | later |
| previously | soon | during | after |
| first | often | until | eventually |
| second | as | now | finally |
| third | when | then | last |

As a student, you will see time order used frequently. Textbooks in all fields describe events and processes, such as the events leading to the uprisings in Egypt in 2011, the steps involved in writing a paper, the growth of Henry Ford's auto empire, or the stages in the development of a tadpole into a frog.

In addition to time transitions, signals for the time order pattern include dates, times, and such words as *stages, series, steps,* and *process.*

The two most common kinds of time order are 1) a series of events or stages and 2) a series of steps (directions for how to do something). Each is discussed below and on the pages that follow.

## Series of Events or Stages

**Time Order: Events**

Event 1
Event 2
Event 3

**Time Order: Stages**

Stage 1
Stage 2
Stage 3

Authors sometimes describe a series of events—for example, the financial mistakes that led to the major recession that began in 2008 in the United States. Or authors may explain a series of stages, such as those that turn a caterpillar into a butterfly. In both cases, they use time order. They discuss the first event or stage, then the second, and so on until the final event or stage in the series is reached.

## ✔ *Check Your Understanding*

Here is a paragraph that is organized according to time order. Complete the outline of the paragraph by listing the missing stages in the order in which they happen.

To help you find the stages, do two things to the paragraph:

- Underline the time words that introduce each stage in the process;
- Number (*1, 2, . . .*) each stage in the process.

    ¹Very young children in a hospital often go through three stages of separation anxiety. ²In the first stage,¹ "protest," these children try actively to get the parent (especially the mother) back. ³For instance, they may shake their cribs and hurl themselves about. ⁴In the second stage,² "despair," the babies and children become inactive and withdrawn. ⁵They may cry, but generally they are so quiet that they are mistakenly assumed to have accepted the hospital. ⁶In the final stage, ³"detachment," they respond to hospital workers—they eat, play with toys, and are friendly. ⁷But they fail to respond to a visiting parent.

**Main idea: Very young children in a hospital often go through three stages of separation anxiety.**

1. Protest _____
2. Despair _____
3. Detachment _____

### Explanation

You should have added the following stages to the outline:

1. Protest. (The author signals this stage with the time transition *first*.)

2. Despair. (The author signals this stage with the time word *second*.)

3. Detachment. (The author signals this stage with the time word *final*.)

As you can see by the transitions used, the relationship between the points is one of time: the second stage happens *after* the first, and the third stage *after* the second.

## PRACTICE 4

The following passage describes a sequence of events. Outline the paragraph by filling in the major details. Note that the major details are signaled by time words.

*Hint:* Underline the time word or words that introduce each major detail, and number each major detail.

[1]All of us have certain fears at different points in our lives. [2]<u>When</u> we are young children, we worry that[1] something bad will happen to our parents. [3]We are afraid of being alone if our parents die or go away. [4]<u>Then</u>, as teenagers, we fear that[2] we will be socially rejected or seen as "uncool" nobodies. [5]We often act against our better instincts in order to be accepted as one of the crowd. [6]<u>Later</u>, if we become parents, our greatest fear is that[3] someone or something will harm our children. [7]Our sense of love and responsibility for our kids makes the thought of our children being hurt our greatest nightmare. [8]<u>Last</u>, when elderly, we fear[4] poor health and death. [9]We worry about losing our independence, being a burden to other people, and, of course, the end of our lives.

*Wording of answers may vary.*

The phrase *different points in our lives* suggests a time order.

**Item 1:** Childhood fear of parents being harmed (introduced with the time word *When*)

**Item 2:** Teenage fear of social rejection (introduced with the time word *Then*)

**Main idea:** **All of us have certain fears at different points in our lives.**

1. Young children worry about something bad happening to their parents.

2. Teenagers fear social rejection.

3. Parents fear that their children will be harmed.

4. Elderly people are afraid of poor health and death.

**Item 3:** Parents' fear of children being harmed (introduced with the time word *Later*)

**Item 4:** Elderly fear of poor health and death (introduced with the time word *Last*)

# Series of Steps (Directions)

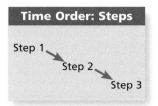

**Time Order: Steps**

Step 1
Step 2
Step 3

When authors give directions, they use time order. They explain step 1, then step 2, and so on through the entire series of steps that must be taken toward a specific goal.

## ✓ *Check Your Understanding*

Here is a paragraph that gives directions. Complete the outline of the paragraph that follows by adding the missing steps in the correct sequence. Then read the explanation that follows.

To help yourself identify each step, do two things to the paragraph:

- Underline the time words that introduce each item in the sequence;
- Number (*1, 2, . . .* ) each step in the sequence.

[1]To improve your memory for names, follow this procedure. [2]<u>First</u>, when you are introduced to someone,[1] make sure you hear the person's name clearly. [3]<u>Next</u>, [2]repeat the name with your greeting: "Nice to meet you, Ms. Baron." [4]<u>Then</u>[3] take a good look at the person and concentrate on matching the face with the name. [5]<u>Last</u>,[4] repeat the name again when you are leaving the person: "Good meeting you, Ms. Baron."

**Main idea: To improve your memory for names, follow this procedure.**

1. *Make sure you hear the person's name clearly during an introduction.*

2. *Repeat the name as you greet the person.*

3. *Concentrate on matching the name with the face.*

4. *When you leave the person, repeat his or her name.*

### Explanation

You should have added these steps to the outline:

1. Make sure you hear the person's name clearly during an introduction. (The author signals this step with the time word *First*.)

2. Repeat the name as you greet the person. (The author signals this step with the time word *Next*.)

3. Concentrate on matching the name with the face. (The author's signal is the time word *Then*.)

4. When you leave the person, repeat his or her name. (The author signals this final step with the time word *Last*.)

## PRACTICE 5

The following passage gives directions involving several steps that must be done in order. Complete the map below by filling in the three missing steps. To help yourself identify each step, do two things:

● Underline the time words that introduce each item in the sequence;

● Number (*1, 2, . . .*) each step in the sequence.

[margin note:] The four steps are introduced with the time words *First, After, next,* and *last.*

¹To study a textbook effectively, follow a few helpful steps. ²<u>First,</u> ¹preview the reading. ³This means a quick reading of the first and last paragraphs and of the headings in the chapter. ⁴Previewing will help you understand the selection better once you do begin reading. ⁵<u>After</u> previewing, you are ready to ²read and mark the selection. ⁶Mark key definitions with "Def"; useful examples with "Ex"; important lists of items with "1, 2, 3"; and key points with underlines. ⁷Your <u>next</u> step is to ³write study notes for the selection. ⁸By selecting and writing down the important parts of the chapter, you will have already begun to learn them. ⁹The <u>last</u> step of this process is to ⁴study the ideas in your notes. ¹⁰Do so by repeating the material over and over to yourself. ¹¹When you can recite it without looking at your notes, you'll really know the material.        *Wording of answers may vary.*

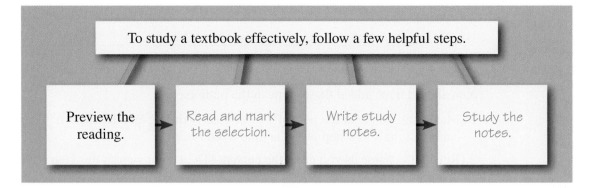

To study a textbook effectively, follow a few helpful steps.

| Preview the reading. | → | Read and mark the selection. | → | Write study notes. | → | Study the notes. |

## A Note on Main Ideas and Patterns of Organization

A paragraph's main idea may indicate its pattern of organization. For example, here's the main idea of the paragraph you just read: "To study a textbook effectively, follow a few helpful steps." The words *a few helpful steps* suggest that this paragraph will be organized according to time order. Another good example is the main idea of the earlier paragraph on the causes of crime: "People have come up with different theories to explain crime." The words *different theories* suggest that this paragraph will be a list of items.

Paying close attention to the main idea, then, can give you a quick sense of a paragraph's pattern of organization. Try, for instance, to guess the pattern of the paragraph with this main idea:

**While there are hundreds of opportunities for volunteering, most fall into four basic categories.**

The statement that volunteer opportunities "fall into four basic categories" is a strong indication that the paragraph will list those categories. The main idea helps us guess that the paragraph will be a list of four items.

## PRACTICE 6

Most of the main ideas below have been taken from college textbooks. In the space provided, write the letter of the pattern of organization that each main idea suggests.

_B_  1. April 12, 1861, marked the beginning of the four years of bloodshed and
     bitterness called the Civil War.     *Time signals: April 12, 1861,*
     A. List of items     B. Time order     *beginning, four years.*

_A_  2. America's highways would be safer if drivers followed three simple
     rules.     *List signal: three simple rules.*
     A. List of items     B. Time order

_A_  3. The widespread use of the Internet has changed American society in a
     number of ways.     *List signal: a number of ways.*
     A. List of items     B. Time order

_B_  4. A series of important world events led to the creation of the United
     Nations in 1945.     *Time signal:*
     A. List of items     B. Time order     *series of . . . events.*

_A_  5. There are several guidelines that every person needs to follow for good
     health.     *List signal:*
     A. List of items     B. Time order     *several guidelines.*

_B_  6. Children pass through various stages on their way to becoming adults.
     A. List of items     B. Time order     *Time signal: stages.*

_A_  7. The students who are most likely to drop out of school often share a few
     characteristics.     *List signal:*
     A. List of items     B. Time order     *a few characteristics.*

_B_  8. In order to create a mummy, ancient Egyptians followed a sequence of
     unusual steps.     *Time signal:*
     A. List of items     B. Time order     *sequence of unusual steps.*

_A_  9. Therapists use a broad variety of methods to help individuals cope with
     their lives.     *List signal:*
     A. List of items     B. Time order     *variety of methods.*

_B_ 10. Income taxes have been part of society throughout history, from the time of the Bible to the present day.

A. List of items          B. Time order

*Time signals:*
*throughout history,*
*from the time of the Bible*
*to the present day.*

## Two Final Points

**1** While many passages have just one pattern of organization, often the patterns are mixed. You may find that part of a passage uses a list of items pattern, and another part of the same passage uses a time order pattern. (For example, in the paragraph on page 156 about studying a textbook, the steps are given in time order, but the second step contains a list of four kinds of items to mark.)

**2** Remember that not all relationships between ideas are signaled by transitions. An author may present a list of items, for example, without using addition words. So as you read, watch for the relationships themselves, not just the transitions.

# RELATIONSHIPS IN READING: Mastery Test 1

**A.** Fill in each blank with an appropriate transition from the box. Use each transition once. Then, in the space provided, write the letter of the transition you have chosen.

| A. after | B. another | C. before |
|---|---|---|
| D. second | E. then | |

*Hint:* Make sure that each word or phrase that you choose fits smoothly into the flow of the sentence. Test your choices by reading each sentence to yourself.

**A** 1. _____ *After* _____ a bad nightmare awakened me in the middle of the night, I decided to turn on the bedroom lights for a while.

> First, the speaker had a nightmare; *after* that, the lights were turned on.

**Item 3:**
The sentences list reasons why today's parents are busy. One reason is that they must raise their children. *Second* introduces another responsibility of busy parents.

**E** 2. ¹Blinking helps to keep your eyes healthy. ²When you close your eyes, your eyelids sweep away dirt and other harmful particles. ³Fluids _____ *then* _____ moisten and bathe the surface of your eyes.

> *Then* introduces the second step in the process of blinking.

**D** 3. ¹Many parents today are busier than ever. ²First of all, they must raise their own children. ³And often their _____ *second* _____ responsibility is to care for aging parents, even to the point of having the parents live with them.

**B** 4. ¹A major trend in education has been the return of adults to the classroom. ²One type of nontraditional student is the adult worker seeking to advance in a job or retrain for a new career. ³_____ *Another* _____ type is the homemaker preparing to enter the job market in middle age. ⁴A third type is the retired person now pursuing interests there was no time for in earlier years.

> *Another* introduces the second item in a list of three major trends in education.

**C** 5. ¹The American custom of dating has changed. ²_____ *Before* _____ the 1970s, dating was more formal. ³Males usually had to ask for a date at least several days in advance. ⁴These days, dating has become more casual. ⁵In fact, the word "date" now sounds a bit old-fashioned to many young people. ⁶"Getting together" and "hanging out" are more likely ways of referring to dating today.

> The sentences describe a series of events in the history of dating, the earliest of which took place *before* the 1970s. Note the other time transitions: *These days, now,* and *today.*

*(Continues on next page)*

**159**

**B.** Fill in each blank with an appropriate transition from the box. Use each transition once.

| after | before | then | when |
|-------|--------|------|------|

¹(6)_____ _When_ _____ President Theodore "Teddy" Roosevelt visited the South in 1902, he was invited to a hunting party. ²The organizers staked a bear cub to the ground so that the President could not miss. ³(7)_____ _After_ _____ he realized that the bear was pinned down, Roosevelt refused to fire. ⁴A political cartoon based on the incident appeared in a number of newspapers. ⁵The cartoon, with a drawing of the small bear, was seen by a shop owner in Brooklyn. ⁶The shop owner (8)_____ _then_ _____ made up a window display version of the little bear in a soft, plush material. ⁷(9)_____ _Before_ _____ offering the bear to customers, the shop owner asked Roosevelt for permission to sell the new toy as "Teddy's Bear." ⁸The President gave his approval but wrote, "I don't think my name is worth much to the toy bear cub business." ⁹He was clearly wrong, for a bear-buying frenzy swept the country, and the teddy bear has been popular ever since.

___B___ 10. The pattern of organization of the above selection is
       A. list of items.
       B. time order.
                        The paragraph presents a series of events showing how the teddy bear originated and became popular. (Note that all the missing transitions are time words.)

# RELATIONSHIPS IN READING: Mastery Test 2

**A.** Fill in each blank with an appropriate transition from the box. Use each transition once. Then, in the spaces provided, write the letter of the transition you have chosen.

| | | |
|---|---|---|
| **A.** also | **B.** another | **C.** before |
| **D.** during | **E.** second | |

___A___ 1. ¹Ice is the safest and most effective immediate treatment for athletic injuries. ²It can be used, for example, on torn ligaments, strained muscles, and bruises. ³Ice relieves pain while slowing the blood flow.

⁴Ice _____ *also* _____ helps reduce internal bleeding and promotes faster healing.

___E___ 2. ¹There are excellent reasons for taking a night class. ²One is that it is a good way to develop a new interest or hobby. ³A _____ *second* _____ reason is that it's a great way to meet people with similar interests.

___D___ 3. ¹Only a little over a century ago, guns were considered a necessity for American pioneers. ²People hunted with guns to provide food for their families. ³Guns were used for protection against threats from the wilderness. ⁴_____ *During* _____ the 1800s and into the early 1900s, a gun was as common as a coffeepot in most American homes.

___C___ 4. ¹Some simple methods can improve your ability to relax. ²One method, called progressive relaxation, involves tensing a muscle group and then slowly relaxing the muscles in that group. ³Your whole body feels relaxed after you repeat this process for all the major muscles. ⁴Another simple relaxation method is to stop what you are doing and take a few deep breaths. ⁵Next time you watch a basketball game, notice how a player will use this technique just _____ *before* _____ shooting a free throw.

___B___ 5. ¹Hispanic Americans, also called Latinos, are the largest minority group in the United States. ²The group includes Mexican Americans, Puerto Ricans, and immigrants from Cuba and other Central and South American countries. ³The Spanish language is the unifying force among Hispanic Americans. ⁴_____ *Another* _____ source of common identification is religion: at least 85 percent are Roman Catholic.

*(Continues on next page)*

**B.** Fill in each blank with an appropriate transition from the box. Use each transition once.

| finally | first of all | moreover | secondly |
|---|---|---|---|

¹United States schools are not entirely to blame for the lower achievements of their students compared with the achievements of Japanese students. ²(6)_____*First of all*_____, our schools deal not just with learning (the only concern of Japanese schools) but also with such social problems as alcohol and drug abuse and teenage pregnancy. ³(7)_____*Secondly*_____, American parents are often too stressed, tired, or self-absorbed to do what Japanese mothers do— help with their children's homework and make sure they study three or four hours a night. ⁴(8)_____*Moreover*_____, many American teenagers hold part-time jobs, reducing their ability to hit the books after school. ⁵Working after school is almost unheard of in Japan. ⁶(9)_____*Finally*_____, American teenagers are under great pressure from their peers to look good, drink, date, or even have sex. ⁷With Japanese teenagers, the pressure instead is to study hard.

___A___ 10. The pattern of organization of the above selection is
    A. list of items.
    B. time order.

The paragraph lists reasons why American schools are not to blame for the lower achievements of their students compared to those of Japanese students. (Note that all the missing transitions are addition words.)

*To the Instructor:*
In the paragraphs in Tests 2–6, the main ideas and transitions relevant to the pattern of organization are underlined.

# RELATIONSHIPS IN READING: Mastery Test 3

**A.** (1–4.) Arrange the scrambled sentences below into a logical paragraph by numbering them *1, 2, 3,* and *4* in an order that makes sense. Then, in the space provided, write the letter of the main pattern of organization used.

Note that transitions will help you by making clear the relationships between sentences.

_3_ Another method is acupuncture, in which a tiny needle is placed in a smoker's earlobe to remove the craving for a cigarette.

_4_ Finally, many feel that being strongly motivated and quitting "cold turkey" is the best way to conquer the habit.

_2_ One method involves chewing a special nicotine gum whose nicotine content decreases at regular intervals.

_1_ Several ways have been suggested to help long-time smokers stop smoking.

*List transitions dictate the order of these items: One, Another, Finally.*

_A_ 5. The pattern of organization of the above selection is
  A. list of items.
  B. time order.

*List signal: Several ways.*

**B.** Read the passage and answer the question that follows. You may find it helpful to underline transitions as you read.

[1]There is a false idea that lemmings, small mouselike creatures that live in northern regions, often commit suicide. [2]The truth is, however, that lemmings end their lives by accident. [3]Normally they live quietly in underground nests, feeding on roots and moss. [4]But every few years, the lemming population grows so large that the food supply becomes too small to feed them all. [5]Then all the lemmings leave their nests and go in search of food. [6]As they travel, the lemmings eat everything in their path. [7]After traveling for weeks, they reach the shore—but they don't stop there. [8]Still searching for food, the tiny rodents plunge into the ocean and begin swimming. [9]In a short time, the little creatures become exhausted and drown.

_B_ 6. The pattern of organization of the above selection is
  A. list of items.
  B. time order.

*The paragraph presents the sequence of events in which lemmings end their lives. The time transitions include Then, As, After, In a short time.*

*(Continues on next page)*

**C.** Fill in each blank with an appropriate transition from the box. Use each transition once.

| after | then | when |
|-------|------|------|

[1]Gary began stealing liquor from his parents at the age of fourteen, and within two years, he regularly came to school drunk. [2](7)_____*When*_____ he was in his early twenties, he realized that he was completely dependent on alcohol, but he continued to drink. [3]Gary's moment of truth came at age twenty-five. [4]He narrowly escaped death in a drunk-driving accident, and he was responsible for injuring someone else. [5]He soon committed himself to the local alcohol-recovery center. [6](8)_____*After*_____ an intensive four-week treatment and a ninety-day follow-up program, Gary was free of alcohol for the first time in over ten years. [7]He (9)_____*then*_____ returned to college and received a degree. [8]Today Gary works as a counselor in the same treatment center that gave him his second chance. [9]Gary's story should inspire many of his own clients at the alcohol-recovery center.

___B___ 10. The pattern of organization of the above selection is

  A. list of items.

  B. time order.    The paragraph narrates a series of events in Gary's life. (Note that all the missing transitions are time words.)

# RELATIONSHIPS IN READING: Mastery Test 4

**A.** (1–4.) Arrange the scrambled sentences below into a logical paragraph by numbering them *1, 2, 3,* and *4* in an order that makes sense. Then, in the space provided, write the letter of the main pattern of organization used.

Note that transitions will help you by making clear the relationships between sentences.

___4___ Then, often quite suddenly, a chimp would grab the stick, poke it through the bars of the cage, and drag the banana within reach.

___1___ A series of experiments showed how chimps solved the problem of reaching a banana placed on the ground outside their cage.

___3___ After a while, the chimps would start looking at what was lying around the cage, including a stick left there by the experimenters.

___2___ The chimps almost always tried <u>first</u> to reach the food with their hands.

___B___ 5. The pattern of organization of the above selection is
    A. list of items.         Solving a problem involves following certain steps.
    B. time order.      The words *solved the problem* suggest a sequence of steps.
The time order pattern is further supported by the time transitions (*first, After, Then*).

**B.** Read the passage and answer the question that follows. You may find it helpful to underline transitions as you read.

[1]Every year, about 35,000 Americans commit suicide. [2]Sadly, research shows that many of these deaths can be avoided. [3]<u>In order to prevent</u> this needless loss of life, people must learn to recognize the warning signs of a potential suicide. [4]Such signs include, <u>first of all</u>, severe depression and withdrawal, often combined with the inability to sleep or eat. [5]Extreme mood swings, from joy to deep depression, are <u>also</u> danger signs. [6]<u>In addition</u>, suicidal people may begin giving away valued belongings. [7]<u>Last</u>, any life crisis, such as the death of a loved one or the loss of a job, may make a potentially suicidal person feel that he or she can't go on.

___A___ 6. The pattern of organization of the above selection is
    A. list of items.
    B. time order.               List signal: *warning signs.*
             Addition words: *first of all, also, In addition, Last.*
        The passage lists four warning signs of a potential suicide.

*(Continues on next page)*

**C.** Fill in each blank with an appropriate transition from the box. Use each transition once.

| later | now | then | when |
|---|---|---|---|

¹Popcorn has long been a favorite food. ²An early Spanish explorer in the Americas wrote of toasted corn that burst and looked very much like white flowers. ³In 1621, Indians brought corn to the first Thanksgiving. ⁴They taught the colonists to hold oiled ears on sticks over the fire and chew the popped kernels off. ⁵Two centuries (7)_____later_____, in 1846, the first cookbook to mention popcorn was published. ⁶The recipe directed the cook to pour corn kernels into a kettle of hot fat. ⁷When the corn popped, it was skimmed off the top. ⁸Popcorn appeared, too, in recipes for soup and beer. ⁹Popcorn balls became a holiday treat, and candied popcorn was flavored with lemon, rose, peppermint, honey, vanilla, or molasses. ¹⁰(8)_____When_____ the first corn poppers were invented in the 1890s, boys in large cities and small towns sold popcorn on street corners. ¹¹It was a good way to make a profit since vendors could buy twenty-five pounds of popping corn for a nickel and sell multiple individual bags for the same price. ¹²Movie theaters (9)_____then_____ brought the taste treat indoors. ¹³During World War II, when sugar was rationed, Americans ate three times as much popcorn as they had before. ¹⁴(10)_____Now_____ we nibble approximately seventy quarts of the snack food per person a year.

The passage presents a sequence of events in the history of popcorn. The events are in time order from past to present.

# RELATIONSHIPS IN READING: Mastery Test 5

Read each textbook passage, and then answer the questions or follow the directions provided.

**A.** ¹People have differing feelings about their work. ²First of all, for some it can be just a job, something done only for the paycheck, with a limited emotional reward. ³For a second type of worker, work is a career and a part of the person's self-image. ⁴A career person is challenged by the work and cares about the power and prestige that the job offers, not just the money. ⁵Last, work can be a calling. ⁶A person with a calling is passionately committed to the work itself, apart from the money or status that it may bring. ⁷In general, people with callings are happier than those with mere jobs or careers.

_A_ 1. The pattern of organization of the above selection is
    A. list of items.
    B. time order.
                *List signal: differing feeings.*

2–3. Two of the transitions that signal major details of the paragraph are
    *Any two of the following:* First of all, second, Last

**B.** ¹In 1814, a military victory was won—not with soldiers or guns, but with animals! ²The battle took place in Chile when a Chilean leader named O'Higgins was fighting to win his country's independence from Spain. ³The Chilean patriots were surrounded by a larger, well-armed Spanish army. ⁴Wounded and seemingly without any options, O'Higgins came up with an idea. ⁵He ordered his soldiers to gather together as many cows, mules, sheep, and dogs as possible. ⁶Then, using gunshots to frighten the herd, O'Higgins got the animals to stampede toward the Spanish camp. ⁷In a short time, the Spanish forces were being attacked by a frightened crowd of charging beasts. ⁸While the Spanish were busy trying to protect themselves from the animals, O'Higgins and his men escaped into the nearby mountains. ⁹Three years later, O'Higgins and an army of four thousand men returned from the mountains and defeated the Spanish once and for all.

_B_ 4. The pattern of organization of the above selection is
    A. list of items.        *The paragraph presents a sequence of events*
    B. time order.             *leading to O'Higgins's victory.*

5–6. Two of the transitions that signal major details of the paragraph are
    *Any two of the following:* In 1814, when, Then, In a short time,
                    *While, Three years later*

*(Continues on next page)*

**C.** ¹A good conclusion should tie a speech together and give the audience the feeling that the speech is complete. ²It should not introduce any new ideas. ³There are several kinds of conclusions to speeches that have proved their value time and time again. ⁴One is a summary of the main ideas of your speech. ⁵This type of conclusion is especially useful if you want your audience to remember your main points. ⁶Another common and useful type of conclusion is a quotation. ⁷If you can find a quotation that fits your subject, the conclusion is one good place to use it. ⁸For example, if your speech was about the importance of reading aloud to little children, you could end with this quotation by Dr. Ruth Love: ⁹"If we could get our parents to read to their preschool children fifteen minutes a day, we could revolutionize the schools." ¹⁰A quotation such as this gives added authority to what you have said. ¹¹A third useful conclusion is one that inspires the audience to action. ¹²When you give a speech, especially a persuasive speech, your goal is often to inspire the audience to some course of action. ¹³If this has been your goal, conclude by telling audience members precisely what they should do.

<u>A</u>    7.  The pattern of organization of the above selection is
    A.  list of items.
    B.  time order.

          *The paragraph lists several kinds of conclusions to speeches.*

8–10.  The paragraph is about three kinds of conclusions to speeches.

● Which transition word signals the first kind of conclusion?

          *One*

● Which transition word signals the second kind of conclusion?

          *Another*

● Which transition word signals the last kind of conclusion?

          *third*

*The three kinds of conclusions—all major details—are signaled by the addition words One, Another, and third.*

# RELATIONSHIPS IN READING: Mastery Test 6

Read each textbook passage, and then answer the questions or follow the directions provided.

**A.** [1]The history of books is marked by many important milestones. [2]Among the earliest of these would have to be the establishment of the first public library. [3]This event took place in Athens, Greece, in 540 B.C. [4]Books then had to be copied by hand until 1456, when another important milestone was reached. [5]The German inventor Johann Gutenberg built a printing press capable of producing multiple copies of one book. [6]After printing presses were established, books spread everywhere. [7]By the 1800s, American publishing houses were pumping out works to satisfy a reading-hungry public. [8]An example of a best-selling book was *Uncle Tom's Cabin*, which was published in 1852 and sold seven million copies. [9]The next chapter in the history of books began in the 1980s, with the publishing of books on audiotape. [10]Today, we even have electronic books that can be downloaded from the Internet.

*The passage presents a sequence of important events in the history of books. Time transitions are used throughout.*

_B_ 1. The pattern of organization of the above selection is
    A. list of items.        B. time order.

2–3. Two of the transitions that signal major details of the paragraph are
   *Any two of the following:* earliest, in 540 B.C., then, until 1456,
   After, By the 1800s, in 1852, next, in the 1980s, Today

**B.** [1]There's no foolproof way to keep a burglar out, but there are precautions you can take. [2]First of all, the best defense against a break-in is lights. [3]Keep an inside and an outside light on at night. [4]Second, if you are going to be home late or away, use timers to turn the lights, radio, and television on and off to give the appearance that someone is home. [5]Also, think of your house as a fort. [6]In many burglaries, thieves simply breeze in through unlocked doors or windows. [7]Keep doors locked even when you are home. [8]A final step is to deprive burglars of what they need. [9]Keep bushes and trees trimmed, if they are near windows and doors, to eliminate places for burglars to lurk. [10]Put away ladders, rakes, brooms, and other equipment that thieves might use to help them break in. [11]These steps won't guarantee that your house will be safe, but they will help minimize the risk.

*The passage lists precautions to prevent burglary. Addition transitions are used throughout.*

_A_ 4. The pattern of organization of the above selection is
    A. list of items.        B. time order.

5–6. Two of the transitions that signal major details of the paragraph are
   *Any two of the following:* First of all, Second, Also, final

*(Continues on next page)*

**C.** ¹For several reasons, some people find it hard to show appreciation or give praise to others. ²One reason is that they may have received little praise or appreciation themselves. ³Not having received it, they don't know how to give it. ⁴Another reason for not making positive remarks about others is insecurity. ⁵Insecure persons often have a need to put others down. ⁶If they can make someone else feel bad, they feel better by comparison. ⁷A final reason for not complimenting others is fear. ⁸Showing affection or appreciation is a way of opening oneself up to someone else, of offering friendship. ⁹But people are afraid they may be rejected, so they decide it is safer not to try.

_A_   7.  The pattern of organization of the above selection is
   A.  list of items.
   B.  time order.

   The passage lists several reasons why people find it hard to give praise. The reasons are signaled by addition words: *One, Another,* and *final.*

8–10.  Complete the map of the selection.

*Wording of answers may vary.*

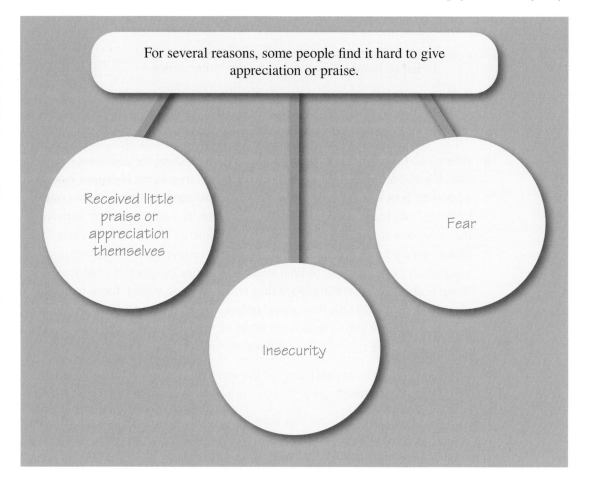

For several reasons, some people find it hard to give appreciation or praise.

Received little praise or appreciation themselves

Insecurity

Fear

# 7 Relationships in Writing

You learned in Chapter Four that the first two goals in writing are to advance a main idea and to support that idea. A third goal in writing is to organize the support you provide for your main idea. This chapter explains the two most common ways to organize your support: listing order and time order. **Just as a knowledge of listing and time order can make you a better reader, it can make you a better writer.**

## Listing Order

Often the supporting material in a paper is organized by using a listing order. A **listing order** uses addition words such as *First, Also, Another,* and *Last of all.* The list might be a list of reasons or of actions or of qualities or of any series of items that are similar in some way. Most of the paragraphs you have looked at so far have had a listing order. For example, here is just one of the paragraphs:

> [1]If you are like most people, you feel that writing is not one of your talents, and there's nothing you can do about it. [2]The truth is that some common-sense tips can help you become a better writer. [3]First of all, write often. [4]Like other crafts, writing improves with practice. [5]Also, organize your material with an outline. [6]An outline will provide you with a good guideline without limiting you, as you can change it at any time. [7]Next, write in a plain style. [8]Don't try to use overly fancy language. [9]Instead, just say what you mean simply and clearly. [10]Finally, tighten your writing. [11]Nothing improves writing more than eliminating unnecessary words.

The paragraph orders its supporting details in a list of the tips that can help people become better writers. The addition words that introduce the items in the list are *First of all, Also, Next,* and *Finally.*

In the previous chapter, you learned that addition words, like all transitions, help writers organize their information and present it clearly to readers. Addition words are as helpful to you as a writer as they are to you as a reader. Here is a cartoon that uses addition words, along with the list of the common addition words you already saw on page 143.

"I can't marry you, Henry. First of all, you're too tall for me.
In addition, I don't like pink."

In the cartoon, the addition words "First of all" and "In addition" present the two reasons that Henry's proposal is being rejected.

Here are words that show addition:

*Addition Words*

| | | | |
|---|---|---|---|
| one | to begin with | in addition | last |
| first | another | next | last of all |
| first of all | second | moreover | final |
| for one thing | also | furthermore | finally |

## PRACTICE 1: Writing a Paragraph with a Listing Order

Write a paragraph that supports one of the following three main ideas:

- There are three mistakes I've made in my life that I'd like to take back.

- There are several advantages (*or* disadvantages) to living alone rather than living with someone.

- There are three ways _____ (name someone you know, or write about yourself) could become a better student.

## A Model Paragraph

Here is one student's response to the assignment.

As I look back at my life from my first year in college, I can think of three mistakes that I wish I could undo. The first mistake was in not taking more challenging classes in high school. I was a decent student, but I didn't want to work any harder than I had to. I only took the basic math and science courses that I needed to graduate. Now, I realize that I'm really pretty interested in some sort of career in health care—maybe nursing or pharmacy. I wish I'd gotten a better foundation in math and science to prepare me for college. A second mistake I'd like to take back—and my mom would have a heart attack if she read this—was quitting music lessons when I was twelve. My mom had me start piano lessons when I was about six. At first I loved them, and I did really well. But as I got older, I didn't want to spend time practicing. When some of the kids I was hanging around with told me that only sissies played the piano, I quit. That was really stupid, and now I want to kick my twelve-year-old self. But the biggest mistake I made was not getting to know my grandfather better. Grandpa lived with us for several years after my grandmother died. He was a really neat guy who had been born in the Dominican Republic and came to this country without a penny. He still managed to make a success of himself and raise a family. I loved him, but I took him for granted and was always too busy to spend much time with him. Now I think about all the stories he could have told me about his life, and about my relatives, and the old days in his country. But he died a year ago, and I missed my chance. Of all the mistakes I've made in my life, I regret that one the most.

● What are the addition transitions used in the model paragraph above? Write them here:

_____first_____    _____second_____

## Writing Your Own Paragraph

**1.** As explained in Chapter 5, there are three prewriting techniques that can help you think about a paper: freewriting, questioning, and list making. Apply one or another of these techniques to each of the three topic sentences at the bottom of page 172. You might, for example:

- Ask yourself what are three mistakes you've made in life, when and where these mistakes happened, why they happened, and what it was that made them mistakes.

- See if you can make a list of advantages or disadvantages of living alone.

- Freewrite for a page or two about how students you know (maybe even yourself) could go about becoming better students.

**2.** These prewriting techniques will help you determine the topic sentence for which you'll be able to provide the best support. Choose that topic sentence to develop in your paper.

**3.** Make a scratch outline in which you list the three supporting items in your paper and the order in which you'll present them.

**4.** Go on to write the first draft of your paper. If you find that you get "stuck" in a major way in providing enough supporting information, remember that you can always go back and choose one of the other topic sentences instead.

**5.** When writing your paper, perhaps in the second draft, remember to use addition transitions—words such as *first, a second, also, another, a third, last of all*—to signal to your readers each of your three supporting items.

**6.** After you have completed your next-to-final draft, read it out loud to yourself. If you come upon snags in your reading, chances are there may be grammar or punctuation problems at those points. Use a grammar handbook, if necessary, to see what corrections are needed. Make the required corrections so that every sentence in your paper reads smoothly and clearly.

*To the Instructor:* There are no correct answers to the practice exercises in this chapter. Instead, students' paragraphs should be evaluated according to the following:
- Is there a clearly expressed main idea?
- Are there enough details to support the main idea? Are the details *relevant?*
- Are transitions used to move from one detail to the next?
- Does the final sentence tie the details together and bring the paragraph to a close?

# Time Order

Time order is another very common way to present supporting details. In **time order**, supporting details are presented in the order in which they occurred.

Read the paragraph below, which is organized in a time order. In the spaces provided, write appropriate transitions to show the time relationships. Use each of the following transitions once: *Before, Then, When, While, After.*

[1]An incident happened yesterday that made me very angry. [2]I got off the bus and started walking the four blocks to my friend's house. [3]___While___ I walked along, I noticed a group of boys gathered on the sidewalk about a block ahead of me. [4]___When___ they saw me, they stopped talking. [5]A bit nervous, I thought about crossing the street to avoid them. [6]But as I came nearer and they began to whistle, a different feeling came over me. [7]Instead of being afraid, I was suddenly angry. [8]Why should I have to worry about being hassled just because I was a woman? [9]I stared straight at the boys and continued walking. [10]___Then___ one of them said, "Oooh, baby. [11]Looking fine today." [12]___Before___ I knew what I was doing, I turned on him. [13]"Do you have a mother? Or any sisters?" I demanded. [14]He looked astonished and didn't answer me. [15]I went on. [16]"Is it OK with you if men speak to them like that? [17]Shouldn't they be able to walk down the street without some creeps bothering them?" [18]___After___ I spoke, he and the other boys looked guilty and backed away. [19]I held my head up high and walked by them. [20]An hour later, I was still angry.

The writer makes the main point of the paragraph in her first sentence: "An incident happened yesterday that made me very angry." She then supports her point with a specific account of just what happened. Time words that are used to help connect her details include the following: "*While* I walked along," "*When* they saw me," "*Then* one of them said," "*Before* I knew," "*After* I spoke."

In the previous chapter, you learned that time words, like all transitions, help writers organize their information and present it clearly to readers. Time words are as helpful to you as a writer as they are to you as a reader. Here is a cartoon that uses time words, along with the list of common time words you already saw on page 145.

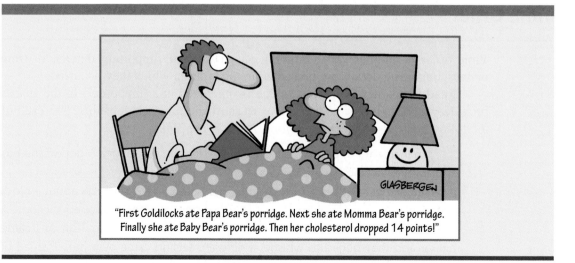

"First Goldilocks ate Papa Bear's porridge. Next she ate Momma Bear's porridge. Finally she ate Baby Bear's porridge. Then her cholesterol dropped 14 points!"

In the cartoon, the time words *First, Next, Finally,* and *Then* indicate the sequence of events in the Goldilocks story. (The joke here is that eating a lot of oatmeal, or "porridge," has been found to lower cholesterol.)

Here are words that show time:

*Time Words*

| | | | |
|---|---|---|---|
| before | immediately | when | until |
| previously | next | whenever | often |
| first (of all) | then | while | frequently |
| second (ly) | following | during | eventually |
| third (ly) | later | as (soon as) | final(ly) |
| now | after | by | last (of all) |

*Note:* Some additional ways of showing time are dates ("In 1890 . . . ," "Throughout the 20th century . . . ," "By 2020 . . .") and other time references ("Within a week . . . ," "by the end of the month . . . ," "in two years . . .").

## PRACTICE 2: Writing a Paragraph with a Time Order

Write a paragraph about a specific experience you've had that was one of the following:

- scary
- embarrassing
- hilarious
- joyful
- frustrating or irritating
- surprising or shocking
- disappointing
- heartbreaking

Note that you will be telling a story in this paragraph—relating in detail something that happened to you that made you feel a certain way.

## A Model Paragraph

Here is one student's response to the assignment.

> Going out to dinner with two of my best friends turned into one of the scariest experiences of my life. Jared, Lisa and I met at a nice pub-type restaurant. I ordered a rib-eye steak, our food was served, and we started to eat. Jared said something funny as I was swallowing a bite of my steak. I guess I laughed and inhaled at the same time, because suddenly the chunk of meat was stuck in my windpipe. I tried to cough, but I couldn't. I could not breathe at all. At first Jared and Lisa continued to talk. Then Lisa caught my eye and looked concerned. "Are you OK?" she asked. I couldn't speak. "Are you OK?" she said again. I shook my head and then I stood up, putting my hand at my throat. The diners at the nearby tables grew quiet as everyone stared at me. All around me I heard people saying, "Are you OK? Are you OK?" but nobody moved to help. My panic grew as I realized what was happening. I was choking to death, and no one was going to do anything. People were concerned, but no one wanted to be the first to come to my aid. They were worried about looking foolish or doing the wrong thing. I remember thinking, "I'm going to die in this restaurant because people are too embarrassed to help." Finally Lisa came behind me and put her arms around me. She was trying to do the Heimlich maneuver, a first-aid move that can save a choking person's life. But she didn't know how to do it properly. Her fists were up around my breastbone rather than in the soft spot between my lower ribs, where they belonged. I grabbed her hands and repositioned them, showing her the upward thrusting movement she needed to make. Soon she understood and did the maneuver several times. It forced enough air upwards in my windpipe that the piece of steak popped out. Coughing and crying, I collapsed back into my chair. It had been a terrifying experience.

● What are three of the time transitions used in the model paragraph above? Write them here:

<u>Any three of the following: as, (At) first, Then, then, as, Finally, Soon</u>

## Writing Your Own Paragraph

**1.** As explained in Chapter 5, there are three prewriting techniques that can help you think about a paper: freewriting, questioning, and list making. Apply one or another of these techniques to the possible topics at the bottom of page 176. You might, for example:

- Ask yourself what was, for example, the most embarrassing or scariest experience in your life, when and where this experience happened, why it happened, and what were the details that made it so embarrassing or scary.

- See if you can make a list of as many details as you can think of about an experience that was, for example, shocking or disappointing.

- Freewrite for a page or two about, for example, a hilarious or frustrating experience in your life.

**2.** These prewriting techniques will help you determine the experience for which you'll be able to provide the best support. Express that experience in your topic sentence. You might write, for example, "The most embarrassing experience of my life took place when I was in fifth grade" or "In my junior year of high school, I had the most disappointing dating experience of my life" or "I have never been as scared as I was when I had to witness a major argument between my parents" or "I have never been as irritated as I was the day I had to go to traffic court."

**3.** Make a scratch outline in which you list the major supporting items in your paper and the time order in which you'll present them.

**4.** Go on to write the first draft of your story. If you find that you get "stuck" in a major way in providing enough supporting information, remember that you can always go back and choose another experience instead.

**5.** To help your experience come alive, include some dialog—words that you said or that someone else said. In the model paragraph, you'll notice, we hear the exact words that Lisa and others speak, "Are you OK?"

**6.** When writing your story, remember to occasionally use time transitions— words such as *first, a second, next, then,* and *eventually*—to help connect one part of your experience with the next as it goes from beginning to end.

**7.** After you have completed your next-to-final draft, read it out loud to yourself. If you come upon snags in your reading, chances are there may be grammar or punctuation problems at those points. Use a grammar handbook, if necessary, to see what corrections are needed. Make the required corrections so that every sentence in your paper reads smoothly and clearly.

# RELATIONSHIPS IN WRITING: Mastery Test 1

**A.** Complete each sentence with a suitable addition word from the box below. Try to use each transition once. Then, in the space provided, write the letter of the transition you have chosen.

| | | |
|---|---|---|
| **A.** another | **B.** finally | **C.** in addition |
| **D.** secondly | **E.** to begin with | |

*Hint:* Make sure that each word or phrase that you choose fits smoothly into the flow of the sentence. Test your choices by reading each sentence to yourself.

___A___ 1. ¹A recent study suggested that parents should be on the lookout for stress in their children. ²There are several signs of stress in young people. ³Unusual tiredness in a child is one sign of stress in young people.

⁴_____Another_____ is temper tantrums.

___C___ 2. ¹That family really believes in volunteering. ²The mother delivers meals to shut-ins, and the father works with Boy Scouts on weekends.

³_____In addition_____, their daughter plays the piano at a nursing home.

___D___ 3. ¹There are proven ways to avoid colds and the flu. ²For one thing, wash your hands frequently. ³_____Secondly_____, don't put your hands to your eyes or nose, the places where germs are most likely to enter your body.

___E___ 4. ¹Walking can be a rewarding experience. ²_____To begin with_____, walking lets you chat with your neighbors and see for yourself what's going on in your neighborhood. ³A regular walk is also a healthy form of exercise.

___B___ 5. ¹There are three reasons why top athletes make so much money. ²First, they receive big salaries just for playing their sport. ³Next, they earn huge fees for personal appearances. ⁴_____Finally_____, they make even more money by endorsing products.

*(Continues on next page)*

**B.** Complete each sentence with a suitable time word from the box below. Try to use each transition once. Then, in the space provided, write the letter of the transition you have chosen.

| A. after | B. before | C. during |
|----------|-----------|-----------|
| D. then | E. while | |

*Hint:* Make sure that each word or phrase that you choose fits smoothly into the flow of the sentence. Test your choices by reading each sentence to yourself.

__A__ 1. _____After_____ Craig got home from school, he checked the refrigerator to see what there was to eat.

__D__ 2. Every night Kris writes down everything she needs to do the next day. _____Then_____ she labels each item as either A (very important), B (important), or C (not important).

__E__ 3. _____While_____ I was taking a shower, a hairy spider crept out of the drain.

__C__ 4. Tanya did her math homework _____during_____ English class.

__B__ 5. The counselor tries to help students _____before_____ their problems get out of control and their grades fall.

## RELATIONSHIPS IN WRITING: Mastery Test 2

Following are four paragraphs that use either a listing order or a time order. Fill in the blanks in each paragraph with an appropriate transition from the box. Use each transition once. Then answer the questions that follow each paragraph.

1.

| after | then | when |
|---|---|---|

All the details of the paragraph support the point that teachers have feelings. The transitions indicate that the details are presented in the order in which they happened.

¹One Monday morning _____ *when* _____ I was in the sixth grade, our teacher came into class looking very tired. ²She was late. ³She looked like she had been crying, and her hair was a mess. ⁴She sat down and, for a minute or two, had her head down, staring at her desk. ⁵_____ *After* _____ she looked up, we could all see there were tears in her eyes. ⁶_____ *Then* _____ she told the class that she was sorry for being late. ⁷She explained that her dad had had a heart attack over the weekend. ⁸I felt really sorry for her. ⁹That was the first time that I realized that teachers have feelings just like everyone else.

- What is the main idea, or point, of the paragraph? _____
  _____ *Teachers have feelings just like everyone else.* _____

- Check (✓) the way in which the paragraph's details are organized:
  ___ Listing order        ✓ Time order

2.

| another | finally | one | third |
|---|---|---|---|

Tailgating, speeding, failure to signal turns, and using cell phones while driving are all examples of dangerous driving habits. The details are organized as a list, in no particular order.

¹Some people have dangerous driving habits. ²_____ *One* _____ dangerous habit is tailgating. ³When the car ahead of a tailgating driver is forced to brake suddenly, a rear-end collision can result. ⁴_____ *Another* _____ unsafe driving habit is speeding. ⁵Since it takes longer for speeding vehicles to slow down or stop, drivers who are going too fast have less time to adjust to unexpected road hazards or sharp curves. ⁶A _____ *third* _____ dangerous driving habit is the failure to signal turns. ⁷Without proper warning, another driver may not have enough time to slow down. ⁸_____ *Finally* _____, it's all too common for today's drivers to talk or text message on their cell phones. ⁹Such distractions prevent drivers from focusing on the road in front of them. ¹⁰Serious accidents may result.

- What is the main idea, or point, of the paragraph? _____
  _____ *Some people have dangerous driving habits.* _____

- Check (✓) the way in which the paragraph's details are organized:
  ✓ Listing order        ___ Time order

*(Continues on next page)*

3.

| also | first | in addition | last of all |
|------|-------|-------------|-------------|

All the details of the paragraph are things to remember when asking someone to behave differently. The transitions indicate that the details are presented as a list of items, in no particular order. (Note that *Also* and *In addition* are interchangeable.)

¹When you want friends to change their behavior, it's best to speak to them in a thoughtful, helpful way. ²Here are some things to remember when you ask a friend to behave differently. ³_____First_____, clearly say what behavior you dislike. ⁴Don't make some general statement such as "Your behavior is awful." ⁵Instead say something like "It upsets me when you get drunk." ⁶_____Also_____, stick to the present and the problem at hand. ⁷Don't drag in things that happened in the past. ⁸_____In addition_____, don't insult your friend. ⁹For example, calling someone "stupid" will only make things worse. ¹⁰Remember to speak in terms of the behavior, not the person. ¹¹_____Last of all_____, speak to your friend in private. ¹²If you speak in front of others, your friend is likely to feel angry and ashamed.

- What is the main idea, or point, of the paragraph? _Here are some things to remember when you ask a friend to behave differently._

- Check (✓) the way in which the paragraph's details are organized:
  ✓ Listing order          ___ Time order

4.

| after | as | before |
|-------|-----|--------|
| then | when | while |

The details of the babysitter's frustrating experience are presented in the order in which they occurred.

¹Working as a babysitter was a frustrating job. ²_____When_____ my sister asked me to stay with her two sons, I thought it would be easy. ³I'd get them dinner, let them watch TV, and put them to bed early. ⁴But just _____as_____ we sat down to a meal of pizza, Rickie let the parakeet out of its cage. ⁵The dog _____then_____ started chasing the parakeet around the house. ⁶I tried to get to the parakeet first, and Rickie and Jeff followed after me. ⁷We had the bird cornered when Rickie jumped up for it and knocked over the hamster cage. ⁸Then the bird escaped again, and the hamsters were scurrying around their cage like crazy creatures. ⁹The dog disappeared _____while_____ I tried to calm down the hamsters. ¹⁰Once I did that, I was able to catch the parakeet and put it back in its cage. ¹¹As Rickie and Jeff and I returned to the kitchen, we discovered that the dog had eaten most of the pizza, and tomato sauce was dripping from his chin. ¹²I cleaned up the mess and made chicken noodle soup and sandwiches for the boys. ¹³_____After_____ I got them to bed, I returned downstairs to find that the dog had thrown up pizza on the living-room rug. ¹⁴_____Before_____ I could finish cleaning the rug, my sister returned. ¹⁵I told her to get someone else to babysit the next time.

- What is the main idea, or point, of the paragraph? _____
  _Working as a babysitter was a frustrating job._

- Check (✓) the way in which the paragraph's details are organized:
  ___ Listing order          ✓ Time order

# RELATIONSHIPS IN WRITING: Mastery Test 3

Write a paragraph that you develop by using a list of three or four items. You may want to choose one of the following ideas that you have not yet written about:

- There are three mistakes I've made in my life that I'd like to take back.

- There are three actions to take in trying to deal with money problems.

- There are three ways _____ (*name someone you know, or write about yourself*) could become a better student.

Or you may choose one of the following topics:

- There are three reasons why people should (*or* should not) be allowed to own guns.

- I have several favorite ways to relax.

- There are several reasons why condoms should (*or* should not) be made available in schools.

## A Model Paragraph

You have already seen a model paragraph on page 173, using listing order, for one of the above topics. Here is a model paragraph for one of the other topics:

> I have several favorite ways to take a break from the everyday grind of things and relax for a bit. One way is to watch one of my favorite television shows on my digital recorder. Between working and going to school, I don't have a lot of time for television, so I simply record shows for whenever I have a break. Grabbing an hour when I can to watch the latest episode of Survivor helps me relax. Another good way to relax for me is to get some exercise. Going for a brisk one-mile walk helps my tense muscles loosen up. Breathing deeply as I walk also makes me feel calmer and less stressed. My final favorite way to relax is to get into the kitchen and start cooking. I know this isn't a tactic that would appeal to everyone, but it works for me. Once I start chopping vegetables, frying up some garlic, and stirring up sauces in my pots and pans, my stress melts away. Making the kitchen smell good and thinking of the delicious meal I'm going to have relaxes me like nothing else.

- What three addition words does the writer use to signal each of her three ways to relax?

  _____One_____     _____Another_____     _____final_____

*(Continues on next page)*

## Writing Your Own Paragraph

Pick out the topic sentence you think you might be able to write about. Then explore that topic by freewriting about it, or asking questions such as *what, when, where, how,* and *why* about it, or making a list of all the details you can think of about it. Prewriting will help you determine the topic for which you can provide the best supporting details.

See if you can develop the topic with even more details and prepare a scratch outline of the paragraph. Then go on to write the first and later drafts of your paper.

*To the Instructor:*
A student's score on this test should be based on your evaluation of whether he or she has written an A, B, C, D, or F paper.

Suggested equivalents:

A = 90 to 100
B = 80 to 89
C = 70 to 79
D = 60 to 69
F = 59 and below

# RELATIONSHIPS IN WRITING: Mastery Test 4

You have probably already written two paragraphs that use a time order and time words: a paper on directions from your school to your house (page 139) and a story about a specific experience (page 176). Now write a paragraph on one of the processes described below. A **process** involves a series of steps carried out in a time order: *first* one does this, *then* this, *next*, this, and so on.

- How to break up gradually with a boyfriend or girlfriend
- How to gradually stop smoking (as opposed to cold turkey)
- How to wash dishes or do some other household chore efficiently
- How to study in a systematic way for a test
- How to stretch your budget when money is tight
- How to begin teaching a young child to read

## A Model Paragraph

Here is a paragraph a student wrote on one of the above topics—how to break up gradually with a boyfriend or girlfriend.

At some point in your life, you're likely to find yourself in a romantic relationship that has stopped being happy or satisfying. You'll want to end the relationship. But how? No one likes to cause pain, especially to someone who has been special to you. Many people break up with a boyfriend or girlfriend in a slow and gradual way. In the first phase, they cut way back on communication with the partner. They stop calling, emailing, and texting, and they are slow to respond to the other person's messages. With the weekend and the usual "date night" coming up, they just don't say anything about getting together, leaving the other person hanging. The second phase begins when the two people do finally get together. The person who wants to break it off—in this case, let's say it's a guy— acts distant and distracted. He doesn't talk much, and he doesn't seem to be listening. He stares off into space a lot. Eventually, of course, the other person says, "What's wrong?" Then the breaker-upper goes into the final phase of the gradual breakup: the excuses. At first he'll insist that nothing's wrong, saying that he's just tired or has a lot on his mind. This phase can go on for days or even weeks. But sooner or later, he'll get around to saying something like, "I think we need some time apart. It's not you; it's me. I'm just in a weird place right now." What he means, of course, is "It's over," but

*(Continues on next page)*

*he thinks it's "less hurtful" to make the breakup sound like a temporary thing. That, in a nutshell, is how the gradual breakup works. But here's a suggestion: If you want to end a relationship, do it directly and honestly. In the long run, ripping off the emotional Band-Aid might be sharply painful, but it's a lot more honest than dragging it out.*

● Underline the topic sentence—the sentence that expresses the main idea of the above paragraph. (You'll note it is not the first sentence.)

● What three transitions (signal words) does the writer use to guide the reader from one part of the process to the next?

<u>    first    </u>    <u>    second    </u>    <u>    final    </u>

## Writing Your Own Paragraph

Pick out the process you think you might be able to write about. Then explore that topic by freewriting about it, or asking questions such as *what, when, where, how,* and *why* about it, or making a list of all the details you can think of about it. Prewriting will help you determine the topic for which you can provide the best supporting details.

See if you can develop the topic with even more details and prepare a scratch outline of the paragraph. In the outline, first write out the point of your paragraph. Here is the scratch outline prepared by the author of the model paragraph shown above:

***To the Instructor:***
A student's score on this test should be based on your evaluation of whether he or she has written an A, B, C, D, or F paper.

Suggested equivalents:

A = 90 to 100
B = 80 to 89
C = 70 to 79
D = 60 to 69
F = 59 and below

*Many people break up with a boyfriend or girlfriend in a slow and gradual way.*
1. *First phase—cut back on communication*
2. *Second phase—when together, act distant*
3. *Final phase—excuses*

After you prepare your scratch outline, go on to write the first and later drafts of your paper. When you think you have the final draft of your paper, read it aloud to make sure that every sentence reads smoothly and clearly. If that is not the case, you still have a bit of work to do. Use a grammar handbook, if necessary, to help remove the trouble spots.

# 8 More Relationships in Reading

Good readers and writers understand the relationships between ideas. This chapter explains four additional basic relationships you should recognize as a reader.

In Chapter 6, "Relationships in Reading" (pages 141–158), you learned about two common types of relationships: ones that involve **addition** and ones that involve **time**. In this chapter, you will learn about more relationships you should recognize as a reader: **illustration, comparison, contrast,** and **cause and effect**.

# 1  Illustration

## Words That Show Illustration

Check (✓) the item that is easier to understand:

_____ Anyone can become a safer driver. Do not talk or send text messages on your cellphone.

_✓_ Anyone can become a safer driver. For instance, do not talk or send text messages on your cellphone.

The second item is easier to understand. The words *For instance* make it clear that not talking or sending text messages on a cellphone is one way to be a safer driver. *For instance* and other words and phrases like it are illustration words.

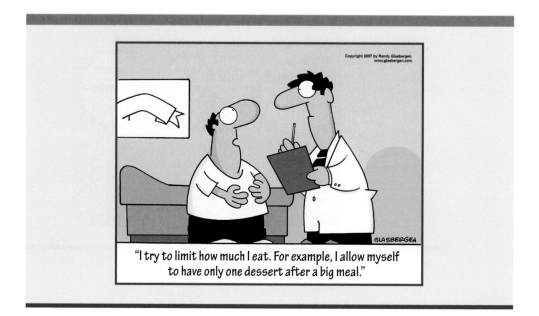

Copyright 2007 by Randy Glasbergen.
www.glasbergen.com

GLASBERGEN

"I try to limit how much I eat. For example, I allow myself to have only one dessert after a big meal."

**Illustration words** tell us that an author will provide one or more *examples* to clarify a given idea. In the cartoon above, the man gives his doctor one example of how he tries to limit what he eats—having only one dessert!

Here are some common words that show illustration:

*Illustration Words*

| (for) example | (for) instance | to illustrate |
|---|---|---|
| including | such as | once |

## Examples

The following items contain illustration words. Notice how these words signal that one or more *examples* are coming.

- Some birds, *such as* the penguin and the ostrich, cannot fly.
- People came to America for many reasons. The Puritans, *for example*, arrived in 1620 seeking religious freedom.
- My mother's love of chocolate has led to some pretty weird combinations. *Once* she put Hershey's syrup on a cheese sandwich.

  *To the Instructor:* Remind students that transitions are **bridges** that connect ideas. For one or more of the example sentences in this chapter, you might wish to put a bridge diagram (similar to the one on page 142) on the board.

### PRACTICE 1

Complete each item with a suitable illustration word or phrase from the box on the previous page. Try to use a variety of transitions.    *Answers may vary.*

*Hint:* Make sure that each word or phrase that you choose fits smoothly into the flow of the sentence. Test each choice by reading the sentence aloud.

1. A large part of what seems to be taste is really smell. _____For example_____, try eating some bread while holding a banana or piece of onion near your nose.

2. When we were young, my older brother liked to tease me. _____Once_____ he put raisins in my cereal and told me they were roaches.

3. The Italian restaurant offers pizza with unusual toppings, _____such as_____ sweet corn, sunflower seeds, and carrots.

4. Some children are very caring. _____For instance_____, they will want to share their toys with others, or they will reach out to comfort a crying friend.

5. Power is the ability to control the behavior of others, even against their will. If a robber forces us to hand over our wallets, that is an _____example_____ of power.

Illustration words are common in all types of writing. One way they are used in textbooks is in the definition and example pattern of organization.

# The Definition and Example Pattern

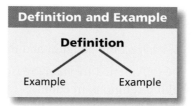

To understand the definition and example pattern, try to arrange the following sentences in an order that makes sense. Put a *1* in front of the sentence that should come first, a *2* in front of the sentence that comes next, and a *3* in front of the sentence that should be last. The result will be a short paragraph. Then read the explanation that follows.

_2_    When acupuncture is used to kill pain, needles are inserted far from the area of pain.

_1_    Acupuncture is a Chinese medical technique that involves inserting special needles in certain places in the body.

_3_    In one stomach operation, for instance, four needles in the patient's outer ears eliminated pain.

This paragraph begins with a definition: "Acupuncture is a Chinese medical technique that involves inserting special needles in certain places in the body." The second sentence further explains acupuncture by discussing a special use: "When acupuncture is used to kill pain, needles are inserted far from the area of pain." Finally, an example of the use of acupuncture for pain is given: "In one stomach operation, for instance, four needles in the patient's outer ears eliminated pain." The third sentence includes the illustration words *for instance*. As you can see, the **definition and example pattern of organization** includes just what its name suggests: a definition and one or more examples.

*An Important Study Hint:* Good textbook authors want to help readers understand the important ideas and terms in a subject—whether it is psychology, sociology, business, biology, or any other field. Such authors often take time, then, to include key definitions. These ideas and terms are usually set off in *italic* or **boldface** type, and the definitions are signaled by such words as *is, are, is called, termed,* and *refers to.* Here are some definitions from a variety of textbooks:

● A **placebo** is a "sugar pill" without any significant medical properties.

● **Hypotheses** are predictions stated in a way that allows them to be tested.

● A low sense of personal worth is what psychologists call **negative self-esteem.**

● The chemical change in which a solid turns into a liquid is termed **melting.**

- Narcolepsy refers to an uncontrollable need to sleep for short periods during the day.
- Many critics argue that tests like the SAT are culturally biased—favoring one ethnic or racial group over others.

(Note: Sometimes a dash is used to signal a definition.)

If an author defines a term, you can assume that it is important enough to learn. So when reading and taking notes on a textbook, always do two things:

1) Write down key definitions.

2) Write down a helpful example for each definition. When a definition is general and abstract, authors often provide examples to help make a meaning clear.

*To the Instructor:*  The terms being defined are double-underlined in this *Instructor's Edition*. Also, throughout this chapter and the tests that follow, transitions relevant to the patterns of organization are underlined.

## ✓ Check Your Understanding

The paragraph below defines a term, explains it a bit, and then gives an example of it. After reading the paragraph, see if you can answer the questions below. Then read the explanation that follows.

¹Self-fulfilling prophecies are predictions that come true because we predict them. ²For example, Tyrone may tell himself, "I bet I can get a good grade in this history class." ³This thought makes Tyrone likely to work hard, making his prediction come true. ⁴Children get their self-fulfilling prophecies from others. ⁵For instance, if someone tells a child that he or she will "never amount to much," there is a good chance that is what will happen. ⁶But if someone keeps saying to a child, "You can be one of the stars of your class," that child is likely to do well.

1. What term is being defined? _____ *Self-fulfilling prophecies* _____

2. Which sentence contains the definition? _____ *1* _____

3. In which sentence does the first example begin? _____ *2* _____

4. How many examples are given in all? _____ *Three* _____

### Explanation

The term *self-fulfilling prophecies* is defined in sentence 1: "predictions that come true because we predict them." (Note that the definition is signaled by the word *are*.) The first example, about Tyrone's self-fulfilling prophecy, begins in sentence 2. A second example, about a child, appears in sentence 5, and a third example begins in sentence 6. Note that the author introduces two of the examples with the transition words *for example* and *for instance*. By providing clear examples, the author helps the reader understand the new term.

## PRACTICE 2

Each of the following passages includes a definition and one or more examples. Underline the term being defined. Then, in the spaces provided, write the number of the definition sentence and the number of the sentence where each example begins.

**A.** [1]Have you ever been up at one o'clock in the morning, trying to finish the last chapter of the text on which you are being tested in the morning? [2]If so, you may have turned to a stimulant to keep you awake. [3]A <u>stimulant</u> is a substance that temporarily increases one's activity or alertness. [4]One common stimulant is caffeine, which is found in coffee, tea, soft drinks, and chocolate. [5]Another <u>example</u> of a common stimulant is nicotine, which is found in cigarettes. [6]Both caffeine and nicotine cause a rise in your heart rate and blood pressure, making you feel more wide-awake.

*Definition* ___3___     *Example 1* ___4___     *Example 2* ___5___

**B.** [1]Frequently, members of a group will develop a <u>jargon</u>, or specialized language, which distinguishes the group from the wider society. [2]The police are well known for their use of distinctive jargons. [3]<u>For instance</u>, members of New York City's police department refer to a suspect as a "perp" (short for "perpetrator"), to a gun as a "piece," and to the police shield as the "tin." [4]Chicago police also have their own terms, <u>such</u> as calling a suspect an "offender"; they call a gun a "biscuit" and the police shield the "button."

*Definition* ___1___     *Example 1* ___3___     *Example 2* ___4___

# 2 Comparison and Contrast

## Words That Show Comparison

Check (✓) the item that is easier to understand:

____ Human infants suck their thumbs; baby elephants suck their trunks.

__✓__ Just as human infants suck their thumbs, baby elephants suck their trunks.

The first item makes us wonder what the author is focusing on—how human infants and baby elephants are alike or how they are different. The words *just as* in the second version show the author is focusing on the similarity. *Just as* and words like them are comparison words.

Copyright 2005 by Randy Glasbergen.
www.glasbergen.com

GLASBERGEN

"Do you realize how much we resemble each other?
We'll both eat anything. We both like to sleep on the furniture.
And we're both overweight."

**Comparison words** signal similarities. Authors use a comparison transition to show that a second idea is *like* the first one in some way. In the above cartoon, the words *resemble* and *both* show the dog is making a comparison between himself and the man. The dog names three ways he and the man are similar: both of them eat anything, sleep on the furniture, and are overweight.

Here are some common words that show comparison:

*Comparison Words*

| | | |
|---|---|---|
| (just) as | in like (similar) manner | same |
| (just) like | similar(ly) | in the same way |
| alike | similarity | resemble |
| likewise | both | equally |

## Examples

The sentences below contain comparison words. Notice how these words show that things are *alike* in some way.

- The carpet was so old and faded it looked *like* a gray shadow.

- Parents today often dislike the music their children listen to, *just as* their own parents disliked the Beatles or the Rolling Stones.

- Tattoos, which used to be seen as lower class, are part of our culture today. *Likewise*, many middle-class people now have body piercings.

*To the Instructor:* Remind students to use the hint on page 189 as they complete these sentences.

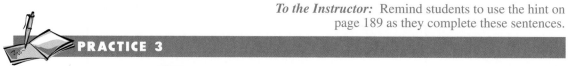

## PRACTICE 3

Complete each sentence with a suitable comparison word or phrase from the box on the previous page. Try to use a variety of transitions.     *Answers may vary.*

1. Bats and frogs hibernate during the winter, _____*just as*_____ bears do.

2. Many Hispanic girls have a special party for their fifteenth birthday. _____*Similarly*_____, Anglo girls often celebrate their sixteenth birthday in a special way.

3. Good teachers are _____*as*_____ skilled in praising what students have accomplished as they are in challenging them to do more.

4. We are often attracted to people who have a social and religious background _____*similar*_____ to our own.

5. As we turned onto the country road, the view in front of us—a bright rainbow rising over a gentle hill—looked _____*just like*_____ a scene in a fairy tale.

## Words That Show Contrast

Check (✓) the item that is easier to understand:

✓ The weather in Florida is usually wonderful, but the summers are hot and humid.

___ The weather in Florida is usually wonderful. The summers are hot and humid.

In the second item, we're not sure if the author feels that the weather in Florida is wonderful *because of* or *in spite of* the hot and humid summers. The transition *but* in the first item makes the relationship clear: the weather in Florida is wonderful in spite of the summer heat and humidity. *But* and words like it are known as contrast words.

"That's the difference between us.
You like to read at meals, and I like to talk."

**Contrast words** signal differences. A contrast word shows that two things *differ* in one or more ways. Contrast words also inform us that something is going to *differ from* what we might expect. In the cartoon above, the woman uses the word *difference* to contrast what her husband likes to do at meals (read) with what she likes to do (talk).

Here are some common words that show contrast:

*Contrast Words*

| | | | |
|---|---|---|---|
| but | instead | still | difference |
| yet | in contrast | as opposed to | different(ly) |
| however | on the other hand | in spite of | differs from |
| although | on the contrary | despite | unlike |
| nevertheless | even though | rather than | while |

## Examples

The sentences below contain contrast words. Notice how these words signal that one idea is *different from* another idea.

- *Although* the movie had an exciting plot, the actors in the lead roles were not very convincing.

- A laptop computer is convenient and portable; *on the other hand*, a desktop computer is usually less expensive.

- Only 10 percent of the population is left-handed. *In contrast*, of babies that are born more than two months prematurely, 54 percent are left-handed.

*To the Instructor:* Remind students to use the hint on page 189 as they complete these sentences.

## PRACTICE 4

Complete each sentence with a suitable contrast word or phrase from the box on the previous page. Try to use a variety of transitions.       *Answers may vary.*

1. Our Toyota is ten years old, _____ but _____ it still runs perfectly.

2. _____ Although _____ many people own running shoes, most of these people are not runners.

3. American women have been dyeing their hair for years. American men, __ on the other hand __, only recently started coloring theirs.

4. _____ Despite _____ the fact that the sign in the corner market window said "Open," the door was locked and no one was in sight.

5. Fast-food chains sell French fries for prices much higher than what they paid for them. The farmer who planted and grew the potatoes, _____ however _____, doesn't get such a good deal. Out of every $1.50 that you spend on a large order of French fries, maybe 2¢ goes to the farmer.

Comparison and contrast transitions often signal the pattern of organization known as the comparison-contrast pattern.

## The Comparison-Contrast Pattern

To understand the comparison-contrast pattern, arrange the following group of sentences in an order that makes sense. Put a *1* in front of the sentence that should come first, a *2* in front of the sentence that comes next, and a *3* in front of the sentence that should be last. The result will be a short paragraph. Then read the explanation that follows.

<u>2</u>    The snakes have <u>similar</u> markings: red, yellow, and black bands.

<u>1</u>    The coral snake and the milk snake may look <u>alike,</u> <u>but</u> there's an important <u>difference</u> between them.

<u>3</u>    <u>However,</u> the milk snake is harmless, <u>while</u> the coral snake is very poisonous.

The first sentence of this paragraph is the general one, the one with the main idea: "The coral snake and the milk snake may look alike, but there's an important difference between them." The words *alike, but*, and *difference* suggest a comparison-contrast pattern. As the comparison word *similar* and the contrast words *however* and *while* suggest, the other two sentences do in fact compare and contrast two things: "The snakes have similar markings: red, yellow, and black bands. However, the milk snake is harmless, while the coral snake is very poisonous."

The **comparison-contrast pattern** shows how two things are alike or how they are different, or both. When things are compared, their similarities are pointed out. When things are contrasted, their differences are discussed.

Authors often find it useful to compare and/or contrast. Here are two examples.

## Comparison

[1]House cats and their larger relatives, jungle cats, have traits in common. [2]Both have eyes suited for night vision, and both prefer to sleep by day and move about at night. [3]Also, just as pet cats use their tails to keep their balance and show emotions, so do lions and other large cats. [4]In addition, both kinds of cats can leap great distances. [5]Finally, cats at home are not the only ones that purr: cats in the wild also purr when content.

## Contrast

[1]Times have changed, and I know this because I have children, two of them, one born in the old days and one in modern times. [2]One was born back before seat belts, when a child might ride standing up in the front seat next to Daddy as he drove 75 mph across North Dakota, and nobody said boo, though nowadays Daddy would do jail time for that. [3]In contrast, my younger child rides in a podlike car seat, belted in like a little test pilot. [4]She likes it. [5]Another difference is that the older child grew up inhaling clouds of secondary smoke, while the younger one lives in a house in which nobody even thinks about smoking.

✓ ### *Check Your Understanding*

In the following paragraph, the main idea is stated in the first sentence. As is often the case, the main idea suggests a paragraph's pattern of organization. Here the transition *differ* is a hint that the paragraph may be organized in a comparison-contrast pattern. Read the paragraph, and answer the questions below. Then read the explanation that follows.

<sup>1</sup>Humans <u>differ</u> from other primates, <u>but</u> not as much as one might think. <sup>2</sup>It's true that there are important <u>differences</u> in size and shape between humans and other primates. <sup>3</sup>And, of course, humans are by far the more intelligent. <sup>4</sup>It is also true that there are striking <u>similarities</u> between the two. <sup>5</sup>To use chimpanzees as an example, <u>both</u> they and humans have the <u>same</u> muscles and bones, located in almost the <u>same</u> places and working in nearly the <u>same</u> ways. <sup>6</sup>The internal organs of <u>both</u> animals are also very much <u>alike</u>, as are their blood and other body fluids. <sup>7</sup>Seen under a microscope, even their genes are strikingly <u>similar</u>.

1. Is this paragraph comparing, contrasting, or both? _____ *Both* _____

2. What two things are being compared and/or contrasted? _____
   *Humans and other primates*

3. Write out four of the comparison and/or contrast words that are used in the
   paragraph. _____ *Any four of the following:* differ, but, differences, _____
   similarities, both, same, alike, similar

#### Explanation

The paragraph both compares and contrasts—it discusses both similarities and differences. First, it contrasts humans and other primates in terms of size, shape, and intelligence. The words used to indicate that contrast are *differ, but*, and *differences*. The paragraph also discusses similarities between humans and other primates—in their muscles, bones, internal organs, body fluids, and genes. The words used to indicate comparison are *similarities*, *both, same, alike*, and *similar*.

*To the Instructor:* In the paragraphs in the practices and tests that follow, the main ideas and transitions relevant to the pattern of organization are underlined in this *Instructor's Edition*.

**PRACTICE 5**

The following passages use the pattern of comparison or contrast. Read each passage and answer the questions which follow.        *Wording of answers may vary.*

**A.** [1]The lives and deaths of two assassinated Presidents, Abraham Lincoln and John F. Kennedy, contain a number of odd <u>similarities</u>. [2]Lincoln was elected to Congress in 1846; Kennedy was elected to Congress in 1946. [3]Lincoln was elected President in 1860, and Kennedy in 1960. [4]<u>Both</u> presidents were shot on a Friday, and <u>both</u> were shot in the head. [5]After their deaths, they were succeeded by men with the <u>same</u> name: Johnson. [6]Lincoln's assassin, John Wilkes Booth, was born in 1839, while Kennedy's killer, Lee Harvey Oswald, was born in 1939. [7]<u>Both</u> presidents' assassins were themselves murdered before they could stand trial.

Check (✓) the pattern used in this paragraph:

_✓_ Comparison        _____ Contrast

*The passage compares the lives and deaths of Presidents Lincoln and Kennedy. Comparison words: similarities, both, and same.*

What two things are being compared or contrasted?

1. _____Abraham Lincoln_____    2. _____John F. Kennedy_____

**B.** [1]High school and college offer very <u>different</u> educational experiences for students. [2]In high school, teachers often treat students like children. [3]For instance, teachers may call parents if a student skips class or fails to hand in an assignment. [4]<u>On the other hand</u>, college teachers treat students like adults. [5]Students are expected to take full responsibility for their attendance and their work. [6]Also, in high school, students typically live at home and depend on their parents. [7]In college, <u>however</u>, students live in apartments (or dorms) and have no one to depend on but themselves.

Check (✓) the pattern used in this paragraph:

_____ Comparison        _✓_ Contrast

What two things are being compared or contrasted?

1. _____High school_____    2. _____College_____

*The passage contrasts students' experiences in high school and college. Contrast words: different, On the other hand, and however.*

# 3  Cause and Effect

## Words That Show Cause and Effect

Check (✓) the item that is easier to understand:

____ Nina cares for her elderly parents. She has very little free time.

_✓_ Because Nina cares for her elderly parents, she has very little free time.

In the first item, we are not sure of the relationship between the two sentences. Does Nina have little free time *with which* to care for her parents? Or does she have little free time *because* she cares for her parents? The word *because* in the second item shows the connection between the two ideas. *Because* and words like it are known as cause and effect words.

Copyright © by Randy Glasbergen.
www.glasbergen.com

"The reason I got the promotion is that I always dress for success."

**Cause and effect words** signal that the author is explaining *the reason* why something happened or *the result* of something happening. In the cartoon above, the dog explains that dressing for success (the *cause*) has led to his promotion (the *effect*).

Here are some common cause and effect words:

*Cause and Effect Words*

| therefore | so | because (of) | thus |
| --- | --- | --- | --- |
| (as a) result | effect | as a consequence | results in |
| cause | explanation | consequently | led to |
| affect | due to | since | reason |

## Examples

The following items contain cause and effect words. Notice how these words introduce a *reason* for something or a *result* of something.

- People eat fewer hamburgers today than they did in the past. *Therefore*, fast-food restaurants have developed new items for their menus.

- *Because* roses are considered the flowers of romance, many people give them for Valentine's Day.

- Digital cameras do not require the use of film; *as a result*, they have become more popular than conventional cameras.

*To the Instructor:* Remind students to use the hint on page 189 as they complete these sentences.

### PRACTICE 6

Complete each sentence with a suitable cause and effect word or phrase from the box on the previous page. Try to use a variety of transitions. *Answers may vary.*

1. _____Because_____ there's no room in your mouth for your wisdom teeth, they will have to be removed.

2. Gail wanted a large wedding reception. _____Therefore_____, her parents had to rent a hall.

3. The construction of a Home Depot and a Wal-Mart right outside of the town _____resulted in_____ the closing of a number of small businesses in the area.

4. Elephants were killed for many years for the valuable ivory in their tusks. _____As a result_____, the elephant population declined significantly.

5. The _____reason_____ our skin wrinkles when we're in the water a long time is that the top layer of skin absorbs much more water than the bottom one.

Cause and effect transitions often signal the cause and effect pattern of organization.

## The Cause and Effect Pattern

Arrange the following group of sentences in an order that makes sense. Put a *1* in front of the sentence that should come first, a *2* in front of the sentence that comes next, and a *3* in front of the sentence that should be last. The result will be a short paragraph. Then read the explanation that follows.

_3_ Accidents are also <u>caused</u> by speeding, as drivers try to get home as quickly as possible.

_1_ Traffic accidents are more likely to <u>result</u> during evening rush hour.

_2_ <u>Because</u> drivers are tired at the end of the day, they are not able to respond quickly enough to changes in traffic.

As the words *result*, *Because*, and *caused* suggest, this paragraph is organized in a cause and effect pattern. In paragraph form, the sentences would read as follows:

> [1]Traffic accidents are more likely to result during evening rush hour. [2]Because drivers are tired at the end of the day, they are not able to respond quickly enough to changes in traffic. [3]Accidents are also caused by speeding, as drivers try to get home as quickly as possible.

The paragraph begins with an effect—that more accidents occur during rush hour—and then follows with two causes.

Information in a **cause and effect pattern** addresses the questions "Why does a behavior or event happen?" and/or "What are the results of a behavior or event?" An author may then discuss causes, or effects, or both causes and effects.

Authors usually don't just tell *what* happened. They both describe what has happened and try to explain *why*. For example, a sociology textbook would not just say that the test scores of American students have declined for most of the last thirty years. The book would also explain the likely *causes* of this decline. Or a health textbook would not just describe the ways that medical care has changed in the last few years. It would also examine the *reasons* for such changes.

## ✓ *Check Your Understanding*

Read the paragraph below and see if you can answer the questions about cause and effect. Then read the explanation to see how you did.

¹Experts point out four reasons why the divorce rate has increased in the United States. ²One explanation is a lack of time for many couples to work at their marriage. ³With husband and wife often holding down jobs outside the home, there may be little energy for everything else that goes into a partnership. ⁴Another cause is the "me-first" attitude in today's society. ⁵Some people put their own personal happiness ahead of the well-being of a spouse and family. ⁶In addition, women now have more freedom of choice. ⁷Their ability to support themselves means that they can more easily leave an unhappy marriage. ⁸Finally, because divorce is so much more common, it has also become more socially acceptable. ⁹People are no longer embarrassed to say they are divorced.

*Wording of answers may vary.*

1. What are the four *causes* described in this paragraph?

   a. Lack of time to work at marriage

   b. "Me-first" attitude

   c. Women's greater freedom of choice

   d. Divorce now more socially acceptable

2. What is the *effect* of these causes?

   Higher divorce rate in the United States

3. What three cause-effect transitions are used?

   a. explanation

   b. cause

   c. because

### Explanation

The paragraph presents four causes: lack of time to work at the marriage, the "me-first" attitude in today's society, more freedom of choice for women, and divorce becoming more socially acceptable. The four causes lead to one effect: the increased divorce rate. The cause-effect transitions used are *explanation, cause,* and *because.*

**PRACTICE 7**

**A.** Read the paragraph below, looking for the **one** effect and the **two** causes. Then complete the map that follows. (The effect has been added for you.)

The *effect:* increase in numbers of overweight Japanese adults (sentences 2–3). The *causes:* lifestyle change (sentence 5) and diet changes (sentences 6–7).

¹For centuries, Japan had one of the lowest rates of obesity in the world. ²But that is changing. ³About a quarter of adult Japanese are now considered significantly overweight. ⁴Two reasons in particular explain this weight gain among the Japanese. ⁵For one thing, lifestyles have become less active as more and more rural Japanese move into cities. ⁶More importantly, many Japanese are turning away from their traditional low-fat diet emphasizing rice, fish, and vegetables. ⁷They are instead adopting a more Western diet that features lots of processed food that is high in fat. *Wording of answers may vary.*

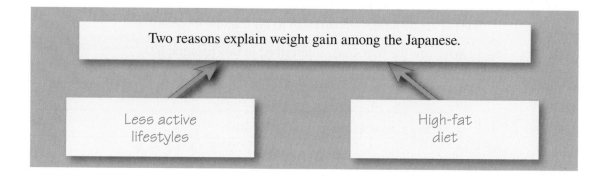

Two reasons explain weight gain among the Japanese.

Less active lifestyles

High-fat diet

**B.** Read the paragraph below, looking for the **one** cause and the **three** effects. Then complete the outline that follows. *Wording of answers may vary.*

¹Increases in the numbers of elderly people will have a major impact in Europe, Canada, and the United States. ²One effect of the aging of these populations is that the number of working-age people will go sharply down, leaving fewer people available to fill jobs. ³Also, as the number of retired people increases, there will be a bigger demand on the countries' pension systems. ⁴A third effect will be an immense strain on national medical services. ⁵Elderly people draw upon far more of a society's health-care services than do young people.

Sentence 1 states the *cause:* increases in the numbers of elderly people. The three *effects* are stated in sentences 2, 3, and 4.

**Main idea** (*the cause*): Increases in the numbers of elderly people will have a major impact in Europe, Canada, and the United States.

**Major supporting details** (*the effects*):

1. Fewer people available to fill jobs

2. Bigger demand on pension systems

3. Great strain on national medical services

## A Note on Main Ideas and Patterns of Organization

As mentioned on page 156, a paragraph's main idea often indicates its pattern of organization. Try, for instance, to guess the pattern of the paragraph with this main idea:

> For various reasons, as many as half of all battered women do not leave their abusive husbands.

The word *reasons* suggests that the author is using a cause-effect pattern. The paragraph will go on to explain the reasons why many abused women stay with their husbands.

Recognizing a main idea, and recognizing the pattern of organization implied in a main idea, are both helpful steps in understanding the material in a paragraph.

### PRACTICE 8

Most of the main ideas below have been taken from college textbooks. In the space provided, write the letter of the pattern of organization that each suggests.

___B___ 1. One of the major <u>differences</u> between men and women is their degree of aggression.

    A. Definition and example     B. Comparison-contrast     C. Cause and effect

___A___ 2. A <u>stereotype</u> is an oversimplified, inaccurate mental picture of others, <u>such as the idea</u> that the poor are lazy.

    A. Definition and example     B. Comparison-contrast     C. Cause and effect

___C___ 3. People often form strong first impressions of others for unusual <u>reasons</u>.

    A. Definition and example     B. Comparison-contrast     C. Cause and effect

___B___ 4. The eyes of newborns are both <u>similar</u> to and <u>different</u> from those of adults.

    A. Definition and example     B. Comparison-contrast     C. Cause and effect

___C___ 5. Strong emotions tend to <u>affect</u> the flow of digestive juices and upset digestion.

    A. Definition and example     B. Comparison-contrast     C. Cause and effect

___A___ 6. <u>Self-esteem</u> refers to how one feels about oneself; people with low self-esteem, <u>for instance</u>, do not like themselves.

    A. Definition and example     B. Comparison-contrast     C. Cause and effect

_C_ 7. Viruses that <u>cause</u> colds and flu are often spread through sneezing, coughing, and unsanitary habits.
   A. Definition and example
   B. Comparison-contrast
   C. Cause and effect

_B_ 8. Irish-Americans were once harshly discriminated against in the United States, <u>just as</u> Italian immigrants were.
   A. Definition and example
   B. Comparison-contrast
   C. Cause and effect

_A_ 9. A <u>closed shop</u> is a business with an employment agreement that requires the company to hire only union workers.
   A. Definition and example
   B. Comparison-contrast
   C. Cause and effect

_C_ 10. Childhood dental problems in the United States have decreased significantly <u>because of</u> the widespread use of fluoride in drinking water and toothpaste.
   A. Definition and example
   B. Comparison-contrast
   C. Cause and effect

## A Final Point

Keep in mind that a paragraph or a longer passage sometimes contains more than one pattern of organization. For instance, the paragraph in this chapter about the reasons for the increased divorce rate in the United States uses a cause-effect pattern. But the reasons themselves—lack of time to work at the marriage, a "me-first" attitude, more freedom of choice for women, and the greater social acceptability of divorce—are presented as a list of items. In other words, the paragraph combines two patterns.

Or consider the following passage:

> [1]People with more wealth tend to have more power. [2]This fact is apparent in the domination of top government positions by the wealthy. [3]Higher-income persons are also more likely to feel a strong sense of power. [4]As a result, they are more likely to be politically active, working to keep or increase their power. [5]In contrast, lower-income people are more likely to feel powerless to influence major political decisions. [6]Therefore, they are more indifferent to politics and less likely to be involved in political activity.

The paragraph partly uses a contrast pattern, noting the *difference* between higher-income people and lower-income people with regard to political activity. But it also uses a cause-effect pattern: it describes the *effect* of feeling a sense of power or feeling no sense of power.

# MORE RELATIONSHIPS IN READING: Mastery Test 1

**A.** Fill in each blank with an appropriate transition from the box. Use each transition once. Then, in the space provided, write the letter of the transition you have chosen.

| | | |
|---|---|---|
| **A. as a result** | **B. because** | **C. for example** |
| **D. however** | **E. just as** | |

*Hint:* Make sure that each word or phrase that you choose fits smoothly into the flow of the sentence. Test your choices by reading each sentence to yourself.

_C_ 1. ¹If you go to a website for medical information, go to one recommended by doctors. ²_____For example_____, the famous Mayo Clinic offers a one-stop health center: **http://mayoclinic.com**.

The website **http://mayoclinic.com** is an example of a site recommended by doctors.

_A_ 2. ¹Small feet were admired in ancient China. ²_____As a result_____, some parents had their female infants' feet tightly bound. ³The feet then grew into a tiny deformed shape. ⁴Some of the women could barely walk.

*As a result* signals the *cause* (small feet were admired) and the *effect* (infants' feet were bound).

_E_ 3. ¹One way to own a book is to take possession by paying for it, _____just as_____ you pay for clothes or furniture. ²But full ownership comes only when you have made the book a part of yourself by reading it closely.

Owning a book is being compared to owning clothes or furniture.

_D_ 4. ¹In many European countries, a kiss on the cheek is used as a greeting by men and women, regardless of the sex of the other person, or of how well they know each other. ²In Britain and Germany, _____however_____, the cheek-kiss is used only between women, or between men and women who know each other well.

A kiss on the cheek in many European countries is being contrasted with a kiss on the cheek in England and Germany.

_B_ 5. ¹In the search for food, wood mice explore fields that don't contain many landmarks such as large rocks and tall trees. ²When they find new food sources, they build their own signposts out of piles of leaves, twigs, and seed casings. ³This method is safer than leaving scents that could be traced by enemies such as weasels. ⁴_____Because_____ of these signposts, wood mice are known as the only mammals other than humans that mark their trail.

*Cause:* Wood mice build signposts to food sources.
*Effect:* Wood mice are known as the only mammals other than humans that mark their trail with "signposts."

*(Continues on next page)*

**B.** Below are the beginnings of five passages. Label each one with the letter of its pattern of organization. (You may find it helpful to underline the transition or transitions in each item.)

    **A**  Definition and example
    **B**  Comparison-contrast
    **C**  Cause and effect

_B_ 6. ¹The first railroad cars were very <u>similar</u> to horse-drawn carriages. ²<u>Both</u> were called "coaches" and held the same number of passengers—just six people. ³<u>Likewise</u>, train cars and horse carriages also featured the same shape, windows, and decorations. ⁴Even though trains could carry many more people than horses, builders simply followed old plans when they built the first cars for the "iron horse." . . .

*Early railroad cars are being compared to horse-drawn carriages.*

_C_ 7. ¹The depression of the 1930s had powerful <u>effects</u> on families. ²It forced many couples to delay marriage. ³Another <u>effect</u> was a sharp drop in the divorce rate <u>because</u> many couples could not afford to keep up separate households. . . .

*Cause: the depression. Effects: delayed marriages, sharp drop in divorce rate.*

_A_ 8. ¹Good listeners can paraphrase well. ²To <u>paraphrase</u> is to state in your own words what someone else has said. ³<u>For instance</u>, after a person has given you directions for getting to a certain place, you might paraphrase, saying, "In other words, what I should do is . . . " ⁴Or if someone tells you a story and you then tell that story to someone else in your own words, you would be paraphrasing the story. . . .

*Term being defined: paraphrase.*

_C_ 9. ¹Various experiments reveal there are several <u>reasons</u> why people will or will not help others. ²One <u>reason</u> is how deserving the victim is thought to be. ³This was shown in an experiment in which people pretended to be in need of help. ⁴If they carried a cane, they were helped more promptly than if they carried a liquor bottle. . . .

*The passage presents a cause (reason) for why people help— or refuse to help— others.*

_B_ 10. ¹<u>In contrast</u> to schools in other countries, the educational system in the United States can be seen as placing limits on teachers. ²Our teachers often cannot choose their own textbooks but must use whatever books are chosen by a local school board or district office. ³<u>On the other hand</u>, teachers in France are free to do their job in almost any way they want. ⁴Teachers are permitted to pick the books for their classes or even not to use any books. . . .

*The passage contrasts the limits on America's teachers with the limits on teachers in other countries.*

# MORE RELATIONSHIPS IN READING: Mastery Test 2

**A.** Read the textbook excerpts that follow and fill in each blank with an appropriate transition from the box. Use each transition once. Then, in the spaces provided, write the letter of the transition you have chosen.

| | | |
|---|---|---|
| A. explanation | B. for instance | C. however |
| D. same | E. therefore | |

_A_ 1. ¹Why is it that about half of America's eligible voters do not take part in national elections? ²One _____explanation_____ may be that many of our political leaders do not appeal to voters.

*Explanation* signals a *cause* (unappealing leaders) and an *effect* (low voter participation).

_B_ 2. ¹Importing is purchasing products in other nations and bringing them into one's own country. ²_____For instance_____, buyers for Target might purchase shirts in India or sneakers in Indonesia or raincoats in England and have them shipped to the United States for sale there.

*For instance* signals an example of *importing*.

_E_ 3. ¹Before the 1900s, it was widely believed that schoolwork "would make women sick" and would take blood away "from their wombs to their brains," so that they would be less suited to have children.

²_____Therefore_____, women were often denied opportunities for higher education and were kept from entering many colleges and universities.

*Therefore* signals a *cause* (the belief that schoolwork would harm women) and an *effect* (women were denied a higher education).

_C_ 4. ¹For twenty years, Asian Americans were the fastest-growing minority in the United States. ²They are now about 4 percent of the U.S. population. ³_____However_____, they are a much smaller minority than African Americans, who are more than 13 percent, and Latino Americans, who are now nearly 16 percent of the population.

*However* signals the contrast between Asian Americans and other minority groups.

_D_ 5. ¹*For example* and *for instance* mean the _____same_____ thing, just as *therefore* and *as a result* do. ²Words and phrases with the same meaning allow authors to include more variety in their writing.

*Same* signals a comparison between the groups of words.

*(Continues on next page)*

**B.** Below are parts of five passages. Label each one with the letter of its pattern of organization. (You may find it helpful to underline the transition or transitions in each item.)

    A  Definition and example
    B  Comparison-contrast
    C  Cause and effect

_B_  6. ¹There are notable <u>differences</u> between people with high self-esteem and those with low self-esteem. ²People with good self-concepts tend to be more accepting of others and also more accepting of their own failures. ³<u>In contrast</u>, people with low self-esteem tend to be very critical of others. . . .   This passage contrasts people with high self-esteem and people with low self-esteem.

*Cause:* Schools teach students to be passive and quiet. *Effect:* Little discussion in college classrooms.

_C_  7. ¹Schools all too often teach students to be passive, viewing instructors as experts who serve up "truth." ²Students are expected to quietly listen and take notes. ³<u>As a result</u>, researchers estimate, just 10 percent of college class time is used for discussion. . . .

_B_  8. ¹Stepfamilies and "natural" families have <u>similarities</u> and <u>differences</u>. ²<u>Both</u> types of families have a <u>similar</u> range of everyday values, and <u>both</u> types have backgrounds that tend to be <u>alike</u> as well. ³<u>However</u>, the stepfamily includes more people—ex-husbands, ex-wives, ex-in-laws, and various other relatives on <u>both</u> sides. ⁴<u>Another difference</u> is that the stepfamily has anger, guilt, and conflicts stemming from issues that "natural" families do not face. . . .   This passage compares and contrasts stepfamilies and "natural" families.

_C_  9. ¹"Let's go shopping!" ²These familiar words echo across America like a battle cry. ³Every day, Americans get another fix of their favorite drug: shopping. ⁴There are probably several <u>causes</u> of this shopping madness. ⁵One <u>reason</u> is that we are competitive. ⁶If our neighbors have something, we want it as well, or we feel like losers or feel that we're losing out. . . .   *Cause:* competitiveness. *Effect:* shopping madness.

_A_  10. ¹Great actors have more than talent. ²They also have a quality known as charisma—a mysterious "x" factor that can't be learned. ³<u>Charisma</u> is that extra something you can't describe but can feel flowing out of them, whether they are on stage or on the screen. ⁴<u>For example</u>, an acting teacher talked about seeing Marlon Brando in a play at the start of his career, before his name was known. ⁵"Suddenly a man came on the stage whom I had never seen or heard of. ⁶Before he even spoke, it was as if a leopard had entered the room." . . .   The passage defines and gives an example of *charisma*.

# MORE RELATIONSHIPS IN READING: Mastery Test 3

**A.** (1–4.) Arrange the scrambled sentences below into a logical paragraph by numbering them *1, 2, 3,* and *4* in an order that makes sense. Then, in the space provided, write the letter of the main pattern of organization used.

Note that transitions will help you by making clear the relationships between sentences.

_3_  Another result is a higher proportion of male children than normal.

_2_  First of all, it has led to a greater number of divorces.

_1_  The Chinese policy of allowing only one child per family has had some disturbing effects.

_4_  The major reason for this imbalance in the sexes seems to be abortions of female fetuses, because male children are preferred.

_C_  5. The primary pattern of organization in the selection is
     A. comparison.
     B. contrast.                     The passage discusses effects of China's policy
     C. cause and effect.             to allow just one child per family. *First of all*
     D. definition and example.       and *another* signal the two effects.

**B.** Read the paragraph and answer the questions that follow.

¹Have you ever heard the term "sandwich generation"? ²Some people might guess that it refers to a generation that spends more time eating sandwiches than sitting down to meals. ³In fact, the term refers to adults who are "caught in the middle," so that they have to care for both their own children and their aging parents at the same time. ⁴As people live longer, more and more adults end up taking care of their elderly parents. ⁵For instance, a single mother named Rose has to care for her two children, one just six years old, and the other a troubled thirteen-year-old. ⁶She must also care for her sixty-six-year-old mother, who has not been able to live independently since suffering a stroke.

_A_  6. The main pattern of organization in the selection is
     A. definition-example.             The paragraph defines and gives an
     B. cause-effect.                   example of the term *sandwich generation.*
     C. comparison-contrast.            *For instance* signals the example.

     7. A transition that signals the pattern of organization is __For instance__ .

*To the Instructor:* In the paragraphs in Tests 3–6, the main ideas and transitions relevant to the pattern of organization are underlined in this *Instructor's Edition.*

*(Continues on next page)*

**C.** Read the paragraph and answer the questions that follow.

¹In recent years, health-care costs in the United States have skyrocketed. ²The result is that a large number of people—particularly the poor and those in the lower middle class—have not been able to afford health care. ³There are many reasons for the increase in health-care costs. ⁴One cause is the aging of the U.S. population. ⁵Greater numbers of older Americans have created added demand for medical care, leading to higher prices. ⁶Another reason that health-care costs are so high is that medical care is better. ⁷As a result, patients who once died quickly from conditions such as comas and strokes can now live much longer—but need expensive medical care that often goes on for years. ⁸Soaring costs have been caused as well by the way in which health care is used in the United States. ⁹American medicine tends to focus on treating a disease, not preventing it. ¹⁰Therefore, simple steps that could prevent illness and save money—such things as prenatal care and free exams for the elderly—are often ignored. ¹¹When people finally get to a doctor, they are more likely to have advanced problems that cost more money to treat.

_B_   8. The main pattern of organization in the selection is
    A. definition-example.
    B. cause-effect.               The paragraph discusses the causes (reasons)
    C. comparison-contrast.            for the rapid increase in health-care costs.

9–10. Two transitions that mark the paragraph's pattern of organization are
    _Any two of the following:_ result, reasons, cause, reason,
    _____
    As a result, caused, Therefore

## MORE RELATIONSHIPS IN READING: Mastery Test 4

**A.** (1–4.) Arrange the scrambled sentences below into a logical paragraph by numbering them *1, 2, 3,* and *4* in an order that makes sense. Then, in the space provided, write the letter of the main pattern of organization used.

Note that transitions will help you by making clear the relationships between sentences.

  2   For example, the tailbone is what remains of a tail, something our ancestors once needed to survive.

  3   Body hairs, too thin to keep us warm or protect our skin, are another example.

  1   Vestigial organs are those parts of our body that serve little or no purpose to us today but were useful to our pre-human ancestors.

  4   A final example, the appendix, is believed to have once helped our ancestors digest rough vegetable matter.

  D   5. The primary pattern of organization in the selection is
     A. comparison.
     B. contrast.                        The paragraph defines and gives examples
     C. cause and effect.                    of the term *vestigial organs*.
     D. definition and example.

**B.** Read the paragraph and answer the questions that follow.

¹Streetcars had dramatic effects on the character of city life. ²Before their introduction, cities were limited in size by the distances people could conveniently walk to work. ³The "walking city" could not easily extend more than two and a half miles from its center. ⁴Streetcars increased this radius to six miles or more. ⁵As a result, the area of a city expanded enormously. ⁶A later effect was a shift in population as those who were better off moved away from the center of the city. ⁷In search of air and space, they left the jam-packed older neighborhoods to the poor. ⁸This flight of middle-class people from urban centers led to the growth of inner-city ghettos.

  B   6. The main pattern of organization of the selection is
     A. definition-example.                 The paragraph discusses the effects
     B. cause-effect.                    streetcars had on city life. *As a result,*
     C. comparison.                          *effect,* and *led to* signal effects.

  7. One transition that signals the paragraph's pattern of organization is

     ___effects or As a result or effect or led to___ .

*(Continues on next page)*

**C.** Read the paragraph and answer the questions that follow.

[1]When life brings setbacks and tragedies to optimists, they weather those storms better than pessimists do. [2]Optimists look on the bright side. [3]They bounce back from defeat, and, with their lives perhaps somewhat poorer, they pick up and start again. [4]In contrast, pessimists give up and fall into depression. [5]Optimists take more risks to get what they want, while pessimists are so sure of failure they don't even try. [6]Optimists also have better health and may even live longer. [7]However, even when things go well for pessimists, they are haunted by fears of catastrophe.

___C___ 8. The main pattern of organization in the selection is
- A. cause-effect.
- B. comparison.
- C. contrast.

*The paragraph contrasts optimists and pessimists.*

9. One transition that signals this pattern of organization is
   ___In contrast or while or However___.

10. Another transition that signals the pattern of organization in the selection
    is ___In contrast or while or However___.

# MORE RELATIONSHIPS IN READING: Mastery Test 5

**A.** (1–4.) Arrange the scrambled sentences below into a logical paragraph by numbering them *1, 2, 3,* and *4* in an order that makes sense. Note that transitions will help you by making clear the relationships between sentences.

_4_ Or if you believe that a certain group has a particular talent, you may be disappointed when a member of that group cannot do what you expect.

_3_ For instance, if you believe that a particular group is pushy, you will automatically judge someone belonging to that group as pushy—without waiting to see what that person is really like.

_1_ Stereotyping is holding a set of beliefs about the general nature of a group of people.

_2_ It can greatly interfere with making accurate judgments about others.

_D_ 5. The primary pattern of organization in the selection is
    A. comparison.
    B. contrast.
    C. cause and effect.
    D. definition and example.

*The paragraph defines and illustrates the term stereotyping.*

**B.** Read the paragraph and answer the questions that follow.

¹The Industrial Revolution <u>led to</u> dramatic changes in American society. ²At the beginning of the nineteenth century, it could take weeks to produce a single shirt. ³Wool had to be turned into yarn, then dyed, made into fabric, and sewn into patterns—all by hand. ⁴When machines were introduced, this whole process could be done in a fraction of the time. ⁵Many workers' lives were <u>affected by</u> the industrial changes. ⁶Instead of working in their homes or on farms, men, women, and children were soon working twelve- and fourteen-hour days in factories. ⁷Workers such as tailors or carpenters, who previously had their own trade, found themselves employed in the very places that drove them out of business. ⁸Another <u>result</u> was that whole villages started being built around factories, providing families with jobs, houses, schools, churches, and stores—all in one place.

_B_ 6. The main pattern of organization of the selection is
    A. definition-example.
    B. cause-effect.
    C. comparison-contrast.

*The paragraph discusses the effects the Industrial Revolution had on American society.*

7. One transition that signals this pattern of organization is
    ___led to or affected by or result___.

*(Continues on next page)*

**C.** Read the paragraph and answer the questions that follow.

¹In a book titled *The Art of Loving*, a psychologist describes the difference between "mother love" and "father love." ²Mother love says, "I will always love you no matter what. ³Nothing you ever do or fail to do will make me stop loving you." ⁴On the other hand, father love says, "I will love you if you *earn* my love and respect. ⁵You must do things like obey me, get good grades, make the team, choose the right friends, get into a good college, and earn a good salary." ⁶In contrast to mother love, father love may seem harsh. ⁷But sometimes we want to hear that we are loved because we deserve it, not only because the other person cares for us without conditions.

_C_    8.  The main pattern of organization in the selection is
        A.  cause-effect.
        B.  comparison.                    The paragraph contrasts
        C.  contrast.                       mother love with father love.

9–10.  Two word signals that mark the paragraph's pattern of organization are
        _Any two of the following:_ difference, On the other hand,
                    In contrast, But

# MORE RELATIONSHIPS IN READING: Mastery Test 6

**A.** Read the textbook paragraph below. Then answer the question and complete the outline that follows.

> ¹There are some common <u>reasons</u> that small businesses fail. ²<u>One</u> is managers who don't have enough knowledge or experience. ³Some people think that managing a business is just "common sense." ⁴But if managers do not know how to make basic business decisions, they are unlikely to succeed in the long run. ⁵<u>Another</u> <u>reason</u> for failure is neglect. ⁶After the excitement of the grand opening, some business owners fail to focus on business as much as they should. ⁷Small-business owners who are unwilling to work long hours and perform many jobs are likely to fail. ⁸A <u>third</u> common <u>reason</u> small businesses fail is poor record-keeping. ⁹By keeping careful track of sales and costs, a manager can spot serious troubles and make changes before it is too late to do so. ¹⁰<u>Finally</u>, many small businesses fail <u>because of</u> lack of money. ¹¹Here is a well-known rule of thumb: A new business should have enough money to operate at least six months without earning a profit. ¹²Owners of new businesses are almost certain to fail if they expect to pay the second month's rent from the first month's profits.

_B_ 1. The patterns of organization of the paragraph are list of items and
   A. definition-example.
   B. cause-effect.
   C. comparison.
   D. contrast.

   *The paragraph discusses four causes (reasons) that make small businesses fail. The list words One, Another, third, and Finally signal the causes.*

2–5. Complete the outline of the paragraph by writing in the four major supporting details.        *Wording of answers may vary.*

   **Main idea: There are common reasons that small businesses fail.**

   1. Managers who lack enough knowledge or experience
   2. Neglect
   3. Poor record-keeping
   4. Lack of money

*To the Instructor:* In this test, the addition transitions that signal major details are double-underlined.

*(Continues on next page)*

**B.** Read the textbook paragraph below. Then answer the question and complete the map that follows.

> ¹When people get sick during the flu season, they are not always sure whether what they have caught is the flu or a cold. ²It's true that the symptoms of the two overlap. ³<u>However</u>, there are some distinct <u>differences</u> between cold and flu symptoms. ⁴<u>First of all</u>, people rarely get a fever when they have a cold. ⁵<u>In contrast</u>, people with the flu typically get a fever of about 100 to 104 degrees Fahrenheit, which lasts three to four days. ⁶<u>Also</u>, although a cold is at times accompanied by a headache, headaches are much more likely with the flu. ⁷<u>Third</u>, cold victims experience at most a few slight aches and pains. ⁸<u>But</u> aches and pains are a usual feature of the flu and can often be quite severe. ⁹<u>Finally</u>, even though a cold never exhausts its victims, someone with the flu may suffer extreme fatigue.

_D_    6.  The paragraph lists a series of
   A. definitions.
   B. examples.                    The paragraph contrasts cold and flu symptoms.
   C. comparisons.                     Four main differences are discussed.
   D. contrasts.

7–10.  Complete the map of the paragraph by writing in the missing supporting details.

_Wording of answers may vary._

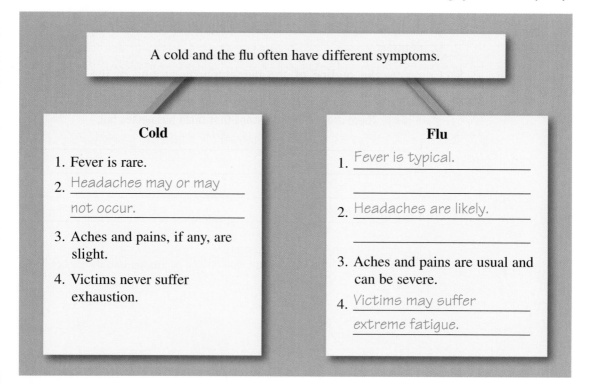

A cold and the flu often have different symptoms.

**Cold**

1. Fever is rare.
2. Headaches may or may not occur.
3. Aches and pains, if any, are slight.
4. Victims never suffer exhaustion.

**Flu**

1. Fever is typical.
2. Headaches are likely.
3. Aches and pains are usual and can be severe.
4. Victims may suffer extreme fatigue.

# 9 More Relationships in Writing

This chapter will show you how to write papers that involve illustration, comparison, contrast, and cause and effect—the patterns of organization you learned about in the previous chapter. **Just as a knowledge of these patterns can make you a better reader, it can also make you a better writer.**

When you learn and practice these new writing patterns, the goals of effective writing will remain the same:

1 Start with a main idea or point.

2 Provide truly specific details that support your main idea or point.

3 Think about your paper by using one or more of the prewriting strategies already discussed: freewriting (writing nonstop about your topic for ten minutes or so without worrying about mistakes while you think on paper); asking questions (*who, when, what, how,* and *why* about your topic); and list making (jotting down a random list of as many details as you can think of about your topic). Keep in mind that effective writing begins with messy prewriting!

4 The eventual result of your prewriting should be a scratch outline that shows at a glance your main idea and the key supporting items that support that main idea.

5 You can then go on to a first draft and later drafts, with revision and editing.

## The Illustration Pattern

Illustration paragraphs use one or more *examples* to clarify and support a main idea. Here is a cartoon that uses illustration, along with a list of the common illustration words you already saw on page 188.

In the cartoon, the man tries to use his statement that he is hungry and tired as an example that he shares deep emotions with his wife. (Of course, the joke in the cartoon is that his example is not a good one!)

Here are words that show illustration:

*Illustration Words*

| (for) example | (for) instance | to illustrate |
| including | such as | once |

Note that if you wrote the paper on page 129 on a good or bad day in your life, you've already done one examples paragraph. You'll now have a chance to do another.

## PRACTICE 1: Writing a Paragraph That Uses Examples

Write a paragraph that uses examples to support one of the following three main ideas:

- I have a friend named _____ who is his/her own worst enemy.

- Some students give the impression they don't want to be in college.

- Rudeness, a lack of concern for another person's feelings or comfort, is all too common in everyday life.

## A Model Paragraph

Here is one student's response to the assignment.

> <u>Rudeness, a lack of concern for another person's feelings or comfort, is all too common in everyday life.</u> For example, when the guy sitting beside you at the movie keeps texting his friends, his rude behavior is saying, "I don't care that you're trying to concentrate on the film and that my flashing screen is distracting you." When two cashiers are busy gossiping and ignore you as you wait to check out, their rude behavior is saying, "We don't care that we're wasting your time. You don't matter to us." When an elderly woman with a cane can't find a seat on the bus, and not one of the other riders stands up to offer her one, their rude behavior is saying, "You're old and have health problems? That's tough. Not my problem." When a group of co-workers make noisy plans to go to lunch together, leaving one employee behind, their rude behavior is saying, "Does being left out hurt your feelings? Who cares?" Whatever its form, rudeness leaves hurt feelings and discomfort behind.

- Underline the topic sentence—the sentence that expresses the main idea of the paragraph.

- Circle the number of examples that are provided in the paragraph to support the topic sentence:    1    2    3    (4)

## Writing Your Own Paragraph

**1.** As explained in Chapter 5, there are three prewriting techniques that can help you think about a paper: freewriting, questioning, and list making. Apply one of these techniques to each of the three topic sentences at the bottom of page 220. You might, for example:

- Ask yourself what are specific examples of how a friend of yours has been his or her worst enemy.

- Make a list of examples of students who reveal—by what they do or don't do—that they don't want to be in college.

- Freewrite for a page or two about examples of rude behavior you observe in everyday life.

**2.** These prewriting techniques will help you determine the topic sentence for which you'll be able to provide the best support. Choose that topic sentence to develop in your paper.

**3.** Make a scratch outline in which you list the three supporting items in your paper and the order in which you'll present them.

**4.** Go on to write the first draft of your paper. If you find that you get "stuck" in a major way in providing enough supporting information, remember that you can always go back and choose one of the other topic sentences instead.

**5.** When writing your paper, perhaps in the second draft, remember to use addition transitions—words such as *first, a second, also, another, a third, last of all*—to signal to your readers each of your three supporting items.

**6.** After you have completed your next-to-final draft, read it out loud to yourself. If you come upon snags in your reading, chances are there may be grammar or punctuation problems at those points. Consult a grammar handbook, if necessary, to see what corrections are needed. Make the required corrections so that every sentence in your paper reads smoothly and clearly.

# The Comparison Pattern

Comparison paragraphs show how two things are *like* each other. Here is a cartoon that uses comparison, along with a list of the common comparison words you already saw on page 193.

"What do you mean you can't marry me? We're perfect for each other. We look exactly alike, and we both love to swim."

In the cartoon, the words *alike* and *both* indicate that a comparison is being made: if the two goldfish are so much like each other, they deserve to be together.

Here are words that show comparison:

*Comparison Words*

| | | |
|---|---|---|
| (just) as | in like (similar) manner | same |
| (just) like | similar(ly) | in the same way |
| alike | similarity | resemble |
| likewise | both | equally |

## PRACTICE 2: Writing a Paragraph That Uses Comparison

Write a paragraph that supports one of the following three main ideas:

- In many ways, I am like my mother/father/grandmother/grandfather.

- All the places where I've lived have had some things in common.

- Two of my bosses/friends/coworkers/instructors/brothers/sisters are (*or* were) very much alike.

### A Model Paragraph

Here is one student's response to the assignment.

As I grow older, I am surprised to see how much I am like my dad. For one thing, I am introverted like Dad. It's not that we're unfriendly. Dad liked people just fine, and so do I. We just don't need to be around people much of the time. As Dad did, I enjoy spending time alone or with just one or two people I know very well. Another way that I am similar to Dad is that we both love to read. When I think of my dad, I picture him sitting in an easy chair in our living room, a book in his hand. There were always two or three books piled on his bedside table. I, too, am always reading at least one book. Right now there are four half-read books beside my bed. And like Dad, I like biographies best of all. The final way that I resemble my dad is my love of nature and gardening. Dad worked at a plant nursery all his life, and he had a big garden at home, where he grew vegetables and flowers. While he was outside, he was always noticing the wildlife around him and would comment on the deer or rabbit that he saw, or the red-tailed hawk that was soaring overhead. As

I have grown older, I have discovered a <u>similar</u> love for gardening and for observing wildlife. As soon as the weather becomes warm in the spring, I am outdoors digging, planting, and weeding. As I work outside, I love watching the birds build their nests and the curious rabbits watching me from a distance. Whether I'm spending time alone, reading, or gardening, I feel my dad is with me.

- Underline the topic sentence—the sentence that expresses the main idea of the above paragraph.

- Underline the comparison words that are used in the paragraph.

- Circle the addition words that move the reader from one point of comparison to the next.

### Writing Your Own Paragraph

Pick out—or create from scratch—a topic sentence you think you might be able to write about. Then explore that topic by freewriting about it, or asking questions such as *what, when, where, how,* and *why* about it, or making a list of all the details you can think of about it. Prewriting will help you determine the topic for which you can provide the best supporting details.

See if you can develop the topic with even more details, and prepare a scratch outline of the paragraph. Then go on to write the first and later drafts of your paper. When you think you have the final draft of your paper, read it aloud to make sure that every sentence reads smoothly and clearly. If that is not the case, you still have a bit of work to do. Use a grammar handbook, if necessary, to see what corrections are needed. Make the required corrections to remove these trouble spots.

# The Contrast Pattern

Contrast paragraphs show how two things are *different*. We might, for example, contrast two instructors, two jobs, or two friends. Contrast helps us understand the two things more clearly and why we feel the way we do about them. Here is a cartoon that uses contrast, along with the common contrast words you already saw on page 195.

"Smoking may kill me. On the other hand, the non-smokers
are inside working themselves to death."

In the cartoon, the speaker is contrasting two possible ways to die.
Here are common words that show contrast:

*Contrast Words*

| | | | |
|---|---|---|---|
| but | instead | still | difference |
| yet | in contrast | as opposed to | different(ly) |
| however | on the other hand | in spite of | differs from |
| although | on the contrary | despite | unlike |
| nevertheless | even though | rather than | while |

## PRACTICE 3: Writing a Paragraph That Uses Contrast

Write a paragraph about two quite different people or events or things. You may
use one of the following main ideas, or start with a topic sentence of your own:

- In many ways, I am different from my mother/father/grandmother/
grandfather.

- Two people I know have sharply different driving habits (*or* spending
habits)/ways of relaxing/approaches to studying (*or* approaches to work).

- My attitudes and behavior today are different from my attitudes and
behavior in the past.

## A Model Paragraph

Here is one student's response to the assignment.

> My daughter's way of doing homework is very, very different from the way I did my homework, years ago. First of all, I did my homework in the family den, because that is where the typewriter (for writing my papers) and the telephone (for keeping in touch with my friends) were. However, my daughter does her homework in her room, in coffee shops, at friends' houses, or wherever else she wants, because her laptop computer and her cell phone are portable. A second difference is that when I did homework, especially research papers, I spent a lot of time at the library. That's where the encyclopedias and other research materials were. But my daughter does all of her research on the Internet; she only visits the library to check out books. In addition, I kept track of homework assignments the only way I could—by writing them down in a notebook. My daughter, on the other hand, can go online to her teachers' websites to see what work is assigned. And finally, I handed in homework by, well, handing it to my teacher. In many cases, my daughter e-mails her assignments to her instructors.

- Underline the topic sentence—the sentence that expresses the main idea of the above paragraph.

- Underline the contrast words that are used in the paragraph.

- Circle the addition words that move the reader from one point of contrast to the next.

## Writing Your Own Paragraph

Pick out—or create from scratch—a topic sentence you think you might be able to write about. Then explore that topic by freewriting about it, or asking questions such as *what, when, where, how,* and *why* about it, or making a list of all the details you can think of about it. Prewriting will help you determine the topic for which you can provide the best supporting details.

See if you can develop the topic with even more details, and prepare a scratch outline of the paragraph. Then go on to write the first and later drafts of your paper. When you think you have the final draft of your paper, read it aloud to make sure that every sentence reads smoothly and clearly. If that is not the case, you still have a bit of work to do. Use a grammar handbook, if necessary, to see what corrections are needed. Make the required corrections to remove these trouble spots.

# The Cause and Effect Pattern

Cause and effect paragraphs show *reasons* or *results*. They seek to explain the *causes* of some behavior or event. Or they describe the *effects* or *consequences* of some behavior or event. Here are two cartoons that use cause and effect.

In the first cartoon, the doctor explains that the man's red spots are caused by pepperoni pizza. In the second cartoon, the doctor says the man's cactus appearance is the result of not drinking enough water.

Here are words that show cause and effect:

### Cause and Effect Words

| | | | |
|---|---|---|---|
| therefore | so | owing to | because (of) |
| thus | (as a) result | effect | reason |
| (as a) consequence | results in | cause | explanation |
| consequently | leads to | if . . . then | accordingly |
| due to | since | affect | |

## PRACTICE 4: Writing a Paragraph That Uses Cause and Effect

Write a paragraph that uses one of the following main ideas, or start with a topic sentence of your own:

- For three reasons, working as a waitress/in the office/as a stock boy (*or fill in another job:* _____ ) was the worst job I ever had.

- A family member/teacher/friend has greatly influenced my education.

- Working while I'm going to school makes for real challenges in my life.

## A Model Paragraph

Here is one student's response to the assignment.

> I'm the first person in my family to ever go to college. When I graduate—and I will—it will be due to the influence of my older sister, Marisa. (One) reason I want to stay in college is her honesty about her own life. Like many women in my family, Marisa had a baby when she was very young. Marisa loves her daughter, but she's truthful about how being a mom has caused her to limit her choices. "With a baby, I don't have the time or money to go to school," she says. "Get your education before you have a kid." (Secondly), Marisa defends me when other people criticize what I'm doing. When people say I'm acting like I'm better than them, or that I should be helping more around the house instead of studying, Marisa gets in their faces. "You're just jealous since she's making something of herself," she'll say. "You should support what she's doing, not criticize." And (last), Marisa gives me material help whenever she can. Her money is tight, but if she knows I need to buy a textbook, then she'll slip me some money out of her paycheck. She noticed that my backpack was falling apart and surprised me with a new one. Because of Marisa's love and help, I have the courage to keep going.

- Underline the topic sentence—the sentence that states the main idea of the paragraph. (You'll note it is not the first sentence. Sometimes a paragraph begins with an introductory sentence or two.)
- Underline the cause and effect words that are used in the paragraph.
- Circle the addition words that move the reader from one cause to the next.

## Writing Your Own Paragraph

Pick out—or create from scratch—a topic sentence you think you might be able to write about. Then explore that topic by freewriting about it, or asking questions such as *what, when, where, how,* and *why* about it, or making a list of all the details you can think of about it. Prewriting will help you determine the topic for which you can provide the best supporting details.

See if you can develop the topic with even more details, and prepare a scratch outline of the paragraph. Then go on to write the first and later drafts of your paper. When you think you have the final draft of your paper, read it aloud to make sure that every sentence reads smoothly and clearly. If that is not the case, you still have a bit of work to do. Use a grammar handbook, if necessary, to see what corrections are needed. Make the required corrections to remove these trouble spots.

# MORE RELATIONSHIPS IN WRITING: Mastery Test 1

**A.** Complete each sentence with a suitable illustration word from the box below. Use each transition once. Then, in the space provided, write the letter of the transition you have chosen.

| | | |
|---|---|---|
| **A. for example** | **B. for instance** | **C. including** |
| **D. once** | **E. such as** | |

*Hint:* Make sure that each word or phrase that you choose fits smoothly into the flow of the sentence. Test each choice by reading the sentence to yourself.

_D_ 1. A cat's curiosity can get it into ridiculous situations. _____*Once*_____ my cat got its head stuck in our garbage disposal.

_B_ 2. Our grandmother doesn't hear well anyone. ____*For instance*____, whenever I say, "Hi, Granny," she answers, "Fine, just fine."

_A_ 3. Some soap opera fans take the shows too seriously. There are viewers, _____*for example*_____, who actually send threats to soap opera "villains."

_C_ 4. Because I hope to work with children, I am considering a number of career choices, _____*including*_____ teaching, school counseling, and working at a day-care center.

_E_ 5. Camping in the woods is not like sleeping in your bed at home. You have to worry about matters _____*such as*_____ insects, snakes, and what to use as a bathroom in the middle of the night.

*(Continues on next page)*

**B.** Complete each sentence with a suitable comparison word from the box below. Try to use each transition once. Then, in the space provided, write the letter of the transition you have chosen.

| | | |
|---|---|---|
| **A. in the same way** | **B. just as** | **C. likewise** |
| **D. resembles** | **E. similarly** | |

*Hint:* Make sure that each word or phrase that you choose fits smoothly into the flow of the sentence. Test each choice by reading the sentence to yourself.

___E___  1.  Driving a car is a skill that we learn through practice. ____Similarly____, writing a paper is a skill that we learn through hands-on experience.

___A___  2.  Spicy foods make me very thirsty. Believe it or not, ice cream affects me ____in the same way____.

___C___  3.  Texting on your lighted cell phone in a darkened theater will not win you any friends. ____Likewise____, talking out loud with your movie partner will soon make people scowl in your direction.

___B___  4.  ____Just as____ rats become hostile when they live in a crowded cage, humans become aggressive in crowded conditions.

___D___  5.  I tell my teenage brother he ____resembles____ a cockroach—he enjoys going out at night and eating junk food.

# MORE RELATIONSHIPS IN WRITING: Mastery Test 2

**A.** Complete each sentence with a suitable contrast word from the box below. Use each transition once. Then, in the space provided, write the letter of the transition you have chosen.

| | | |
|---|---|---|
| **A. although** | **B. but** | **C. despite** |
| **D. in contrast** | **E. on the other hand** | |

*Hint:* Make sure that each word or phrase that you choose fits smoothly into the flow of the sentence. Test each choice by reading the sentence to yourself.

__E__ 1. A cup of coffee can give you a quick energy boost. _On the other hand_, too much coffee can make you irritable and unable to sleep at night.

__A__ 2. _Although_ climbing up a ladder is easy enough, looking down from the top can be difficult.

__B__ 3. At first my family planned on vacationing at a campground, _but_ then we decided to save money by relaxing at home.

__C__ 4. I was not satisfied with the paper _despite_ the fact I had already written three drafts.

__D__ 5. We use seventeen muscles to smile. _In contrast_, we have to use forty-three muscles to frown.

*(Continues on next page)*

**B.** Complete each sentence with a suitable cause and effect word from the box below. Use each transition once. Then, in the space provided, write the letter of the transition you have chosen.

| | | |
|---|---|---|
| A. as a result | B. because | C. if |
| D. reason | E. therefore | |

*Hint:* Make sure that each word or phrase that you choose fits smoothly into the flow of the sentence. Test each choice by reading the sentence to yourself.

___B___  1. Students who have to work full-time sometimes nap during classes _____because_____ they are tired after work.

___D___  2. One _____reason_____ for our lower electric bills is that we stopped using air conditioning.

___A___  3. My sister decided she didn't want to eat anything that had a mother; _____as a result_____, she became a vegetarian.

___C___  4. _____If_____ the weather gets too humid, the wooden doors and windows in our house swell up and begin to stick.

___E___  5. I didn't want to graduate from college with a lot of debt. _____Therefore_____, I worked my way through school at a local community college.

## MORE RELATIONSHIPS IN WRITING: Mastery Test 3

Following are four paragraphs that use either illustration, comparison, contrast, or cause and effect. Fill in the blanks in each paragraph with an appropriate transition from the box. Use each transition once. Then answer the questions that follow each paragraph.

1.

| but | in contrast | however |
|---|---|---|

The paragraph contrasts how children behave at home with how they have to behave at school. The transitions in the box are all contrast words.

¹Young children in school have to make important adjustments. ²At home, children may have been able to do what they wanted. ³____In contrast____, in school they are given set times to work, talk, play, or even go to the bathroom. ⁴At home, they are corrected in private for their mistakes. ⁵_____But_____ in school, there may be a public method of discipline, and they may be scolded in front of their classmates. ⁶Finally, at home children may not have to compete for attention. ⁷____However____, in school children may have to compete to get stars on a paper or approving glances or words from the teacher.

● What is the main idea, or point, of the paragraph? _Young children in_ _school have to make important adjustments._

● __C__ Which pattern of organization is used in the paragraph?

A. Illustration      C. Contrast
B. Comparison      D. Cause and effect

2.

| example | for instance |
|---|---|

The paragraph presents several examples of tell signs, each introduced with an illustration transition.

¹"Tell signs" are nonverbal clues that a person may be lying. ²____For instance____, if a person is making more obvious hand gestures than normal, or scratching the head or neck, he or she may not be telling the truth. ³These gestures suggest a subconscious effort to rub out an untrue statement. ⁴Another ____example____ of a tell sign is a repeated shrugging of the shoulders, which may be a subconscious way to contradict what has just been said.

● What is the main idea, or point, of the paragraph? _"Tell signs" are_ _nonverbal clues that a person may be lying._

● __A__ Which pattern of organization is used in the paragraph?

A. Illustration      C. Contrast
B. Comparison      D. Cause and effect

*(Continues on next page)*

233

3.

| both | just like | resemble | similar |
|------|-----------|----------|---------|

The paragraph compares the writer to his or her brother: they have similar physical qualities, tastes, dislike of phone conversations, sense of humor, and politics. The transitions in the box are all comparison words.

¹As different as we are, my brother and I still ____resemble____ each other in some ways. ²We are somewhat ____similar____ in appearance, with our fair skin, sandy-colored hair, and green eyes. ³We also tend to like the same music, books, and movies, and often recommend those to each other. ⁴____Just like____ my brother, I don't much like talking on the phone, so we usually communicate through e-mail. ⁵We share the same sense of humor, too; something that makes one of us laugh will almost always amuse the other. ⁶In addition, we ____both____ generally vote for the same candidates.

● What is the main idea, or point, of the paragraph? _As different as we are, my brother and I still resemble each other in some ways._

● __B__ The pattern of organization of the above selection is
   A. illustration.          C. contrast.
   B. comparison.          D. cause and effect.

4.

| caused | lead to | result |
|--------|---------|--------|

The paragraph gives four causes ("various reasons") for hair loss among young people: normal bodily changes, medical problems, undernourishment, and allergic reactions to hair products. The transitions in the box are all cause and effect words.

¹Teens and young adults lose hair for various reasons. ²As part of the normal changes in the body, they can expect to lose about one hundred hairs per day. ³Medical problems may ____lead to____ more hair loss. ⁴Abnormal hair loss may also be ____caused____ by undernourishment, so teens should be mindful of their diet. ⁵And significant hair loss can ____result____ from allergic reactions to dyes or hair straighteners.

● What is the main idea, or point, of the paragraph? _Teens and young adults lose hair for various reasons._

● __D__ The pattern of organization of the above selection is
   A. illustration.          C. contrast.
   B. comparison.          D. cause and effect.

## MORE RELATIONSHIPS IN WRITING: Mastery Test 4

Write a paragraph that uses examples to support its point. You may want to choose one of the following ideas that you have not written about:

- I have a friend named _____ who is his/her own worst enemy.
- Some students give the impression they don't want to be in college.
- Many television commercials appear to assume that people are complete idiots.

### A Model Paragraph

You have already seen on page 221 a model paragraph that uses *illustration*. Here is another model paragraph:

I have a friend named Victor who is charming, intelligent, and talented. I like him very much, but I am also so frustrated with him I can hardly stand it. Of Victor I can truly say, "He is his own worst enemy." Victor is now in his late twenties, and he's just moved back in with his parents for the fourth or fifth time. Almost every time I talk with Victor, he has an ambitious new life plan. At one point he decided, for instance, that he wanted to sell luxury automobiles. Because Victor is so smooth and charming, he actually got an entry-level sales job at a BMW dealership. True to form, he did extremely well at it . . . for about six months. Then he decided he wasn't really interested in selling cars. Instead, he wanted to go to nursing school. "Terrific!" all his friends said. "You're smart; you're compassionate; you'll make a wonderful nurse!" He got all his paperwork done, enrolled in nursing school, and dropped out after a semester. Again, he decided that nursing wasn't really his thing. Next, I think, he went to work at an electronics store. He got off to such a great start that within a couple of months, his boss was talking about sending him to open a new store out of state. But guess what? Right. He lost interest and quit. Now he's living with his parents, sleeping in the bedroom he lived in when he was twelve, and thinking up another great life plan. But unless he makes a radical change, he'll find a way to ruin that plan as well.

*(Continues on next page)*

● Underline the topic sentence—the sentence that expresses the main idea of the above paragraph. (It is not the first sentence. Sometimes a paragraph can begin with an introductory sentence or two.)

● Circle the number of examples that are provided in the paragraph to support the topic sentence:  1    2    ③    4

## Writing Your Own Paragraph

Pick out—or create from scratch—a topic sentence you think you might be able to write about. Then explore that topic by freewriting about it, or asking questions such as *what, when, where, how,* and *why* about it, or making a list of all the details you can think of about it. Prewriting will help you determine the topic for which you can provide the best supporting details.

See if you can develop the topic with even more details, and prepare a scratch outline of the paragraph. Then go on to write the first and later drafts of your paper. When you think you have the final draft of your paper, read it aloud to make sure that every sentence reads smoothly and clearly. Use a grammar handbook, if necessary, to see what corrections are needed. Make the required corrections to remove the trouble spots.

*To the Instructor:*
A student's score on this test should be based on your evaluation of whether he or she has written an A, B, C, D, or F paper.

Suggested equivalents:

A = 90 to 100
B = 80 to 89
C = 70 to 79
D = 60 to 69
F = 59 and below

# MORE RELATIONSHIPS IN WRITING: Mastery Test 5

Write a paragraph that uses *comparison* or *contrast* to support its point. You may want to choose one of the following ideas that you have not yet written about:

- In many ways, I am like my mother/father/grandmother/grandfather.

- All the places where I've lived have had some things in common.

- Two of my bosses/friends/coworkers/instructors/brothers/sisters are (*or* were) very much alike.

- In many ways I am very different from my mother/father/grandmother/grandfather.

- Two people I know have sharply different driving habits (*or* spending habits), ways of relaxing, approaches to studying (*or* approaches to work).

- My attitudes and behavior today are different from my attitudes and behavior in the past.

## A Model Paragraph

You have already seen on pages 223–224 and 226 model paragraphs that use comparison and contrast. Here is another model paragraph—one that uses contrast:

> When I began attending community college this fall, I thought I knew what to expect. After all, I'd been in school for years. I thought college would be just an extension of high school. But I have found college to be much different than I had expected. For one thing, I had expected to make a bunch of new college friends quickly. I thought I'd be in many of the same classes with the same students, and that we'd get to know each other easily. Instead, I rarely see my fellow students outside of the particular class we take together. They either leave campus or go to class in another building, and I don't see them again until our next class. I'm also surprised by how quickly my classes became demanding. In high school, we'd spend a week or so getting settled before the real work would begin. However, in college the instructors expect us to show up to the first class ready to work, with our textbooks purchased and our notebooks open. And finally, as one of my instructors said on the first day, "Your instructors are not your mom." In high school, I was used to our teachers reminding us several times when assignments were due and

*(Continues on next page)*

> giving us extra chances if we forgot something. *But in college, the instructors hand out the syllabus and expect us to keep track of due dates without reminders.*

- Underline the topic sentence that expresses the main idea of the above paragraph. (It is not the first sentence. Sometimes a paragraph can begin with an introductory sentence or two.)

- Underline the contrast words used in the paragraph.

- Circle the addition words that move the reader from one point of contrast to the next.

## Writing Your Own Paragraph

Pick out—or create from scratch—a topic sentence you think you might be able to write about. Then explore that topic by freewriting about it, or asking questions such as *what, when, where, how,* and *why* about it, or making a list of all the details you can think of about it. Prewriting will help you determine the topic for which you can provide the best supporting details.

See if you can develop the topic with even more details, and prepare a scratch outline of the paragraph. Then go on to write the first and later drafts of your paper. When you think you have the final draft of your paper, read it aloud to make sure that every sentence reads smoothly and clearly. Use a grammar handbook, if necessary, to see what corrections are needed. Make the required corrections to remove the trouble spots.

*To the Instructor:*
A student's score on this test should be based on your evaluation of whether he or she has written an A, B, C, D, or F paper.

Suggested equivalents:

A = 90 to 100
B = 80 to 89
C = 70 to 79
D = 60 to 69
F = 59 and below

# MORE RELATIONSHIPS IN WRITING: Mastery Test 6

Write a paragraph that uses *cause* or *effect* to support its point. You may want to choose one of the following ideas that you have not yet written about:

- For three reasons, working as a waitress/in the office/as a stock boy/ [*other job*_____] was the worst job I ever had.

- My bad habit of smoking cigarettes/eating junk food [*or some other bad habit*] has had several effects in my life.

- A family member/teacher/friend has been a major influence on my education.

- Working at the same time I'm going to school makes for real challenges in my life.

- Several events in my life help explain why I've become the person I am today.

- For several reasons, I have changed the political/religious views I used to hold.

## A Model Paragraph

You have already seen on page 228 a model paragraph that uses cause/effect. Here is another model paragraph.

> I've had jobs that were boring. I've had jobs that were hard. But I've had only one job that I've really, truly hated. For three unforgettable reasons, working as a waitress at DaVinci's Italian Restaurant was the worst job I've ever had. The first awful thing about the job was that the management was completely disorganized. At least twice I showed up for work only to be told, "Oh, you're on a different shift this week. Didn't anybody tell you?" The kitchen staff was constantly changing; half the time I didn't know who was cooking and if I could rely on them. The second awful thing about the job was that that DaVinci's food was terrible. I dreaded seeing the disgusted look on diners' faces as they called me over to complain about the greasy veal parmesan or the meatballs that still had ice crystals in them. Even though I had nothing to do with the cooking, the customers took out their frustration on me, and sometimes I'd get no tip at all. But the absolute worst thing about the job was that the restaurant was dirty. It looked presentable in the dining area, but behind the scenes, it was horrible.

*(Continues on next page)*

> There were mouse droppings and cockroaches in the kitchen. The cooks never washed their hands, even after using the bathroom or blowing their noses. If food fell on the floor, they would pick it up and put it back on the customer's plate. Needless to say, I did not work at DaVinci's for very long. And needless to say, I never ate there.

- Underline the topic sentence—the sentence that expresses the main idea of the above paragraph. (It is not the first sentence. Sometimes a paragraph can begin with an introductory sentence or two.)

- Circle the addition words that move the reader from one reason to the next.

## Writing Your Own Paragraph

Pick out—or create from scratch—a topic sentence you think you might be able to write about. Then explore that topic by freewriting about it, or asking questions such as *what, when, where, how,* and *why* about it, or making a list of all the details you can think of about it. Prewriting will help you determine the topic for which you can provide the best supporting details.

See if you can develop the topic with even more details, and prepare a scratch outline of the paragraph. Then go on to write the first and later drafts of your paper. When you think you have the final draft of your paper, read it aloud to make sure that every sentence reads smoothly and clearly. Use a grammar handbook, if necessary, to see what corrections are needed. Make the required corrections to remove the trouble spots.

*To the Instructor:*
A student's score on this test should be based on your evaluation of whether he or she has written an A, B, C, D, or F paper.
Suggested equivalents:
  A = 90 to 100
  B = 80 to 89
  C = 70 to 79
  D = 60 to 69
  F = 59 and below

# Inferences in Reading and Writing

## Inferences in Reading

**A** good reader is able to recognize not only directly stated ideas but also implied ideas. This chapter will help develop your ability to make inferences—ideas that are not stated directly.

### An Introduction to Inferences

**Inferences** are ideas that are suggested, but not stated. They are conclusions we draw from what we see, hear, and read.

Look at the cartoon below. What conclusions can you draw about it? Check (✓) the **two** inferences that are most logically based on the information suggested by the cartoon. Then read the explanation on the next page.

"It's Junior's report card. The good news is that he's passing his gym class."

_____ 1. The parents have several children in school.

✓ 2. Junior is not doing well in most subjects.

_____ 3. The parents are angry about Junior's grades.

✓ 4. The wife is trying to be positive about a bad situation.

_____ 5. The parents were both good students when they were in school.

*Explanation*

1. Nothing in the cartoon indicates that the husband and wife have other children. The only child they are talking about is Junior.

2. If "the good news" is that Junior is passing gym, we can infer that there is also bad news: he is not passing some, or even all, of his other classes. You should have checked this item.

3. Nothing suggests that the husband or the wife is angry. They might, for example, be used to Junior's poor performance in academic subjects.

4. By presenting "the good news" about gym class first, the wife is trying to be as positive as possible. You should also have checked this item.

5. There is no evidence that the husband and wife were good students. In fact, they might have had the same kind of academic difficulties as their son, but there's no way to tell.

We make inferences all the time. We hear a sound in the night and infer it is just a squirrel on the roof. We walk into a friend's house for dinner, and the smells coming from the kitchen help us infer that we are about to have a delicious meal. We greet someone and infer from that person's body language or tone of voice that something is troubling him or her. We sense the air suddenly getting cooler and the light changing in the sky and infer that a storm is approaching.

With visual material such as cartoons, book covers, and photographs, we can infer a great deal from all the clues provided. With written material, we can "read between the lines" and pick up ideas the author only suggests, or implies. This chapter will give you practice in making inferences from a variety of reading materials.

## Inferences about Reading Materials

You have already practiced making inferences while reading an earlier chapter of this book. Do you remember, for example, the following sentence from "Vocabulary Development for Reading and Writing"?

In the United States, shaking hands is the *appropriate* way to greet someone; in China, bowing is the right way.

The sentence does not give us a definition of *appropriate*, but it does suggest that *appropriate* is close in meaning to "right." Thus we can infer in this sentence that *appropriate* means "right" or "proper." As you looked at all the sentences in Chapter 1, you inferred the meanings of words by looking closely at the surrounding context.

In all of our everyday reading, we make logical leaps from the information given directly on the page to ideas that are not stated directly. To draw such inferences, we use the clues provided by the writer, and we also apply our own experience, logic, and common sense.

## Inferences in Passages

Read the following passage and then check (✓) the **two** inferences that are most firmly based on the given information.

> [1]I once hired a roofer to put a new roof on my home. [2]He checked the roof and then quoted me a price of $1,000. [3]I agreed. [4]He tore the old roof off, then came back down. [5]I noticed a barely hidden smile on his face.
>
> [6]"Sorry," he said, "it's gonna cost you $1,800. [7]I didn't know it needed so much work."
>
> [8]"No way," I said, folding my arms.
>
> [9]"Whatever you say," the roofer said. [10]He looked up at the sky and commented, "You know, it looks like rain."
>
> [11]I sighed, shook my head, and said, "With my luck, it will rain for three days. [12]Finish the job."

✓   1. At first, the author did not want to spend the extra $800.

____   2. The author's old roof would have held up for another year or two.

✓   3. The roofer may have planned all along to raise the price after the old roof was torn off.

____   4. The author believes that all roofers are con men.

____   5. The roofer had been recommended to the author.

*Explanation*

1. When the roofer first tells the author that the job would cost $1,800, the author says, "No way." Using our common sense, we can conclude that the author of the selection refuses because he doesn't want to spend the extra $800. So you should have checked this item.

2. Nothing in the passage discusses the actual quality of the roof. You should not have checked this item.

3. The roofer says, "I didn't know [the roof] needed so much work." However, in telling us that the roofer had a smile on his face, the author implies that the roofer may have known all along that he planned on charging an extra $800. So you should have checked this item.

4. The passage makes no mention of the author's view of all roofers. We see only his reaction to this roofer. You should not have checked this item.

5. There is no mention in the passage of how the author came to hire the roofer. You should not have checked this item.

## ✓ *Check Your Understanding*

Now read the following textbook passage. Then answer the questions about it by writing the letters of the inferences that are most firmly based on the given information. Hints are provided to help you think through the choices for each question.

> [1]A twenty-eight-year-old woman named Catherine Genovese was returning home from work one day. [2]Kitty, as she was called by almost everyone in her Queens neighborhood, had just parked her car. [3]Then a man with a knife grabbed her. [4]She screamed, "Oh my God, he stabbed me! [5]Please help me! [6]Please help me!"
>
> [7]For more than half an hour, thirty-eight neighbors listened to Kitty's screams as the attack continued. [8]The last time he stabbed her, she was slumped on the foot of the stairs to her apartment. [9]Not one person telephoned the police during the fatal attack. [10]Later, the police gathered statements from the witnesses. [11]Among their comments were, "I didn't want to get involved," "We thought it was a lovers' quarrel," and "I was tired. [12]I went back to bed."

_B_ 1. We can infer that Kitty was attacked
   A. while she was on vacation.
   B. in her own neighborhood.
   C. on her way from work to her car.

   *Hint:* The passage tells us that Genovese "was returning home from work" and that she "had just parked her car."

_B_ 2. We can conclude that the man who stabbed Genovese
   A. was someone she knew.
   B. intended to kill her.
   C. was a convicted criminal.

   *Hint:* Is there evidence that Genovese knew her killer or that he was a convicted criminal? Also, Genovese's killer stabbed her even after he was sure she was wounded and weak.

_A_ 3. We can infer that the witnesses
   A. might have stopped the attack if they had called the police.
   B. wanted the man to kill Genovese.
   C. would not want someone else to get involved if they themselves were being attacked.

   *Hint:* The attack continued for at least half an hour.

### Explanation

Here is an explanation of each item:

1. The answer to the first question is B. We have solid evidence to conclude that Genovese was attacked in her neighborhood: she was returning home from work and had parked her car. Since she was returning home from

work, she was not on vacation. Also, we know she had just parked her car after coming home from work. So the attack could not have taken place before she got into the car to go home.

2. The answer to the second question is B. We can conclude that Genovese's attacker wanted to kill her. If his goal was to rob or rape her, he could have done so long before the last time he stabbed her. And no evidence in the passage indicates that Genovese knew her attacker. Finally, although we cannot be sure the attacker was never convicted of a crime, there is absolutely no evidence in the passage to support the conclusion that he was—his past is not referred to at all.

3. The answer to the third question is A. The crime took at least a half hour; thus we can conclude that if the police had been called, there is a chance they would have arrived in time to save Genovese. However, we have no reason to believe the witnesses actually wanted the man to kill Genovese. Most people, in fact, would be horrified to see someone stabbed to death. And on the basis of our knowledge of human nature, we can be pretty sure the witnesses would have wanted others to get involved if they were victims.

## Guidelines for Making Inferences

The exercises in this chapter provide practice in making careful inferences when you read. Here are three guidelines to that process:

1   **Never lose sight of the available information.**   As much as possible, base your inferences on the facts. For instance, in the paragraph about Kitty Genovese's attack, we are told that she "was returning home from work." On the basis of that fact, we can readily conclude that she was not on vacation.

It's also important to note when a conclusion lacks support. For instance, the idea that the attacker was a convicted criminal has no support in the selection. We are told of only one instance of his criminal behavior, the attack on Genovese.

2   **Use your background knowledge, experience, and common sense to help you in making inferences.**   Our experience with people, for instance, tells us that witnesses would themselves have wanted help if they had been in Genovese's place.

The more you know about a subject, the better your inferences are likely to be. So keep in mind that if your background in an area is weak, your inferences may be shaky. If you are having study problems, for example, the inferences of a tutor about what you need to do are likely to be more helpful than those of another student.

3   **Consider the alternatives.**   Don't simply accept the first inference that comes to mind. Instead, consider all of the facts of a case and all the possible explanations. For example, the tutor may be aware of many helpful study habits that would work for you.

**PRACTICE 1**

Read each of the following passages. Then write the letter of the most logical answer to each question, based on the information given in the passage.

**A.** ¹When Oprah Winfrey was a child, she lived with her mother and two younger half-siblings in a Milwaukee apartment without electricity or running water. ²One Christmas Eve, her mother told her there would be no celebration that year. ³There was no money to buy presents. ⁴"But what about Santa Claus?" Oprah asked. ⁵Her mother answered that there wasn't enough money to pay Santa to come. ⁶As she went to bed that night, Oprah dreaded the following day. ⁷She knew the neighbor children would be outside playing with their toys and comparing presents. ⁸She tried to think of a story she could tell the other kids to explain why she had nothing. ⁹Then she heard the doorbell ring. ¹⁰Three nuns had come to the apartment. ¹¹They brought a turkey, a fruit basket, and toys for the children. ¹²"I've never had a stronger feeling of someone lifting me up," she says today. ¹³"Their kindness made me feel so much better about myself." ¹⁴Oprah remembers that Christmas as the best she ever had.

_C_   1. We can infer that before the nuns came, Oprah dreaded the next day because she
   A. would not have any new toys to play with at home.
   B. now knew Santa Claus was not real.
   C. would be shamed in front of her friends.

   *Hint:* The paragraph tells us Oprah "knew the neighbor children would be outside . . . comparing presents" and that she felt she'd have to "think of a story she could tell the other kids to explain why she had nothing."

_A_   2. We can conclude this was Oprah's best Christmas because
   A. she was so relieved and grateful for what the nuns had done.
   B. the toys she received were exactly what she had wanted.
   C. she had never received Christmas presents before.

   *Hint:* The paragraph says that after the nuns arrived, Oprah had the "feeling of someone lifting" her up and felt "so much better" about herself.

_B_   3. What can we infer Oprah would most likely have done the next day if the nuns had not come?
   A. She would have been angry and hostile toward her mother.
   B. She would have made up a lie about the presents somehow being delayed.
   C. She would have gone out and stolen some toys.

   *Hint:* The passage states that Oprah knew the next day "the neighbor children would be outside playing with their toys and comparing presents" and that she "tried to think of a story she could tell the other kids to explain why she had nothing."

**B.** ¹The British prime minister Winston Churchill was a master of the elegant put-down. ²At one fancy dinner party, he was seated next to a favorite target—a woman whose political views were opposed to his own. ³The two argued more or less continually throughout the meal. ⁴Totally annoyed, the lady said, "Sir Winston, if you were my husband, I'd put poison in your coffee!" ⁵"Madam," replied Churchill, "if you were my wife, I'd drink it."

_B_   4. We can conclude that Churchill

The first sentence suggests that Churchill was known for "the elegant putdown," and the next sentence tells us his "favorite target" was a political opponent.

  A. constantly put people down.
  B. liked to put down his political opponents.
  C. was rarely invited to fancy dinner parties.

**Item 5:**
Answers A and B are not supported. Answer C can be inferred. Churchill so disliked the woman's company, his joke suggests, that he'd rather die than be married to her.

_C_   5. When Churchill said, "If you were my wife, I'd drink it," he meant to imply that
  A. he admired the woman so much he would do whatever she said.
  B. he would never insult the woman by refusing her coffee.
  C. if she were his wife, he would prefer to die.

_C_   6. We can conclude that the author of the passage admires
  A. Churchill's politics.
  B. the woman's politics.
  C. Churchill's wit.

Answers A and B are not supported. Answer C can be inferred. The description of Churchill as "the master of the elegant putdown" reveals the author's admiration for his wit.

## PRACTICE 2

The ability to make inferences will help you in all kinds of reading, including textbook material. Read the following textbook passages. Then, for each passage, check (✓) the **two** inferences that are most logically based on the given facts.

**A.** ¹A question that interests many is why a woman will remain with a husband who abuses her. ²Interviews with violent families revealed that the decision is related to three major factors. ³First, the more severe and more frequent the violence, the more a woman is likely to end her marriage or to seek help from social agencies or the police. ⁴The second factor has to do with how much violence she experienced as a child. ⁵The more she was struck by her own parents, the more inclined she is to stay with an abusive husband. ⁶Third, wives who have not completed high school and those who are unemployed are less likely to leave their husbands. ⁷It appears that the fewer resources a woman has, the fewer alternatives she sees and the more trapped in her marriage she becomes.

____ 1. Abusive husbands tend to be rich.

The passage does not mention the financial status of husbands.

_✓_ 2. People who were beaten as children learn to tolerate being abused.

See sentences 4 and 5.

✓ 3. Women who are dependent on their husbands economically are more
      likely to stay in an abusive marriage.                    See sentence 7.

___ 4. Employed women who are well educated are never abused by their
      husbands.        The passage does not discuss who is abused; it discusses
                                        why women don't leave abusive husbands.
___ 5. The more abused a woman is, the less likely she is to leave her husband.
                                        Sentence 3 refutes this statement.

**B.** [1]It may be important to have a job, but does work make people happy? [2]In many

**Items 1 and 2:**
Since most
people would
continue
working if they
had lots of
money
(sentence 3),
work must offer
rewards other
than pay.
Therefore, item 1
is not supported;
item 2 is.

studies during the last two decades, workers have been asked whether they would
continue to work if they inherited enough money to live comfortably without
working. [3]More than 70 percent replied that they would. [4]Asked how satisfied they
were with their jobs, even more—from 80 to 90 percent—replied that they were
very or moderately satisfied. [5]But asked whether they would choose the same
line of work if they could begin all over again, most said no. [6]Only 43 percent of
white-collar and 24 percent of blue-collar workers said yes. [7]And when asked, "Do
you enjoy your work so much that you have a hard time putting it aside?" only 34
percent of men and 32 percent of women answered positively.

___ 1. The only reason people work is to earn money.

✓ 2. Work provides people with rewards other than money.

**Item 3** is
not supported.

___ 3. For most people, work is as enjoyable as a hobby.

**Item 4:** See
sentences 4–6.

✓ 4. Most people like their jobs but are not thrilled by them.

___ 5. For most people, work is the most important thing in their lives.

**Item 5:** Sentence 7 states most people easily put work aside, suggesting that work is not the most
important thing in their lives.

## PRACTICE 3

**A.** (1.) Read the following passage and check (✓) the **one** inference that is most firmly
based on the given information.

[1]At a White House dinner during the Civil War, an elderly guest waved his hat
and cried out, "Mr. President, I'm from New York State, where we believe that God
Almighty and Abraham Lincoln will save this country."

[2]Lincoln—a modest man whose political thought was guided and shaped by
his religious faith—smiled and nodded. [3]"My friend," he said, "you're half right."

**Item 1:**
Lincoln's
religious faith
and modesty
(sentence 2)
suggest he would
agree that God—
not himself—
would save the
country.

✓ 1. Lincoln believed the guest was right in saying God would save the
      country.

___ 2. Lincoln believed the guest was right in saying that he, Lincoln, would
      save the country.        Lincoln said the guest was only "half right"
                                        (sentence 3).

___ 3. Lincoln believed that the man was supporting the wrong political
      party.        The political party of the man is not mentioned.

**B.** (2–3.) Put a check (✔) by the **two** inferences that are most logically based on the information given in the following passage:

> ¹When I look back at myself in high school, I am amazed by two things: how smart I thought I was, and how much I didn't know. ²It seems to me now that I learned few, if any, important lessons in high school. ³For example, I learned a good deal about "romance." ⁴That is, I learned about fighting, jealousy, spreading rumors, breaking up, gossip, and using other people. ⁵I don't think I learned anything about genuine love and concern for a partner. ⁶I learned about "fun." ⁷That meant partying, drinking, smoking, putting off work, and lying to my parents. ⁸I learned very little about the satisfaction of doing a job well or the rewards of discipline. ⁹Finally, I learned all about fitting in and going along with the crowd and being one of the cool people. ¹⁰I didn't learn anything about standing up for what I believed, or even figuring out what that was. ¹¹I learned almost nothing about being me.

_____ 1. The author had low self-esteem in high school.   Not mentioned.

_____ 2. The author was not popular in high school.   Refuted by sentence 9.

✓ 3. Schoolwork was not a priority for the author during high school.
   The author does not mention schoolwork.
_____ 4. The author is proud of his or her behavior in high school.

✓ 5. If the author could go to high school again, he or she would do things differently.   Because the author missed so many important lessons in high school, it can be inferred that he or she would do things differently a second time.

**C.** (4–5.) Read the following textbook passage and check (✔) the **two** inferences that are most firmly based on the given information.

> ¹In America during the 1700s, the typical woman gave birth to her children at home. ²Female relatives and neighbors would gather at her bedside to offer support and encouragement. ³Records show that the daughter of a Puritan official gave birth to her first child on the last day of January 1701. ⁴At least eight other women were present at her bedside, including her mother and four or more other neighbors. ⁵Most women were assisted in childbirth not by a doctor, but by a midwife. ⁶Skilled midwives were highly valued. ⁷Communities tried to attract experienced midwives by offering a salary or a house rent-free. ⁸In addition to assisting in childbirth, midwives helped farm animals give birth and attended the baptisms and burials of infants. ⁹During labor, midwives gave no painkillers except alcohol. ¹⁰Pain in childbirth was considered God's punishment for Eve's sin of eating the forbidden fruit in the Garden of Eden. ¹¹After delivery, new mothers were often treated to a banquet. ¹²Women from well-to-do families were then

**Item 1:** The passage does not say there were no doctors, just that they did not assist with childbirth (sentence 5).

expected to spend three to four weeks in bed recovering. ¹³Women from poorer families were generally back at work in one or two days.

_____ 1. In colonial America, there were no doctors.

_____ 2. Giving birth in colonial America was typically a lonely experience.

✓ 3. In colonial America, midwives filled several community roles.

✓ 4. Society's view of pain in childbirth has changed since the 1700s.

**Item 2:** See sentence 2.

**Item 3:** See sentence 8.

_____ 5. Poor women recovered more slowly from childbirth than rich women.

**Item 4:** Today pain is treated with medication and not viewed as God's punishment.

**Item 5:** The passage does not mention how long the women took to recover—just how long they were "out of work." (Since the poor women returned to work in a day or two, they might have actually been forced to recover faster than the rich women, who, by contrast, were encouraged to stay in bed "recovering" for weeks.)

# Inferences in Writing

An excellent way to enrich your writing is to practice creative writing techniques that encourage readers to make inferences. Three such techniques, described on the pages that follow, are:

**1** Details that show rather than tell

**2** Figures of speech

**3** Dialog

The techniques add to a reader's experience by asking him or her to make inferences about what has been read.

## Details That Show Rather Than Tell

Creative writers provide verbal pictures that _show_ us what they mean. It is up to the reader to infer the point of what the creative writer has said. For instance, a nonfiction writer might write the following:

The little boy was in a stubborn mood.

But the creative writer might say:

When Jamal's mother asked him to stop playing in the yard and come indoors, he didn't even look up but shouted "NO!" and then spelled it out, "N ... O!"

Rather than merely stating that Jamal was stubborn, the author _shows_ the stubbornness with specific details. To get the most out of creative writing and literature, you must often infer meanings—just as you do in everyday life.

Now look at the following statement that a nonfiction writer might produce:

A man got angry at the person using a cell phone in the theater.

But a novelist might write this:

> Thomas turned to face the laughing red-haired girl sitting behind him in the theater. A vein on his forehead was throbbing. "Would you mind very much turning off that cell phone?" he hissed. "A few of us are here to actually see the movie."

Rather than merely stating that Thomas was angry, the author shows the anger with vivid details. To get the most out of literature, you must often infer meanings—just as you do in everyday life. Your may have inferred, for example, that the laughing girl is insensitive to the rights of others in the theater. You could also have concluded that Thomas has probably been waiting a while for her to quiet down, but she has not, and his temper is now boiling.

Now look at the following statement that a nonfiction writer might produce:

> A farmer is about to kill a small pig, but his daughter objects, so the farmer decides to let his daughter learn for herself that a small pig can be a problem.

Compare the above line with the following scene from *Charlotte's Web*, a literary classic that is beloved by young and old alike:

> [1]"Fern," said Mr. Arable, "I know more about raising a litter of pigs than you do. [2]A weakling makes trouble. [3]Now run along!"
>
> [4]"But it's unfair," cried Fern. [5]"The pig couldn't help being born small, could it? [6]If I had been very small at birth, would you have killed me?"
>
> [7]Mr. Arable smiled. [8]"Certainly not," he said, looking down at his daughter with love. [9]"But this is different. [10]A little girl is one thing, a little runty pig is another."
>
> [11]"I see no difference," replied Fern, still hanging on to the ax. [12]"This is the most terrible case of injustice I ever heard of."
>
> [13]A queer look came over John Arable's face. [14]He seemed almost ready to cry himself.
>
> [15]"All right," he said. [16]"You go back to the house and I will bring the runt when I come in. [17]I'll let you start it on a bottle, like a baby. [18]Then you'll see what trouble a pig can be."

---

## Check Your Understanding

See if you can answer the following inference questions about the excerpt.

_C_    1. Fern and Mr. Arable probably live
   A. in a city.
   B. in a small town.
   C. on a farm.

_A_    2. We can infer from the excerpt that Mr. Arable
    A. has probably raised many pigs in his lifetime.
    B. has had little experience raising pigs.
    C. does not like pigs.

_C_    3. Mr. Arable appears almost ready to cry because he
    A. gets worried about how difficult it would be to raise the pig.
    B. does not like to lose an argument with his daughter.
    C. is touched by his daughter's willingness to stand up for the small pig.

_B_    4. We can conclude that Mr. Arable agrees to spare the pig because
    A. Fern has convinced him that it is unfair to kill pigs, no matter what their size.
    B. he believes that raising a pig will teach Fern some lessons.
    C. he realizes that taking care of a runt pig is not that difficult.

_B_    5. By the end of this passage, we can infer that Mr. Arable is
    A. a cruel man.
    B. a reasonable man.
    C. not a very patient man.

## Explanation

1. Fern and Mr. Arable live in a place where pigs are born and raised. That strongly suggests that they live on a farm. The correct answer, then, is C.

2. Mr. Arable mentions that he knows about "raising a litter of pigs." He also tells Fern how to begin feeding the pig. These details suggest that he has raised pigs before. Therefore, the answer is A.

3. Mr. Arable seems near crying after Fern insists there's no difference between killing a runt pig and killing a small daughter. And the passage has already described Mr. Arable looking at his daughter with love. So we can conclude the plea for justice from the young daughter he adores is what touched him so. Thus the answer is C.

4. When Mr. Arable agrees to let his daughter raise the pig, he says "you'll see what trouble a pig can be." His words suggest that he expects Fern to learn a lesson. Therefore B is the answer.

5. Mr. Arable talks to Fern, listens to her opinions, and agrees to allow her to do something he does not fully support. These actions suggest he is a fair and reasonable man. So answer B is correct.

The excerpt from *Charlotte's Web* is a small example of how inference skills can increase your appreciation of literary forms—fiction, poetry, autobiographies, and other imaginative literature.

## Figures of Speech

Creative writers often use comparisons known as **figures of speech** to imply their meanings and give us a fresh and more informed way of looking at something. The two most common figures of speech are similes and metaphors.

**Simile**—a stated comparison, introduced with *like, as,* or *as if.*

"The boss was really angry about the suggestion I made. He chewed me out! I feel like a piece of old bubble gum!"

Copyright © Glasbergen 2008

In the cartoon, the man says that because the boss chewed him out, he feels "like a piece of old bubble gum." The simile clearly shows that the man's feelings have been hurt.

Here is another example. Instead of saying, "My stepfather shouted at me," you could express it vividly by saying, "When my stepfather shouted at me, it was like a fist in my face." The simile shows that the stepfather's shout was shocking, violent, and painful. It gives us much more information than the line that simply tells us that the stepfather shouted.

Following are some other similes:

- Many of the players on the football team have arms *as big as tree trunks.*

- In the recently planted garden, I saw tomato plants starting to come out of the ground, curled up *like a hand unfolding.*

- I loved my mother, but she was about *as huggable as a cactus.*

- After I lost my job, my material possessions soon disappeared *like so much dandelion fluff in a wind.*

- When my new boyfriend arrived, my parents stared at him *as if he were a cockroach that had just crawled under the door.*

**Metaphor**—an implied comparison, with *like, as,* or *as if* omitted.

In this cartoon, the boy, Linus, is using a metaphor when he says that big sisters are "the crab grass in the lawn of life." He means that big sisters (like his own sister, Lucy, who just insulted his cartoon) spoil things and are a nuisance.

In another example, the thought "Life is a struggle" was memorably expressed in metaphor by the ancient writer Plotinus, who wrote: "Be kind, for everyone you meet is fighting a hard battle." His comparison says that even though we may not be aware of it, everyone we meet is dealing with difficulties, just as we are.

Here are some other metaphors:

● From the airplane, I looked down on Manhattan, *an anthill of frantic life*.

● Looking westward, I saw an *army of dark clouds* massed on the horizon.

● Our boss is always a *bear* on Monday morning.

● None of the players on the demoralized football team were strong enough to withstand *the gale-force winds* of the coach's personality.

● My aunt's home was a *pack rat's nest* of everything she had collected during her life.

## PRACTICE 4

Use a check (✓) to identify each figure of speech as a simile or a metaphor. Then, in the space provided, answer each inference question that follows.

__C__ 1. The head of that corporation needs money as much as a bat needs sunglasses.

   __✓__ simile        ___ metaphor

*As much as* signals the simile. The head of a corporation, who does not need money, is being compared to the bat, which does not need sunglasses.

You can infer that the head of the corporation
   A. is bankrupt.
   B. always has been wealthy.
   C. doesn't need any more money.

__B__ 2. When I emerged from the air-conditioned building, the air hit me in the face like a steaming washcloth.

   __✓__ simile        ___ metaphor

You can infer that the air outside was
   A. cool and dry.
   B. hot and humid.
   C. hot and dry.

*Like* signals the simile. A steaming washcloth is hot and damp.

__A__ 3. Marlo and Scott's relationship was first a race car, then a stalled sedan, and finally scrap metal.

   ___ simile        __✓__ metaphor

Metaphors make comparisons without the use of words such as *like* or *as*. The relationship started out strong like the race car, but then it slowed down (stalled) and finally fell apart (became scrap in the junkyard).

You can infer that Marlo and Scott's relationship
   A. started out strong but fell apart.
   B. slowly grew to a strong and lasting one.
   C. had a rapid start and an equally rapid end.

__C__ 4. My job interview went as smoothly as a drive down a street filled with potholes.

   __✓__ simile        ___ metaphor

You can infer that the interview went
   A. extremely well.
   B. fairly well.
   C. poorly.

*As smoothly as* signals the simile. A drive down a potholed road goes poorly.

___B___  5. There was nothing uncertain about the voice inside that told me what to do. It spoke with the clearness and certainty of church bells heard on bright Sundays.

___ simile          ✓ metaphor          The clear sound of the church bells is compared to the clear sound of the speaker's conscience.

You can infer that the author
A. could not make up his mind.
B. felt very sure about what the voice was telling him to do.
C. experienced a moment of insanity.

## Dialog

Another way to write creatively is to use dialog that presents the exact words of the persons in your writing. Seeing and hearing speakers' exact words makes it seem as if we are present in a scene—or listening to the words in a film. Exact words can often help readers infer more about what a character is thinking and feeling than a great deal of description would.

### PRACTICE 5

To appreciate the power of dialog, read the following short story by Langston Hughes, a poet and fiction writer who emerged as a major literary figure during the Harlem Renaissance of the 1920s. After reading the story, answer the inference questions about it.

## Early Autumn

[1]When Bill was very young, they had been in love. [2]Many nights they had spent walking, talking together. [3]Then something not very important had come between them, and they didn't speak. [4]Impulsively, she had married a man she thought she loved. [5]Bill went away, bitter about women.

[6]Yesterday, walking across Washington Square, she saw him for the first time in years.

[7]"Bill Walker," she said.

[8]He stopped. [9]At first he did not recognize her; to him she looked so old.

[10]"Mary! Where did you come from?"

[11]Unconsciously, she lifted her face as though wanting a kiss, but he held out his hand. [12]She took it.

[13]"I live in New York now," she said.

[14]"Oh"—smiling politely. [15]Then a little frown came quickly between his eyes.

[16]"Always wondered what happened to you, Bill."

[17]"I'm a lawyer. Nice firm, way downtown."

[18]"Married yet?"

[19]"Sure. Two kids."

[20]"Oh," she said.

[21]A great many people went past them through the park. [22]People they didn't know. [23]It was late afternoon. [24]Nearly sunset. [25]Cold.

[26]"And your husband?" he asked her.

[27]"We have three children. [28]I work in the bursar's office at Columbia."

[29]"You're looking very . . . " (he wanted to say *old*) ". . . well," he said.

[30]She understood. [31]Under the trees in Washington Square, she found herself desperately reaching back into the past. [32]She had been older than he then in Ohio. [33]Now she was not young at all. [34]Bill was still young.

[35]"We live on Central Park West," she said. [36]"Come and see us sometime."

[37]"Sure," he replied. [38]"You and your husband must have dinner with my family some night. [39]Any night. [40]Lucille and I'd love to have you."

[41]The leaves fell slowly from the trees in the Square. [42]Fell without wind. [43]Autumn dusk. [44]She felt a little sick.

[45]"We'd love it," she answered.

[46]"You ought to see my kids." [47]He grinned.

[48]Suddenly the lights came on up the whole length of Fifth Avenue, chains of misty brilliance in the blue air.

[49]"There's my bus," she said.

[50]He held out his hand. [51]"Good-by."

[52]"When . . . " she wanted to say, but the bus was ready to pull off. [53]The lights on the avenue blurred, twinkled, blurred. [54]And she was afraid to open her mouth as she entered the bus. [55]Afraid it would be impossible to utter a word.

[56]Suddenly she shrieked very loudly, "Good-by!" [57]But the bus door had closed.

[58]The bus started. [59]People came between them outside, people crossing the street, people they didn't know. [60]Space and people. [61]She lost sight of Bill. [62]Then she remembered she had forgotten to give him her address—or ask him for his—or tell him that her youngest boy was named Bill, too.

_B_  1. Authors of fiction often choose settings that symbolically reflect their story. In this case, the characters' stage of life is echoed in the author's choices of

The two characters were at a later stage of life than when they had last met.

A. city and park.
B. season and time of day.
C. transportation and temperature.

_C_  2. Hughes portrayed the awkwardness of the meeting by indicating a contrast between

Bill wanted to say she looked old, but instead said she looked well. Also, he said he'd love to have her over for dinner, but he didn't take her phone number or address.

A. the woman's and Bill's jobs.
B. New York City and Ohio.
C. what Bill said and what he meant.

_B_  3. The suggestion that Bill was still young but the woman was not implies that

A. she was actually many, many years older than he.
B. her life has aged her more rapidly than his life has aged him.
C. he was an exercise buff who had taken especially good care of himself.

Life experiences have influenced the way Bill and Mary have aged.

_A_  4. The story suggests that Bill

A. did not regret having married someone else.
B. plans on inviting the woman and her husband over for dinner.
C. still wished nothing had come between him and the woman when they were young.

She "looked so old" to him, and he held out his hand instead of kissing her.

_C_  5. The last few words of the story suggest that

A. the boy was really Bill's son.
B. the woman regretted naming her youngest son Bill.
C. the woman had thought of Bill with so much longing that she named a son after him.

Mary's strong memories and powerful reaction to Bill suggest that she purposely named her son after him.

# INFERENCES IN READING AND WRITING: Mastery Test 1 (Reading)

**A.** (1–4.) Shown below is a note that was actually found on a car windshield in Chicago. Put a check (✓) by the **four** inferences that are most logically based on the information given in the note.

_____ 1. The note was written by Mario's girlfriend.

_____ 2. The car was not really Mario's.

_____ 3. Mario had gotten out of work early.

_____ 4. Mario's car was parked at another woman's house.

_____ 5. Mario had lied to his girlfriend.

_____ 6. The author of the note will never speak to Mario again.

_____ 7. The author of the note thinks Mario is cheating on her.

_____ 8. Mario and the author of the note are married.

**Logical inferences:**
**Item 1:** Who else but a girlfriend would say things such as were written in the note?
**Item 4:** "HER place" suggests that Mario's car was parked at another woman's house.
**Item 5:** The note says, "You said you had to work then whys your car . . . ."
**Item 7:** Clues: "HER place" and "I hate you, you slime."

**Items that are not logical inferences:**
**Item 2:** There is no way to know who owns the car.
**Item 3:** There is no way to know what Mario's work hours are or when he works.
**Item 6:** The note indicates the opposite: "text me later."
**Item 8:** Nothing indicates the marital status of either.

*(Continues on next page)*

**B.** After reading each short passage, check (✓) the **two** inferences that are most logically based on the given information.

5–6.   ¹There's an old story about a certain state legislator who had spent some time in a mental institution. ²For years after, when debate in the legislature got heated, he would wave his release papers and declare, "I've got papers that prove I'm sane! ³What about the rest of you?"

_____ A. The legislator was ashamed of having been in a mental institution.
    *For years he had been telling everyone.*

✓   B. When he left the institution, the legislator was considered sane.
    *Sentence 2: "I've got papers that prove I'm sane!"*

✓   C. The legislator had been reelected despite his mental problems.
    *He was in the legislature "for years after."*

_____ D. The legislator should never have been released from the mental institution.     *Nothing in the passage indicates that the legislator is still mentally ill.*

7–8.   ¹"Most people don't believe me when I tell them that reading aloud is the single most important factor in reading success," author Jim Trelease says as he prepares to speak to an audience of parents and teachers. ²"They don't believe me for three reasons: One, it's simple. ³Two, it's free. ⁴And three, the child enjoys it. ⁵But if reading required a $149 machine, we'd have it in half the homes of America. ⁶And if kids hated it, we'd have it in every classroom."

**Statement C:** Sentence 1 identifies Trelease as an author speaking to parents and teachers. We can assume his book is about children and reading.

_____ A. The use of a machine is the best way to teach a child to read.     *Not supported. Sentence 1 states that reading aloud is the best way.*

✓   B. If something is simple, free, and enjoyable, people believe it's too good to be true.     *See sentences 2–4.*

✓   C. Jim Trelease has probably written a book about children and reading.

_____ D. Learning to read is a complex and difficult challenge for any child.     *Not mentioned.*

9–10.   ¹A well-known prayer goes as follows: "Oh, God, grant me the courage to change what I must change, the patience to bear what I must bear, and the wisdom to know the difference."

✓   A. It sometimes takes courage to change one's life.     *The fact that the prayer asks for courage suggests that courage is needed for change.*

_____ B. Courage is more important than patience.

_____ C. Courage and patience are much the same.     *Neither courage nor patience is evaluated in the passage.*

✓   D. We sometimes aren't wise enough to know when we must simply accept a situation.     *The fact that the prayer asks for wisdom suggests that people sometimes don't have enough wisdom to know when to accept a situation.*

# INFERENCES IN READING AND WRITING: Mastery Test 2 (Reading)

**A.** (1–4.) Put a check (✓) by the **four** inferences that are most logically based on the information given in the following cartoon.

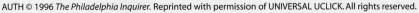

**Items 1–2:** The figure on the left is muscular, suggesting he works out regularly.

**Item 3:** The different shapes of the two figures suggest they do different things.

**Item 4:** Not supported.

**Item 5:** The figure's large head suggests that his time at the library caused his mind to grow—an important effect.

**Item 6:** The right figure's large head suggests he has a strong mind, just as the left figure's large muscles suggest he has a strong body.

**Item 7:** The differences in the two figures show that their "workouts" have different effects.

**Item 8:** The size of the right figure's large head and small body suggest his work is mental, not physical.

_____ 1. The figure on the left does not work out at all.

✓ 2. The figure on the left probably spends lots of time working out.

✓ 3. The two figures do very different things when they work out.

_____ 4. The two figures do not like each other.

_____ 5. Spending time at the library has had no effect on the figure on the right.

✓ 6. Spending time at the library has made the figure on the right mentally strong.

_____ 7. Working out at the library has the same effect as working out at the gym.

✓ 8. Working out at the library involves mental—not physical—effort.

*(Continues on next page)*

**B.** After reading each short passage, check (✓) the **two** inferences that are most logically based on the given information.

5–6. ¹A doctor calls a patient into his office to reveal the results of some recent tests. ²"I have some bad news and some worse news," says the doctor. ³"The bad news is that you only have 24 hours to live."

⁴"Oh no," says the patient. ⁵"What could be worse than that?"

⁶The doctor answers, "I've been trying to reach you since yesterday."

_____ A. The patient learns he has cancer.    The doctor does not tell the patient what his medical problem is.

✓ B. The patient learns he will die that very day.    See sentences 3 and 6.

_____ C. The patient learns he will die a painless death.    Not mentioned.

✓ D. The patient at first cannot believe anything is worse than having only one day to live.    See sentence 5.

7–8. ¹Americans tend to see old age negatively, as a time of physical and mental decline. ²In Japan, the situation is very different. ³For instance, elderly guests arriving at a hotel in Japan are asked their age—a tradition meant to ensure that they will receive the proper respect. ⁴Japanese grandmothers wear red to show their high status. ⁵And to celebrate reaching age sixty, a Japanese man wears a red vest. ⁶This, too, is a sign of great honor.

✓ A. The Japanese tend to view old age more positively than Americans do.    See sentences 1 and 2.

_____ B. Old people in Japan do not experience as much physical or mental decline as old people in the United States.    The passage does not discuss people's decline in old age.

_____ C. Guests at a Japanese hotel would probably be embarrassed to state their age.    See sentences 4–5. In Japan, people don't hide old age; they show it off.

✓ D. The color red apparently has a special meaning in Japan.    See sentences 4–6.

9–10. ¹"I hate war," said U.S. General Dwight Eisenhower, "as only a soldier who has lived it can, as one who has seen its brutality, its futility, its stupidity. ²Every gun that is made, every warship launched, every rocket fired, signifies in the final sense a theft from those who hunger and are not fed, those who are cold and not clothed."

_____ A. Eisenhower did not like the military.    Not supported. He speaks of war, not the military.

✓ B. Eisenhower's involvement in war made him hate war.    See the last part of sentence 1.

✓ C. Eisenhower believed that the money spent on war could be put to better use.    See sentence 2.

_____ D. Eisenhower believed the military was directly responsible for poverty and hunger.    Not supported. He says war steals from the poor and the hungry, not that the military is responsible for hunger and poverty.

# INFERENCES IN READING AND WRITING: Mastery Test 3 (Reading)

**A.** (1–4.) After reading each short passage, check (✓) the **two** inferences that are most firmly based on the given information.

1–2. ¹For centuries, coca leaves have been chewed by South American Indians to combat fatigue, hunger, and thirst. ²When processed into cocaine, coca becomes much more powerful. ³Cocaine was once believed to be a safe painkiller and was prescribed by doctors. ⁴In fact, Coca-Cola originally contained a small amount of cocaine. ⁵In recent times, cocaine has been recognized as a dangerous addictive drug.

_____ A. Cocaine is not an effective painkiller.   The fact that cocaine was once prescribed by doctors suggests it was effective.

__✓__ B. Coca grows naturally in South America.   Since coca has been chewed in South America for centuries, it must grow there naturally.

_____ C. Coca leaves are more dangerous than processed cocaine.   Cocaine is more powerful (sentence 2); it is probably more dangerous.

__✓__ D. Cocaine was once legal in the United States.   Since cocaine was prescribed by doctors and used in Coca-Cola, it must have once been legal in the U.S.

3–4. ¹A small private plane developed engine trouble while still many miles from a suitable landing strip. ²The pilot, realizing there was nothing he could do to keep the plane in the air, rushed back to where his three passengers sat and explained the situation. ³He added, "I am a married man with two small children. ⁴I regret to tell you there are only three parachutes aboard." ⁵And with that, he grabbed one of the parachutes and bailed out.

⁶One of the passengers reacted quickly to the pilot's exit. ⁷"I am a brilliant scientist!" he announced. ⁸"I am the world's smartest man! ⁹The world cannot do without me!" ¹⁰And with that, he too bailed out.

¹¹The other two passengers, an elderly priest and a Boy Scout, were quiet for a moment. ¹²"Son," the priest said finally, "I am old and have lived a full life. ¹³I am ready to meet my Maker."

¹⁴"You'll have to cancel the meeting, Father," the Boy Scout answered, smiling. ¹⁵"The world's smartest man just bailed out with my backpack!"

_____ A. Scientists tend to think highly of themselves.   One scientist's self-assessment cannot be applied to all scientists.

__✓__ B. The "world's smartest man" wasn't as smart as he thought.   He wasn't smart enough to grab the parachute.

_____ C. Scientists are more important to the world than priests and Boy Scouts.   The passage doesn't make judgments about people's importance.

__✓__ D. No matter how smart someone is, he or she needs to examine the facts closely before acting.   The "brilliant scientist" should have looked—to make sure he had a parachute—before he leaped.

*(Continues on next page)*

**B.** After reading each short passage, check (✓) the **three** inferences that are most firmly based on the given information.

5–7.  [1]A disk jockey in Dallas asked his listeners to send him money, and they did. [2]One day, Ron Chapman of station KVIL simply told his listeners, "Go to your checkbooks. [3]Write a check payable to KVIL Fun and Games. [4]Make it in the amount of $20 and mail it to this address." [5]He never stated why listeners should send the money, only that they should. [6]Chapman expected that about three or four hundred listeners would respond. [7]He intended to return their checks and send them a bag of goodies from his sponsors. [8]However, instead of four hundred checks, over twelve thousand were received, amounting to $244,240. [9]The station donated the money to charity.

**Statement C:**
The fact that Chapman had planned to return the money with "goodies" suggests his announcement was meant to be a trick on listeners.

✓  A. People will sometimes do what they're told without knowing exactly why.       Many people sent money (sentence 8) even though they were not told why (sentence 5) they should.

___  B. The station gave the money to the homeless.       Not mentioned.

✓  C. Chapman made his announcement to play a trick on his listeners.

___  D. Chapman's sponsors were furious about the stunt.       Not mentioned.

✓  E. Chapman assumed that a small percentage of his listeners would send money without knowing why.       See sentence 6.

8–10.  [1]At Wellness Community meetings, cancer patients give each other various types of support, including the opportunity to laugh. [2]They laugh with each other about things that would make outsiders uneasy. [3]One joke told by patients is about a man with cancer who has just learned that he has only one more night to live. [4]He asks his wife to come to the bedroom with him for one last sexual encounter. [5]His wife says, "Gosh, Hugo, I'd love to, but I'm too tired." [6]Hugo says, "Oh, come on." [7]And his wife says, "That's easy for you to say. [8]You don't have to get up in the morning."

___  A. In real life, cancer patients cannot participate in sex.

✓  B. Cancer patients can laugh about their problems.       See sentence 2.

✓  C. The author feels that healthy people may be uncomfortable over jokes about death.       See sentence 2.

✓  D. The wife in the joke is aware that Hugo will die the next morning.

___  E. All cancer patients in the Wellness Community meeting will die from their illness.

**Statement A:** Whether cancer patients can or cannot participate in sex is not mentioned.

**Statement D:** See sentence 8. The wife's words "you don't have to get up" suggests she knows Hugo will die.

**Statement E:** The passage does not comment about the death of the patients. It just tells a joke about the death of one man.

# INFERENCES IN READING AND WRITING: Mastery Test 4 (Writing)

**A.** Use a check (✓) to identify the sentence in each pair that shows us sharp and vivid details rather than vague and general ones.

Specific items the cousin worries about: apples (not organic), hot dogs (preservatives), ice cream (sugar).

1. \_\_\_\_ A. My cousin worries about everything her children eat and passes judgment on every bite of food that goes into their mouths.

   ✓ B. At lunch today, my cousin wouldn't let her kids eat the apples (not organic), the hot dogs (too many preservatives), or the ice cream (too much sugar).

Vivid detail: the speaker was so ugly that the dog needed an incentive (the pork chop) to play with him.

2. \_\_\_\_ A. When I was a boy, my older brother would tease me by saying I was so ugly that no one would play with me.

   ✓ B. My brother said I was so ugly as a kid that my mother had to tie a pork chop around my neck to get our dog to play with me.

Specific commitments: choir rehearsal, soccer practice, paper, tests, doctor's appointments.

3. ✓ A. I wish I could join you for lunch, but this week I have a choir rehearsal, soccer practice, a paper due on Tuesday, tests on Thursday and Friday, and two doctor's appointments.

   \_\_\_\_ B. I'm sorry, but I can't join you for lunch this week. I'm just too busy these days. I have a lot of commitments already, and there's not enough time in my day to do all the things I'd like to do.

Specific ways Tony seems distracted and unfriendly: doesn't look at the other person, stares out the window, naps at his desk, tells the same joke four times.

4. ✓ A. Something must be wrong with Tony. He doesn't look at me when I talk to him, he spends a lot of time staring out the window, and at times he naps at his desk. Just this week, he told me the same joke four times.

   \_\_\_\_ B. I'm afraid there's something wrong with Tony. For a while now, he's seemed distracted and even a little unfriendly, and he's not always working at his desk. Sometimes he even repeats himself.

Vivid (and possibly exaggerated) description of the pest problem: three hundred cockroaches and a dozen mice.

5. \_\_\_\_ A. Our apartment has had a pest problem that has existed from when we first moved in, and it's been difficult to deal with, to say the least.

   ✓ B. When we leave this apartment, we plan to release about three hundred cockroaches and a dozen mice so we can leave the place exactly as we found it.

*(Continues on next page)*

**B.** Use sharp and specific details—visual details and actions, sounds, smells, tastes, and textures—to turn any five of the following sentences into vivid ones. Use the spaces provided.

*Example*

A girl was in the hall.

The little girl with pigtails skipped and jumped her way down the

brightly-lit hall.

1. The food was unappetizing.
2. Traffic was heavy.
3. I spent quite a bit of time studying for the test.
4. A man approached me.
5. The room was messy.
6. Parking on campus can be a challenge.
7. I ate and drank too much.
8. The old woman was tired.
9. I looked through the window at the view outside.
10. My friend and I stopped for a snack.

*Answers will vary.*

*To the Instructor:* Answers will vary. Give credit to sentences that contain the kinds of sharp, specific details mentioned in the directions.

## INFERENCES IN READING AND WRITING: Mastery Test 5 (Writing)

Use a check (✓) to identify each figure of speech as a simile or a metaphor. Then, in the space provided, answer each inference question that follows.

__B__ 1. His friendship is as genuine as a plastic Christmas tree.

✓ simile        ___ metaphor

You can infer that the friendship is
A. easy to maintain.
B. fake and cheap.
C. seasonal and glittery.

> The word indicating the simile is underlined. A plastic Christmas tree is a fake and cheap substitute for a real tree.

__C__ 2. A gang of teenaged boys moved through the mall like a pack of wild dogs.

✓ simile        ___ metaphor

You can infer that the boys were
A. polite and friendly.
B. sneaky and quiet.
C. loud and disruptive.

> The word indicating the simile is underlined. Wild dogs would be loud and disruptive.

__B__ 3. The executives did not admit that the company was a sinking ship until after they had taken millions of dollars for themselves.

___ simile        ✓ metaphor

You can infer that the company
A. was well-managed.
B. was failing.
C. was going in more than one direction.

> The company is being compared to a sinking ship without using like or as. The metaphor of a sinking ship suggests the company will not last much longer.

__C__ 4. Everyone at work thinks that Jasmine is a real gem.

___ simile        ✓ metaphor

You can infer that Jasmine is
A. disliked and unfriendly.
B. shy and quiet.
C. admired and valued.

> A gem is something that is admired and valued.

__C__ 5. I'm writing a family history so that my grandparents' stories do not go up in smoke and ashes.

___ simile        ✓ metaphor

You can infer that the grandparents' stories are
A. full of fire and passion.
B. uneventful and unimportant.
C. in danger of being lost forever.

> Something that goes up in smoke and ashes would be lost forever.

*(Continues on next page)*

_C_ 6. To Jennifer, the psychology course was a banquet of ideas.

___ simile   ✓ metaphor

It is a comparison without *like* or *as*. Just as a banquet can provide many tasty foods, so the psychology course provides many interesting ideas.

You can infer that Jennifer
A. finds her psychology course rather tedious.
B. likes to eat during her psychology course.
C. finds her psychology course quite interesting.

_B_ 7. After I ate that meal, I felt as if I had swallowed a barbell.

✓ simile   ___ metaphor

You can infer that the meal was
A. sweet.
B. heavy.
C. spicy.

*As if* signals a simile. A barbell is heavy, suggesting that the meal was heavy.

_A_ 8. When Don started to run track again after his knee operation, he felt like a bus on the racetrack at the Indy 500.

✓ simile   ___ metaphor

You can infer that Don
A. felt slow and awkward.
B. felt cheerful and optimistic.
C. knew he would never regain his old form.

*Like* signals a simile. Both Don after his knee operation and a bus on a racetrack are comparatively slow and awkward.

_A_ 9. Tina says that her first boyfriend was an economy car, but her current one is a luxury sedan.

___ simile   ✓ metaphor

You can infer that Tina's current boyfriend
A. is a big improvement over her first one.
B. is an auto mechanic.
C. is a family man.

This metaphor implies that Tina's first boyfriend was only average (an economy car), but her current boyfriend is way above average, perhaps rich (a luxury sedan).

_C_ 10. The CEO of the company gave a talk to his employees that was one part sugar and one part sandpaper.

___ simile   ✓ metaphor

You can infer that the CEO
A. was hard to understand.
B. led a company that sold both groceries and home products.
C. was both encouraging to and critical of his employees.

To speak in a sugary way suggests encouragement. Sandpaper suggests harshness (criticism).

## INFERENCES IN READING AND WRITING: Mastery Test 6 (Writing)

Make up and write a *realistic and lively* dialog between two or more people. Don't have your characters talk like cardboard figures; have them talk the way people would in real life. Also, make sure their voices are consistent. (Don't have them suddenly talk out of character.)

The dialog might, for example, be a discussion or an argument between two friends, or a husband and wife, or a parent and child, or a brother and sister, or a clerk and customer, or a doctor and patient, or a police officer and suspect. The verbal exchange might lead to an action or decision of some kind.

You should begin by describing the setting—the time, the place, and what is happening there—in which the dialog takes place. Also, you should briefly describe the characters involved and the relationship between them. Enclose characters' exact words within quotation marks; enclose descriptions or other comments within parentheses. Use the example that follows as a guide.

*SETTING: A television news truck parks in front of a small row home. Two camera people get out and set up a camera. Some children from the neighborhood run up and look on curiously. Then a man in a sharp-looking suit gets of the truck and knocks on the door of the home. A distracted-looking woman opens the door.*

"My name is Tod Hunter," the reporter says. "I'm with *Action News*, and I'd like to talk to the woman who lost a child in the school fire yesterday."

The woman at the door says, "Oh, I'm sorry, but my daughter is not in the mood for visitors."

"I understand," the reporter says. "But please tell her that we only want a moment of her time."

When the woman goes to find her daughter, the reporter whispers to his crew: "You can shoot from this angle, but let's try to get inside. If she cooperates, let's gradually move in through the doorway."

Meanwhile, some of the children begin to shout, "Those are TV cameras! Wow, real TV cameras!"

Then the mother of the fire victim appears at the door, looking drawn and exhausted. "What do you want?"

"I'm really, really sorry for your great loss, Ma'am," the reporter says. "I'm here for *Action News*. Has the school explained to you what caused the fire?"

"Please, no interviews," the mother says.

But the reporter steps closer. "Our viewers want to know how you feel."

*(Continues on next page)*

"I don't care about you or your viewers!" the mother shouts. She looks at the reporter with sudden fire and disgust in her eyes. "My pain is none of your business! Please get out of here."

"All I want is a minute," the reporter pleads. "Please, just give me a minute."

The door slams in his face.

The reporter says to his crew, "So much for that. Let's get out of here. I'm starved."

One of the camera people says, "I've got to get another job."

*To the Instructor:*
A student's score on this test should be based on your evaluation of whether he or she has written an A, B, C, D, or F paper.

Suggested equivalents:

A = 90 to 100
B = 80 to 89
C = 70 to 79
D = 60 to 69
F = 59 and below

# 11 Longer Selections in Reading and Writing

## Reading Longer Selections

Just as a paragraph has a main idea, a longer selection has a **central point**, also known as a **central idea**, or **thesis**. The longer selection might be an essay, a reading, or a section of a textbook chapter. As a reader, you can find a central point in the same way that you find a main idea—by identifying the topic (which is often suggested by the title of the selection) and then looking to see what idea is advanced about that topic, and what support is provided for that idea. Often the paragraphs within a longer reading will provide supporting details for the central point.

### ✔ Check Your Understanding

In the following essay, the central point is stated in one sentence. See if you can find and underline this sentence. Then write its number in the space provided.

#### Peer Pressure

¹We often hear about the dangers of peer pressure to teenagers. ²Teens take drugs, skip school, get drunk, or have sex to impress their friends. ³However, there is another, perhaps equally bad, effect of peer pressure. ⁴Desperate to conform to their friends' values, teens may give up their interests in school, in hobbies, and even in certain people.

⁵Teens may lose or hide their interest in school in order to be like their friends. ⁶They adopt a negative attitude in which school is seen as a battlefield, with teachers and other officials regarded as the enemy. ⁷In private, they may enjoy certain teachers, but in front of their friends, they put on a sarcastic or hostile act. ⁸In addition, teenagers may stop participating in class. ⁹They may refuse to join in class discussions, even when the topic interests them. ¹⁰They may decide it is cool to show up without the assigned homework. ¹¹If their peers demand it, they may interfere with others' learning by disrupting class. ¹²Conforming also means not joining in after-school activities.

¹³Teenagers also give up private pleasures and hobbies to be one of the crowd. ¹⁴Certain pastimes, such as writing poems, practicing piano, reading books, or joining an after-school club may be off-limits because the crowd laughs at them.

¹⁵Most sadly, teenagers sometimes give up the people they love in order to be accepted. ¹⁶If necessary, they sacrifice the old friend who no longer dresses

well enough, listens to the wrong kind of music, or refuses to drink or take drugs. [17]Potential boyfriends or girlfriends may be rejected, too, if the crowd doesn't like their looks or values. [18]Teens can even cut their families out of their lives if they are too poor, too conventional, or too different from their friends' parents.

_____4_____ is the number of the sentence that states the central point.

## Explanation

The central point is a general statement that covers all or most of the details in a reading. To find the central point of the essay above, look first at its topic. Since the title is "Peer Pressure," and every paragraph is about that subject, we can say "peer pressure" is the topic. Then decide on what point is being made about the topic by looking at the major details of the essay. The first major detail, presented in the second paragraph, is about giving up interest in school as a result of peer pressure. The next major detail, in the third paragraph, is about giving up interest in hobbies; and the third major detail, in the fourth paragraph, is about giving up interest in certain people.

The central point, then, will be a general statement that covers all of the major details presented. As is often the case, the central point is stated in the first paragraph. Sentence 4 in that paragraph expresses the idea that peer pressure may cause students to give up interest in school, in hobbies, and in certain people.

## PRACTICE

The author has stated the central point of the following textbook selection in one sentence. Find that sentence, and write its number in the space provided.

### Prewriting Strategies

[1]Prewriting refers to strategies you can use to generate ideas before starting the first draft of a paper. [2]Prewriting techniques have various advantages. [3]They encourage imaginative exploration and therefore also help you discover what interests you most about your subject. [4]Having such a focus early in the writing process keeps you from plunging into your initial draft without first giving some thought to what you want to say. [5]Prewriting thus saves you time in the long run by keeping you on course.

[6]Prewriting can help in other ways, too. [7]When we write, we often interfere with our ability to generate material because we continually critique what we put down on paper. [8]"This makes no sense," "This is stupid," "I can't say that," and other critical thoughts pop into our minds. [9]Such negative, self-critical comments stop the flow of our thoughts and reinforce the fear that we have nothing to say and aren't very good at writing. [10]During prewriting, you deliberately ignore your internal critic. [11]Your purpose is simply to get ideas down on paper without evaluating their effectiveness. [12]Writing without immediately judging what you produce can be liberating. [13]Once you feel less pressure, you'll probably find that you can generate a good deal of material. [14]And that can make your confidence soar.

¹⁵One final advantage of prewriting: The random associations typical of prewriting tap the mind's ability to make unusual connections. ¹⁶When you prewrite, you're like an archaeologist going on a dig. ¹⁷On the one hand, you may not unearth anything; on the other hand, you may stumble upon one interesting find after another. ¹⁸Prewriting helps you appreciate—right from the start—this element of surprise in the writing process.

_____2_____   is the number of the sentence that states the central point.

*Sentence 1 explains what the word* prewriting *means. Sentence 2 contains the list words* various advantages. *The remainder of the passage describes advantages of prewriting.*

Part Two of this book will consist of fifteen longer selections that you will be able to use for both reading and writing practice. In every case, you will find that an author advances an idea (or ideas) about a topic and then supports that idea.

# Writing Longer Selections and Essays

As a writer, you will be expected to write essays as well as paragraphs. As you know, a **paragraph** is a series of sentences about a main idea. An **essay**, on the other hand, is a series of *paragraphs* about a main idea—called the **central idea** or **central point** or **thesis**. Since an essay is much longer than a paragraph, a writer can develop a topic in more detail. To see clearly the difference between a paragraph and an essay, look at the model paragraph and essay below.

## A Paragraph about Bullies

Here is a paragraph written by a student named Carla.

### Three Kinds of Bullies

There are three kinds of bullies in schools. First of all, there are the physical bullies. They are the bigger or meaner kids who try to hurt kids who are smaller or unsure of themselves. They'll push other kids off swings, trip them in the halls, or knock books out of their hands. Another kind of bully is the verbal bully. This kind tries to hurt with words rather than fists. Kindergartners may call each other "dummy" or "weirdo" or "fatty," and as kids get older, their words carry even more sting. "You are such a loser," those bullies will tell their victim, making sure there is a crowd nearby to hear. The worst kind of bully is the social bully. Social bullies realize that they can make themselves feel powerful by making others feel unwanted. Bullies choose their victims and then do all they can to isolate them. They move away if a victim sits near them at lunch

> or stands near them in gym. They make sure the unwanted ones are not
> invited to games or parties.  Physical, verbal, and social bullies all have
> the same ugly goal: to hurt and humiliate others.

● What is the main idea of Carla's paragraph? _____
_____
*There are three kinds of bullies in schools.*

● What are the three supporting details that Carla has provided to back up her
point?
1. *Physical bullies* _____
2. *Verbal bullies* _____
3. *Social bullies* _____

Carla's paragraph, like many effective paragraphs, starts by stating a main
idea, or point. In this case, the clear point is that there are three kinds of bullies in
schools. An effective paragraph must not only make a point but also support it with
**specific evidence**—reasons, examples, and other details. Such specifics help prove
to readers that the point is a reasonable one. Even if readers do not agree with the
writer, at least they have the writer's evidence in front of them. Readers are like
juries: they want to see the evidence for themselves so that they can make their
own judgments.

As you have seen, the author of the paragraph provides plenty of examples to
support the idea that there are physical, verbal, and social bullies. It's an effective
paragraph, beginning with a main idea and then backing up that idea with strong
specific evidence.

## An Essay about Bullies

Now look at the following essay, written by Carla after she was asked to develop
her paragraph about bullies into a longer paper.

### A Hateful Activity: Bullying

Eric, a new boy at school, was shy and physically small. He quickly
became a victim of bullies. Kids would wait after school, pull out his
shirt, and punch and shove him around. He was called such names as
"Mouse Boy" and "Jerk Boy." When he sat down during lunch hour,
others would leave his table. In gym games he was never thrown the ball,
as if he didn't exist. Then one day he came to school with a gun. When
the police were called, he told them he just couldn't take it anymore.
Bullying had hurt him badly, just as it hurts so many other students.

As Eric's experience shows, there are three hateful forms of bullying in schools: physical, verbal, and social.

First of all, there is physical bullying. Bigger or meaner kids try to hurt kids who are smaller or unsure of themselves. They'll push kids into their lockers, knock books out of their hands, or shoulder them out of the cafeteria line. In gym class, a popular bully move is to kick someone's legs out from under him while he is running. In the classroom, bullies might kick the back of the chair or step on the foot of the kids they want to intimidate. Another classic bully move is to corner a kid in a bathroom. There the victim will be slapped around, will have his or her clothes half pulled off, and might even be shoved into a trash can. Bullies will also wait for kids after school and bump or wrestle them around, often while others are looking on. The goal is to frighten kids as much as possible and try to make them cry. The victims are left bruised, hurting, and feeling emotional pain.

Perhaps even worse than physical attack is verbal bullying, which uses words, rather than hands or fists, as weapons. We may be told that "sticks and stones may break my bones, but names can never harm me," but few of us are immune to the pain of a verbal attack. Like physical bullies, verbal bullies tend to single out certain targets. From that moment on, the victim is subjected to a hail of insults and put-downs. These are usually delivered in public, so the victim's humiliation will be greatest: "Oh, no; here comes the nerd!" "Why don't you lose some weight, blubber boy?" "You smell as bad as you look!" "Weirdo." "Fairy." "Creep." "Dork." "Slut." "Loser." Meanwhile, the victim retreats into a painful shell, hoping to escape further notice.

As bad as verbal bullying is, perhaps the most painful type of bullying is social bullying. Many students have a strong need for the comfort of being part of a group. For social bullies, the pleasure of belonging to a group is increased by not allowing others into the group. So, like wolves targeting the weakest sheep in a herd, the bullies lead the pack in isolating people they select as victims. They roll their eyes and turn away in disgust if those people try to talk to them. They move away if a victim sits near them at lunch or stands near them in a school hallway or at a bus stop. No one volunteers to work with these victims on class activities, and they are the ones that no one wants as part of gym teams. Bullies make sure the unwanted ones are never invited to games or parties. As the victims sink into isolation and depression, the social bullies feel all the more puffed up by their own popularity.

Whether bullying is physical, verbal, or social, it can leave deep and lasting scars. If parents, teachers, and other adults were more aware of the types of bullying, they might help by stepping in before the situation becomes too extreme. If students were more aware of the terrible pain that bullying causes, they might think twice about being bullies themselves.

- Which sentence in the introductory paragraph expresses the central point of the essay?

  *As Eric's experience shows, there are three hateful forms of bullying in schools: physical, verbal, and social.*

- How many supporting paragraphs are provided to back up the central point?

  *3*

## The Parts of an Essay

Each of the parts of an essay is explained below.

### Introductory Paragraph

A well-written introductory paragraph will normally do the following:

- Gain the reader's interest by using one of several common methods of introduction.

- Present the **thesis statement**. The thesis statement expresses the central point of an essay, just as a topic sentence states the main idea of a paragraph. The central idea in Carla's essay is expressed in the last sentence of the introductory paragraph.

### Four Common Methods of Introduction

Four common methods of introduction are (1) telling a brief story, (2) asking one or more questions, (3) shifting to the opposite, or (4) going from the broad to the narrow. Following are examples of all four.

**1 Telling a brief story.** An interesting story is hard for a reader to resist. In an introduction, the story should be no more than a few sentences, and it should relate meaningfully to the central idea. The story can be an experience of your own, of someone you know, or of someone you have read about. Carla uses this method of introduction for her essay on bullying:

> Eric, a new boy at school, was shy and physically small. He quickly became a victim of bullies. Kids would wait after school, pull out his shirt, and punch and shove him around. He was called such names as "Mouse Boy" and "Jerk Boy." When he sat down during lunch hour, others would leave his table. In gym games he was never thrown the ball, as if he didn't exist. Then one day he came to school with a gun. When the police were called, he told them he just couldn't take it anymore. Bullying had hurt him badly, just as it hurts so many other students. As Eric's experience shows, there are three hateful forms of bullying in schools: physical, verbal, and social.

**2 Asking one or more questions.** These questions may be ones that you intend to answer in your essay. They may also indicate that your topic is relevant to readers—it is something they care about. If Carla had used this approach, here is how her introductory paragraph might have looked:

> When you were a kid, were you ever pushed around by bigger children? Were you shoved aside in hallways or knocked out of your seat in classrooms? Were you ever called hurtful names like "fatso," "worm," "dogface," or "retard"? Or were you coldly ignored by other students? Did they turn their backs on you, pretending you didn't exist? If the answer to any of these questions is "yes," then you were a victim of one of three forms of bullying: physical, verbal, or social.

**3 Shifting to the opposite.** Another way to gain the reader's interest is to first present an idea that is the opposite of what will be written about. Using this approach, Carla could have begun her essay like this:

> For many children, school is a happy experience. They like their teachers, they see their friends on a daily basis, and they feel comfortable and welcome. But for the victims of bullies, school is a nightmare. Every day they must face someone bigger or meaner than they are and endure humiliation in a variety of forms—physical, verbal, and social.

**4 Going from the broad to the narrow.** Broad, general observations can capture your reader's interest; they can also introduce your general topic and provide helpful background information. If Carla had used this method of introduction, she might have written first about typical problems in growing up and then narrowed her focus down to one problem: bullying.

> Many unpleasant parts of growing up seem unavoidable. Pimples happen, voices crack, and students worry all the time about their looks and their changing bodies. In time, the pimples disappear, the voices deepen, and the worries recede. But one all-too-common aspect of growing up, bullying, can have lasting negative results. Young people should not have to put up with bullying in any of its forms—physical, verbal, or social.

## Supporting Paragraphs

The traditional school essay has three supporting paragraphs. But some essays will have two supporting paragraphs, and others will have four or more. Each supporting paragraph should have its own main idea (also called a **topic sentence**) stating the point to be developed in that paragraph.

Notice that the essay on bullying has clear main ideas for each of the three supporting paragraphs:

- First of all, there is physical bullying.
- Perhaps even worse than physical attack is verbal bullying, which uses words, rather than hands or fists, as weapons.
- As bad as verbal bullying is, perhaps the most painful type of bullying is social bullying.

## Transitional Words and Sentences

In a paragraph, **transitional words** like *first, another, also, in addition,* and *finally* are used to help connect supporting ideas. In an essay, **transitional sentences** are used to help tie the supporting paragraphs together. Such transitional sentences often occur at the beginning of a supporting paragraph.

- Look at the main ideas (topic sentences) for the second and third supporting paragraphs in the essay on bullying. Explain how those sentences are also transitional sentences.

  *The first few words in each sentence refer to the main idea of the*

  *paragraph immediately before it.*

(As you may have realized, the topic sentences are also transitional sentences because each introduces another type of bullying while restating the type of bullying already mentioned. The second topic sentence introduces verbal bullying, saying it may be even worse than physical bullying. The third topic sentence introduces social bullying, saying it may be the most painful type of bullying.)

## Concluding Paragraph

The concluding paragraph often summarizes the essay by briefly restating the thesis and, at times, the main supporting points. It may also provide a closing thought or two (which may include a recommendation) as a way of bringing the paper to a natural and graceful end.

Look again at the concluding paragraph of the essay on bullies.

- Which sentence summarizes the essay? _____ *First* _____
- Which sentences provide closing thoughts? _____ *Second and third* _____
- How many closing thoughts are there? __ *Two* __

(The sentence that summarizes the essay is the first sentence of the concluding paragraph. And the last two sentences of the essay present two closing thoughts.)

Three essay-writing assignments are provided in the writing mastery tests that follow. The readings in Part Two of this book will then offer many opportunities for writing both paragraphs and essays.

# LONGER SELECTIONS IN READING AND WRITING: Mastery Test 1 (Reading)

In each of the passages that follow, the authors state their central point on one sentence. Find that sentence, and write its number in the space provided.

**A.**    ¹Those who are fortunate enough not to live in poverty may equate "being poor" with "not having enough money to buy the things I'd like." ²Certainly, being poor does mean doing without many of life's material pleasures. ³But the impact of poverty goes far beyond the inability to buy goods.

⁴One fundamental effect of poverty is that the poor often live in substandard housing. ⁵They rent from landlords who may neglect the property, even to a criminal extent. ⁶The houses are often unsafe, with dangerous electrical wiring, non-functioning plumbing, and inadequate heat.

⁷Poverty also profoundly affects people's ability to receive an education. ⁸Public schools in poor areas are underfunded, poorly staffed, and supplied with outdated textbooks and sparse supplies. ⁹Classrooms are crowded and often chaotic; the schools function more as warehouses than as places of education. ¹⁰Children coming out of these schools are inadequately prepared for college, so they rarely advance beyond high school.

¹¹A third way in which poverty profoundly affects people's lives is in the area of employment. ¹²Without the career preparation that quality education provides, poor people are often qualified only for jobs with no future, no benefits, and a high chance of being laid off. ¹³When the poor do lose their jobs, they must deal with the tangled mess of unemployment insurance and welfare, adding stress and the increasing sense of failure to their lives.

    __3__    is the number of the sentence that states the central point.

> Sentences 1–2 introduce the topic of what poverty means. The word *But* in sentence 3 signals the main idea—that "the impact of poverty goes far beyond the inability to buy goods." Sentences 4–13 present details of three specific areas of people's lives impacted by poverty—housing, education, and employment.

*(Continues on next page)*

**B.**    ¹Can people modify their own behavior? ²Researchers have found that it is possible to change one's behavior—but only by following certain steps.

³The first thing to do is to decide what behavior you want to acquire—the desired "target" behavior. ⁴What if you want to get rid of some behavior? ⁵Behavior modification specialists emphasize a positive approach called "ignoring." ⁶Much better results are achieved when the emphasis is on the new behavior to be acquired rather than on the behavior to be eliminated. ⁷For example, instead of setting a target of being less shy, you might define the target behavior as becoming more outgoing or more sociable. ⁸Other possible target behaviors are behaving more assertively, studying more, and getting along better with your roommate. ⁹In each case, you have focused on the behavior that you want to acquire, rather than on the behavior that you want to reduce or eliminate.

¹⁰The next step is to define the target behavior precisely: What exactly do you mean by "assertive" or by "sociable"? ¹¹One way to do this is to imagine situations in which the target behavior could be performed. ¹²Then describe in writing these situations and the way in which you now respond to them. ¹³For example, in the case of shyness, you might write: "When I am sitting in the lecture hall, waiting for class to begin, I don't talk to the people around me." ¹⁴Next, write down how you would rather act in that situation: "Ask the people sitting next to me how they like the class or the professor; or ask if they have seen any particularly good movies recently."

¹⁵The last step—which gets to the heart of self-modification—is to provide yourself with a positive reinforcer that is gained only upon specific improvements in the target behavior. ¹⁶You may be able to use the same reinforcer that now maintains your undesirable behavior, or you may want to pick a new reinforcer. ¹⁷Researchers use the example of a student who wanted to improve his relationship with his parents. ¹⁸He first counted the times he said something pleasant to them and then rewarded himself for improvement by making his favorite pastime, playing pool, dependent on predetermined increases in the number of pleasant remarks he made. ¹⁹You can also use tokens: Give yourself one token for every thirty minutes of studying, and cash in those tokens for reinforcement. ²⁰For instance, the privilege of going to a movie might require ten tokens.

_____2_____    is the number of the sentence that states the central point.

Sentence 1 introduces the topic of behavior modification. The list words *certain steps* in sentence 2 signal the main idea—that "it is possible to change one's behavior—but only by following certain steps." Sentences 3–20 present details of three of these steps.

# LONGER SELECTIONS IN READING AND WRITING: Mastery Test 2 (Reading)

In each of the passages that follow, the central idea is implied rather than stated, and the passage is followed by four sentences. In the space provided, write the letter of the sentence that best expresses the unstated central idea.

**A.**    ¹Today's world puts a lot of pressure on teenagers to work. ²By working, they gain more independence from their families, and they also get the spending money needed to keep up with their peers. ³Many people argue that working can be a valuable experience for the young.

⁴However, schoolwork and the benefits of extracurricular activities tend to go by the wayside when adolescents work more than fifteen hours a week. ⁵Teachers are then faced with the problems of keeping the attention of tired pupils and of giving homework to students who simply don't have the time to do it. ⁶In addition, educators have noticed less involvement in the extracurricular events many consider healthy influences on young people. ⁷School bands and athletic teams are losing players to work, and sports events are poorly attended by working students. ⁸Those teenagers who try to do it all—homework, extracurricular activities, and work—may find themselves exhausted and prone to illness.

⁹Another drawback of too much work is that it may promote materialism and an unrealistic lifestyle. ¹⁰Some parents say that work teaches adolescents the value of a dollar. ¹¹Undoubtedly, it can, and it's true that some teenagers work to help out with the family budget or save for college. ¹²But surveys have shown that the majority of working teens use their earnings to buy luxuries—stereos, tape decks, clothing, even cars. ¹³These young people, some of whom earn $300 and more a month, don't worry about spending wisely—they can just about have it all. ¹⁴In many cases, experts point out, they are becoming accustomed to a lifestyle they won't be able to afford several years down the road, when they'll no longer have parents to pay for car insurance, food and lodging, and so on. ¹⁵At that point, they'll be hard pressed to pay for necessities as well as luxuries.

_____D_____ Write the letter of the sentence that best expresses the implied main idea.
   A. Teenagers who work more than fifteen hours a week find that they have little or no time for homework and extracurricular activities.
   B. Some people believe that work teaches teenagers the value of a dollar, but others believe that it leads to materialism.
   C. These days, students who work often use their earnings to buy luxuries that they will not be able to afford when they're no longer living at home.
   D. By limiting their working hours, teenagers can benefit from both work *and* school—and also avoid an unrealistic lifestyle.

Answer A covers only sentences 4–7. Answer B covers only sentences 9–15. Answer C covers only sentences 12–15.

*(Continues on next page)*

**B.** ¹If exercise could be packed into a pill, it would be the single most widely prescribed and beneficial medicine in the nation. ²In a survey, eight in ten undergraduates realized that physical activity can prevent heart disease and prevent and treat obesity. ³However, fewer than half knew that it maintains bone density and can help prevent diabetes.

⁴With regular exercise, your heart muscles become stronger and pump blood more efficiently. ⁵Your heart rate and resting pulse slow down. ⁶Your blood pressure may drop slightly from its normal level.

⁷Exercise thickens the bones and can slow the loss of calcium that normally occurs with age. ⁸Physical activity increases flexibility in the joints and improves digestion and elimination. ⁹It speeds up metabolism and builds lean body mass, so the body burns more calories and body fats decrease. ¹⁰It heightens sensitivity to insulin (a great benefit for diabetics) and may lower the risk of developing diabetes. ¹¹In addition, exercise enhances clot-dissolving substances in the blood, helping to prevent strokes, heart attacks, and pulmonary embolisms (clots in the lungs), and it helps lower the risk of certain cancers. ¹²Regular exercise can actually extend your lifespan and sharpen your memory and mind.

¹³Even your eyes benefit from physical activity. ¹⁴Individuals who exercise three or more times a week may reduce by 70 percent their risk of age-related macular degeneration, which destroys the sharp central vision needed for tasks such as reading and driving.

_B_ Which sentence best expresses the implied central idea of the entire selection?
   A. Few undergraduates realize all the health benefits of exercise.
   B. Nothing is better than exercise to help your body function at its best.
   C. Science needs to develop a pill that will provide all the benefits of exercise.
   D. Exercise can make your heart pump more efficiently and improve your digestion and elimination.

   Answer B works because each detail in the passage describes a way that exercise helps the body function well. Answers A and D are too narrow; each covers only one or two of the details in the passage. Answer C is not discussed.

# LONGER SELECTIONS IN READING AND WRITING: Mastery Test 3 (Reading)

In each of the passages that follow, the central idea is implied rather than stated, and the passage is followed by four sentences. In the space provided, write the letter of the sentence that best expresses the unstated central ideas.

**A.** ¹Ben Franklin said that the only sure things in life are death and taxes. ²He left something out, however: disappointment. ³No one gets through life without experiencing many disappointments.

⁴Depression is a common negative response to disappointment. ⁵Yvonne, for example, works hard for over a year in her department, trying to win a promotion. ⁶However, the boss names one of her coworkers to the spot. ⁷Deeply depressed, Yvonne decides that all her goals are doomed to defeat. ⁸She loses her enthusiasm for her job and can barely force herself to show up every day. ⁹She tells herself that she is a failure and that doing a good job just isn't worth the work.

¹⁰Another negative reaction to disappointment is escape. ¹¹Kevin fails to get into the college his brother is attending, the college that was the focus of all his dreams, and reacts to his disappointment by escaping his circumstances. ¹²He covers up his real feelings by giving up on his schoolwork and getting completely involved with friends, parties, and "good times." ¹³Or Linda doesn't make the varsity basketball team—something she wanted very badly—and so refuses to play sports at all. ¹⁴She decides to forget her disappointment by hanging out with a new set of friends who get high every day.

¹⁵The positive way to react to disappointment is to use it as a chance for growth. ¹⁶Yvonne, the woman who wasn't promoted, could have handled her disappointment by looking at other options. ¹⁷If her boss doesn't recognize talent and hard work, perhaps she could transfer to another department. ¹⁸Or she could ask the boss how she could improve her performance so that she would be a shoo-in for the next promotion. ¹⁹Kevin, the young man who didn't get into the college of his choice, should look into other schools. ²⁰Going to another college may encourage him to be his own person, step out of his brother's shadow, and realize that being turned down by one college isn't a final judgment on his abilities or potential. ²¹Rather than escape into drugs, Linda could improve her basketball skills for a year or pick up another sport, like swimming or tennis, that might turn out to be more useful to her as an adult.

²²Disappointments are unwelcome but regular visitors to everyone's life. ²³The best response is to step over the unwelcome visitor on the doorstep and get on with life.

Only answer ____D____ Write the letter of the sentence that best expresses the implied central idea.
D covers both
negative and
positive reactions
to disappointment.
Answer A covers
only the first sentence.
Answer B covers
sentences 4–14. Answer C covers only sentences 15–23.

A. Death, taxes, and disappointment are three inevitable parts of life.

B. Many people react to disappointment in a negative way.

C. One of life's challenges is to react to disappointment in a positive way.

D. Many people react to disappointment with depression or escape, rather than using it as an opportunity for growth.

*(Continues on next page)*

**B.**    ¹For many people, the image of the woman in movies about the old West is a gentle one of a mother quietly tending to her kitchen, shopping at the general store, and raising her children.

²But preparing even a simple meal was a time- and energy-consuming chore. ³In the 1800s, cooking was performed on a coal- or wood-burning stove. ⁴Unlike an electric or a gas range, which can be turned on with the flick of a single switch, cast-iron and steel stoves were especially difficult to use. ⁵A housewife would first have to clean out the ashes left from previous fires. ⁶Then, she had to set paper and kindling inside the stove, carefully adjust the dampers and flues, and light a fire. ⁷Any time the fire slackened, she had to adjust a flue or add more fuel. ⁸All day long, the stove had to be fed with new supplies of coal or wood—an average of fifty pounds or more. ⁹At least twice a day, the ash box under the fire had to be emptied. ¹⁰All together, a housewife spent four hours every day rubbing the stove with thick black wax to keep it from rusting, lighting the fire, adjusting dampers, sifting ashes, and carrying wood or coal.

¹¹A housewife also had to know how to prepare unprocessed foods for consumption. ¹²Prior to the 1890s, there were few factory-prepared foods. ¹³Shoppers bought poultry that was still alive and then had to kill and pluck the birds. ¹⁴Fish had to have scales removed. ¹⁵Green coffee had to be roasted and ground. ¹⁶Loaves of sugar had to be pounded, flour sifted, nuts shelled, and raisins seeded.

¹⁷Cleaning was an even more arduous task than cooking. ¹⁸The soot and smoke from coal- and wood-burning stoves blackened walls and dirtied drapes and carpets. ¹⁹Gas and kerosene lamps left smelly deposits of black soot on furniture and curtains. ²⁰Each day, the lamps' glass chimneys had to be wiped and the wicks trimmed or replaced. ²¹And periodically floors had to be scrubbed, rugs beaten, and windows washed.

²²Since only the wealthy had indoor plumbing, chores that involved water were especially demanding. ²³Even bringing water into the house was a challenge. ²⁴According to calculations made in 1886, a typical North Carolina housewife had to carry water from a pump or well or a spring eight to ten times each day. ²⁵Washing, boiling, and rinsing a single load of laundry used about fifty gallons of water. ²⁶Over the course of a year, she walked 148 miles toting over 36 tons of water! ²⁷Homes without running water also lacked sinks with drains. ²⁸That meant that women had to remove dirty dishwater, kitchen slops, and, worst of all, the contents of chamber pots from their house by hand.

_____C_____    Write the letter of the sentence that best expresses the implied central idea.

All of the details in the passage describe harsh physical labor. Answers A and D cover only sentences 2–16. Answer B covers only sentences 22–28.

A. In the 1800s, preparing even a simple meal was a time- and energy-consuming chore.

B. During the 1800s, only the wealthy had indoor plumbing, so a typical housewife walked 148 miles, carrying over 36 tons of water, every year.

c. In America in the 1800s, a housewife's days were spent in harsh physical labor.

D. Because coal-and wood-burning stoves were especially difficult to use and because most foods required intensive preparation, most American housewives in the 1800s were tied to their kitchens.

# LONGER SELECTIONS IN READING AND WRITING: Mastery Test 4 (Writing)

Write an essay about three people who have been important influences in your life.

## How to Proceed

**1.** To help decide which three people to focus on, first use one or more of the prewriting techniques: (1) freewrite, and/or (2) ask questions such as *what, when, where, how,* and *why* about each person, and/or (3) make a list of all the details you can think of about each person you might want to include. Prewriting will help you determine the three people for whom you can provide the best supporting details.

**2.** Make a scratch outline consisting of the thesis (central point) of your paper and the names of the three people who have influenced you.

**3.** Decide on what approach you will use in your introductory paragraph. As shown on pages 276–277, will you (1) tell a brief story, (2) ask one or more questions, (3) shift to the opposite, or (4) go from broad to narrow? Whatever method you choose, be sure to end your introductory paragraph with your thesis statement. Here is an example of an introduction that goes from broad to narrow:

> As you go through life, how many people do you suppose you meet? Certainly the number is in the hundreds, even the thousands. But how many of them do you remember for the rest of your life? How many of them affect you in such a way that you never forget them? For me, that number is small. When I see the question, "Who has had a major impact on your life?" I think of three people: my first-grade teacher, my junior-high basketball coach, and my first boss.

**4.** Then begin each of your three supporting paragraphs with a topic sentence that states your main idea in that paragraph. For example:

> The first person I think of as being an important influence in my life, believe it or not, was my first-grade teacher, Mrs. Bertram.

> The second person who was a big influence on me was Mr. Mulholland, my junior-high basketball coach.

> Finally, the third person who was a major influence on me was Rick Sanchez, my first boss.

*(Continues on next page)*

**5.** End with a short concluding paragraph that summarizes your essay and/or provides a closing thought or two. For example:

> As I think of the three people I've mentioned above, I am struck by how very different they were. Mrs. Bertram was a grandmother who spoke very softly and kindly. Mr. Mulholland was a lifelong bachelor whose bellowing voice echoed through the gym. Mr. Sanchez was a husband and father who treated us like members of his own family.  But they all had something in common: me. In their three very separate ways, each of them contributed something unforgettable to my life.

**6.** After you have edited and proofread your paper, be sure to *read it out loud*. Hearing how your writing sounds is an excellent way to pick up grammar and punctuation problems in your writing. Chances are that you'll find sentence mistakes at spots where your paper does not read smoothly and clearly. Use a grammar handbook, if necessary, to help you remove these trouble spots.

*To the Instructor:*
A student's score on this test should be based on your evaluation of whether he or she has written an A, B, C, D, or F paper.

Suggested equivalents:

A = 90 to 100
B = 80 to 89
C = 70 to 79
D = 60 to 69
F = 59 and below

# LONGER SELECTIONS IN READING AND WRITING: Mastery Test 5 (Writing)

Write an essay about three challenges in your life—either ones you have resolved or ones that you are still dealing with.

## How to Proceed

**1.** To help decide which challenges to focus on, first use one or more of the prewriting techniques: (1) freewrite, and/or (2) ask questions such as *what, when, where, how,* and *why* about each challenge, and/or (3) make a list of all the details you can think of about each challenge. The prewriting techniques will help you determine the three challenges for which you can provide the best supporting details.

**2.** Make a scratch outline consisting of the thesis (central point) of your paper and a brief list of the three challenges.

**3.** Decide on what approach you will use in your introductory paragraph. As shown on pages 276–277, will you (1) tell a brief story, (2) ask one or more questions, (3) shift to the opposite, or (4) go from broad to narrow? Whatever method you choose, be sure to end your introductory paragraph with your thesis statement. Here is an example of an introduction that shifts to the opposite:

> Some people are born with a silver spoon in their mouths. They have happy, stable families. Their parents are loving and supportive. They're surrounded by encouragement and opportunities. School comes easily to them. Everything and everyone around them seems golden. They glide through life with no bumps along the way. But my life hasn't been like that. From my early childhood, I've been dealing with three significant challenges.

**4.** Then begin each of your three supporting paragraphs with a topic sentence that states your main idea in that paragraph. For example:

> A big challenge in my life has been that I have dyslexia, which has made it extra hard for me to succeed in school.

> Another challenge that I've had to deal with is my difficult relationship with my father.

> But by far the biggest challenge in my life is having lost my mother at an early age.

*(Continues on next page)*

**5.** End with a short concluding paragraph that summarizes your essay and/or provides a closing thought or two. For example:

> Dyslexia, my relationship with my dad, and the death of my mother are all very real and very difficult challenges I've had to deal with. But I've made progress in dealing with all three. I'm a better reader, I've worked to improve the relationship with my dad, and I'm trying to live a life that would make my mom proud of me.

**6.** After you have edited and proofread your paper, be sure to *read it out loud*. Hearing how your writing sounds is an excellent way to pick up grammar and punctuation problems in your writing. Chances are that you'll find sentence mistakes at spots where your paper does not read smoothly and clearly. Use a grammar handbook, if necessary, to help you remove these trouble spots.

*To the Instructor:*
A student's score on this test should be based on your evaluation of whether he or she has written an A, B, C, D, or F paper.

Suggested equivalents:

A = 90 to 100
B = 80 to 89
C = 70 to 79
D = 60 to 69
F = 59 and below

# LONGER SELECTIONS IN READING AND WRITING: Mastery Test 6 (Writing)

Write an essay about three of the biggest mistakes (*or* best decisions) you have made in your life. (*Note:* You may have already written a paragraph on mistakes in your life, as presented on page 172. If so, you may want to expand your treatment of those mistakes and develop the paragraph into an essay.)

## How to Proceed

**1.** To help decide which mistakes or decisions to focus on, first use one or more of the prewriting techniques: (1) freewrite, and/or (2) ask questions such as *what, when, where, how,* and *why,* and/or (3) make a list of all the details you can think of about your biggest mistakes or best decisions. The prewriting techniques will help you determine the mistakes or decisions for which you can provide the best supporting details.

**2.** Make up a scratch outline consisting of the thesis of your paper and a brief list of your three mistakes or decisions.

**3.** Decide on what approach you will use in your introductory paragraph. As shown on pages 276–277, will you (1) tell a brief story, (2) ask one or more questions, (3) shift to the opposite, or (4) go from broad to narrow? Whatever method you choose, be sure to end your introductory paragraph with your thesis statement. Here is an example of an introduction that begins with a story:

> I was standing somewhere I'd never wanted to be—in front of a judge in a criminal courtroom. I was wearing an orange prison jumpsuit. The judge was a stern-looking woman wearing a black robe. Surrounding me were armed police officers, ready to tackle me if I made a wrong move. The judge looked over her steel-rimmed glasses at me and said, "How do you plead to the charges against you?" As my lawyer and I had agreed, I said, "Guilty, Your Honor." The judge nodded briefly, then said, "Is there anything you would like to say before the court considers your sentence?" I looked at her stern face and thought, yes, there is a lot I'd like to say. Mostly I'd like to explain that along the way, I had made three terrible decisions.

**4.** Then begin each of your three supporting paragraphs with a topic sentence that states your main idea in that paragraph. For example:

> I made a terrible mistake when I was sixteen and decided to drop out of high school.

> A second bad mistake I made was hanging out with people who were involved in illegal activities.

> A third bad mistake I made was fathering a child when I was pretty much still a kid myself.

*(Continues on next page)*

**5.** End with a short concluding paragraph that summarizes your essay and/or provides a closing thought or two. For example:

> There in the courtroom, I didn't have time to tell the judge any details about my three bad decisions. All I could say was, "I know what I did was wrong. I take full responsibility and am working hard to turn my life around." I meant every word of that, and I mean it today. I'm determined not to let three bad decisions rule the rest of my life.

**6.** After you have edited and proofread your paper, be sure to *read it out loud*. Hearing how your writing sounds is an excellent way to pick up grammar and punctuation problems in your writing. Chances are that you'll find sentence mistakes at spots where your paper does not read smoothly and clearly. Use a grammar handbook, if necessary, to help you remove these trouble spots.

*To the Instructor:*
A student's score on this test should be based on your evaluation of whether he or she has written an A, B, C, D, or F paper.

Suggested equivalents:

A = 90 to 100
B = 80 to 89
C = 70 to 79
D = 60 to 69
F = 59 and below

# Part Two

**Fifteen Selections
for Readers and Writers**

# Introduction to the Reading Selections

**P**art Two of the book is made up of fifteen high-interest essays that will provide extensive practice in reading and writing. This introduction will describe the format of the fifteen essays. It will briefly review the concept of point and support that is the key to becoming a better reader and writer. Finally, it will offer strategies for reading and writing about the essays.

## Format of the Readings

Each of the fifteen essays contains the following:

- A *Preview* that presents helpful background information and arouses your interest in the selection.

- A *Words to Watch* section that gives the definitions of some of the words in the selection.

- An activity called *First Impressions* that asks you to write for ten minutes about the selection you have just finished reading.

- A *Vocabulary Check* that helps you learn words in a research-proven way: by seeing how they are actually used in the selection.

- A *Reading Check* that helps you practice and develop important reading skills: recognizing main ideas and the central point; identifying key supporting details; making inferences; and being aware of the writer's craft.

- *Discussion Questions* to help you deepen your understanding of a reading.

- *Two Paragraph Assignments* and *two Essay Assignments*—giving you a choice of topics for writing practice. As a general rule, you will be given both a paragraph and an essay assignment that involve a first-person "I" point of view, in which you are asked to provide evidence from your own personal experience. You will also be given a paragraph and an essay assignment that involve an objective point of view, in which you will be asked to provide evidence from research or your own general reasoning.

# Point and Support

The most important principle in this book is that effective reading and writing share two basic parts: (1) a *point* and (2) *support* for that point. By keeping this principle in mind, you can become a better reader and writer. When you read, remember that an author's purpose is to make a point and support it with reasons, examples, and details. When you write, remember that to communicate effectively, you should follow the same basic plan: make a point and support it.

# Reading Strategies

To become a better reader, get actively involved in each stage of the reading process. Here are ways to do so.

1  **Preview the selection.** In other words, look over what you will read—quickly but alertly—before you start to read it. Follow these steps:

   ● *Turn the title into a question.* For example, before reading the selection "Adult Children at Home," you might ask the question, "Why are adult children still at home?" or "Why have adult children returned home?" Searching for the answer to your question will give you a reason for reading.

   ● *Read through the first several paragraphs and the last several paragraphs.* They will give you a quick general sense of what the selection is about.

**2    Read the selection straight through to enjoy whatever it has to say about life and human nature.** Don't get bogged down; instead, just try to understand as much as you can the first time through.

**3    Now reread the selection, marking key information with a pen or pencil.** Marking material will keep your mind alert and show you what to come back to later. Here are some suggestions on how and what to mark:

- Underline ideas that seem important.

- Write *Ex* in the margin to set off helpful examples.

- Put question marks beside any material you don't understand.

- Number any major series of items or ideas.

   Following each selection is a set of questions that help you apply important reading skills, almost all of which you have already practiced in this book. As you strengthen these skills enough to make them habits, your reading ability is sure to improve. Here are the skills:

- Understanding vocabulary in context

- Recognizing main ideas and the central point

- Identifying key supporting details

- Making inferences

- Being aware of the writer's craft

**4    Note techniques that the author uses to communicate ideas.** In this book, questions on these techniques appear under the head "The Writer's Craft." Being aware of these strategies will increase your understanding of what you read as well as improve your own writing. Questions on the writer's craft include the following:

- *Introductions and Conclusions.* What does an author do at the start of an essay to interest you in reading what he or she has written? And what kind of "caboose," or conclusion, does the author use at the end of an essay?

- *Types of Support.*   How has the author supported his or her central point? As you've already learned, common methods of support include reasons, examples, details, and personal experiences.

- *Patterns of Organization.* How have the supporting details been arranged? As you have seen, authors often use a **time order**—telling the parts of a story in the order that they happened. Common word signals (also called *transitions*) that mark time order are *first, then, before, as, after, next,* and *finally.* (See also pages 175–178.)

An equally popular pattern of organization is a **listing order**—providing a series of reasons, examples, or details. Common word signals or transitions that mark listing order are *first of all, another, in addition, also,* and *finally. (*See also pages 171–174.)

Another pattern of organization is **illustration**—supporting an idea with one or more examples, and using transitions such as *for instance, for example,* and *such as*. (See also pages 219–222.)

A fourth pattern is **comparison or contrast**—showing how things are alike or (more often) different. Typical transitions for this pattern are (for comparison) *like, just as, similarly* and (for contrast) *but, however, in contrast,* and *on the other hand*. (See also pages 222–226.)

A fifth pattern worth noting is **cause-effect**—explaining the reasons why something happened or the results of something. Typical transitions for this pattern are *because, therefore, effect, consequently,* and *as a result*. (See also pages 227–228.)

- *Tone.* Just as a speaker's tone of voice reveals how he or she feels, a writer's tone communicates feelings. You can get a sense of how an author feels about his or her subject by looking at the wording of the selection. It will often indicate whether a selection's tone is humorous or serious, angry or friendly, formal or informal, sentimental or sarcastic, hopeful or discouraging, or simply objective (detached and factual).

- *Purpose.* Decide what type of writing you are reading. Is it intended to **inform** (give people information), to **entertain** (give people pleasure), or to **persuade** (change people's minds about an issue)? Or does it have a combination of these purposes?

- *Audience.* Decide for what kind of reader the selection was probably written. Was it meant for the general reader (anyone)? Or was the author writing for a smaller audience, such as researchers, parents, or students?

- *Titles.* Most authors choose their titles very carefully. Many times, a title clearly describes the topic of the essay, and sometimes it is the shortest possible summary of the central point of an essay. Look closely at titles for excellent clues about authors' ideas and their attitudes toward their topics.

# Writing Strategies

You have already practiced in Part One the steps you should take to write effectively. In a nutshell, you should:

**1**  Use the prewriting strategies of freewriting, asking questions, and list making to begin to write about your topic. Remember that the heart of the matter is to advance an idea or point of some kind and to provide solid support for that idea.

**2**  Make a scratch outline.

**3**  Write several drafts, aiming all the while to make a clear point, to provide strong support for that point, and to organize your support. A pattern of organization and transitions will help you organize your support.

**4**  When you have revised and edited and think you are almost finished, read your paper out loud. It should read smoothly and clearly. Look closely for grammar and punctuation problems at any rough spots. Use a grammar and punctuation handbook to help identify and correct mistakes that you may be making.

Here are some other tips that will help you with your writing.

**1**  Learn from your instructor whether you should be writing a paragraph or an essay in response to a given selection.

**2**  When you have a choice, write about what you know. You will note that for many of the writing topics in Part Two, you are given the opportunity to draw upon your personal experiences and use an "I" or "my" point of view.

But you may also be expected to write papers on objective topics, for which you will not draw upon personal experience but, instead, on your own reasoned opinions. You may be asked, for example, to take a position on abortion or handguns or marijuana or teenage parents or alcohol advertising on TV or texting while driving or bullying—or any other topic.

**3**  If you don't know much about your topic, you should do some quick research and read about your topic. The easiest way to do this is to simply go onto the Internet, using the search engine Google (**www.google.com**) to get more information. For example, if you Googled "bullying," you would immediately have access to over forty million articles on that topic!

Using Google will help you get more information quickly about a given topic; it will also suggest ways you can narrow down your potential topic. For example, you might decide, after looking through a number of articles about bullying, that you will write an essay on the steps that schools should take to prevent bullying.

Keep in mind two notes of caution about use of the Internet:

- Never for a moment believe that "If it's on the Internet, it must be true." Technology today allows anyone to publish anything at any time. For a given article, an author or information provider should be clearly identified. That author or information provider should be a knowledgeable, qualified, impartial, and reliable authority on the data presented.

- Do not use someone else's words in writing your paper. That would be *plagiarizing*—in a word, stealing. Use other people's ideas only as a springboard for developing your own thoughts about a given topic.

# The Yellow Ribbon

## Pete Hamill

## Preview

When the United States is involved in overseas military actions, U.S. communities often display yellow ribbons to symbolize the hope that their sons and daughters will return home safely. That practice was probably inspired by this story, which first appeared as a column in the *New York Post*. Read it to learn what message a yellow handkerchief conveyed to a worried, lonely man.

## Words to Watch

*cocoon* (2):  protective covering
*bluntness* (13):  abruptness
*solitude* (21):  the state of being alone
*exaltation* (22):  joy

1   They were going to Fort Lauderdale, the girl remembered later. There were six of them, three boys and three girls, and they picked up the bus at the old terminal on 34th Street, carrying sandwiches and wine in paper bags, dreaming of golden beaches and the tides of the sea as the gray cold spring of New York vanished behind them. Vingo was on board from the beginning.

2   As the bus passed through Jersey and into Philly, they began to notice that Vingo never moved. He sat in front of the young people, his dusty face masking his age, dressed in a plain brown ill-fitting suit. His fingers were stained from cigarettes and he chewed the inside of his lip a lot, frozen into some personal cocoon° of silence.

3   Somewhere outside of Washington, deep into the night, the bus pulled into a Howard Johnson's, and everybody got off except Vingo. He sat rooted in his seat, and the young people began to wonder about him, trying to imagine his life: Perhaps he was a sea captain, maybe he had run away from his wife, he could be an old soldier going home. When they went back to the bus, the girl sat beside him and introduced herself.

4   "We're going to Florida," the girl said brightly. "You going that far?"

5   "I don't know," Vingo said.

6   "I've never been there," she said. "I hear it's beautiful."

7   "It is," he said quietly, as if remembering something he had tried to forget.

8     "You live there?"

9     "I did some time there in the Navy. Jacksonville."

10     "Want some wine?" she said. He smiled and took the bottle of Chianti and took a swig. He thanked her and retreated again into his silence. After a while, she went back to the others, as Vingo nodded in sleep.

11     In the morning they awoke outside another Howard Johnson's, and this time Vingo went in. The girl insisted that he join them. He seemed very shy and ordered black coffee and smoked nervously, as the young people chattered about sleeping on the beaches. When they went back on the bus, the girl sat with Vingo again, and after a while, slowly and painfully and with great hesitation, he began to tell his story. He had been in jail in New York for the last four years, and now he was going home.

12     "Four years!" the girl said. "What did you do?"

13     "It doesn't matter," he said with quiet bluntness°. "I did it and I went to jail. If you can't do the time, don't do the crime. That's what they say and they're right."

14     "Are you married?"

15     "I don't know."

16     "You don't know?" she said.

17     "Well, when I was in the can I wrote to my wife," he said. "I told her, I said, Martha, I understand if you can't stay married to me. I told her that. I said I was gonna be away a long time, and that if she couldn't stand it, if the kids kept askin' questions, if it hurt her too much, well, she could just forget me. Get a new guy—she's a wonderful woman, really something—and forget about me. I told her she didn't have to write me or nothing. And she didn't. Not for three and a half years."

18     "And you're going home now, not knowing?"

19     "Yeah," he said shyly. "Well, last week, when I was sure the parole was coming through, I wrote her. I told her that if she had a new guy, I understood. But if she didn't, if she would take me back, she should let me know. We used to live in this town, Brunswick, just before Jacksonville, and there's a great big oak tree just as you come into town, a very famous tree, huge. I told her if she would take me back, she should put a yellow handkerchief on the tree, and I would get off and come home. If she didn't want me, forget it, no handkerchief, and I'd keep going on through."

20     "Wow," the girl said. "Wow."

21     She told the others, and soon all of them were in it, caught up in the approach of Brunswick, looking at the pictures Vingo showed them of his wife and three children, the woman handsome in a plain way, the children still unformed in a cracked, much-handled snapshot. Now they were twenty miles from Brunswick and the young people took over window seats on the right side, waiting for the approach of the great oak tree. Vingo stopped looking, tightening his face into the ex-con's mask, as if fortifying himself against still another disappointment. Then it was ten miles, and then five and the bus acquired a dark hushed mood, full of

silence, of absence, of lost years, of the woman's plain face, of the sudden letter on the breakfast table, of the wonder of children, of the iron bars of solitude°.

22    Then suddenly all of the young people were up out of their seats, screaming and shouting and crying, doing small dances, shaking clenched fists in triumph and exaltation°. All except Vingo.

23    Vingo sat there stunned, looking at the oak tree. It was covered with yellow handkerchiefs, twenty of them, thirty of them, maybe hundreds, a tree that stood like a banner of welcome blowing and billowing in the wind, turned into a gorgeous yellow blur by the passing bus. As the young people shouted, the old con slowly rose from his seat, holding himself tightly, and made his way to the front of the bus to go home.

## First Impressions

Freewrite for ten minutes on one of the following.

1. Did you enjoy reading this selection? Why or why not?

2. Have you ever gotten into an interesting conversation with a stranger? What did you learn about him or her?

3. Why do you think the young people were so excited when they saw the tree? What did it mean to them? If you had been on the bus, how would you have reacted?

## Vocabulary Check

_A_  1. In the sentence below, the word *fortifying* means
   A. strengthening.
   B. watching.
   C. hurrying.
   D. losing.

If he is expecting a disappointment, he would strengthen himself to prepare for it.

"Vingo stopped looking, tightening his face into the ex-con's mask, as if fortifying himself against still another disappointment." (Paragraph 21)

_B_ 2. In the excerpt below, the word *acquired* means

    A. needed.

    B. took on.

    C. stopped.

    D. lost.

> As the people anticipated reaching the tree, the bus would take on a hushed mood.

"Then it was ten miles, and then five and the bus acquired a dark hushed mood...." (Paragraph 21)

_A_ 3. In the excerpt below, the word *hushed* means

    A. quiet.

    B. evil.

    C. surprising.

    D. pleasant.

> If the mood is "full of silence," it must be quiet.

"[T]he bus acquired a dark hushed mood, full of silence, of absence, of lost years, of the woman's plain face, of the sudden letter on the breakfast table...." (Paragraph 21)

# Reading Check

## Central Point and Main Ideas

Answer A is not supported. Answer B covers only paragraph 13. Answer C covers only paragraphs 14–21; it overlooks the outcome.

_D_ 1. Which sentence best expresses the central point of the entire selection?

    A. Prison sentences can ruin marriages.

    B. If you commit a crime, you must pay for it.

    C. Vingo did not know what to expect.

    D. Vingo returned from prison to find that his wife still loved him.

Answers A and D cover only sentence 1. Answer C covers only sentence 2.

_B_ 2. Which sentence best expresses the main idea of paragraph 3?

    A. The bus stopped at a Howard Johnson's.

    B. The young people began to be curious about Vingo.

    C. Vingo might have been a sea captain.

    D. Everyone got off the bus except Vingo.

Answer A covers only sentence 2. Answer B covers only sentence 1. Answer C covers only sentence 3.

_D_ 3. Which sentence best expresses the main idea of paragraph 21?

    A. The young people watched out the window more than Vingo did as the bus neared Brunswick.

    B. Vingo showed the young people photographs of his wife and children.

    C. Vingo tightened his face as if to prepare himself for a disappointment.

    D. The suspense built as the bus neared Brunswick and the oak tree.

## Supporting Details

_B_    4.  When the young girl asks what he was in prison for, Vingo answers that
    A. it is none of her business.
    B. it doesn't matter.
    C. he is too ashamed to tell her.
    D. he was imprisoned for a crime he didn't commit.

See paragraph 13.

_B_    5.  Vingo describes his wife as
    A. not much of a letter writer.
    B. a wonderful woman.
    C. an ex-convict like himself.
    D. very beautiful.

See paragraph 17.

## Inferences

_C_    6.  We can infer that the young people were going to Florida
    A. on business.
    B. to visit relatives.
    C. on vacation.
    D. to get married.

Hamill states that the young people were "dreaming of golden beaches and the tides of the sea" (paragraph 1).

_B_    7.  The author implies that Vingo thought

Vingo's nervousness and the fact that his wife hadn't written imply the possibility that she might not want him back.

    A. he would someday be in prison again.
    B. there might be no yellow handkerchief on the tree.
    C. his wife was wrong for not writing to him in prison.
    D. his wife was sure to want him back.

_C_    8.  By writing "[Vingo] slowly rose from his seat, holding himself tightly" (paragraph 23), the author implies that Vingo
    A. has suffered a physical injury.
    B. does not want to get off the bus.
    C. is trying to control his emotions.
    D. is angry about something.

We already know that Vingo wants to be reunited with his family, so answer B is incorrect. Answers A and D are unsupported.

_C_    9.  By telling us that the picture of Vingo's family was a "cracked, much-handled snapshot," the author implies that
    A. Vingo didn't know how to take good care of photos.
    B. the pictures were not really of Vingo's family.
    C. Vingo had looked at the snapshot a great deal while in jail.
    D. the photo was relatively new.

For the four years that Vingo was in jail, the photo may have been his only concrete connection with his family.

## The Writer's Craft

_C_ 10. The introductory paragraph indicates that Hamill
   A. was one of the young people on the bus.
   B. heard the story from Vingo years later.
   C. interviewed one of the young girls who had been on the bus.
   D. knew Vingo personally.     The words "the girl remembered later" reveal that Hamill had spoken to one of the girls who had been on the bus.

# Discussion Questions

1. According to the information in the selection, what is Vingo's attitude toward his wife? What else do you learn about her at the conclusion of the story?

2. Why do you think the young people first became interested in Vingo? How do you think their attitude about him changed after they'd learned his story?

3. While there is much we don't learn about Vingo in this very short narrative, Hamill does provide us with clues to some important aspects of his personality. What evidence is there that he is a decent man, a person who we could feel deserves a second chance?

4. Many people are thrilled, some even to tears, by this story. How did you and your classmates react when you first read it? Why do you think "The Yellow Ribbon" has such a powerful effect on readers?

# Paragraph Assignments

1. In "The Yellow Ribbon," Hamill provides various clues to Vingo's character. Vingo's body language, his conversation with his fellow passengers, what he has to say about his past and his family, and his attitude as the bus nears his hometown all contribute to the reader's opinion of what kind of man he is. Write a paragraph that supports the following topic sentence: "Details in the story suggest that Vingo is a decent man who deserves a second chance." Alternatively, you may favor an opposing topic sentence: "The overall impression I am left with after reading this story is that Vingo does not deserve a second chance." Present specific evidence from the story to back up the main idea you have chosen.

2. For some reason, it is not unusual for fellow passengers in a bus, train, or airplane to enter into quite personal conversations. The same thing sometimes happens in public waiting spaces, like a doctor's office. Perhaps it is because people feel free to confide in someone they do not expect to ever see again. Write a paragraph about a personal conversation you have had with a stranger. As Hamill does, include details that make your reader able to picture where you were, how you started talking with the person, and what your first impression was of him or her. Then narrate the conversation that occurred. Include nonverbal information, such as body language, to paint the most vivid word picture that you can.

Here is one student's response to the assignment:

I never thought I'd get choked up at a mall food court, but last year a conversation with a stranger in that very place almost made me cry. I was on my lunch break and in a bad mood, staring at my phone so that I wouldn't have to talk to anyone. At that moment, an elderly woman sat down across from me. She wore a faded old dress that had been patched in several places. "Lovely day, isn't it?" she asked in a thin voice. "Um, I guess," I replied, hoping she'd go away. "I don't mean to bother you," she apologized, "but you just look so much like my daughter when she was your age." Then I felt kind of bad for being rude. "Really?" I asked with a smile. She leaned across the table and touched my arm while she stared at me. "Same dark eyes and smile. It's amazing." Then I asked, "Do you see your daughter very often?" "I'm going to see her today," the woman replied as she sat back, still looking at me. "So she's nearby, then?" I asked. The woman nodded her head. "In Grace Cemetery. She passed on three years ago. But now she lies next to her father. I visit them every Friday. So, you see, it's a lovely day." I was stunned. I felt a lump in my throat. I couldn't recall what I'd been in a bad mood about. I looked the old lady right in the eyes and smiled. Yes, it was a lovely day.

## Essay Assignments

1. Many readers see the tree full of yellow handkerchiefs as a symbol of unconditional love. Write an essay about what the world would be like if we loved each other unconditionally—taking to heart the message of Jesus and other timeless religious figures that we love our neighbor as ourselves. Specifically, describe three ways that the world would be different from the world as it is today. Begin your essay with an introductory paragraph in which you state your thesis, follow it with three supporting paragraphs in which you detail three differences in everyday life, and end in a final paragraph with a concluding thought or two.

2. Vingo made serious mistakes in life, and he then had to deal with the consequences of his mistakes. It appears he was able to receive forgiveness and experience redemption. Write an essay about three mistakes that you've made in your life and what happened—for better or worse—as a result.

## Check Your Performance                    THE YELLOW RIBBON

| Activity | Number Right | Points | Score |
|---|---|---|---|
| **Vocabulary Check**  (3 items) | _____ | x   10  = | _____ |
| **Reading Comprehension Questions** | | | |
| Central Point and Main Ideas  (3 items) | _____ | x   7  = | _____ |
| Supporting Details  (2 items) | _____ | x   7  = | _____ |
| Inferences  (4 items) | _____ | x   7  = | _____ |
| The Writer's Craft  (1 item) | _____ | x   7  = | _____ |
| | | TOTAL SCORE   = | _____% |

Enter your total score into the **Performance Chart: Fifteen Reading Selections** on the inside back cover.

# 2 Adult Children at Home
## Marilyn Mack

## Preview

Parents used to expect their children to leave home not long after high school or college. Nowadays, however, children leave home later than ever, and even then they may not be gone for good. Marilyn Mack explains this new pattern and its ups and downs.

## Words to Watch

*ruefully* (2): with regret
*phenomenon* (10): noteworthy situation or event
*cope* (12): manage

1  Ruth Patterson remembers the day the last of her children left home. "Dan was 18 and headed off to the state university," said the Pennsylvania housewife. "I cried awhile, and then told myself, 'Cheer up! At last you and Dave have the house to yourselves!'"

2  Six years later, Mrs. Patterson laughs a little ruefully° at that memory. Since her youngest son left for college, three of her four children—one with a three-year-old daughter—have moved back to the family home for at least six months at a time.

3  "The 'empty nest' hasn't been quite as empty as we expected," says Mrs. Patterson.

4  The Pattersons' situation is becoming less unusual all the time. Adult children have been "nesting," or moving back to the family home, in increasing numbers in recent years. In 1970, according to the U.S. Census Bureau, 54 percent of men and 41 percent of women between the ages of 18 and 24 depended on their parents for housing. Lately, those figures have risen much higher. One survey in 2010 found that as many as 85 percent of students graduating from college in the spring planned to move back home.

5  Why are adult children coming home? The case of the Pattersons provides some typical reasons.

6  Their oldest daughter, Suzanne, 35, a bank teller, returned home with her toddler after a painful divorce. Two years later, she is still there, with her mother caring for her little girl. "She needed a place to lick her wounds,"

said her mother. "We thought it would be for just a few months, but when we realized what it would cost her to keep Jenny in day care while she worked, it didn't make sense for them to move out again."

7      Five years after high school, their son Peter, now 28, moved back in. The plan was for him to spend a year working on a painting crew while he and his fiancée saved money for the down payment on a house. One year turned into three; long stretches between jobs made it impossible for Peter to make the kind of money he needed. Eventually he and his fiancée married and moved into a tiny apartment. They still hope to buy a house someday, but fear that "someday" may never come.

8      Their daughter Lesley, 30, has moved in and out of the house so many times "we've lost count," says her mother. A legal secretary, Lesley "earns enough to have her own place, if she'd learn to live within her means. But she wants to live like the lawyers she works with." That translates into an expensive car, lots of evenings out, and a wardrobe that bursts the limits of her modest salary.

9      Only the Pattersons' youngest child, Dan, now 24, has followed the route his parents expected. He graduated from college, found a job teaching high-school social studies, and lives on his own in a city apartment.

10      Many factors have contributed to the phenomenon° of nesting. First and foremost is the general slump in the economy. As many commentators have noted, "The rich are getting richer; the poor are getting poorer; and the middle class is disappearing." Even for college graduates, the prospect of easily finding employment and starting on the path toward home ownership is doubtful. Other contributing factors include the rise in the divorce rate, increased housing costs, college debts, and the trend to delay marriage. Once out on their own, many young people are finding it unexpectedly difficult to maintain the standard of living they hoped for. Apartment rentals, particularly in major cities, can make living alone an impossible option. Even for those fortunate enough to have found steady employment, buying a house can seem unlikely—a first-time home-buyer can expect to pay over 40 percent more today than twenty years ago.

11      Returning home can be a financial lifesaver for struggling young people. Some credit counselors recommend nesting as a solution for people who've gotten in over their heads with credit cards and rent payments and utility bills. "I was really in a mess financially when I moved back in with Mom and Dad," said Tony Woelk, a 28-year-old Best Buy salesman. "I don't know what I would have done if they hadn't helped me pay off my bills and make a fresh start." Today, after two years of living with his parents, Tony is on his own again and determined to keep his spending under control.

12      Another advantage mentioned by some nesters is the emotional support they were shown by their parents in a time of need. Judy Loewen, 22, moved

back in with her family for a month after breaking up with her long-time boyfriend. "I quit my job and left the city where he was," she remembers today. "I really felt that I couldn't cope° unless I got away immediately, and where could I go with no money and no job except to my folks? And bless them, they said, 'Just take it easy here for a while and don't rush into anything.' After a few weeks, I was ready to take a lot more realistic view of the situation and make some good decisions."

13    Parents, too, can find some practical and emotional benefits when their adult children return home. A child's contribution to room and board can help out with household expenses, particularly if the parents are living on a fixed income. In addition, parents may enjoy having a younger person around to help out with household repairs and other chores. "As I get older, taking care of the house and yard has become more of a burden for me," said Bill Robinson, a widower whose 35-year-old son has been sharing the house for the last two years. "Joseph pays some rent, but his real contribution has been to take a lot of those worries off my shoulders."

14    But the nesting phenomenon has its gloomy side as well. Parents and children report the number-one problem as the lack of space and privacy experienced by everyone involved.

15    "Never, never, never again," vowed Vicki Langella, 23, who lived with her parents for six months after losing her job in a township clerk's office. "We get along fine when we visit, but within ten minutes of moving back in, I felt

like a twelve-year-old. It was constantly, 'Where are you going? When will you be back? Who are you going to be with?' And I found myself reacting to them as if I really were 12. The worst part of it was knowing that it was my own fault—I'd chosen to move back in with them."

16    "Believe it or not, sixty-year-olds enjoy some privacy too," said Ella Purcell, whose two adult daughters have both returned home for brief periods. "Coming into my own living room to find my daughter and a date smooching on the couch made me feel like an intruder. I finally had to say, 'I love you—but out already!'"

17    Finances can be another difficult area for parents and returned children. Parents often struggle with the decision of whether to ask their children for rent. "When you're letting them stay with you in order to save money, it seems silly to charge rent. But when we saw the way Ed was throwing money around, we began to feel taken advantage of," said the mother of one adult nester.

18    Despite its possible pitfalls, psychologists, family counselors, and others believe that nesting can succeed for many families if some precautions are taken. They offer the following tips on maintaining a happy "nest."

- Regardless of their financial situation, adult children should pay some room and board. Monica O'Kane, the author of *Living with Adult Children,* admits that this can be difficult. "It's hard to squeeze blood from a turnip, especially when it's your own turnip. But paying for room and board helps children grow in financial independence."

20 • Establish clear expectations about household duties. "I remembered all too well being treated like the family servant when the kids were teenagers," said one experienced mother of a nester. "So when Rob moved back in, I said, 'Fine. Here is your share of the laundry, grocery-shopping, and cleaning duties.' Once it was clear that I was serious, he pitched right in."

21 • Respect one another. Children should not expect to be treated as guests or to use the parental home as a hotel, coming and going at all hours with no explanations. Parents, on the other hand, should recognize that the nester is no longer a youngster whose activities need constant supervision.

22 • And, most importantly: Don't let it go on forever. "When a child returns home, everyone should agree on a tentative date for him to move out again," said one family therapist. "If that date is changed later by the mutual consent of everyone concerned, that's OK, but everyone should understand that this isn't a permanent arrangement."

## First Impressions

Freewrite for ten minutes on one of the following.

1. Did you enjoy reading this selection? Why or why not?

2. Among your acquaintances, is it common for adult children to move back in with their parents? What are some reasons they give for doing so?

3. If you were a parent, would you want your adult children to move back in with you? Why or why not?

# Vocabulary Check

_B_ 1. In the excerpt below, the word *maintain* means
   A. avoid.
   B. keep up.
   C. remember.
   D. sum up.

   What would one want to do to a hoped-for standard of living?

   "...many young people are finding it unexpectedly difficult to maintain the standard of living they hoped for." (Paragraph 10)

_A_ 2. In the excerpt below, the word *option* means
   A. choice.
   B. discovery.
   C. failure.
   D. limit.

   High apartment rentals make it impossible to choose to live alone.

   "Apartment rentals . . . can make living alone an impossible option." (Paragraph 10)

_D_ 3. In the excerpt below, the word *tentative* means
   A. unchangeable.
   B. public.
   C. according to law.
   D. agreed upon for the time being.

   A date that can be "changed later" is one "agreed upon for the time being."

   "'When a child returns home, everyone should agree on a tentative date for him to move out again,' said one family therapist. 'If that date is changed later ... that's OK....'" (Paragraph 22)

# Reading Check

## Central Point and Main Ideas

_C_ 1. Which sentence best expresses the central point of the selection?
   A. Parents are not sure if they should ask for rent money from their grown children who live at home.
   B. The Pattersons are a good example of nesting.
   C. Nesting, which has increased, has advantages and disadvantages, but it can succeed if families take precautions.
   D. Between 1970 and 2010, nesting has greatly increased among adult children.

   Answers A, B, and D are too narrow. Each covers only one detail of the selection.

_____A_____ 2. The main idea of paragraph 10 is expressed in its
    A. first sentence.
    B. second sentence.
    C. third sentence.
    D. last sentence.

*The first sentence has a list signal: many factors. The rest of the paragraph lists factors that contribute to nesting.*

_____A_____ 3. The main idea of paragraph 13 is
    A. in the first sentence.
    B. in the second sentence.
    C. in the last sentence.
    D. implied.

*The first sentence has a list signal: some practical and emotional benefits. The rest of the paragraph details some of the benefits.*

## Supporting Details

_____D_____ 4. Adult children return home
    A. after divorces.
    B. when it's hard to find a job.
    C. so that they can pay their bills.
    D. for all of the above reasons.

*See paragraph 10.*

_____D_____ 5. According to the article, when adult children return home, they
    A. gain privacy.
    B. should be allowed to stay indefinitely.
    C. should be treated like guests.
    D. should help out with finances and household chores.

*See paragraphs 19–22.*

## Inferences

_____T_____ 6. *True or False?* The author implies that money problems are the main reason that adult children return home to live.

*See paragraph 10.*

*Most of the factors contributing to nesting are related to financial problems, suggesting that money is the key reason for the increase in nesting.*

_____D_____ 7. The reading suggests that
    A. only "losers" return home to live with their parents.
    B. going to college is a waste of time and money for many Americans.
    C. most young Americans will never own their own homes.
    D. returning home to live with one's parents is a growing trend.

*Answers A, B, and C are not supported.*

_____C_____ 8. We can conclude from the selection that
    A. the negative aspects of returning home to live far outweigh the advantages for both parents and their adult children.
    B. parents should refuse to let their adult children return home to live.
    C. clear communication between parents and their adult children is essential to maintaining a happy "nest."
    D. it is silly for parents to ask their adult children to pay rent.

*See paragraphs 18–22, which indicate that with clear expectations, nesting can work for both parents and children.*

## The Writer's Craft

Ruth's comment, that she and her husband will now have the house to themselves, turns out to be the opposite of what happens.

_B_ 9. Which of the following best describes how the writer introduces this selection?

A. She makes a broad statement that narrows down to a specific point.

B. She introduces an idea that is the opposite of the point of the story.

C. She provides an anecdote that illustrates the point of the story.

D. She asks a challenging question.

For reasons, see paragraphs 5–12; for guidelines, see paragraphs 18–22. Answers C and D are too narrow; answer A is unsupported.

_B_ 10. Which of the following statements best describes the writer's purpose?

A. To warn parents against allowing their adult children to return home after moving out.

B. To explore reasons adult children are moving home and suggest guidelines for making the arrangement work.

C. To criticize parents for being overly demanding of their adult children who need to return home.

D. To cite the financial and emotional benefits of having adult children move back home.

## Discussion Questions

1. Do you know about any cases of nesting? Why did the children return home? How did it work out?

2. Do you think today's young adults are having a harder time financially than their parents' generation? Or is the "standard of living they hoped for" higher? Or both?

3. Mack mentions the "people who've gotten in over their heads with credit cards and rent payments and utility bills." Why do you think people get into this situation? What advice would you give them?

4. Do you agree that adult children who return home, "regardless of their financial situation," should pay some room and board? If not, what financial situations should excuse adult children from paying room and board?

## Paragraph Assignments

1. If you are not living with a parent or parents, would you consider doing so? Under what circumstances? Alternatively, if you had adult children, would you allow them to move back in with you? If so, under what circumstances? Write a paragraph in which you answer one of these questions and explain the reasons for your answer.

2. Think of a family you know in which an adult child has moved back into the parents' home.  Does the situation seem to be a positive or a negative one? Write a paragraph in which you describe the situation and tell why you think it is a good or a bad arrangement.

## Essay Assignments

1. Overall, do you think it is a good or a bad thing for adult children to return home? Write an essay in which you develop one of these two thesis statements:

   ● There are three reasons I think it is a bad idea for adult children to return to live with their parents.

   *or*

   ● There are three reasons I think it can be a good idea for adult children to return to live with their parents.

2. The selection ends with a list of suggestions for making the adult-children-at-home living situation go smoothly. Write an essay in which you focus on a different living situation: living with a roommate, living with a spouse or partner, living with teenagers, or living alone. Develop a list of guidelines to make your living situation work well. Devote each of the essay's three main paragraphs to a guideline, giving specific instructions on how that guideline should be put into practice.

   Here is one student's response to this assignment:

   > Have you ever shared a place with a roommate? Was it a good, practical arrangement? Or did it become a nightmare of conflict? In order to have a workable roommate situation, it's important to have clear guidelines from the beginning about housekeeping, privacy, and finances.
   >
   > First of all, roommates need to agree on standards of housekeeping. If Roommate A is used to living with piles of laundry on the sofa, wet towels draped over chairs, and mountains of empty pizza boxes on the floor, while Roommate B prefers neatness and order, that is going to be a problem. From the beginning, roommates need to be clear about how they will maintain common areas, such as the bathroom, kitchen, and living room. Once you're living with a roommate, it isn't cool to say, "I don't mind clutter—I know where everything is." That's fine if you're living alone, but when you're sharing a living space, you have to respect the

other person's expectations that it be reasonably clean and orderly.

Secondly, roommates should talk frankly from the outset about how they will respect one another's privacy. Is it okay to bring dates over? How about overnight guests? How long is it okay for a houseguest to stay? What if one roommate wants to host a party that doesn't involve the other one? Are public displays of affection in the common areas okay, or should they be reserved for behind closed doors? These questions may feel awkward to talk about, but it's better to get them out of the way before one roommate gets angry, for instance, about the other hogging the living room with the romantic partner who is "always" there.

And finally, roommates absolutely have to come up with a financial agreement. Sure, there's the question of how they will split the rent. But there are a number of questions beyond that. Whose name will the utilities be in? If Roommate A pays the utilities, how and when will Roommate B reimburse him or her? If the roommates are cooking and eating together, how will the grocery bill be split? How about the random errands? It might not seem like a big deal the first time or two a roommate says, "Can you pick up a pizza on your way home?" but those little expenses add up and can lead to tensions between roommates. Come up with a plan, save receipts, and be businesslike about splitting expenses. It might feel weird, but it will keep the roommate relationship running smoothly.

Housekeeping, privacy, and money—these are three essential areas that can make or break a peaceful roommate relationship. If you set aside some time to talk with your new roommate to make sure you are on the same page, you will save yourself a lot of potential trouble.

- *Circle one answer:* Does the introduction (a) go from broad to narrow, (b) tell a story, (c) ask questions, or (d) shift to the opposite?

- Underline the thesis statement.

- Underline the topic sentences for the three supporting paragraphs.

- *Circle one answer:* Does the conclusion end with (a) a summary, (b) a final thought, or (c) both?

## Check Your Performance        ADULT CHILDREN AT HOME

| Activity | Number Right | Points | Score |
|---|---|---|---|
| **Vocabulary Check** (3 items) | _____ | x   10   = | _____ |
| **Reading Check** | | | |
|    Central Point and Main Ideas (3 items) | _____ | x   7   = | _____ |
|    Supporting Details (2 items) | _____ | x   7   = | _____ |
|    Inferences (3 items) | _____ | x   7   = | _____ |
|    The Writer's Craft (2 items) | _____ | x   7   = | _____ |
| | | **TOTAL SCORE**   = | _____ % |

Enter your total score into the **Performance Chart: Fifteen Reading Selections** on the inside back cover.

# 3 Rowing the Bus
## Paul Logan

## Preview

If you could go back in time and undo one thing you are sorry for, what would it be? Such a long-regretted moment is the focus of Paul Logan's essay. While we can never turn back the clock, this story illustrates how we can do the next best thing: we can turn our regrets into valuable lessons in living.

## Words to Watch

*musty* (3): stale or moldy in odor
*brunt* (6): greatest part
*sinister* (7): evil
*stoic* (13): emotionless
*stricken* (25): affected by painful emotions

1   When I was in elementary school, some older kids made me row the bus. Rowing meant that on the way to school I had to sit in the dirty bus aisle littered with paper, gum wads, and spitballs. Then I had to simulate the motion of rowing while the kids around me laughed and chanted, "Row, row, row the bus." I was forced to do this by a group of bullies who spent most of their time picking on me.

2   I was the perfect target for them. I was small. I had no father. And my mother, though she worked hard to support me, was unable to afford clothes and sneakers that were "cool." Instead she dressed me in outfits that we got from "the bags"—hand-me-downs given as donations to a local church.

3   Each Wednesday, she'd bring several bags of clothes to the house and pull out musty°, wrinkled shirts and worn bell-bottom pants that other families no longer wanted. I knew that people were kind to give things to us, but I hated wearing clothes that might have been donated by my classmates. Each time I wore something from the bags, I feared that the other kids might recognize something that was once theirs.

4   Besides my outdated clothes, I wore thick glasses, had crossed eyes, and spoke with a persistent lisp. For whatever reason, I had never learned to say the "s" sound properly, and I pronounced words that began with "th" as if they began with a "d." In addition, because of my severely crossed eyes, I

317

lacked the hand and eye coordination necessary to hit or catch flying objects.

5    As a result, footballs, baseballs, soccer balls and basketballs became my enemies. I knew, before I stepped on the field or court, that I would do something clumsy or foolish and that everyone would laugh at me. I feared humiliation so much that I became skillful at feigning illnesses to get out of gym class. Eventually I learned how to give myself low-grade fevers so the nurse would write me an excuse. It worked for a while, until the gym teachers caught on. When I did have to play, I was always the last one chosen to be on any team. In fact, team captains did everything in their power to make their opponents get stuck with me. When the unlucky team captain was forced to call my name, I would trudge over to the team, knowing that no one there liked or wanted me. For four years, from second through fifth grade, I prayed nightly for God to give me school days in which I would not be insulted, embarrassed, or made to feel ashamed.

6    I thought my prayers were answered when my mother decided to move during the summer before sixth grade. The move meant that I got to start sixth grade in a different school, a place where I had no reputation. Although the older kids laughed and snorted at me as soon as I got on my new bus— they couldn't miss my thick glasses and strange clothes—I soon discovered that there was another kid who received the brunt° of their insults. His name was George, and everyone made fun of him. The kids taunted him because he was

skinny; they belittled him because he had acne that pocked and blotched his face, and they teased him because his voice was squeaky. During my first gym class at my new school, I wasn't the last one chosen for kickball; George was.

7    George tried hard to be friends with me, coming up to me in the cafeteria on the first day of school. "Hi. My name's George. Can I sit with you?" he asked with a peculiar squeakiness that made each word high-pitched and raspy. As I nodded for him to sit down, I noticed an uncomfortable silence in the cafeteria as many of the students who had mocked George's clumsy gait during gym class began watching the two of us and whispering among themselves. By letting him sit with me, I had violated an unspoken law of school, a sinister° code of childhood that demands there must always be someone to pick on. I began to realize two things. If I befriended George, I would soon receive the same treatment that I had gotten at my old school. If I stayed away from him, I might actually have a chance to escape being at the bottom.

8    Within days, the kids started taunting us whenever we were together. "Who's your new little buddy, Georgie?" In the hallways, groups of students began mumbling about me just loud enough for me to hear, "Look, it's George's ugly boyfriend." On the bus rides to and from school, wads of paper and wet chewing gum were tossed at me by the bigger, older kids in the back of the bus.

9    It became clear that my friendship with George was going to cause me

several more years of misery at my new school. I decided to stop being friends with George. In class and at lunch, I spent less and less time with him. Sometimes I told him I was too busy to talk; other times I acted distracted and gave one-word responses to whatever he said. Our classmates, sensing that they had created a rift between George and me, intensified their attacks on him. Each day, George grew more desperate as he realized that the one person who could prevent him from being completely isolated was closing him off. I knew that I shouldn't avoid him, that he was feeling the same way I felt for so long, but I was so afraid that my life would become the hell it had been in my old school that I continued to ignore him.

10    Then, at recess one day, the meanest kid in the school, Chris, decided he had had enough of George. He vowed that he was going to beat up George and anyone else who claimed to be his friend. A mob of kids formed and came after me. Chris led the way and cornered me near our school's swing sets. He grabbed me by my shirt and raised his fist over my head. A huge gathering of kids surrounded us, urging him to beat me up, chanting "Go, Chris, go!"

11    "You're Georgie's new little boy-friend, aren't you?" he yelled. The hot blast of his breath carried droplets of his spit into my face. In a complete betrayal of the only kid who was nice to me, I denied George's friendship.

12    "No, I'm not George's friend. I don't like him. He's stupid," I blurted out. Several kids snickered and mumbled under their breath. Chris stared at me

for a few seconds and then threw me to the ground.

13    "Wimp. Where's George?" he demanded, standing over me. Someone pointed to George sitting alone on top of the monkey bars about thirty yards from where we were. He was watching me. Chris and his followers sprinted over to George and yanked him off the bars to the ground. Although the mob quickly encircled them, I could still see the two of them at the center of the crowd, looking at each other. George seemed stoic°, staring straight through Chris. I heard the familiar chant of "Go, Chris, go!" and watched as his fists began slamming into George's head and body. His face bloodied and his nose broken, George crumpled to the ground and sobbed without even throwing a punch. The mob cheered with pleasure and darted off into the playground to avoid an approaching teacher.

14    Chris was suspended, and after a few days, George came back to school. I wanted to talk to him, to ask him how he was, to apologize for leaving him alone and for not trying to stop him from getting hurt. But I couldn't go near him. Filled with shame for denying George and angered by my own cowardice, I never spoke to him again.

15    Several months later, without telling any students, George transferred to another school. Once in a while, in those last weeks before he left, I caught him watching me as I sat with the rest of the kids in the cafeteria. He never yelled at me or expressed anger, disappointment, or even sadness. Instead he just looked at me.

16    In the years that followed, George's silent stare remained with me. It was there in eighth grade when I saw a gang of popular kids beat up a sixth-grader because, they said, he was "ugly and stupid." It was there my first year in high school, when I saw a group of older kids steal another freshman's clothes and throw them into the showers. It was there a year later, when I watched several seniors press a wad of chewing gum into the hair of a new girl on the bus. Each time that I witnessed another awkward, uncomfortable, scared kid being tormented, I thought of George, and gradually his haunting stare began to speak to me. No longer silent, it told me that every child who is picked on and taunted deserves better, that no one—no matter how big, strong, attractive or popular—has the right to abuse another person.

17    Finally, in my junior year, when a loudmouthed, pink-skinned bully named Donald began picking on two freshmen on the bus, I could no longer deny George. Donald was crumpling a large wad of paper and preparing to bounce it off the back of the head of one of the young students when I interrupted him.

18    "Leave them alone, Don," I said. By then I was six inches taller and, after two years of high-school wrestling, thirty pounds heavier than I had been in my freshman year. Though Donald was still two years older than me, he wasn't much bigger. He stopped what he was doing, squinted and stared at me.

19    "What's your problem, Paul?"

20    I felt the way I had many years earlier on the playground when I watched the mob of kids begin to surround George.

21    "Just leave them alone. They aren't bothering you," I responded quietly.

22    "What's it to you?" he challenged. A glimpse of my own past, of rowing the bus, of being mocked for my clothes, my lisp, my glasses, and my absent father flashed in my mind.

23    "Just don't mess with them. That's all I am saying, Don." My fingertips were tingling. The bus was silent. He got up from his seat and leaned over me, and I rose from my seat to face him. For a minute, both of us just stood there, without a word, staring.

24    "I'm just playing with them, Paul," he said, chuckling. "You don't have to go psycho on me or anything." Then he shook his head, slapped me firmly on the chest with the back of his hand, and sat down. But he never threw that wad of paper. For the rest of the year, whenever I was on the bus, Don and the other troublemakers were noticeably quiet.

25    Although it has been years since my days on the playground and the school bus, George's look still haunts me. Today, I see it on the faces of a few scared kids at my sister's school—she is in fifth grade. Or once in a while I'll catch a glimpse of someone like George on the evening news, in a story about a child who brought a gun to school to stop the kids from picking on him, or in a feature about a teenager who killed herself because everyone teased her. In each school, in almost every classroom, there is a George with a stricken° face, hoping that someone nearby will be

strong enough to be kind—despite what the crowd says—and brave enough to stand up against people who attack, tease or hurt those who are vulnerable.

26      If asked about their behavior, I'm sure the bullies would say, "What's it to you? It's just a joke. It's nothing." But to George and me, and everyone else who has been humiliated or laughed at or spat on, it is everything. No one should have to row the bus.

## First Impressions

Freewrite for ten minutes on one of the following.

1. Did you enjoy reading this selection? Why or why not?

2. What do you think would have happened if Paul had stood up for George? Would it have made any difference?

3. Did your elementary or high school have bullies and victims similar to the ones in this story? How did they behave?

## Vocabulary Check

_C_  1. In the sentence below, the word *simulate* means

   A. sing.
   B. ignore.
   C. imitate.
   D. stop.

   What would the bullies have forced Paul to do while they chanted about rowing the bus?

   "Then I had to simulate the motion of rowing while the kids around me laughed and chanted, 'Row, row, row the bus.'" (Paragraph 1)

_B_  2. In the sentence below, the word *feigning* means

   A. escaping.
   B. faking.
   C. recognizing.
   D. curing.

   If he wanted to get out of gym class, he would have faked an illness.

   "I feared humiliation so much that I became skillful at feigning illnesses to get out of gym class." (Paragraph 5)

_C_ 3. In the excerpt below, the word *rift* means
- A. friendship.
- B. agreement.
- C. break.
- D. joke.

> If he has stopped being friends with George, there would be a break between him and George.

"I decided to stop being friends with George. . . . Our classmates, sensing that they had created a rift between George and me, intensified their attacks on him." (Paragraph 9)

## Reading Check

### Central Point and Main Ideas

Answers A, B, and D are too narrow. Answer A omits all the details about George as well as the story of Paul's eventually standing up to a bully. Answer B covers only paragraphs 6–7. Answer D covers only paragraphs 14–17 and 25–26.

_C_ 1. Which sentence best expresses the central point of the entire selection?
- A. Although Paul Logan was a target of other students' abuse when he was a young boy, their attacks stopped as he grew taller and stronger.
- B. When Logan moved to a different school, he discovered that another student, George, was the target of more bullying than he was.
- C. Logan's experience of being bullied and his shame at how he treated George eventually made him speak up for someone else who was teased.
- D. Logan is ashamed that he did not stand up for George when George was being attacked by a bully on the playground.

_A_ 2. Which sentence best expresses the implied main idea of paragraph 5?
- A. Because of Logan's clumsiness, gym was a miserable experience for him in elementary school.

Answers B, C, and D each cover only one or two sentences of the paragraph.

- B. Because Logan hated gym so much, he made up excuses to avoid it.
- C. The gym teacher caught on to Logan's excuses.
- D. Other students did not want Logan to be a member of their team when games were played.

### Supporting Details

_D_ 3. When Chris attacked George, George reacted by
- A. fighting back hard.
- B. shouting for Logan to help him.
- C. running away.
- D. accepting the beating.

See paragraph 13.

_A_ 4. Logan finally found the courage to stand up for abused students when he saw

A. Donald about to throw paper at a younger student.

See paragraph 17.

B. older kids throwing a freshman's clothes into the shower.

C. seniors putting bubble gum in a new student's hair.

D. a gang beating up a sixth-grader whom they disliked.

## Inferences

_C_ 5. We can conclude that when Logan began sixth grade at the new school, he

See paragraphs 5–7. George is the answer to Logan's prayers that he not be the target of bullying.

A. became quite popular.

B. began to dress more fashionably.

C. was relieved to find someone who was more unpopular than he was.

D. became a bully himself.

_B_ 6. We can infer that by the time Logan was a high-school junior, he

See paragraph 18. Logan's new height and weight have given him the courage to stand up to a bully.

A. had gained a reputation for being a "psycho."

B. had gained self-confidence as a result of becoming taller and stronger.

C. had done his best to locate George in order to apologize to him.

D. had gotten into several fistfights with bullies.

_B_ 7. The author implies that

A. the kids who picked on George did not really intend to be cruel.

B. bullying can lead to terrible tragedies at schools.

C. his sister is the victim of teasing, much as he was.

D. George grew up to be a confident, well-adjusted person.

See paragraph 25. (Sadly, stories about the tragic results of bullying are becoming increasingly common in the news.) Answers A, C, and D are not supported.

## The Writer's Craft

_A_ 8. Logan begins his essay with

Logan does not describe the school, ask questions, or mention George in his introduction.

A. an anecdote that illustrates the humiliation he suffered in elementary school.

B. a description of his elementary school.

C. a series of questions about the nature of bullying.

D. a comparison of his school experience with George's.

Logan mentions his small size, outdated clothing, thick glasses, crossed eyes, lisp, and lack of coordination—

_C_ 9. In paragraphs 2–4, the author

A. describes how his mother did her best to support him.

B. contrasts his appearance with that of his classmates.

C. lists specific reasons he was bullied while in elementary school.

D. explains how he felt about being the target of a group of bullies.

all traits that made him a "perfect target" for bullying. Answers A and B are too narrow; answer D is not supported.

_D_ _10. Logan's tone in paragraph 25 can best be described as
  A. nostalgic.
  B. detached.
  C. depressed.
  D. regretful.

> The phrases "still haunts me" and "a stricken face" indicate that Logan still sympathizes with the targets of bullying and regrets he did not do more to help them.

## Discussion Questions

1. Paul Logan titled his selection "Rowing the Bus." Yet very little of the essay actually deals with the incident the title describes—only the first and last paragraphs. Why do you think Logan chose that title?

2. Logan wanted to be kind to George, but he wanted even more to be accepted by the other students. Have you ever found yourself in a similar situation—where you wanted to do the right thing but felt that it had too high a price? Explain what happened.

3. Logan refers to "a sinister code of childhood that demands there must always be someone to pick on." What does the phrase "a sinister code of childhood" mean to you? Why do children need someone to pick on?

4. The novelist Henry James once said, "Three things in human life are important. The first is to be kind. The second is to be kind. And the third is to be kind." Are there things that teachers, school administrators, parents, and other concerned adults can do to encourage young people to treat one another with kindness rather than cruelty?

## Paragraph Assignments

1. Logan writes, "In each school, in each classroom, there is a George with a stricken face." Think of a person who filled the role of George in one of your classes. In a paragraph, describe why he or she was the target of bullying and what form that bullying took. Include a description of your own thoughts and actions regarding the student who was bullied. Your topic sentence could be something like the following: "In my eighth-grade class, _____ was a student who was often bullied."

   Here is one student's response to this assignment:

   > Jenny was a target of bullying in my fifth-grade class. There were a number of reasons she attracted cruel attention. She was at least a head taller than any other girl in the class, and her long, skinny limbs made her look

*like Olive Oyl in the old Popeye cartoons. She was physically awkward, too, and wore thick glasses that magnified her eyes. I think Jenny probably had below-average intelligence, and her bad grades and frequent wrong answers in class provided more reasons to sneer at her. Jenny wanted to have friends, and she would trail other girls, including me, around on the playground, trying to involve herself in our games and conversation. In the way that mean girls bully, we would stare coldly at Jenny, ignore her attempts to talk to us, and even run away from her. At the time I probably didn't think of myself as a bully, because I didn't physically harm her, but I see now how awfully cruel my friends and I were.*

2. Because he was afraid that his life would be made miserable, the author decided to stop being friends with George. How do you feel about that decision? Do you think it was cruel? Understandable? Were there other options Logan might have tried? Write a paragraph in which you explain what you think of Logan's decision and why. Suggest at least one other way he could have acted, and describe what you think the consequences might have been.

## Essay Assignments

1. In this essay, Logan provides vivid descriptions of incidents in which bullies attack other students. Reread those descriptions and consider what they tell you about the nature of bullies and bullying. Then write an essay that supports the following thesis: "Evidence in 'Rowing the Bus' and elsewhere suggests that most bullies share certain characteristics."

    From reading this essay, and from your own observations, see if you can pick out several characteristics that many bullies share. You might also research this topic by Googling "characteristics of bullies." In your essay, describe three qualities of bullies. Support your claim with examples from the essay, from stories you have discovered in your research, or from your own experience. Include an introductory paragraph for your essay as well as a final paragraph with concluding thoughts.

2. Imagine that you are a high-school guidance counselor who has been asked to come up with ideas to help students treat one another better. Write an essay in which you make several detailed suggestions for what teachers and students could do to make your school a friendlier, gentler place.

---

**Check Your Performance**                                    **ROWING THE BUS**

| Activity | Number Right | Points | | Score |
|---|---|---|---|---|
| **Vocabulary Check** (3 items) | _____ | x  10  = | | _____ |
| **Reading Check** | | | | |
| Central Point and Main Ideas (2 items) | _____ | x  7  = | | _____ |
| Supporting Details (2 items) | _____ | x  7  = | | _____ |
| Inferences (3 items) | _____ | x  7  = | | _____ |
| The Writer's Craft (3 items) | _____ | x  7  = | | _____ |
| | | TOTAL SCORE | = | _____% |

Enter your total score into the **Reading Performance Chart: Ten Reading Selections** on the inside back cover.

# 4 All Washed Up?

## Sara Hansen

## Preview

Each year Americans spend millions, if not billions, of dollars on medications designed to combat common illnesses. What many don't realize is that a simple, inexpensive method to prevent illness lies at their very fingertips.

## Words to Watch

*correlation* (2): relationship
*entities* (5): creatures
*innocuous* (8): harmless
*hygiene* (15): cleanliness

1   If you've heard it once, you've heard it a thousand times: "Did you wash your hands?" Warnings about the need for hand-washing are given regularly, usually by parents, but proliferate at certain times of year—for example, you'll hear them more often in cold and flu season. The sad truth, though, is that frequent hand-washing is right up there with flossing your teeth on the list of "Things You Know You Ought to Do—But Probably Don't."

2   Why "probably don't"? Research has uncovered a surprising truth: Even though most people have heard that there's a correlation° between hand-washing and staying healthy, they still don't wash their hands thoroughly—or frequently—enough. In fact, the American Society of Microbiology and the Soap and Detergent Association, in a recent study, discovered that 23% of adults observed in public restrooms did not bother to wash their hands at all. Furthermore, those that do wash their hands spend only a few seconds on this activity—insufficient time for the hand-washing to do any good.

3   It's understandable that adults balk a little at the idea that they should lather up on a regular basis. After all, we consider ourselves fastidious adults, not small children prone to the sticky messes of childhood. We are not usually smeared with jelly or melted chocolate; we rarely play in the mud. Many adults quite reasonably think, "I'll wash my hands when they need washing—when they're dirty."

4   Unfortunately, "dirty" is defined by many people as "showing visible signs of dirt." The fact is that in terms

327

of spreading disease, invisible "dirt" is far more dangerous than, say, a streak of mud. In order to understand why, a quick biology lesson is in order.

5    In general, infectious diseases are spread when bacteria and viruses—those microscopic entities° that we lump into the category of "germs"—are transmitted from one person to another. There are three basic ways by which germs can travel:

6    **Direct contact.** Just a few examples of direct contact are shaking hands, kissing, and hugging. Any sort of touching qualifies as direct contact.

7    Most people realize that if they have direct contact with a person who has a cold, they had better wash their hands quickly to avoid being contaminated with that person's cold germs. The problem with that reasoning is that it assumes that healthy people cannot infect you. The exact opposite is true; when you shake hands (or otherwise have direct contact) with those healthy people, you are, in effect, having direct contact with all the people *they* have had recent contact with, and all the people *those* people have had contact with, and on and on. You have no way of knowing whether your healthy friend is transferring someone else's disease-causing germs to you.

8    **Airborne transmission.** Infection can also be spread through the very air we breathe. Germs can hang in the air or be distributed as moisture droplets—by a cough, a sneeze, or merely the movement of an object. Something as seemingly innocuous° as the sleeve on your doctor's white coat could be covered with dangerous germs, left there by previous patients.

9    **Indirect contact.** Most sneakily of all, germs can survive on an inanimate object, waiting to be picked up by the next person who touches that object. Can you imagine how many such objects you touch over the course of an average day? A few that come to mind instantly are tabletops, pens, phones, ATMs, doorknobs, toilets, light switches, money, supermarket carts, elevator buttons, parking meters, staplers, computer keyboards, and books. Each of those objects and hundreds more may be full of germs capable of causing anything from the common cold to chicken pox to pneumonia. And don't forget how sneaky germs are. Because they are invisible to the naked eye, the surface that they inhabit may well look perfectly clean.

10    So now let's return to our original subject: hand-washing. Washing our hands frequently and doing it thoroughly (more on that later), according to the federal Centers for Disease Control and Prevention, is the single most effective way we have of protecting ourselves against the thousands of germs lurking in our daily environment. Actually, the fact that the germs end up on our hands is not the real problem; it's what we *do* with our hands that puts us in danger. And what is that? We touch our faces—regularly and frequently, without even being aware we are doing it. We rub our eyes, scratch our noses, chew our nails, wipe lipstick off our teeth, and rest our chins on our fists, giving the germs on our hands a convenient bridge directly

into our eyes, noses, and mouths, and then straight into our bloodstreams. People who study disease estimate that more than 80 percent of common illnesses develop as a result of face-touching with germ-laden hands.

11    Now that you know *why* hand-washing is so crucial, let's talk about *how*. Yes, you've been washing your hands since you were a toddler, but no, "how to wash your hands" is not a really stupid topic. Too many of us think that a swipe under the faucet is sufficient. But those few seconds under a faucet are simply not enough to get rid of those pesky germs. Instead, here is what you have to do:

12    **1. Use hot water.** Why hot water? You may have heard "to kill the germs." However, that's not the reason; water hot enough to kill germs would be too hot for you to touch. But there are two genuine reasons. One is that hot water does a better job than cold of dissolving the natural oils on your skin that trap bacteria. The second reason is simply that hot water feels better than cold, leading you to spend more time washing.

13    **2. Use lots of soap, and take time to work up a good lather.** Again, you have probably heard that soap "kills germs." But again, that's not true (unless it's an "antibacterial" soap, and even then, it won't kill viruses). The actual function of soap is to form a thin layer around germs so they can be easily dislodged from your skin. In order to get the full effect, you need plenty of soap, plenty of lather (scrub for a minimum of 20 seconds—some experts say "Long

enough to recite the ABCs twice"), and plenty of hot water to wash all the trapped germs down the drain.

14    (By the way, you've undoubtedly seen the many "hand sanitizers" for sale. These small bottles of alcohol-based liquid, conveniently sized for pocket or purse, can be helpful if you need to disinfect your hands and you don't have access to soap and water. But plain old soap-and-water washing is still the most effective, and certainly the cheapest, way of insuring that your hands are clean.)

15    **3. Dry your hands.** The final step in good hand-washing hygiene° is to dry your hands and then exit the washing area without re-contaminating yourself. After all, you've just spent at least 20 seconds carefully washing up. What will happen when you use your nice clean hands to turn off the water faucet and grab the door handle to exit the restroom? That's right—you will pick up brand new germs, many of them left there by people who did not wash *their* hands properly. The solution is simple: grab a paper towel before you turn off the faucet. Use the towel to both turn off the faucet and open the door; then dispose of the towel. Many public restrooms have trash cans right outside the door for this very purpose.

16    How often should you wash your hands? There are some obvious times of day—after you use the restroom, before eating, and before preparing food. But think back to the earlier discussion of where and how we pick up germs, and you'll realize that the more frequently you wash (within reason, of course), the

better. In particular, find time to wash up whenever you've been in an area where many people gather, or when you've been handling objects that have been touched by lots of people. Spending a few extra minutes each day washing your hands—and doing it right—will almost certainly save you from the discomfort and inconvenience of preventable illnesses.

## First Impressions

Freewrite for ten minutes on one of the following.

1. Did you enjoy reading this selection? Why or why not?

2. Which facts about hand-washing presented here did you already know? Which ones were new to you?

3. Will reading this article cause you to change your own hand-washing habits? In what way will you change them?

## Vocabulary Check

_B_ 1. In the sentence below, the word *proliferate* means
   A. slow down.
   B. increase.
   C. become more surprising.
   D. are ignored.

"Warnings about the need for hand-washing are given regularly, usually by parents, but proliferate at certain times of year—for example, you'll hear them more often in cold and flu season." (Paragraph 1)

Synonym-like clue: "hear them more often."

___D___  2.  In the excerpt below, the word *fastidious* means
   A. sloppy.
   B. hard-working.
   C. successful.
   D. fussy about cleanliness.

> "It's understandable that adults balk a little at the idea that they should lather up on a regular basis. After all, we consider ourselves fastidious adults, not small children prone to the sticky messes of childhood. We are not usually smeared with jelly or melted chocolate; we rarely play in the mud." (Paragraph 3)          Antonym clue: The excerpt lists several unclean situations.

___B___  3.  In the excerpt below, the word *inanimate* means
   A. boring.
   B. non-living.
   C. very small.
   D. wooden.

> "Most sneakily of all, germs can survive on an inanimate object, waiting to be picked up by the next person who touches that object. Can you imagine how many such objects you touch over the course of an average day? A few that come to mind instantly are tabletops, pens, phones, ATMs, doorknobs, toilets, light switches, money, supermarket carts, elevator buttons, parking meters, staplers, computer keyboards, and books." (Paragraph 9)          Tabletops, pens, and the other items mentioned are examples of non-living objects.

# Reading Check

## Central Point and Main Ideas

___D___  1.  Which sentence best expresses the central point of the entire selection?
   A. Most people do not wash their hands often enough or long enough to avoid being contaminated by germs.
   B. Airborne transmission, direct contact, and indirect contact are three ways in which germs can travel.
   C. When washing your hands, you should use hot water, plenty of soap, take time to work up a good lather, and dry your hands.
   D. Spending a few extra minutes thoroughly washing your hands will reduce the chances that you'll become ill.
          Answers A, B, and C are too narrow.

___B___ 2. Which sentence best expresses the main idea of paragraph 7?

Most of the paragraph is about the dangers of contact with healthy people. Answer A is too narrow; answers C and D are supporting details.

   A. Most people wrongly assume that they cannot become infected by contact with healthy people.

   B. It is possible to become infected by contact with healthy people as well as contact with unhealthy people.

   C. When you shake hands with a person, you are, in effect, having contact with all the people they've had recent contact with.

   D. You have no way of knowing who the person you've had direct contact with has had contact with.

___B___ 3. Which sentence best expresses the main idea of paragraph 9?

   A. It is difficult to imagine the number of objects we touch in the course of a day.

   B. Because germs can survive on inanimate objects, we can become ill from the things we touch.

   C. Tabletops, pens, phones, ATMs, door-knobs, toilets, and other objects are just a few of the many things we touch in an average day.

   D. Even though inanimate objects may look perfectly clean, they may be full of germs.   Answers A, C, and D are too narrow.

## Supporting Details

___C___ 4. The author recommends that people wash their hands for

   A. at least a few seconds.

   B. 10 seconds.

   C. 20 seconds.        See paragraph 13.

   D. about a minute.

___C___ 5. According to the selection, you should

   A. avoid using public restrooms.

   B. wash your hands with a hand sanitizer after using a public restroom.

   C. use a paper towel to turn off the faucet and open the door after washing your hands in a public restroom.

   D. dry your hands with a blow dryer rather than a paper towel when using a public restroom.        See paragraph 15.

## Inferences

___D___ 6. Which of the following inferences is best supported by paragraphs 1 and 2?

See the second sentence of paragraph 2. Answer A is contradicted by paragraph 2; answers B and C are not supported.

   A. Most people don't know why they should wash their hands.

   B. More people floss their teeth regularly than wash their hands regularly.

   C. Most outbreaks of disease occur because some people didn't wash their hands.

   D. Most people believe that washing their hands for a few seconds is enough to get them clean.

The author __A__ 7. On the basis of paragraph 8, we can conclude that
states that even the
doctor's coat sleeve
could harbor germs.
Answers A, B, and C
are not supported.

7. On the basis of paragraph 8, we can conclude that
   A. it is possible to get sick from the germs found in doctors' offices.
   B. white is a color that attracts germs.
   C. most doctors don't wash their hands nearly enough.
   D. people should wear face masks while visiting doctors' offices.

__B__ 8. We can infer that the author of the selection
   A. is a microbiologist.
   B. washes her hands more often and more thoroughly than the average person.
   C. once became seriously ill as a result of not washing her hands.
   D. works for the Soap and Detergent Association.

The author is aware of the dangers of not washing hands, so we can assume she does wash hers properly—and, as she states, the average person does not.

## The Writer's Craft

__D__ 9. In paragraphs 6–9, the author

Note the boldfaced
heads, each of which
introduces a different
way germs travel.
Answers A and B are
too narrow; answer C
is not mentioned.

   A. compares the dangers of direct and indirect contact with cold germs.
   B. contrasts people's common but false beliefs about germs with the facts about germs.
   C. defines and gives examples of several dangerous diseases, including chicken pox and pneumonia.
   D. lists the three basic ways that germs can travel from one person to another.

__C__ 10. Which of the following best describes the author's purpose in writing this piece?
   A. To entertain the reader with a description of how people behave in a public restroom when they don't know they're being watched.
   B. To inform people that food preparers, doctors, and others they encounter may actually be making them ill.
   C. To inform people of the reasons for hand-washing and the proper technique for doing so.
   D. To persuade people to avoid touching objects that might transmit disease-causing germs.

The focus of the article is on the ease with which germs are transmitted and, therefore, the necessity and technique of hand-washing. Answers A and B are too narrow; answer D is not supported.

## Discussion Questions

1. About how many times a day—and for how long—do you usually wash your hands? Do you think your hand-washing habits will change as a result of reading this selection? Why or why not?

2. Do you agree with Hansen's conclusion that spending more time every day washing your hands will "almost certainly" save you from contracting preventable illnesses? Or are there other factors to take into consideration? Explain.

3. In the course of the selection, Hansen refutes the belief that hot water kills germs. What are some other health theories you've heard that may or may not be true? How could you find out whether or not they are true?

4. Hansen points out that frequent hand-washing and flossing one's teeth are two things that people know they ought to do, but probably don't. Can you add some more examples to this list? What do you think are the main reasons people don't do what they should when it comes to questions of health?

## Paragraph Assignments

1. This essay mentions washing hands and flossing teeth as examples of "Things You Know You Ought to Do—but Probably Don't." Are there other habits or practices that you know would be good for you but that you don't do (at least not often)? Write a paragraph about one such practice. Explain why you feel you should do it and why you fail to do so.

   Here is one student's response to this assignment:

   > Something I know is good for me but that I rarely do is get enough sleep. I know from (rare) experience that when I get about eight hours of sleep, I feel better, I work better, and I think better. I wake up refreshed and ready to greet the day. However, it is much more common for me to get about six hours of shuteye. I don't get home from work until about 6. By the time I get some dinner and clean up the kitchen, it's close to 7:30. Then I generally have two hours of schoolwork to do. What I should do at that point is read for a half hour and then go to sleep, but the temptations to watch some TV, check my e-mail and the Internet, and maybe make a phone call or two are too strong. Before I know it, it's close to midnight, and my alarm clock is set to ring at 6 a.m. So at this point in my life, it looks like I'm going to be sleep-deprived more often than not.

2. Imagine that you are training health inspectors whose job it will be to visit restaurants and make recommendations for improving the cleanliness of their kitchens and restrooms. Write a paragraph about specific areas they should pay close attention to during an inspection.

## Essay Assignments

1. What are three changes you could make in your life that could improve your health and well-being? Those changes might be physical, such as giving up an unhealthy habit. Or they might be lifestyle changes, such as getting a more fulfilling job or improving a relationship. Write an essay in which you describe each of those changes and how it could benefit you. Include details about what you would have to do in order to make these changes a reality.

2. In this essay, you learned that several widespread beliefs about hand-washing are not true—specifically, that soap doesn't "kill germs," and neither does hot water (at least not at the temperature you use to wash). What are some other beliefs about health or disease that you have heard, but know are not true? Write an essay in which you describe several of those beliefs and explain what about them is false. Include any thoughts you have about why people believe those false theories. You may want to research this topic first by Googling "common misconceptions about health" or "false beliefs about disease" or some related phrase.

---

### Check Your Performance                                    ALL WASHED UP?

| Activity | Number Right | Points | Score |
|---|---|---|---|
| **Vocabulary Check** (3 items) | _____ | x  10  = | _____ |
| **Reading Check** | | | |
| Central Point and Main Ideas  (3 items) | _____ | x  7  = | _____ |
| Supporting Details  (2 items) | _____ | x  7  = | _____ |
| Inferences  (3 items) | _____ | x  7  = | _____ |
| The Writer's Craft  (2 items) | _____ | x  7  = | _____ |
| | | TOTAL SCORE   = | _____% |

Enter your total score into the **Performance Chart: Fifteen Reading Selections** on the inside back cover.

# 5 The Scholarship Jacket

## Marta Salinas

## Preview

All of us have suffered disappointments and moments when we have felt we've been treated unfairly. In "The Scholarship Jacket," originally published in *Growing Up Chicana: An Anthology*, Marta Salinas writes about one such moment in her childhood in southern Texas. By focusing on an award that school authorities decided she should not receive, Salinas shows us the pain of discrimination as well as the need for inner strength.

## Words to Watch

*agile* (2): able to move quickly
*eavesdrop* (4): secretly listen
*mesquite* (15): a sweet-smelling thorny tree
*gaunt* (25): thin and bony
*adrenaline* (31): a hormone that raises the blood pressure and stimulates the heart

1 The small Texas school that I attended carried out a tradition every year during the eighth grade graduation: a beautiful gold and green jacket, the school colors, was awarded to the class valedictorian, the student who had maintained the highest grades for eight years. The scholarship jacket had a big gold S on the left front side, and the winner's name was written in gold letters on the pocket.

2 My oldest sister, Rosie, had won the jacket a few years back, and I fully expected to win also. I was fourteen and in the eighth grade. I had been a straight-A student since the first grade, and the last year I had looked forward to owning that jacket. My father was a farm laborer who couldn't earn enough money to feed eight children, so when I was six I was given to my grandparents to raise. We couldn't participate in sports at school because there were registration fees, uniform costs, and trips out of town; so even though we were quite agile° and athletic, there would never be a sports school jacket for us. This one, the scholarship jacket, was our only chance.

3 In May, close to graduation, spring fever struck, and no one paid any attention to class; instead we stared

out the windows and at each other, wanting to speed up the last few weeks of school. I despaired every time I looked in the mirror. Pencil thin, not a curve anywhere, I was called "Beanpole" and "String Bean," and I knew that's what I looked like. A flat chest, no hips, and a brain, that's what I had. That really isn't much for a fourteen-year-old to work with, I thought, as I absentmindedly wandered from my history class to the gym. Another hour of sweating during basketball and displaying my toothpick legs was coming up. Then I remembered my P.E. shorts were still in a bag under my desk where I'd forgotten them. I had to walk all the way back and get them. Coach Thompson was a real bear if anyone wasn't dressed for P.E. She had said I was a good forward and once she even tried to talk Grandma into letting me join the team. Grandma, of course, said no.

4     I was almost back at my classroom door when I heard angry voices and arguing. I stopped. I didn't mean to eavesdrop°; I just hesitated, not knowing what to do. I needed those shorts and I was going to be late, but I didn't want to interrupt an argument between my teachers. I recognized the voices: Mr. Schmidt, my history teacher, and Mr. Boone, my math teacher. They seemed to be arguing about me. I couldn't believe it. I still remember the shock that rooted me flat against the wall as if I were trying to blend in with the graffiti written there.

5     "I refuse to do it! I don't care who her father is, her grades don't even begin to compare to Martha's. I won't lie or falsify records. Martha has a straight-A-plus average and you know it." That was Mr. Schmidt, and he sounded very angry. Mr. Boone's voice sounded calm and quiet.

6     "Look, Joann's father is not only on the Board, he owns the only store in town; we could say it was a close tie and—"

7     The pounding in my ears drowned out the rest of the words, only a word here and there filtered through. ". . . Martha is Mexican . . . resign . . . won't do it. . . ." Mr. Schmidt came rushing out, and luckily for me went down the opposite way toward the auditorium, so he didn't see me. Shaking, I waited a few minutes and then went in and grabbed my bag and fled from the room. Mr. Boone looked up when I came in but didn't say anything. To this day I don't remember if I got in trouble in P.E. for being late or how I made it through the rest of the afternoon. I went home very sad and cried into my pillow that night so Grandmother wouldn't hear me. It seemed a cruel coincidence that I had overheard that conversation.

8     The next day when the principal called me into his office, I knew what it would be about. He looked uncomfortable and unhappy. I decided I wasn't going to make it any easier for him, so I looked him straight in the eye. He looked away and fidgeted with the papers on his desk.

9     "Martha," he said, "there's been a change in policy this year regarding the scholarship jacket. As you know, it has always been free." He cleared his throat and continued. "This year the Board

decided to charge fifteen dollars—which still won't cover the complete cost of the jacket."

10    I stared at him in shock and a small sound of dismay escaped my throat. I hadn't expected this. He still avoided looking in my eyes.

11    "So if you are unable to pay the fifteen dollars for the jacket, it will be given to the next one in line."

12    Standing with all the dignity I could muster, I said, "I'll speak to my grandfather about it, sir, and let you know tomorrow." I cried on the walk home from the bus stop. The dirt road was a quarter of a mile from the highway, so by the time I got home, my eyes were red and puffy.

13    "Where's Grandpa?" I asked Grandma, looking down at the floor so she wouldn't ask me why I'd been crying. She was sewing on a quilt and didn't look up.

14    "I think he's out back working in the bean field."

15    I went outside and looked out at the fields. There he was. I could see him walking between the rows, his body bent over the little plants, hoe in hand. I walked slowly out to him, trying to think how I could best ask him for the money. There was a cool breeze blowing and a sweet smell of mesquite° in the air, but I didn't appreciate it. I kicked at a dirt clod. I wanted that jacket so much. It was more than just being a valedictorian and giving a little thank-you speech for the jacket on graduation night. It represented eight years of hard work and expectation. I knew I had to be honest with Grandpa; it was my only chance. He saw me and looked up.

16    He waited for me to speak. I cleared my throat nervously and clasped my hands behind my back so he wouldn't see them shaking. "Grandpa, I have a big favor to ask you," I said in Spanish, the only language he knew. He still waited silently. I tried again. "Grandpa, this year the principal said the scholarship jacket is not going to be free. It's going to cost fifteen dollars and I have to take the money in tomorrow, otherwise it'll be given to someone else." The last words came out in an eager rush. Grandpa straightened up tiredly and leaned his chin on the hoe handle. He looked out over the field that was filled with the tiny green bean plants. I waited, desperately hoping he'd say I could have the money.

17    He turned to me and asked quietly, "What does a scholarship jacket mean?"

18    I answered quickly; maybe there was a chance. "It means you've earned it by having the highest grades for eight years and that's why they're giving it to you." Too late I realized the significance of my words. Grandpa knew that I understood it was not a matter of money. It wasn't that. He went back to hoeing the weeds that sprang up between the delicate little bean plants. It was a time-consuming job; sometimes the small shoots were right next to each other. Finally he spoke again.

19    "Then if you pay for it, Marta, it's not a scholarship jacket, is it? Tell your principal I will not pay the fifteen dollars."

20    I walked back to the house and locked myself in the bathroom for a long time. I was angry with Grandfather even though I knew he was right, and I was angry with the Board, whoever they were. Why did they have to change the rules just when it was my turn to win the jacket?

21    It was a very sad and withdrawn girl who dragged herself into the principal's office the next day. This time he did look me in the eyes.

22    "What did your grandfather say?"

23    I sat very straight in my chair.

24    "He said to tell you he won't pay the fifteen dollars."

25    The principal muttered something I couldn't understand under his breath, and walked over to the window. He stood looking out at something outside. He looked bigger than usual when he stood up; he was a tall, gaunt° man with gray hair, and I watched the back of his head while I waited for him to speak.

26    "Why?" he finally asked. "Your grandfather has the money. Doesn't he own a small bean farm?"

27    I looked at him, forcing my eyes to stay dry. "He said if I had to pay for it, then it wouldn't be a scholarship jacket," I said and stood up to leave. "I guess you'll just have to give it to Joann." I hadn't meant to say that; it had just slipped out. I was almost to the door when he stopped me.

28    "Martha—wait."

29    I turned and looked at him, waiting. What did he want now? I could feel my heart pounding. Something bitter and vile tasting was coming up in my mouth; I was afraid I was going to be sick. I didn't need any sympathy speeches. He sighed loudly and went back to his big desk. He looked at me, biting his lip, as if thinking.

30    "Okay, damn it. We'll make an exception in your case. I'll tell the Board, you'll get your jacket."

31    I could hardly believe it. I spoke in a trembling rush. "Oh, thank you, sir!" Suddenly I felt great. I didn't know about adrenaline° in those days, but I knew something was pumping through me, making me feel as tall as the sky. I wanted to yell, jump, run the mile, do something. I ran out so I could cry in the hall where there was no one to see me. At the end of the day, Mr. Schmidt winked at me and said, "I hear you're getting a scholarship jacket this year."

32    His face looked as happy and innocent as a baby's, but I knew better. Without answering I gave him a quick hug and ran to the bus. I cried on the walk home again, but this time because I was so happy. I couldn't wait to tell Grandpa and ran straight to the field. I joined him in the row where he was working and without saying anything I crouched down and started pulling up the weeds with my hands. Grandpa worked alongside me for a few minutes, but he didn't ask what had happened. After I had a little pile of weeds between the rows, I stood up and faced him.

33    "The principal said he's making an exception for me, Grandpa, and I'm getting the jacket after all. That's after I told him what you said."

34    Grandpa didn't say anything; he just gave me a pat on the shoulder and

a smile. He pulled out the crumpled red handkerchief that he always carried in his back pocket and wiped the sweat off his forehead.

35        "Better go see if your grandmother needs any help with supper."

I gave him a big grin. He didn't fool  36 me. I skipped and ran back to the house, whistling some silly tune.

## First Impressions

Freewrite for ten minutes on one of the following.

1. Did you enjoy reading this selection? Why or why not?

2. Have you ever felt that you were treated unfairly simply because of your gender, age, ethnicity, or financial situation? Explain.

3. Which person in this story do you admire the most? Why?

## Vocabulary Check

_B_ 1. In the excerpt below, the words *fidgeted with* mean
   A. folded neatly.
   B. fussed nervously with.
   C. played happily with.
   D. calmly examined.

   Synonym-like clues for *nervously: uncomfortable, unhappy, looked away.*

   "He looked uncomfortable and unhappy.... He looked away and fidgeted with the papers on his desk." (Paragraph 8)

_D_ 2. In the excerpt below, the word *dismay* means
   A. joy.
   B. comfort.
   C. relief.
   D. disappointment.

   If Marta was "shocked" and received unexpected information, she would make a sound of sudden disappointment.

   "I stared at him in shock and a small sound of dismay escaped my throat. I hadn't expected this." (Paragraph 10)

_D_ 3. In the sentence below, the word *withdrawn* means
   A. not healthy.
   B. curious.
   C. amused.
   D. not responsive.

People who are sad and have to drag themselves to appointments are often quiet and unresponsive.

"It was a very sad and withdrawn girl who dragged herself into the principal's office the next day." (Paragraph 21)

# Reading Check

## Central Point and Main Ideas

_C_ 1. Which sentence best expresses the central point of the selection?
   A. It is more important to be smart than good-looking or athletic.
   B. People who are willing to pay for awards deserve them more than people who are not.
   C. By refusing to give in to discrimination, the author finally received the award she had earned.
   D. Always do what the adults in your family say, even if you don't agree.        Answers A, B, and D are not supported.

_B_ 2. Which sentence best expresses the main idea of paragraph 2?
   A. Marta wanted to win the scholarship jacket to be like her sister Rosie.
   B. The scholarship jacket was especially important to Marta because she was unable to earn a jacket in any other way.
   C. The scholarship jacket was better than a sports school jacket.
   D. Marta resented her parents for sending her to live with her grandparents.        Answers A, C, and D are not supported.

_B_ 3. Which sentence best expresses the main idea of paragraph 7?
   A. Marta didn't want her grandmother to know she was crying.
   B. Marta was shocked and saddened by the conversation she overheard.
   C. Mr. Schmidt didn't see Marta when he rushed out of the room.
   D. Marta didn't hear every word of Mr. Schmidt's and Mr. Boone's conversation.   Expressions like "ears pounded," "shaking," "fled from the room," and "don't remember" show that Marta was shocked and saddened.

## Supporting Details

_B_ 4. Marta was raised by her grandparents because
   A. she wanted to learn to speak Spanish.
   B. her father did not earn enough money to feed all of his children.
   C. she wanted to learn about farming.
   D. her parents died when she was six.        See paragraph 2.

## Inferences

We suspect ___C___ 5. We can infer from paragraph 8 that the principal was "uncomfortable
the principal is going          and unhappy" because
to tell Marta that
there is some sort              A. the students had not been paying attention in class during the last few
of problem with the                weeks before graduation.
scholarship jacket that     B. his office was very hot.
he knows she deserves,     C. he was ashamed to tell Marta that she had to pay fifteen dollars for a
so it is logical to infer          jacket that she had earned.
that this is why he
looks "uncomfortable        D. Mr. Boone and Mr. Schmidt were fighting in the hallway.
and unhappy."

___B___ 6. The author implies that the Board members were not going to give Marta
            the scholarship jacket because
            A. she was late for P.E. class.
            B. they wanted to award the jacket to the daughter of an important local
               citizen.
            C. another student had better grades.
            D. they didn't think it was fair to have two members of the same family
               win the jacket.    See paragraphs 5–6. Answers A and D are unsupported;
                                              answer C is contradicted by paragraph 5.

___T___ 7. *True or False?* The author implies that the Board's new policy to require
            a fee for the scholarship jacket was an act of discrimination.
                   See paragraph 7. Mentioning Marta's ethnicity suggests that it might
                            be a factor in the decision. Also, imposing a fee for something that
**The Writer's Craft**    should be free discriminates against poor students and their families.

___A___ 8. The main pattern of organization in this story is a
            A. narrative, in time order, of the events leading up to Marta's winning
Starting in paragraph          the scholarship jacket.
3, the events of the
story are shown in         B. definition of *discrimination* and several examples of it.
the order in which        C. comparison and contrast of Marta's and Joann's backgrounds and
they happened.                 classroom performance.
            D. list of reasons why Marta should have gotten the jacket.

___D___ 9. The author begins her story with a description of the scholarship jacket
            in order to
If the jacket is
beautiful, it is           A. get readers interested in who will win the jacket.
desirable. If the author  B. show that the jacket is desirable.
"fully expected to        C. let readers see exactly what the jacket looks like.
win" it, we want to
find out if she does.     D. do all of the above.

___C___ 10. The tone of paragraph 31 is best described as
            A. accepting and contented.
            B. angry and resentful.              Words like "great," "as tall as the sky,"
            C. joyous and excited.        and "I wanted to yell, jump, run the mile"
            D. disappointed and distressed.              indicate joy and excitement.

## Discussion Questions

1. In her first meeting with the principal, Marta could have challenged him by telling what she had overheard the two teachers saying. Why do you think she stayed silent? What do you think the principal would have said or done if she'd told him she knew the real reason she wasn't being given the jacket?

2. Why do you think the principal gave in during his second meeting with Marta? What do you think will happen when he has to face the Board again? If you were the principal, what would you say to the Board?

3. What values did Marta learn from her grandfather? Where in the story do they demonstrate similar values?

4. Marta implies that she was discriminated against because of her racial background (she was Mexican) and her family's economic condition (they were poor). Have you ever experienced discrimination, or do you know of a friend who has experienced it? Explain.

## Paragraph Assignments

1. Early in the selection, we learn that Marta and her older sister, Rosa, couldn't participate in sports at school because of the expense involved. Thus, becoming valedictorian and winning the scholarship jacket was the only way they could earn a school jacket. Write a paragraph that supports one of the following topic sentences:

   ● It would be a good thing if schools focused more on academics and less on sports.

   *or*

   ● Overall, sports play a positive role in middle school, high school, and college.

   Before you start writing, you may wish to brainstorm ways that a focus on sports in schools can either help or harm students. Then, organize your supporting details using transition words such as *one*, *another*, and *finally*.

2. Marta stresses again and again how important the scholarship jacket was to her and how hard she worked to win it. Write a paragraph about something you worked hard to achieve when you were younger. How long did you work toward that goal? How did you feel when you finally succeeded? Or as an alternative, write about not achieving the goal. How did you cope with the disappointment? What lessons, if any, did you learn from the experience?

Here is one student's response to the assignment:

> When I was in third grade, a lady came to my school and said that she would teach any kid who wanted lessons to play the violin. I was very excited about learning. I imagined myself standing on a concert stage and amazing everyone with my beautiful music. So I signed up for lessons, and the lady gave me a kid-sized violin to use. Every week she met with me and the other third graders and tried to teach us to play. I watched her very carefully and tried hard to do exactly what she told us. But what I didn't do is practice much at home. The day after the lesson, when I was still feeling inspired, I might practice a little. But for the rest of the week I would rather play with my friends or watch TV. Gradually I noticed that some other kids in our group were making much better progress than I was. They were actually able to play little songs, while the sounds my violin made were more like a dying cat. I got embarrassed and finally said I didn't want to take lessons anymore. I didn't achieve my goal. But I did learn something, and that is that wanting the goal is not enough. I learned I had to do the work to reach that goal.

## Essay Assignments

1. This story contains several examples of authority figures—specifically, the two teachers, the principal, and Marta's grandfather. Write an essay describing three qualities that you think an authority figure should possess. Such qualities might include honesty, fairness, compassion, and knowledge, among others.

Devote each of the supporting paragraphs in the body of your essay to one of those qualities. Within each paragraph, give an example or examples of how an authority figure in your life has demonstrated that quality.

You may write about three different authority figures that have demonstrated those three qualities to you. Alternatively, one authority figure may have demonstrated all three.

Your thesis statement might be similar to one of these:

● My older brother, my grandmother, and my football coach have been models of admirable behavior for me.

● My older brother's honesty, courage, and kindness to others have set a valuable example for me.

2. In paragraph 3, Marta recalls her self-consciousness about her skinny body, which made the other students call her "Beanpole" and "String Bean." Her reaction reflects the importance placed on physical appearance in our society.

Think about the messages teenagers receive regarding their appearance. ("Appearance" could include their bodies, dress, and hairstyles, among other things.) These messages can come from any of the following:

● other students
● magazine, billboard, and Internet advertisements
● television commercials
● talk shows
● television shows and movies
● sports figures

Write an essay about the types of pressure that teenagers face to look or act a certain way. Examine the consequences—for example, low self-esteem, eating disorders, steroid use—that result when these ideals are not achieved.

Focus your essay on three different influences—for example, fashion magazines, popular TV shows, and professional sports—and the consequences of each.

## Check Your Performance                    THE SCHOLARSHIP JACKET

| Activity | Number Right | Points | Score |
|---|---|---|---|
| **Vocabulary Check** (3 items) | _____ | x  10  = | _____ |
| **Reading Check** | | | |
| Central Point and Main Ideas (3 items) | _____ | x  7  = | _____ |
| Supporting Details (1 item) | _____ | x  7  = | _____ |
| Inferences (3 items) | _____ | x  7  = | _____ |
| The Writer's Craft (3 items) | _____ | x  7  = | _____ |
| | | TOTAL SCORE  = | _____% |

Enter your total score into the **Performance Chart: Fifteen Reading Selections** on the inside back cover.

## Preview

Many of us have an anger problem. We may snap at slow-moving clerks, swear at aggressive drivers, or steam at the general incompetence that many people (including ourselves) show in the matters of everyday life. Why are we so irritable? Is there anything we can do about it? This article explores the roots of our anger and suggests some ways of coping.

## Words to Watch

*designated* (3): set apart for a particular purpose
*chronic* (15): continuous
*diffuse* (15): not confined to one area; present everywhere
*self-perpetuating* (15): causing itself to continue
*catharsis* (15): a release of tension

1 Laura Houser remembers the day with embarrassment.

2 "My mother was visiting from Illinois," she says. "We'd gone out to lunch and done some shopping. On our way home, we stopped at an intersection. When the light changed, the guy ahead of us was looking at a map or something and didn't move right away. I leaned on my horn and automatically yelled—well, what I generally yell at people who make me wait. I didn't even think about what I was doing. One moment I was talking and laughing with my mother, and the next I was shouting curses at a stranger. Mom's jaw just dropped. She said, 'Well, I guess you've been living in the city too long.' That's when I realized that my anger was out of control."

3 Laura has plenty of company. Here are a few examples plucked from the headlines of recent newspapers:

- Amtrak's Washington–New York train: When a woman begins to use her cell phone in a designated° "quiet car," her seatmate grabs the phone and smashes it against the wall.
- Reading, Massachusetts: Arguing over rough play at their ten-year-old sons' hockey practice, two fathers begin throwing punches. One of the dads beats the other to death.
- Westport, Connecticut: Two supermarket shoppers get into a fistfight

over who should be first in a just-opened checkout line.

4    Reading these stories and countless others like them that happen daily, it's hard to escape the conclusion that we are one angry society. An entire vocabulary has grown up to describe situations of out-of-control fury: road rage, sideline rage, computer rage, biker rage, air rage. Bookstore shelves are filled with authors' advice on how to deal with our anger. Court-ordered anger management classes have become commonplace, and anger-management workshops are advertised in local newspapers.

5    Human beings have always experienced anger, of course. But in earlier, more civil decades, public displays of anger were unusual to the point of being aberrant. Today, however, whether in petty or deadly forms, episodes of unrepressed rage have become part of our daily landscape.

6    What has happened to us? Are we that much angrier than we used to be? Have we lost all inhibitions about expressing our anger? Are we, as a society, literally losing our ability to control our tempers?

## WHY ARE WE SO ANGRY?

7    According to Sybil Evans, a conflict-resolution expert in New York City, there are three components to blame for our societal bad behavior: time, technology and tension.

8    What's eating up our time? To begin with, Americans work longer hours and are rewarded with less vacation time than people in any other industrial society. Over an average year, for example, most British employees work 250 hours less than most Americans; most Germans work a full 500 hours less. And most Europeans are given four to six weeks of vacation each year, compared to the average American's two weeks. And to top it all off, many Americans face long, stressful commutes at the beginning and end of each long workday.

9    Once we Americans do get home from work, our busy day is rarely done. We are involved in community activities; our children participate in sports, school programs, and extracurricular activities; and our houses, yards and cars cry out for maintenance. To make matters worse, we are reluctant to use the little bit of leisure time we do have to catch up on our sleep. Compared with Americans of the nineteenth and early twentieth centuries, most of us are chronically sleep-deprived. While our ancestors typically slept nine and a half hours a night, many of us feel lucky to get seven. We're critical of "lazy" people who sleep longer, and we associate naps with toddlerhood. (In doing so, we ignore the examples of successful people, including Winston Churchill, Albert Einstein, and Napoleon, all of whom were devoted to their afternoon naps.)

10    The bottom line: we are time-challenged and just plain tired—and tired people are cranky people. We're ready to blow—to snap at the slow-moving cashier, to tap the bumper of the slowpoke ahead of us, or to do something far worse.

11    Technology is also to blame for the bad behavior so widespread in our culture. Amazing gadgets were supposed to make our lives easier—but have they? Sure, technology has its positive aspects. It is a blessing, for instance, to have a cell phone on hand when your car breaks down far from home or to be able to "instant message" a friend on the other side of the globe. But the downsides are many. Cell phones, pagers, fax machines, handheld computers and the like have robbed many of us of what was once valuable downtime. Now we're always available to take that urgent call or act on that last-minute demand. Then there is the endless pressure of feeling we need to keep up with our gadgets' latest technological developments. For example, it's not sufficient to use your cell phone for phone calls. Now you must learn to use the phone for text-messaging and downloading games. It's not enough to take still photos with your digital camera. You should know how to shoot ultra high-speed fast-action clips. It's not enough to have an enviable CD collection. You should be downloading new songs in MP3 format. The computers in your house should be connected by a wireless router, and online via high-speed DSL service. In other words, if it's been more than ten minutes since you've updated your technology, you're probably behind.

12    In fact, you're not only behind; you're a stupid loser. At least, that's how most of us end up feeling as we're confronted with more and more unexpected technologies: the do-it-yourself checkout at the supermarket, the telephone "help center" that offers a recorded series of messages, but no human help. And feeling like losers makes us frustrated and, you guessed it, angry. "It's not any one thing but lots of little things that make people feel like they don't have control of their lives," says Jane Middleton-Moz, an author and therapist. "A sense of helplessness is what triggers rage. It's why people end up kicking ATM machines."

13    Her example is not far-fetched. According to a survey of computer users in Great Britain, a quarter of those under age 25 admitted to having kicked or punched their computers on at least one occasion. Others confessed to yanking out cables in a rage, forcing the computer to crash. On this side of the Atlantic, a Wisconsin man, after repeated attempts to get his daughter's malfunctioning computer repaired, took it to the store where he had bought it, placed it in the foyer, and attacked it with a sledgehammer. Arrested and awaiting a court appearance, he told local reporters, "It feels good, in a way." He had put into action a fantasy many of us have had—that of taking out our feelings of rage on the machines that so frustrate us.

14    Tension, the third major culprit behind our epidemic of anger, is intimately connected with our lack of time and the pressures of technology. Merely our chronic exhaustion and our frustration in the face of a bewildering array of technologies would be enough to cause our stress levels to skyrocket, but we are dealing with much more.

Our tension is often fueled by a reserve of anger that might be the result of a critical boss, marital discord, or (something that many of today's men and women experience, if few will admit it) a general sense of being stupid and inadequate in the face of the demands of modern life. And along with the annoyances of everyday life, we now live with a widespread fear of such horrors as terrorist acts, global warming, and antibiotic-resistant diseases. Our sense of dread may be out of proportion to actual threats because of technology's ability to constantly inundate us with worrisome information. Twenty-four-hour-a-day news stations bring a stream of horror into our living rooms. As we work at our computers, headlines and graphic images are never more than a mouse click away.

## THE RESULT OF OUR ANGER

15    Add it all together—our feeling of never having enough time; the chronic° aggravation caused by technology; and our endless, diffuse° sense of stress—and we become time bombs waiting to explode. Our angry outbursts may be briefly satisfying, but afterward we are left feeling—well, like jerks. Worse, flying off the handle is a self-perpetuating° behavior. Brad Bushman, a psychology professor at Iowa State University, says, "Catharsis° is worse than useless." Bushman's research has shown that when people vent their anger, they actually become more, not less, aggressive. "Many people think of anger as the psychological equivalent of the steam in a pressure cooker. It has to

be released, or it will explode. That's not true. The people who react by hitting, kicking, screaming, and swearing just feel more angry."

16    Furthermore, the unharnessed venting of anger may actually do us physical harm. The vigorous expression of anger pumps adrenaline into our system and raises our blood pressure, setting the stage for heart attack and strokes. Frequently angry people have even been shown to have higher cholesterol levels than even-tempered individuals.

## HOW TO DEAL WITH OUR ANGER

17    Unfortunately, the culprits behind much of our anger—lack of time, frustrating technology, and megalevels of stress—are not likely to resolve themselves anytime soon. So what are we to do with the anger that arises as a result?

18    According to Carol Tavris, author of *Anger: The Misunderstood Emotion*, the keys to dealing with anger are common sense and patience. She points out that almost no situation is improved by an angry outburst. A traffic jam, a frozen computer, or a misplaced set of car keys is annoying. To act upon the angry feelings those situations provoke, however, is an exercise in futility. Shouting, fuming, or leaning on the car horn won't make traffic begin to flow, the screen unlock, or keys materialize.

19    Patience, on the other hand, is a highly practical virtue. People who take the time to cool down before responding to an anger-producing situation are far less likely to say or do something they

will regret later. "It is true of the body as of arrows," Tavris says, "that what goes up must come down. Any emotional arousal will simmer down if you just wait long enough." When you are stuck in traffic, in other words, turn on some soothing music, breathe deeply, and count to ten—or thirty or forty, if need be.

20      Anger-management therapist Doris Wild Helmering agrees. "Like any feeling, anger lasts only about three seconds," she says. "What keeps it going is your own negative thinking." As long as you focus on the idiot who cut you off on the expressway, you'll stay angry. But if you let the incident go, your anger will go with it. "Once you come to understand that you're driving your own anger with your thoughts," adds Helmering, "you can stop it."

21      Experts who have studied anger also encourage people to cultivate activities that effectively vent their anger. For some people, it's reading the newspaper or watching TV, while others need more active outlets, such as using a treadmill, taking a walk, hitting golf balls, or working out with a punching bag. People who succeed in calming their anger can also enjoy the satisfaction of having dealt positively with their frustrations.

22      For Laura Houser, the episode in the car with her mother was a wake-up call. "I saw myself through her eyes," she said, "and I realized I had become a chronically angry, impatient jerk. My response to stressful situations had become habitual—I automatically flew off the handle. Once I saw what I was doing, it really wasn't that hard to develop different habits. I simply decided I was going to treat other people the way I would want to be treated." The changes in Laura's life haven't benefited only her former victims. "I'm a calmer, happier person now," she reports. "I don't lie in bed at night fuming over stupid things other people have done and my own enraged responses." Laura has discovered the satisfaction of having a sense of control over her own behavior—which ultimately is all any of us can control.

# First Impressions

Freewrite for ten minutes on one of the following.

1. Did you enjoy reading this selection? Why or why not?

2. Would you describe yourself as a person who gets angry easily? What sort of things set off your anger?

3. Do you agree with the author that technology is to blame for some of our anger? Why or why not?

# Vocabulary Check

_B_   1.  In the sentence below, the word *aberrant* means
     A.  amusing.
     B.  abnormal.
     C.  common.
     D.  beneficial.

     Synonym-like clue: *unusual*. Displays of anger that were "unusual" were also considered aberrant.

     "But in earlier, more civil times, public displays of anger were unusual to the point of being aberrant." (Paragraph 5)

_A_   2.  In the sentence below, the word *discord* means
     A.  disagreement.
     B.  harmony.
     C.  absence.
     D.  energy.

     General-sense-of-the-sentence clue: A disagreement in marriage might result in anger.

     "Our tension is often fueled by a reserve of anger that might be the result of a critical boss, marital discord, or (something that many of today's men and women experience, if few will admit it) a general sense of being stupid and inadequate in the face of the demands of modern life." (Paragraph 14)

_C_   3.  In the excerpt below, the word *inundate* means
     A.  interest.
     B.  entertain.
     C.  overwhelm.
     D.  surprise.

     What would 24-hour-a-day news horror stories and a large supply of clickable headlines and images do to us?

     "Our sense of dread may be out of proportion to actual threats because of technology's ability to constantly inundate us with worrisome information. Twenty-four-hour-a-day news stations bring a stream of horror into our living rooms. As we work at our computers, headlines and graphic images are never more than a mouse click away." (Paragraph 14)

# Reading Check

## Central Point and Main Ideas

__B__  1.  Which sentence best expresses the central point of the selection?
   A.  People today have lost their ability to control their anger and behave in a civil fashion.
   B.  Our out-of-control anger has understandable causes, but common sense and patience are more satisfying than outbursts of rage.
   C.  Anger would last only a few seconds if we didn't keep it going with negative thinking.
   D.  While technology has its positive aspects, it has made us constantly available to others and challenged us to master the endless new developments.    Answers A, C, and D are too narrow.

__A__  2.  The main idea of paragraph 9 is expressed in its
   A.  first sentence.
   B.  second sentence.
   C.  third sentence.
   D.  fourth sentence.

   The first sentence states that our busy day is not done when we get home from work. The details following list some of the things that keep us busy after work.

__C__  3.  Which sentence best expresses the implied main idea of paragraph 11?
   A.  Cell phones, computers, and other technological gadgets can be very convenient.
   B.  We would all be better off living without technological gadgets.
   C.  Despite their good points, technological gadgets have added stress to our lives.
   D.  Cell phones, digital cameras, and computers need to be made simpler to use.    Answer A is too narrow. Answers B and D are not indicated in the selection.

## Supporting Details

__C__  4.  Sybil Evans says that the three forces to blame for our anger are
   A.  finances, technology, and tension.
   B.  technology, marital discord, and money.
   C.  time, technology, and tension.
   D.  tension, incompetence, and critical employers.    See paragraph 7.

__D__  5.  According to psychology professor Brad Bushman,
   A.  "blowing off steam" is a psychological necessity.
   B.  people who do not express their anger become seriously depressed.
   C.  the emotion of anger lasts only a few seconds.
   D.  venting our anger does us more harm than good.    See paragraph 15.

**Inferences**

A, B, and C are not
indicated in ___D___
the passage.
Answer D is supported
by Laura's mother's
statement, "I guess
you've been living in
the city too long."

___D___  6.  From paragraph 2 we can infer that

A.  Laura's mother was a bad-tempered woman.

B.  Laura's mother was proud of her daughter's behavior.

C.  Laura's mother knew the driver of the car ahead of them.

D.  Laura had not always been so quick-tempered.

Paragraph  ___A___  7.  In paragraph 11, the author suggests that
11 mentions
the "endless
pressure of feeling we
need to keep up with
our gadgets' latest
technological developments" and then gives several examples.

A.  it is nearly impossible to keep up with technological advances.

B.  only lazy people ignore the wonderful advantages of technology.

C.  text messaging is a waste of time.

D.  most digital cameras and cell phones do not work very well.

___B___  8.  We can infer from the excerpt that follows that

A.  being well-informed about bad news gives us a sense of control.

B.  we would be less worried about problems if we were not constantly reminded of them.

C.  the news media deliberately exaggerate the problems in the world.

D.  it is irresponsible not to keep up with world news.

> "Our sense of dread may be out of proportion to actual threats because of technology's ability to so constantly inundate us with worrisome information. Twenty-four-hour-a-day news stations bring a stream of horror into our living rooms. As we work at our computers, headlines and graphic images are never more than a mouse click away." (Paragraph 14)

The word *dread* refutes answer A.
Answers C and D are not indicated in the excerpt.

## The Writer's Craft

___C___  9.  The section "Why Are We So Angry?" (paragraphs 7–14)

The paragraphs list
and provide examples
of three causes of
angry behavior: time,
technology, and
tension.

A.  compares people's reasons for being angry.

B.  presents a series of steps in the process of becoming angry.

C.  lists and discusses causes of the angry behavior in our society.

D.  contrasts time with technology.

___A___ 10.  The author's purpose in writing this selection is to

A.  inform readers about the causes of anger and ways to control their anger.

B.  entertain readers with stories about people who have lost their tempers in dramatic ways.

C.  persuade people to be kinder to one another.

D.  persuade people that modern life is more stressful than they realize.

The selection describes, in a straightforward way, the reasons people are angry and what they can do to control their anger. Answer B is too narrow. Answers C and D are incorrect because the author does not urge readers to change their behavior or their opinion of modern life.

## Discussion Questions

1. What kinds of things make you most angry? Is your anger directed mostly at others, or at yourself? What steps do you think you should take, or what steps have you taken, to control anger?

2. If you were teaching a class to students on what they should do to control anger, what would be your advice?

3. Of the three sources of our anger identified in the reading—time, technology, and tension—which do you think is the greatest problem for you? Why?

4. Do you agree with Carol Tavris, author of *Anger: The Misunderstood Emotion*, that almost no situation is improved by an angry outburst? Is anger ever helpful? Explain your answer.

## Paragraph Assignments

1. Think of a time you lost your temper. What made you angry? How did you express your anger? Write a paragraph about the incident. Include your thoughts about how you felt later. Are you satisfied with how you handled the situation, or do you wish you'd done something different?

2. Davidson begins the selection by describing an incident in which a woman becomes so angry with another driver that she shouts curses at him. Write a paragraph in which you discuss three reasons why this kind of anger, called road rage, has increased so significantly in recent years. In other words, what is it about driving today that seems to bring out the worst in people? Be sure to begin your paragraph with a clear topic sentence and to use transition words such as *one*, *another*, and *finally* to introduce each of your major supporting details.

## Essay Assignments

1. In this selection, Davidson identifies three main components behind most people's anger: time, technology, and tension. Write an essay in which you give specific examples of how those three components have contributed to your own feelings of anger. Your thesis statement might be something like this: "In my own life, problems with time, technology, and tension have definitely made me lose my temper." Then devote one paragraph to each of those three components. In your final paragraph, draw some conclusions about how the three affect you.

Here is one student's response to this assignment:

Some people never get extremely upset or raise their voices or say a single word in anger, no matter what happens. In contrast, I do get very angry at times, and my anger seems to come out of nowhere. But when I read "Taming the Anger Monster," I recognized the three important components that the author wrote about. I realized that problems with time, technology, and tension often do make me lose my temper.

When it comes to time, I hate to feel that I'm wasting it, especially when it's out of my control. Recently, for instance, I went to renew my driver's license. The office in my town is open only two mornings a week, so there is usually a crowd. When I got there, there was only one clerk working, and there were seven people ahead of me. As I sat waiting for my turn, I felt myself getting more and more irritated. I focused on the clerk and thought all kinds of critical things about how slowly she was working and how stupid I thought she was. By the time I finally reached the head of the line, I was in a truly foul mood. The clerk tried to be friendly with me, but I snapped at her about the long wait and generally acted like a jerk.

Problems with technology can definitely bring out my inner anger monster. I actually love technology—when a new smartphone or tablet comes out, I immediately want one. And when everything is working right, I'm very happy. But when something goes wrong and I can't immediately figure out how to fix it, I become very frustrated. The other day, I was trying to set up my e-mail account on my new phone. To do so, I needed to remember the password for the account, which of course would not come to mind just when I needed it. Within five minutes of trying various passwords that didn't work, I was furious and even slammed my expensive phone on the desk. Finally my brother said, "Just change the password!" I said, "I can't, you idiot! I don't remember the old one!" He said, "You don't need to remember. When you signed up, you probably set a security question to answer to prove your identity. Just answer the question, and you'll be able to get a new password." He was right. I was able to very quickly set a new password, and everything was OK. But I know that the next time a technology problem puzzles me, I'll lose it again.

And tension, of course, can make any frustrating situation worse. If I've already had a tough day at school, or a fight with my boyfriend, or I'm worried about money, it won't take much to send me over the edge into full-blown anger. Recently I'd had "one of those days"—my car was making a scary, expensive-sounding noise; my advisor hadn't liked my plan for an upcoming project; and I hadn't slept well the night before. By the time I got home that evening, my shoulder muscles were so tight they felt like they were made of granite. That's when I saw my younger sister heading out wearing my favorite jacket. Now, she and I trade clothes all the time, although we usually ask each other ahead of time. On any other day, it wouldn't have been a big deal at all. But on this day, I was looking for a target for my general tension-induced anger. I yelled at her, demanding that she take my jacket off that minute. She was shocked at my anger, and so was I. It wasn't really her that I was angry at—it was the world in general.

Now that I've recognized how easily problems with time, technology, and tension can trigger my anger, I hope to be more aware of them. I don't like myself or the things I do when I am angry, and I hope to spend less time feeling angry in the future.

- *Circle one answer:* Does the introduction (a) go from broad to narrow, (b) tell a story, (c) ask questions, or (d) shift to the opposite?

- Underline the thesis statement.

- Underline the topic sentences for the three supporting paragraphs.

- *Circle one answer:* Does the conclusion end with (a) a summary, (b) a final thought, or (c) both?

2. Imagine that you are a counselor who runs anger workshops for people who have trouble managing their anger. Write an essay in which you describe three techniques that people can use to help deal with their anger. In each case, first describe a situation that can trigger anger. Then follow that description with an explanation of a technique that can be used to help defuse that anger.

To help you develop ideas for your paper, you may want to Google "ways to deal with anger" or "coping with anger" or "anger management." You'll find many millions of entries on this universal topic!

Be sure to begin your essay with an introductory paragraph and to follow your three supporting paragraphs with a concluding paragraph.

## Check Your Performance

## TAMING THE ANGER MONSTER

| Activity | Number Right | Points | | | Score |
|---|---|---|---|---|---|
| **Vocabulary Check** (3 items) | _____ | x | 10 | = | _____ |
| **Reading Check** | | | | | |
|    Central Point and Main Ideas (3 items) | _____ | x | 7 | = | _____ |
|    Supporting Details (2 items) | _____ | x | 7 | = | _____ |
|    Inferences (3 items) | _____ | x | 7 | = | _____ |
|    The Writer's Craft (2 items) | _____ | x | 7 | = | _____ |
| | | **TOTAL SCORE** | | = | _____% |

Enter your total score into the **Performance Chart: Fifteen Reading Selections** on the inside back cover.

# 7 All the Good Things

## Sister Helen Mrosla

## Preview

Teachers must often wonder if their efforts on behalf of their students are appreciated—or even noticed. In this article, Sister Helen Mrosla, a Franciscan nun from Little Falls, Minnesota, tells the story of a moment when she learned the answer to that question in a most bittersweet way. Her simple but powerful story has been reprinted many times, as well as widely circulated on the Internet.

## Words to Watch

*mischievousness* (1): minor misbehavior
*novice* (3): new
*deliberately* (5): slowly and on purpose
*concept* (8): idea
*taps* (16): a bugle call sounded at night and at a military funeral
*sheepishly* (20): with embarrassment
*frazzled* (20): worn-out; ragged

1   He was in the first third-grade class I taught at Saint Mary's School in Morris, Minnesota. All thirty-four of my students were dear to me, but Mark Eklund was one in a million. He was very neat in appearance but had that happy-to-be-alive attitude that made even his occasional mischievousness° delightful.

2   Mark talked incessantly. I had to remind him again and again that talking without permission was not acceptable. What impressed me so much, though, was his sincere response every time I had to correct him for misbehaving— "Thank you for correcting me, Sister!" I didn't know what to make of it at first, but before long I became accustomed to hearing it many times a day.

3   One morning my patience was growing thin when Mark talked once too often, and then I made a novice° teacher's mistake. I looked at him and said, "If you say one more word, I am going to tape your mouth shut!"

4   It wasn't ten seconds later when Chuck blurted out, "Mark is talking again." I hadn't asked any of the students to help me watch Mark, but since I had stated the punishment in front of the class, I had to act on it.

5   I remember the scene as if it had occurred this morning. I walked to my desk, very deliberately° opened my drawer, and took out a roll of masking tape. Without saying a word, I proceeded to Mark's desk, tore off two pieces of

tape and made a big X with them over his mouth. I then returned to the front of the room. As I glanced at Mark to see how he was doing, he winked at me.

6    That did it! I started laughing. The class cheered as I walked back to Mark's desk, removed the tape, and shrugged my shoulders. His first words were, "Thank you for correcting me, Sister."

7    At the end of the year I was asked to teach junior-high math. The years flew by, and before I knew it, Mark was in my classroom again. He was more handsome than ever and just as polite. Since he had to listen carefully to my instruction in the "new math," he did not talk as much in ninth grade as he had talked in the third.

8    One Friday, things just didn't feel right. We had worked hard on a new concept° all week, and I sensed that the students were frowning, frustrated with themselves—and edgy with one another. I had to stop this crankiness before it got out of hand. So I asked them to list the names of the other students in the room on two sheets of paper, leaving a space after each name. Then I told them to think of the nicest thing they could say about each of their classmates and write it down.

9    It took the remainder of the class period to finish the assignment, and as the students left the room, each one handed me the papers. Charlie smiled. Mark said, "Thank you for teaching me, Sister. Have a good weekend."

10    That Saturday, I wrote down the name of each student on a separate sheet of paper, and I listed what everyone else had said about that individual.

11    On Monday I gave each student his or her list. Before long, the entire class was smiling. "Really?" I heard whispered. "I never knew that meant anything to anyone!" "I didn't know others liked me so much!"

12    No one ever mentioned those papers in class again. I never knew if the students discussed them after class or with their parents, but it didn't matter. The exercise had accomplished its purpose. The students were happy with themselves and one another again.

13    That group of students moved on. Several years later, after I returned from a vacation, my parents met me at the airport. As we were driving home, Mother asked me the usual questions about the trip—the weather, my experiences in general. There was a slight lull in the conversation. Mother gave Dad a sideways glance and simply said, "Dad?" My father cleared his throat as he usually did before something important. "The Eklunds called last night," he began. "Really?" I said. "I haven't heard from them in years. I wonder how Mark is."

14    Dad responded quietly. "Mark was killed in the war," he said. "The funeral is tomorrow, and his parents would like it if you could attend." To this day I can still point to the exact spot on I-494 where Dad told me about Mark.

15    I had never seen a serviceman in a military coffin before. Mark looked so handsome, so mature. All I could think at that moment was, Mark, I would give all the masking tape in the world if only you would talk to me.

16    The church was packed with Mark's friends. Chuck's sister sang "The Battle

Hymn of the Republic." Why did it have to rain on the day of the funeral? It was difficult enough at the graveside. The pastor said the usual prayers, and the bugler played taps°. One by one those who loved Mark took a last walk by the coffin and sprinkled it with holy water.

17    I was the last one to bless the coffin. As I stood there, one of the soldiers who had acted as pallbearer came up to me. "Were you Mark's math teacher?" he asked. I nodded as I continued to stare at the coffin. "Mark talked about you a lot," he said.

18    After the funeral, most of Mark's former classmates headed to Chuck's farmhouse for lunch. Mark's mother and father were there, obviously waiting for me. "We want to show you something," his father said, taking a wallet out of his pocket. "They found this on Mark when he was killed. We thought you might recognize it."

19    Opening the billfold, he carefully removed two worn pieces of notebook paper that had obviously been taped, folded and refolded many times. I knew without looking that the papers were the ones on which I had listed all the good things each of Mark's classmates had said about him. "Thank you so much for doing that," Mark's mother said. "As you can see, Mark treasured it."

20    Mark's classmates started to gather around us. Charlie smiled rather sheepishly° and said, "I still have my list. It's in the top drawer of my desk at home." Chuck's wife said, "Chuck asked me to put his list in our wedding album." "I have mine too," Marilyn said. "It's in my diary." Then Vicki, another classmate, reached into her pocketbook, took out her wallet, and showed her worn and frazzled° list to the group. "I carry this with me at all times," Vicki said without batting an eyelash. "I think we all saved our lists."

21    That's when I finally sat down and cried. I cried for Mark and for all his friends who would never see him again.

## First Impressions

Freewrite for ten minutes on one of the following.

1. Did you enjoy reading this selection? Why or why not?

2. Do you have any special keepsake or souvenir that you have saved for a long time? What is it? Why is it special to you?

3. Name one teacher you are likely to remember years from now. What is it that you will remember about him or her?

## Vocabulary Check

_B_   1. In the excerpt below, the word *incessantly* means
    A. slowly.
    B. constantly.
    C. quietly.
    D. pleasantly.

    *If Mark had to be reminded over and over again to stop talking, how did he talk?*

    "Mark talked incessantly. I had to remind him again and again that talking without permission was not acceptable." (Paragraph 2)

_A_   2. In the sentence below, the words *blurted out* mean
    A. said suddenly.
    B. watched for.
    C. ran away.
    D. looked at.

    *How did Chuck tell Sister Helen about Mark?*

    "It wasn't ten seconds later when Chuck blurted out, 'Mark is talking again.'" (Paragraph 4)

_C_   3. In the sentence below, the word *edgy* means
    A. funny.
    B. calm.
    C. easily annoyed.
    D. happy.

    *What describes frustrated and frowning students?*

    "We had worked hard on a new concept all week, and I sensed that the students were frowning, frustrated with themselves—and edgy with one another." (Paragraph 8)

## Reading Check

### Central Point and Main Ideas

_B_   1. Which sentence best expresses the central point of the entire selection?
    A. Mark Eklund was a charming, talkative student who appreciated Sister Helen's efforts to teach him.
    B. Sister Helen found out that an assignment she had given years ago had been very important to a beloved former student and his classmates.
    C. When Sister Helen was a young teacher, she had some unusual classroom techniques.
    D. A promising young man, whom Sister Helen had taught and loved, lost his life in the war.

    *Answers A, C, and D are too narrow.*

_C_   2.   Which sentence best expresses the main idea of paragraphs 1–2?
     A.   Mark Eklund was in the first third-grade class Sister Helen taught at Saint Mary's School.
     B.   Mark Eklund was the most talkative of all Sister Helen's students.
     C.   Although Mark Eklund was talkative and mischievous, he was also very sweet-natured.
     D.   Although Sister Helen kept reminding Mark that talking without permission was not permitted, she was unable to stop him from talking.      *Answers A, B, and D are too narrow.*

_B_   3.   Which sentence best expresses the main idea of paragraphs 8–12?
     A.   A difficult math concept had made Sister Helen's students irritable.
     B.   The "good things" assignment made the students feel happy with themselves and others.
     C.   Sister Helen gave up part of her weekend to write out a list of good things about each student.
     D.   At the end of Friday's class, both Charlie and Mark seemed to be in good moods.      *Answers A, C, and D are too narrow.*

## Supporting Details

_B_   4.   When the students didn't mention the lists after the day they received them, Sister Helen
     A.   assumed that the assignment had been a failure.
     B.   didn't mind, because the assignment had done what she hoped.
     C.   called a few students to ask what they thought of the lists.
     D.   felt angry that the students didn't appreciate what she had done.
     *See paragraph 12.*

_D_   5.   At the funeral, Sister Helen learned that
     A.   Mark was the only student who had saved his list.
     B.   Vicki and Mark were the only students who had saved their lists.
     C.   the lists were more important to the male students than the female students.
     D.   all the students in attendance at Mark's funeral had saved their lists.
     *See paragraph 20.*

## Inferences

_C_   6.   The author implies that
     A.   she had known all along how important the lists were to her students.
     B.   she did not support the war.
     C.   the lists meant more to the students than she had ever realized.
     D.   Mark's parents were jealous of her relationship with him.
     *See paragraphs 18–21. Answer A is contradicted by paragraph 12.*
     *Answers B and D are not supported.*

_A_ 7. It is reasonable to conclude that Mark
   A. cared as much for Sister Helen as she cared for him.
   B. never talked much about his past.
   C. planned to become a math teacher himself.
   D. had not stayed in touch with his classmates.

See paragraphs 2, 6, 9, and 17–20.

_C_ 8. We can infer that Sister Helen

See paragraphs 8–12. The "good things" exercise ended the students' frustration and made it possible for them to learn.

   A. liked teaching junior-high math more than she had liked teaching third grade.
   B. was very old at the time of Mark's death.
   C. believed that if students feel good about themselves, they will be more likely to succeed in school.
   D. was an extremely strict teacher.

## The Writer's Craft

_C_ 9. Sister Helen's tone in paragraphs 14–15 is
   A. self-pitying.
   B. matter-of-fact.
   C. sorrowful.
   D. bitter.

Sister Helen remembers exactly where she was when she learned of Mark's death and wishes he could still talk to her—both suggest sadness.

_B_ 10. The author titles this selection "All the Good Things." Which of the following *best* explains her choice of a title?
   A. After years of teaching, Sister Helen chose only to remember good things about her former students.
   B. By asking her students to write good things about each other, Sister Helen had a positive impact on their lives.
   C. At Mark's funeral, Sister Helen learned about all the good things her former students had accomplished in their lives.
   D. Sister Helen believes it was a good thing that she had Mark Eklund as a student.

Sister Helen didn't realize, at the time, how much the students' lists would mean to them. She might have wanted readers to think about the powerful effects of kind words. Answers A, C, and D are not supported.

# Discussion Questions

1. In this story, we read of two classroom incidents involving Sister Helen and her students. In one, she briefly taped a third-grader's mouth closed. In another, she encouraged junior-high students to think of things they liked about one another. In your opinion, what do these two incidents tell about Sister Helen? What kind of teacher was she? What kind of person?

2. Why do you think so many of Sister Helen's students kept their lists for so long? Why were the lists so important to them—even as adults?

3. At the end of the story, Sister Helen tells us that she "cried for Mark and for all his friends who would never see him again." Do you think she might have been crying for other reasons, too? Explain what they might be.

4. "All the Good Things" has literally traveled around the world. Not only has it been reprinted in numerous publications, but many readers have sent it out over the Internet for others to read. Why do you think so many people love this story? Why do they want to share it with others?

## Paragraph Assignments

1. Write a paragraph that develops the following topic sentence: "There are several effective ways of showing appreciation to others." Try to write two or three sentences about each of the methods of appreciation that you describe.

2. Although Sister Helen didn't want to do it, she felt she had to tape Mark's mouth shut after announcing that she would do so. When have you done something you didn't really want to do because others expected it? Write a paragraph about that incident. Explain why you didn't want to do it, why you felt pressure to do it, and how you felt about yourself afterward. Here are sample topic sentences for such a paragraph:

    ● Even though I knew it was wrong, I told my friend's parents a lie to keep my friend out of trouble.

    ● Last year, I pretended I didn't like a guy that I really did like because my friends convinced me he wasn't cool enough.

    ● Recently I've gotten into debt because my friends kept encouraging me to just use my credit card.

# Essay Assignments

1. A recent poll indicated that almost three-fourths of American voters believe that the United States has been involved in too many overseas wars. Write an essay in which you agree or disagree with this poll and, in either case, support your position with specific details. Your thesis statement might be:

   ● There are several reasons why the United States should end its involvement in overseas wars.

   *or*

   ● There are several reasons why the United States must continue its involvement in overseas wars.

   In either case, you should use Google to research the topic. You will find positions for and against our military involvement, and you should explore the many supporting reasons and arguments to clarify and then present your own position. Go on then to write an essay that includes an introduction with a thesis statement, three paragraphs that support your position, and a conclusion.

2. Mark Eklund obviously stood out in Sister Helen's memory. She paints a vivid "word portrait" of Mark as a third-grader. Write an essay about three fellow students who, for positive or negative reasons, you have always remembered. The three may have been your classmates at any point in your life. Your essay should be confined to your memories of those students in the classroom—not on the playground, in the cafeteria, or outside of school. As you describe your memories of those three classmates in that setting, include details that appeal to as many senses as possible—hearing, sight, touch, smell—to make your readers vividly picture those individuals and that time and place in your history.

   Alternatively, you may write an essay about three teachers whom you will always remember.

   Here is one student's response to the assignment:

   > There are some classmates that you just never forget. In many ways, I probably remember a lot more about some of the people in my classes than I do about what was taught! Looking through yearbooks and seeing the faces of certain fellow students, I'm right back in that year and that class. From first grade through high school, there have been some pretty memorable classmates, and three in particular stand out in my memory.

In my third grade class, no one got in more trouble than Stan. Stan was always getting sent to the principal's office for talking, throwing paper airplanes, or just running around. He was a freckled, good-natured kid who, in spite of his troublemaking, was really likeable. I enjoyed him even though I didn't think I was supposed to. One morning during "quiet time," he passed me a note with a drawing of a woman with a big nose and hair sticking straight out. He leaned forward in his seat and whispered, "Mrs. Jennings." I tried hard not to, but I burst out laughing. That morning, both Stan and I were sent to the principal's office after our little secret note was read by our teacher—Mrs. Jennings.

Several years later, in eighth grade, a very quiet student named Cara stands out in my memory. Cara was so shy that she always tried to hide in the back row of our English class so that she'd never get called on. She was very thin, wore old hand-me-downs, and kind of smelled like mothballs. Thankfully, no one really picked on her, but no one talked to her either. I think everyone just figured she wasn't too bright. One day, our teacher paired me with Cara to work on a project. Cara looked like she was going to jump out of her skin at first, but once we got into the work, I realized that Cara was really smart. When I told her that and she smiled, she looked like a completely different person. It was the first time that it occurred to me that just because some kids don't speak in class, it doesn't mean they're not smart.

Finally, one of the most memorable students my senior year in high school was Jorge, a boy whose family had moved to the United States from Puerto Rico three years earlier. Jorge still struggled with speaking English sometimes, but that never kept him from asking a million questions. He used to drive our history teacher insane, and when he'd finally ask a question that our teacher couldn't answer, he'd look around the classroom with a huge grin and say, "Aha!" To say that our history teacher was not amused is putting it lightly. Sometimes I wasn't sure if Jorge was brave or crazy, but all of his questioning must have helped him. He graduated near the top of our class and went on to study law at a good university. I can definitely picture Jorge grilling some poor defendant with a long line of questions!

> A likeable troublemaker, a painfully shy girl, and a curious kid from Puerto Rico—these are three students from my past who still stand out in my memory. I guess if there's a common thread with these three very different people, it's that each was unusual and stood out in his or her own way. They made me laugh or think or admire. That's why I still remember them today.

- *Circle one answer:* Does the introduction (a) go from broad to narrow, (b) tell a story, (c) ask questions, or (d) shift to the opposite?
- Underline the thesis statement.
- Underline the topic sentences for the three supporting paragraphs.
- *Circle one answer:* Does the conclusion end with (a) a summary, (b) a final thought, or (c) both?

## Check Your Performance                          ALL THE GOOD THINGS

| Activity | Number Right | Points | Score |
|---|---|---|---|
| **Vocabulary Check** (3 items) | _____ | x   10 = | _____ |
| **Reading Check** | | | |
| Central Point and Main Ideas (3 items) | _____ | x   7 = | _____ |
| Supporting Details (2 items) | _____ | x   7 = | _____ |
| Inferences (3 items) | _____ | x   7 = | _____ |
| The Writer's Craft (2 items) | _____ | x   7 = | _____ |
| | | TOTAL SCORE   = | _____% |

Enter your total score into the **Reading Performance Chart: Ten Reading Selections** on the inside back cover.

# Shame

## Dick Gregory

## Preview

This excerpt from the autobiography of African American comedian and social activist Dick Gregory describes what it is like to live in poverty. The time was different—Harlem in the 1940s—as were the prices of things, but the human theme of the story resonates in America today. Estimates are that almost 47 million Americans are now living in poverty as our country continues to cope with the longest and deepest recession since the Great Depression of the 1930s.

## Words to Watch

*nappy* (2): kinky, or tightly curled
*stoop* (2): an outside stairway, porch, or platform at the entrance to a house
*mackinaw* (28): a short, plaid coat or jacket
*googobs* (29): Gregory's slang for *gobs*, a large amount

1  I never learned hate at home, or shame. I had to go to school for that. I was about seven years old when I got my first big lesson. I was in love with a little girl named Helene Tucker, a light-complected little girl with pigtails and nice manners. She was always clean and she was smart in school. I think I went to school then mostly to look at her. I brushed my hair and even got me a little old handkerchief. It was a lady's handkerchief, but I didn't want Helene to see me wipe my nose on my hand. The pipes were frozen again, there was no water in the house, but I washed my socks and shirt every night. I'd get a pot, and go over to Mister Ben's grocery store, and stick my pot down into his soda machine. Scoop out some chopped ice. By evening the ice melted to water for washing. I got sick a lot that winter because the fire would go out at night before the clothes were dry. In the morning I'd put them on, wet or dry, because they were the only clothes I had.

2  Everybody's got a Helene Tucker, a symbol of everything you want. I loved her for her goodness, her cleanness, her popularity. She'd walk down my street and my brothers and sisters would yell, "Here comes Helene," and I'd rub my tennis sneakers* on the back of my pants and wish my hair wasn't so nappy° and

_____
\* All sneakers used to be called "tennis sneakers."

369

the white folks' shirt fit me better. I'd run out on the street. If I knew my place and didn't come too close, she'd wink at me and say hello. That was a good feeling. Sometimes I'd follow her all the way home, and shovel the snow off her walk and try to make friends with her Momma and her aunts. I'd drop money on her stoop° late at night on my way back from shining shoes in the taverns. And she had a Daddy, and he had a good job. He was a paper hanger.

3    I guess I would have gotten over Helene by summertime, but something happened in that classroom that made her face hang in front of me for the next twenty-two years. When I played the drums in high school it was for Helene and when I broke track records in college it was for Helene and when I started standing behind microphones and heard applause I wished Helene could hear it, too. It wasn't until I was twenty-nine years old and married and making money that I finally got her out of my system. Helene was sitting in that classroom when I learned to be ashamed of myself.

4    It was on a Thursday. I was sitting in the back of the room, in a seat with a chalk circle drawn around it. The idiot's seat, the troublemaker's seat.

5    The teacher thought I was stupid. Couldn't spell, couldn't read, couldn't do arithmetic. Just stupid. Teachers were never interested in finding out that you couldn't concentrate because you were so hungry, because you hadn't had any breakfast. All you could think about was noontime, would it ever come? Maybe you could sneak into the cloakroom and steal a bite of some kid's lunch out of a coat pocket. A bite of something. Paste. You can't really make a meal of paste, or put it on bread for a sandwich, but sometimes I'd scoop a few spoonfuls out of the big paste jar in the back of the room. Pregnant people get strange tastes. I was pregnant with poverty. Pregnant with dirt and pregnant with smells that made people turn away, pregnant with cold and pregnant with shoes that were never bought for me, pregnant with five other people in my bed and no Daddy in the next room, and pregnant with hunger. Paste doesn't taste too bad when you're hungry.

6    The teacher thought I was a troublemaker. All she saw from the front of the room was a little black boy who squirmed in his idiot's seat and made noises and poked the kids around him. I guess she couldn't see a kid who made noises because he wanted someone to know he was there.

7    It was on a Thursday, the day before the Negro payday. The eagle always flew on Friday.* The teacher was asking each student how much his father would give to the Community Chest**. On Friday night, each kid would get the money from his father, and on Monday he would bring it to the school. I decided I was going to buy a Daddy right then. I had money in my pocket from shining shoes and selling papers, and whatever

---

* In Gregory's day, ten-dollar bills were known as "eagles." On payday, people would have some ten-dollar bills to spend.

** In Gregory's day, the charitable organization we call the United Way was known as the Community Chest.

Helene Tucker pledged for her Daddy I was going to top it. And I'd hand the money right in. I wasn't going to wait until Monday to buy me a Daddy.

8    I was shaking, scared to death. The teacher opened her book and started calling out names alphabetically.

9    "Helene Tucker?"

10   "My Daddy said he'd give two dollars and fifty cents."

11   "That's very nice, Helene. Very, very nice indeed."

12   That made me feel pretty good. It wouldn't take too much to top that. I had almost three dollars in dimes and quarters in my pocket. I stuck my hand in my pocket and held onto the money, waiting for her to call my name. But the teacher closed her book after she called everybody else in the class.

13   I stood up and raised my hand.

14   "What is it now?"

15   "You forgot me."

16   She turned toward the blackboard. "I don't have time to be playing with you, Richard."

17   "My Daddy said he'd . . ."

18   "Sit down, Richard, you're disturbing the class."

19   "My Daddy said he'd give . . . fifteen dollars."

20   She turned around and looked mad. "We are collecting this money for you and your kind, Richard Gregory. If your Daddy can give fifteen dollars you have no business being on relief*."

21   "I got it right now, I got it right now, my Daddy gave it to me to turn in today, my Daddy said . . ."

------

* welfare

22   "And furthermore," she said, looking right at me, her nostrils getting big and her lips getting thin and her eyes opening wide, "we know you don't have a Daddy."

23   Helene Tucker turned around, her eyes full of tears. She felt sorry for me. Then I couldn't see her too well because I was crying, too.

24   "Sit down, Richard."

25   And I always thought the teacher kind of liked me. She always picked me to wash the blackboard on Friday, after school. That was a big thrill, it made me feel important. If I didn't wash it, come Monday the school might not function right.

26   "Where are you going, Richard!"

27   I walked out of school that day, and for a long time I didn't go back very often. There was shame there.

28   Now there was shame everywhere. It seemed like the whole world had been inside that classroom, everyone had heard what the teacher had said, everyone had turned around and felt sorry for me. There was shame in going to the Worthy Boys Annual Christmas Dinner for you and your kind, because everybody knew what a worthy boy was. Why couldn't they just call it the Boys Annual Dinner, why'd they have to give it a name? There was shame in wearing the brown and orange and white plaid mackinaw° the welfare gave to three thousand boys. Why'd it have to be the same for everybody so when you walked down the street the people could see you were on relief? It was a nice warm mackinaw and it had a hood, and my Momma beat me and called me

a little rat when she found out I stuffed it in the bottom of a pail full of garbage way over on Cottage Street. There was shame in running over to Mister Ben's at the end of the day and asking for his rotten peaches, there was shame in asking Mrs. Simmons for a spoonful of sugar, there was shame in running out to meet the relief truck. I hated that truck, full of food for you and your kind. I ran into the house and hid when it came. And then I started to sneak through alleys, to take the long way home so the people going into White's Eat Shop wouldn't see me. Yeah, the whole world heard the teacher that day, we all know you don't have a Daddy.

29     It lasted for a while, this kind of numbness. I spent a lot of time feeling sorry for myself. And then one day I met this wino in a restaurant. I'd been out hustling all day, shining shoes, selling newspapers, and I had googobs° of money in my pocket. Bought me a bowl of chili for fifteen cents, and a cheeseburger for fifteen cents, and a Pepsi for five cents, and a piece of chocolate cake for ten cents. That was a good meal. I was eating when this old wino came in. I love winos because they never hurt anyone but themselves.

30     The old wino sat down at the counter and ordered twenty-six cents worth of food. He ate it like he really enjoyed it. When the owner, Mister Williams, asked him to pay the check, the old wino didn't lie or go through his pocket like he suddenly found a hole.

31     He just said: "Don't have no money."

32     The owner yelled: "Why in hell you come in here and eat my food if you don't have no money? That food cost me money."

33     Mister Williams jumped over the counter and knocked the wino off his stool and beat him over the head with a pop bottle. Then he stepped back and watched the wino bleed. Then he kicked him. And he kicked him again.

34     I looked at the wino with blood all over his face and I went over. "Leave him alone, Mister Williams. I'll pay the twenty-six cents."

35     The wino got up, slowly, pulling himself up to the stool, then up to the counter, holding on for a minute until his legs stopped shaking so bad. He looked at me with pure hate. "Keep your twenty-six cents. You don't have to pay, not now. I just finished paying for it."

36     He started to walk out, and as he passed me, he reached down and touched my shoulder. "Thanks, sonny, but it's too late now. Why didn't you pay it before?"

37     I was pretty sick about that. I waited too long to help another man.

## First Impressions

Freewrite for ten minutes on one of the following.

1. Did you enjoy reading this selection? Why or why not?

2. When you were in elementary school did you, like Gregory, ever have a crush on a classmate? What was it about this person that you liked so much?

3. Were you ever badly embarrassed by a teacher (or did you witness someone else embarrassed by a teacher)? What happened?

## Vocabulary Check

_A_    1. In the excerpt below, the word *pregnant* means

    A. full of.

    B. empty of.

    C. sick of.

    D. pleased with.

> Pregnant women's wombs are full of the babies they are carrying, and these women often have strange food cravings. Gregory is full of poverty and hunger, so even paste tastes good to him.

"Pregnant people get strange tastes. I was pregnant with poverty . . . and pregnant with hunger. Paste doesn't taste too bad when you're hungry." (Paragraph 5)

_C_    2. In the sentence below, the word *pledged* means

    A. repeated.

    B. studied.

    C. promised to give.

    D. brought home.

> Each child has been asked how much his or her father would give, so Dick Gregory plans to top whatever amount Helene promises her father will give.

"I had money in my pocket . . . and whatever Helene Tucker pledged for her Daddy, I was going to top it." (Paragraph 7)

_D_    3. In the sentence below, the word *hustling* means

    A. complaining.

    B. relaxing.

    C. studying hard.

    D. working energetically.

> Shining shoes and selling newspapers all day are examples of working energetically.

"I'd been out hustling all day, shining shoes, selling newspapers, and I had googobs of money in my pocket." (Paragraph 29)

# Reading Check

## Central Point and Main Ideas

_C_  1.  Which sentence best expresses the central point of the entire selection?

Answer A covers only paragraphs 1–3. Answer B covers only paragraph 28. Answer D covers only paragraphs 1–2.

    A.  Dick Gregory had a long-standing crush on a girl named Helene Tucker.

    B.  The charity Gregory received was given in a way that labeled him as poor, which made him ashamed.

    C.  As both a receiver and a giver, Gregory learned that giving something the wrong way can cause shame.

    D.  Gregory grew up in a fatherless, poor family.

_A_  2.  Which sentence best expresses the main idea of paragraph 2?

Answer B covers only the first sentence. Answer C covers only sentence 3. Answer D covers only the last sentence.

    A.  The author adored Helene Tucker, a symbol of everything he wanted.

    B.  Everybody has a symbol of everything he or she wants.

    C.  Helene Tucker made the author feel ashamed of his looks.

    D.  Unlike the author, Helene Tucker had a father.

_D_  3.  Which sentence best expresses the main idea of paragraph 5?

Answer A is incorrect because he does not say he liked to eat it, only that it doesn't taste bad if you are hungry. Answer B covers only sentences 1–3. Answer C covers only sentence 4.

    A.  Gregory liked to eat paste.

    B.  The teacher assumed that Gregory was stupid.

    C.  The teacher never realized that Gregory was hungry all the time.

    D.  The teacher assumed that Gregory was stupid and never realized that his poor work was the result of hunger.

## Supporting Details

_D_  4.  Gregory could afford to contribute to the Community Chest because he had

See paragraph 7.

    A.  worked as a paperhanger.

    B.  stolen money out of the pockets of coats in the school cloakroom.

    C.  earned money by cleaning the blackboard for the teacher.

    D.  earned money by shining shoes and selling papers.

_A_  5.  Gregory's mother beat him when he

See paragraph 28.

    A.  threw away the jacket that he'd gotten from welfare.

    B.  dropped his money on Helene's stoop.

    C.  didn't stop Mister Williams from beating the wino.

    D.  walked out of school.

## Inferences

_____F_____ 6. *True or False?* In the classroom scene, the author implies that Helene is not sensitive.    See paragraph 23. Helene's crying reveals her sensitivity.

Gregory _____C_____ 7. In paragraph 5, the author implies that
writes that teachers
"were never interested    A. he is stupid.
in finding out that you    B. teachers understood him well.
couldn't concentrate
because you were so    C. it was difficult for him to concentrate in school.
hungry."    D. the only way he ever got food was to steal it.

_____B_____ 8. When the wino says, "I just finished paying for [the food]," he is
When Mister Williams implying that he
realizes he isn't going    A. had found some money to give Mister Williams.
to get money from the    B. had paid for it by taking a beating.
wino, he beats him.
The beating takes the    C. had paid for the meal before he ate.
place of money.    D. would work for Mister Williams to pay for the meal.

## The Writer's Craft

The first _____B_____ 9. Gregory organizes his essay by
incident is related in    A. listing the types of behavior demonstrated by victims of poverty.
paragraphs 4–27; the
second, in paragraphs    B. relating, in time order, two incidents that taught him the meaning of
29–37. Each incident's    shame.
details are organized in    C. showing the effects of poverty on a person's educational level.
the order in which they    D. contrasting the ways rich people and poor people relate to others.
happened.

_____D_____ 10. The word that best describes the tone of the last paragraph of the
selection is
A. angry.
B. objective.
C. sentimental.    The words "pretty sick about that" indicate regret.
D. regretful.

## Discussion Questions

1. The Community Chest incident could have had very different results if Gregory's teacher had handled the situation in another way. What do you think she should have done when Gregory said, "You forgot me"? Or could she have used a different method of collecting money from students? Explain.

2. Why do you think Gregory included both the classroom story and the restaurant story in his article? In what ways are the two incidents similar? What is the difference between the shame he felt in the first incident and the shame he felt in the second?

3. We say that something is ironic when it has an effect that is the opposite of what might be expected. In this reading, Gregory uses irony in several places. In what ways are the following quotations from "Shame" ironic?

   ● "I never learned hate at home, or shame. I had to go to school for that."

   ● "If I knew my place and didn't come too close, she'd wink at me and say hello. That was a good feeling."

   ● "I looked at the wino with blood all over his face and I went over. 'Leave him alone, Mister Williams. I'll pay the twenty-six cents.'
   "The wino got up. . . . He looked at me with pure hate."

4. Have the hard economic times and job shortages of today affected your life or the lives of people you know? In what ways? What do you think needs to be done to help turn these situations around?

## Paragraph Assignments

1. When have you, like Gregory, regretted the way you acted in a particular situation? Perhaps you didn't speak up when someone was being teased, or perhaps you spoke harshly to someone because you were in a bad mood. Write a paragraph that describes the situation and how you acted. You might want to start the paragraph with a sentence like "I still regret the way I acted when _____." Conclude by explaining why you feel you acted wrongly and what you wish you had done instead.

Here is one student's response to the assignment:

> I still feel bad about a situation I let go on for years. I went to a very small school, meaning that the same dozen or so kids were together in one class through elementary and middle school. One of those kids, I'll call him Keith, was pretty strange. Looking back, I think he may have had mild autism or something. He was overweight and messy, and he had a lot of odd habits. He constantly rocked back and forth in his chair, and when he got anxious or excited, he would rock faster. He would blurt out odd comments at inappropriate times. He had a collection of little-kid action figures that he played with. So yes, he was strange, and I admit I laughed at him behind his back. But there was another student named Ben who teased and bullied him constantly. Ben would sit behind him and imitate Keith's strange movements and comments. He would give him meaningless little jobs to do at recess, promising Keith that if he did them right, he'd be accepted by the "cool" kids. After Keith finished the jobs, of course, Ben would say he'd changed his mind. Ben would get written up for bullying Keith, but he never stopped. During all the years that Ben was bullying Keith, and all the other kids in our tiny class were watching, not one of us did a thing about it. No one ever told Ben to knock it off. No one ever tried to be a friend to Keith. Even though I was one of the popular kids, it never occurred to me that I could have made a difference. I think if I had stood up for Keith, other students would have followed me. But I didn't, and I feel ashamed about that to this day.

2. Teachers are powerful figures in children's lives. At times—perhaps because of impatience, poor judgment, a misunderstanding, or anger—a teacher may hurt a student's feelings. Write a paragraph about a situation you witnessed in which you believe a teacher acted inappropriately and made a student feel bad. Be sure to explain not only what the teacher did but also how the student was affected.

## Essay Assignments

1. A dictionary defines a word by briefly explaining its meaning. But in an essay, an author can define a term in a different, more personal manner. In this reading, Dick Gregory defines *shame* by describing two incidents in his life in which shame played a central part.

   Write an essay in which you define *poverty* by presenting several real-life examples of people in America today coping with poverty. Your central point might be stated something like this: "Many people in America today endure the heartbreak of coping with poverty." Perhaps you can provide an example that comes out of your own life or the life of someone you have heard about or know. Otherwise, or in addition, if you Google "Examples of poverty in the US," you will find over 100 million articles on the topic! Look for articles that present vivid specific examples from the real lives of real people dealing with poverty, and use them as the basis for the supporting paragraphs in your essay. In a concluding paragraph, present your thoughts and reactions to what you have learned in researching your paper.

2. By embarrassing him in front of the class, Gregory's teacher demonstrated the negative effect that a teacher can have on a student. But teachers also have the potential to be very positive figures in their students' lives. Write an essay about three qualities that you think a good teacher should possess. Some of these qualities might be patience, a sense of humor, insight into students' feelings, and the ability to make a lesson interesting. Illustrate each of those qualities with examples of behavior you have witnessed from real-life teachers. Include your observations on how students benefit when a teacher has the qualities you're writing about.

---

## Check Your Performance                                    SHAME

| Activity | Number Right | Points | Score |
|---|---|---|---|
| **Vocabulary Check** (3 items) | _____ | x  10  = | _____ |
| **Reading Check** | | | |
| Central Point and Main Ideas (3 items) | _____ | x  7  = | _____ |
| Supporting Details (2 items) | _____ | x  7  = | _____ |
| Inferences (3 items) | _____ | x  7  = | _____ |
| The Writer's Craft (2 items) | _____ | x  7  = | _____ |
| | | TOTAL SCORE  = | _____ % |

Enter your total score into the **Performance Chart: Fifteen Reading Selections** on the inside back cover.

# 9 "Extra Large, Please"

## Alice M. Davies

## Preview

Americans are getting fatter. The statistics keep coming out, and they are steadily worse. As a people, our weight keeps climbing, while our physical fitness is declining. What is going on? In this essay, the author encourages us to look at the point where most obesity begins: childhood.

## Words to Watch

*diabetes* (4): a chronic health condition in which the body is unable to break down sugar in the blood

*coma* (12): a state of prolonged unconsciousness

*staple* (14): a basic item or feature

1   School lunches have always come in for a lot of criticism. When I was a kid, we complained about "mystery meat" and "leftover surprise casserole." Half a canned pear in a shaky nest of Jell-O didn't do much to excite our taste buds. I hid my share of limp green beans under my napkin, the better to escape the eagle eye of lunchroom monitors who encouraged us to eat our soggy, overcooked vegetables.

2   But the cafeteria lunches were there, and so we ate them. (Most of them. OK, I hid the gooey tapioca pudding, too.) I think we accepted the idea that being delicious was not the point. The meals were reasonably nutritious, and they fueled our young bodies for the mental and physical demands of the day. In my case, that demand included walking a quarter mile to and from school, enjoying three recesses a day, and taking part in gym class a couple of times a week. After-school hours, at least when the weather was good, were spent outdoors playing kickball or tag with neighbor kids.

3   You're thinking, "Who cares?"— aren't you? I don't blame you. My memories of school days in northern Indiana forty-some years ago aren't all that fascinating, even to me. And yet I think you should care, because of one fact I haven't mentioned yet. When I was a kid and looked around at other kids my age, I saw all kinds of differences. There were tall ones and short ones and black and white and brown ones, rude ones

and polite ones, popular ones and geeky ones, athletic ones and uncoordinated ones. But you know what? There weren't many heavy ones. The few there were stood out because they were unusual. I think that if you had asked me at the time, I would have told you that kids are just naturally skinny.

4      Flash forward to the present. Walk down any city street in America. Sit in a mall and watch the people stream by. You don't need to be a pediatrician to notice something's changed. Whether you call them big-boned, chubby, husky, or plus-sized, kids are heavy, lots of them. If your own eyes don't convince you, here are the statistics: Since 1980, the number of American kids who are dangerously overweight has tripled. Nearly one-third of American kids qualify as "overweight" or "obese." In 2011, the U.S. military released a study showing that 27 percent of young people ages 17 to 24 are too fat to join the armed forces. Hordes of kids are developing Type-2 diabetes°, a diet-related disease that used to be called "adult onset diabetes" because it was virtually never seen in children. When Texas schools conducted a statewide physical fitness test in 2010, two-thirds of the students failed. The same test in California showed similar results—only one child in three scored in the "physically fit" range. Schools are ordering larger desks to accommodate extra-big kids. Clothing stores for plus-size kids—from toddlers on up—are multiplying.

5      Part of the problem is that many kids don't have good opportunities to exercise. They live in neighborhoods without sidewalks or paths where they can walk, bike, or skate safely. Drug activity and violent crime may make playing outside dangerous. They can reach their schools only by car or bus. Many of those schools are so short of money they've scrapped their physical-fitness classes. Too few communities have athletic programs in place.

6      Electronic entertainment also plays a role in the current state of affairs. Kids used to go outside to play with other kids because it was more fun than sitting around the house. Today's sedentary kids don't mind sitting around the house; they have access to hundreds of cable TV channels, YouTube, Facebook, Hulu, instant streaming movies, DVD players, and a dizzying assortment of video games.

7      Still another cause is the lack of parental supervision. When I was a kid, most of us had a mom or an older sibling at home telling us to get off our butts and go outside. (The alternative was often to stay inside and do chores. We chose to go out and play.) Now, most American parents work outside the home. During the daylight hours, those parents just aren't around to encourage their kids to get some exercise. A related problem is that parents who can't be home much may feel guilty about it. One way of relieving that guilt is to buy Junior the game system of his dreams and a nice wide-screen TV to play it on.

8      These are all complicated problems whose solutions are equally complicated. But there is one cause of the fattening of America's kids that can be dealt with more easily. And that

cause is the enormous influence that fast-food restaurants and other sources of calorie-laden junk food have gained over America's kids.

9     I'm no health nut. I like an occasional Quarter Pounder as well as the next mom. When my kids were young, there was no quicker way to their hearts than to bring home a newly-released DVD, a large pepperoni pizza, and a bag of Chicken McNuggets. But in our home, an evening featuring extra mozzarella and bottles of 7-Up was a once-in-a-while treat—sort of a guilty pleasure.

10     To many of today's kids, fast food is not a treat—it's their daily diet. Their normal dinnertime equals McDonalds, Pizza Hut, Domino's, Burger King, Taco Bell, or KFC, all washed down with Pepsi. And increasingly, lunchtime at school means those foods too. About 20 percent of our nation's schools have sold chain restaurants the right to put their food items on the lunch line. A majority of middle schools and high schools allow snack and soft-drink vending machines on their campuses. The National Soft Drink Association reports that 60 percent of public and private middle schools and high schools make sodas available for purchase.

11     Believe me, when I was a kid, if the lunch line had offered me a couple of slices of double-crust stuffed pepperoni-sausage pizza instead of a Turkey Submarine, I would have said yes before you could say the words "clogged arteries." And when I needed a mid-afternoon pick-me-up, I would have gladly traded a handful of change for a sugar-and-caffeine-laden "energy drink" like Red Bull or Monster and a Snickers bar.

12     And then I would have gone back into algebra class and spent the hour bouncing between a sugar high and a fat-induced coma°.

13     Advertising for fast foods has also sneaked its way into many schools, increasingly giving kids the idea that junk food is their friend. In one notorious example in Seminole, Florida, kids' report cards came enclosed in Ronald McDonald envelopes. Inside was a promise for a free Happy Meal for good grades. (Concerned parents soon put an end to that particular promotion.) Pizza Hut's "Book It" program rewards frequent readers with Pizza Hut products. McDonald's sponsors a popular "Passport to Play" program, which brings Ronald McDonald into elementary schools to introduce games, dances, and other physical activities from foreign lands.

14     All these factors help hook kids on what's become the Standard American Diet, which is indeed SAD. It's one thing to stop off at Taco Bell for an occasional Seven-Layer Burrito. But when fast food becomes the staple° of young people's diets, it's the kids who become Whoppers. And it has become the staple for many. According to researchers at Children's Hospital in Boston, during any given week, three out of four children eat a fast-food meal one or more times a day. The beverages they chug down are a problem, too. The U.S. Department of Agriculture says that every day, the average adolescent drinks enough soda, "energy drinks," and fruit beverages to

equal the sugar content of 50 chocolate-chip cookies.

15      The problem isn't only that burgers, fries, and sodas aren't nutritious to begin with—although they aren't. What has made the situation much worse is the increasingly huge portions sold by fast-food restaurants. Back when McDonald's began business, its standard meal consisted of a hamburger, two ounces of French fries, and a 12-ounce Coke. That meal provided 590 calories. But today's customers don't have to be satisfied with such modest portions. For very little more money, diners can end up with a Double Quarter Pounder with cheese (730 calories), large fries (570), and a 32-ounce Coke (310). That adds up to 1,610 calories. A whole generation of kids is growing up believing that this massive shot of fat, sugar, and sodium equals a "normal portion." As a result, they're becoming extra large themselves.

16      As kids sit down to watch the after-school and Saturday-morning shows designed for them, they aren't just taking in the programs themselves. They're seeing at least an hour of commercials for every five hours of programming. On Saturday mornings, nine out of ten of those commercials are for sugary cereals, fast food, and other non-nutritious junk. Many of the commercials are tied in with popular toys or beloved cartoon characters or movies aimed at children. Watching those commercials makes the kids hungry—or at least they *think* they're hungry. (Thanks to all the factors mentioned here, many children can no longer tell if they're genuinely hungry or not. They've been programmed to eat for many reasons other than hunger.) So they snack as they sit in front of the TV set. Then at mealtime, they beg to go out for more junk food. And they get bigger, and bigger, and bigger.

17      There is no overnight solution to the problem of American children's increasing weight and decreasing level of physical fitness. But can anything be done?

18      Yes. Let's start with the good news. With major input from First Lady Michelle Obama, the federal government began paying serious attention to increasing physical activity and combating obesity in children. Mrs. Obama's "Let's Move!" campaign and the Partnership for a Healthier America, a nonprofit organization working with the private sector and the Obama administration, helped raise awareness that childhood obesity is a problem that affects everyone. In 2010, Congress passed the Healthier, Hunger-Free Kids Act. Under this bill, the United States Department of Agriculture released new school meal regulations—the first significant changes to school meals in fifteen years. As the regulations are put into place, school lunches will contain more fruits and vegetables, less fat and salt, and more whole grains than ever before. Eventually, new nutritional guidelines will be released for all foods sold on a school campus, including those obtained from vending machines or available in the à la carte section of the cafeteria.

19      These changes are an excellent beginning. Fast-food meals and junk-

food vending machines have no place in our schools. (One study in Florida showed that about one in five middle-school kids routinely skipped the school lunch altogether and instead ate a snack and beverage from a school vending machine.) Our educational system should be helping children acquire good nutritional habits, not assisting them in committing slow nutritional suicide.

20    In addition, commercials for junk food should be banned from TV during children's viewing time, specifically Saturday mornings.

21    And finally, fast-food restaurants should be required to do what tobacco companies—another manufacturer of products known to harm people's health—have been mandated to do. They should display in their restaurants, and in their TV and print ads as well, clear nutritional information about their products. For instance, a young woman at Burger King who was considering ordering a Double Whopper with Cheese, a king-size order of fries and a king-size Dr. Pepper could read something like this:

- *Your meal will provide 1860 calories, 880 of those calories from fat.*
- *Your recommended daily intake is 2000 calories, with no more than 600 of those calories coming from fat.*

22    At a glance, then, the customer could see that in one fast-food meal, she was taking in almost as many calories and more fat than she should consume in an entire day.

23    There are opponents to many if not all of these measures. Such opponents say that eating well and staying healthy and active are personal responsibilities; that government intervention in the obesity epidemic is an example of a "nanny state" intruding where it does not belong.

24    They are wrong.

25    The well-funded, well-researched efforts of junk-food producers have, in just a couple of generations, contributed to a public health crisis whose effects are only now beginning to be felt—all in the name of a quick profit. If a foreign invader had damaged the health of as many American children, we would be at war.

26    Overweight kids today become overweight adults tomorrow. Overweight adults are at increased risk for heart disease, diabetes, stroke, and cancer. Schools, fast-food restaurants, and the media are contributing to a public-health disaster in the making. Anything that can be done to decrease the role junk food plays in kids' lives needs to be done, and done quickly.

## First Impressions

Freewrite for ten minutes on one of the following.

1. Did you enjoy reading this selection? Why or why not?

2. Did any of the facts or statistics in this article surprise you? Which ones?

3. Do you agree with the author that childhood obesity is a social problem that schools and the government should get involved with? Or is it strictly a personal matter?

## Vocabulary Check

_B_ 1. In the excerpt below, the word *hordes* means

    A. small groups.

    B. large groups.

    C. selected groups.

    D. concerned groups.

> If the number of American kids who are dangerously overweight has tripled, large groups of them must be developing diet-related diabetes.

"Since 1980, the number of American kids who are dangerously overweight has tripled....Hordes of kids are developing Type-2 diabetes, a diet-related disease that used to be called 'adult onset diabetes' because it was virtually never seen in children." (Paragraph 4)

_D_ 2. In the excerpt below, the word *sedentary* means

    A. playful.

    B. bored.

    C. well-behaved.

    D. inactive.

> Synonym clue: *sitting around the house.*

"Kids used to go outside to play with other kids because it was more fun than sitting around the house. Today's sedentary kids don't mind sitting around the house; they have access to hundreds of cable TV channels, YouTube, Facebook, Hulu, instant streaming movies, DVD players, and a dizzying assortment of video games." (Paragraph 6)

_A_ 3. In the sentence below, the word *mandated* means

    A. ordered.

    B. likely.

    C. forbidden.

    D. eager.

> Synonym clue: *required.*

"And finally, fast-food restaurants should be required to do what tobacco companies—another manufacturer of products known to harm people's health—have been mandated to do." (Paragraph 21)

# Reading Check

## Central Point and Main Ideas

__B__  1.  Which sentence best expresses the central point of the selection?
   A.  This generation of children is heavier than previous generations.
   B.  Our kids' growing obesity is a serious public health problem that has several causes.
   C.  The fast-food industry should be more closely regulated.
   D.  Nothing is more important for today's generation of children than getting more exercise.    Answers A covers only paragraph 4; answer C covers only paragraph 18. Answer D is not supported.

__A__  2.  The main idea of paragraph 10 is stated in the
   A.  first sentence.
   B.  second sentence.    The remainder of the paragraph supports the idea
   C.  third sentence.    that fast food is many kids' daily diet.
   D.  last sentence.

__B__  3.  The main idea of paragraph 15 is stated in the
   A.  first sentence.
   B.  second sentence.    The first sentence tells what the main idea *isn't*,
   C.  third sentence.    but not what it is. The third and last sentences
   D.  last sentence.    are too narrow.

## Supporting Details

__C__  4.  Which of the following is *not* presented as a reason that kids are growing heavier?
   A.  Lack of exercise    Answer A is mentioned in paragraphs 5–7,
   B.  Overly large portions of food    answer B in paragraph 15,
   C.  Genetics    and answer D in paragraph 14.
   D.  Overconsumption of soda

__B__  5.  The Healthier, Hunger-Free Kids Act requires that
   A.  TV stations broadcast public service messages that promote healthy eating.
   B.  school lunches contain more fruits and vegetables, less salt and fat, and more whole grains.
   C.  schools ban vending machines that sell junk food and sugary soft drinks.
   D.  commercials for junk food be banned from TV during children's viewing time.

See paragraph 18, sentences 5–7.

## Inferences

___C___ 6. Which sentence best expresses the implied main idea of paragraph 4?
A. Kids today spend too much time in malls.
B. Diabetes is the most serious health threat today.
C. Kids today are heavier and less physically fit than ever before.
D. Kids in California and Texas are heavier and less fit than children elsewhere.

*Answers A, B, and D are not supported.*

___D___ 7. Which sentence best expresses the implied main idea of paragraphs 5–7?
A. Moms should stay home and supervise their kids rather than join the work force.
B. Electronic entertainment influences kids to stay inside and get less physical exercise than they need.
C. Kids are only going to get heavier and less fit as the years go on.
D. There are at least three major reasons for young people's increased obesity.

*Answers A and C are not supported by paragraphs 5–7. Answer B covers only paragraph 6.*

___A___ 8. The implied main idea of paragraph 16 is that

*Answers B, C, and D are too narrow. Each covers only one detail of the paragraph.*

A. kids are pushed to overeat by the commercials that they see.
B. children's television has one hour of commercials for every five hours of programs.
C. many commercials aimed at children feature tie-ins with toys and movies.
D. children do not always realize when they are genuinely hungry.

## The Writer's Craft

___B___ 9. Which of the following does Davies rely on most heavily to make her points?
A. Anecdotes
B. Facts and statistics
C. Personal opinion
D. Humor

*See paragraphs 5–7, 10, 13, 18 (facts) and paragraphs 4, 14–16, 19, and 21–22 (statistics).*

*Statements* ___A___ 10. The author's purpose in writing this selection is to
A. persuade readers that childhood obesity is a health crisis that demands action.
B. inform people about the possible health effects of being significantly overweight.
C. entertain readers with memories of the author's childhood and school experiences.
D. persuade readers to get more exercise and to eat a healthier diet.

*like "Our educational system should be helping children acquire good nutritional habits, not assisting them in committing slow nutritional suicide" and "Anything that can be done to decrease the role junk food plays in kids' lives needs to be done, and done quickly" reveal the author's persuasive purpose.*

## Discussion Questions

1. When you were a child, how much—and what kinds of—exercise did you typically get? Did you grow up in a place where kids could and did play outside? If not, were you able—or encouraged—to find opportunities to exercise?

2. The author of the selection proposes that fast-food restaurants should be required to display clear nutritional information about their products. Do you think that the presentation of this information would result in a significant reduction in the amount of fast food that people consume? Would it change your eating habits? Why or why not?

3. The author of the selection believes that it's a good idea for the federal government to get involved in trying to get Americans, especially kids, to eat healthier. Do you agree with her? Or do you believe, as opponents of government intervention say, that staying healthy and active are personal responsibilities with which the government should not interfere? Explain your reasoning.

4. The author admits that when she was a kid, she probably would have preferred pizza to something more nutritious. She also mentions that two-thirds of Texas students failed a statewide physical fitness test. Given the fact that most kids prefer fast foods and passive entertainment, what can be done to promote healthier lifestyles to young people?

## Paragraph Assignments

1. Alice Davies provides a number of reasons that help explain why childhood obesity is more widespread today than ever before. Of the reasons she mentions, which one do you think is most significant? Write a paragraph that explains your answer.

2. In your opinion, should schools contain vending machines that sell soda pop, candy, and snacks? Why or why not? Write a paragraph defending your answer.

## Essay Assignments

1. The parents of children who are overweight are in a difficult situation. They don't want to make the kids feel as though they are less loved because of their size. On the other hand, they worry about their children's health and social acceptance.

   What advice would you give the parents of children who are significantly overweight? Should they ignore the situation, allowing the children to deal with it themselves? Should they encourage the child to lose weight? How should they do that? Write an essay in which you describe what you think is the best way for a parent to deal with the situation. Begin with a thesis statement similar to this: "In dealing with an overweight child, a parent should keep several things in mind."

2. Think about the children who live in your own neighborhood. What issues do you observe that concern you? Those issues might include their physical fitness, discussed in this article. They might include concerns about how they play, treat their peers, or relate to their parents or neighbors. The issues might involve the environment they are growing up in. Think of three things that concern you about the kids in your own community. Write an essay whose thesis is similar to this: "Three things worry me about the kids growing up in my neighborhood."

   Here is one student's response to this assignment:

   > We're fortunate to live in a fairly nice neighborhood. By "nice," I mean it's relatively safe and clean, and the homes have decent-sized yards. So my concerns about the kids in our neighborhood aren't the same concerns I'd have if we lived in a high-crime or drug area. <u>Still, I have several concerns about the kids who live here.</u>
   >
   > <u>First, the kids don't seem to know how to play outdoors.</u> One reason for this may be that there aren't sidewalks in our area, so kids can't easily walk to a friend's house. But even when kids get together, they stay in the houses playing video or computer games or watching TV. As I said, they have yards they could play baseball or touch football or tag or soccer in. They could build forts or make snowmen or do the other activities that kids have enjoyed for generations. But they don't. It's as if they've lost the ability to enjoy any activity that doesn't have an electrical cord or a battery. I think that's sad.

Secondly, and this is related to my first point, the kids are not in good shape. Many of them are overweight, and even the ones who aren't fat often look flabby and inactive. By the time they're adolescents, they seem sort of pasty and middle-aged. They move slowly, shuffling around as if they're trying to save energy. When they're already out of shape in their teens, it's hard to imagine them ever becoming fit and healthy.

Finally, I'm concerned about the way the kids relate—or don't relate—to the adults in their lives. From observing the families coming and going in the neighborhood, and the rare times I see them outside together in their yards, I get the sense that the kids don't really feel much connection or affection for their parents. When they talk, all I hear is the exchange of information, such as, "What time is the game?" or "Do we have any soda?" I wish I would hear them really talking together, laughing and teasing, or even arguing sometimes. Instead, I get the sense that they're just a bunch of near strangers living together.

I guess what it comes down to is that even though they're not poor or neglected, I don't see the kids in my neighborhood as having very happy, healthy lives. I don't know what is at the root of that, but it makes me feel bad for them.

- *Circle one answer:* Does the introduction (a) go from broad to narrow, (b) tell a story, (c) ask questions, or (d) shift to the opposite?
- Underline the thesis statement.
- Underline the topic sentences for the three supporting paragraphs.
- *Circle one answer:* Does the conclusion end with (a) a summary, (b) a final thought, or (c) both?

## Check Your Performance                    "EXTRA LARGE, PLEASE"

| Activity | Number Right | Points | | Score |
|---|---|---|---|---|
| **Vocabulary Check** (3 items) | _____ | x   10 | = | _____ |
| **Reading Check** | | | | |
| Central Point and Main Ideas  (3 items) | _____ | x    7 | = | _____ |
| Supporting Details  (2 items) | _____ | x    7 | = | _____ |
| Inferences  (3 items) | _____ | x    7 | = | _____ |
| The Writer's Craft  (2 items) | _____ | x    7 | = | _____ |
| | | **TOTAL SCORE** | = | _____% |

Enter your total score into the **Performance Chart: Fifteen Reading Selections** on the inside back cover.

# ⑩ A Change of Attitude
## Grant Berry

## Preview

No one was more surprised than Grant Berry to find himself in college. His high-school experience did little to prepare him for a life of learning. But somehow, as a father of two with a full-time job, he returned to school to pursue a college degree. Berry's transformation from a reluctant student to a passionate one is the subject of this essay.

## Words to Watch

*striven* (3): tried
*suavely* (4): in a sophisticated manner
*immaculately* (4): perfectly clean
*tedious* (6): boring
*trudging* (6): moving with great effort
*nil* (6): zero
*smugly* (8): in a way that demonstrates self-satisfaction
*deprivation* (16): state of being without possessions
*battering* (22): pounding

1  For me to be in college is highly improbable. That I am doing well in school teeters on the illogical. Considering my upbringing, past educational performance, and current responsibilities, one might say, "This guy hasn't got a chance." If I were a racehorse and college was the track, there would be few who would pick me to win, place, or show.

2  When I told my dad that I was going back to school, the only encouragement he offered was this: "Send me anywhere, but don't send me back to school." For my father, school was the worst kind of prison, so I was raised believing that school at its best was a drag. My dad thought that the purpose of graduating from high school was so you never had to go back to school again, and I adopted this working stiff's philosophy.

3  I followed my dad's example like a man who double-crossed the mob follows a cement block to the bottom of the river. My dad has been a union factory worker for more than two decades, and he has never striven° to be anything more than average.

Nonetheless, he is a good man; I love him very much, and I respect him for being a responsible husband and father. He seldom, if ever, missed a day of work; he never left his paycheck at a bar, and none of our household appliances were ever carted off by a repo-man. He took his family to church each week, didn't light up or lift a glass, and he has celebrated his silver anniversary with his first, and only, wife. However, if he ever had a dream of being more than just a shop rat, I never knew about it.

4   On the other hand, my dreams were big, but my thoughts were small. I was not raised to be a go-getter. I knew I wanted to go to work each day in a suit and tie; unfortunately, I could not define what it was I wanted to do. I told a few people that I wanted to have a job where I could dress suavely° and carry a briefcase, and they laughed in my face. They said, "You'll never be anything," and I believed them. Even now I am envious of an immaculately° dressed businessman. It is not the angry type of jealousy; it is the "wish it were me" variety.

5   Since I knew I was not going to further my education, and I didn't know what I wanted to do except wear a suit, high school was a disaster. I do not know how my teachers can respect themselves after passing me. In every high school there are cliques and classifications. I worked just hard enough to stay above the bottom, but I did not want to work hard enough to get into the clique with the honor roll students.

6   Also, I had always had a problem with reading. When I was a kid, reading for me was slow and tedious°. My eyes walked over words like a snail trudging° through mud. I couldn't focus on what I was reading, which allowed my young, active mind to wander far from my reading material. I would often finish a page and not remember a single word I had just read. Not only was reading a slow process, but my comprehension was nil°. I wasn't dumb; in fact, I was at a high English level. However, reading rated next to scraping dog poop from the tread of my sneakers. I didn't yet know that reading could be like playing the guitar: the more you do it, the better you get. As far as reading was concerned, I thought I was stuck in the same slow waltz forever.

7   In junior high and high school, I read only when it was absolutely essential. For example, I had to find out who Spiderman was going to web, or how many children Superman was going to save each month. I also had to find out which girls were popular on the bathroom walls. I'm ashamed to say that my mother even did a book report for me, first reading the book. In high school, when I would choose my own classes, I took art and electronics rather than English.

8   Even though I was raised in a good Christian home, the only things I cared about were partying and girls. I spent all of my minimum-wage paycheck on beer, cigarettes, and young ladies. As a senior, I dated a girl who was twenty. She had no restrictions, and I tried to keep pace with her lifestyle. I would stay out drinking until 3:00 a.m. on school nights. The next morning I would sleep through

class or just not show up. It became such a problem that the school sent letters to my parents telling them that I would not be joining my classmates for commencement if I didn't show up for class once in a while. This put the fear of the establishment in me because I knew the importance of graduating from high school. Nonetheless, I never once remember doing homework my senior year. Yet in June, they shook my hand and forked over a diploma as I smugly° marched across the stage in a blue gown and square hat.

9      Since I felt I didn't deserve the piece of paper with the principal's and superintendent's signatures on it, I passed up not only a graduation party, but also a class ring and yearbook. If it were not for my diploma and senior pictures, there would not be enough evidence to convince a jury that I am guilty of attending high school at all. I did, however, celebrate with my friends on graduation night. I got loaded, misjudged a turn, flattened a stop sign, and got my car stuck. When I pushed my car with my girlfriend behind the steering wheel, mud from the spinning tire sprayed all over my nice clothes. It was quite a night, and looking back, it was quite a fitting closure for the end of high school.

10      After graduation I followed my father's example and went to work, plunging into the lukewarm waters of mediocrity. All I was doing on my job bagging groceries was trading dollars for hours. I worked just hard enough to keep from getting fired, and I was paid just enough to keep from quitting.

11      Considering the way my father felt about school, college was a subject that seldom came up at our dinner table. I was not discouraged, nor was I encouraged to go to college; it was my choice. My first attempt at college came when I was nineteen. I had always dreamed of being a disc jockey, so I enrolled in a broadcasting class. However, my experience in college was as forgettable as high school. My habit of not doing homework carried over, and the class was such a yawner that I often forgot to attend. Miraculously, I managed to pull a C, but my dream was weak and quickly died. I did not enroll for the next term. My girlfriend, the one who kept me out late in high school, became pregnant with my child. We were married two days after my final class, which gave me another excuse not to continue my education.

12      My first job, and every job since, has involved working with my hands and not my head. I enjoyed my work, but after the money ran out, the month would keep going. One evening my wife's cousin called and said he had a way that we could increase our income. I asked, "How soon can you get here?" He walked us through a six-step plan of selling and recruiting, and when he was finished, my wife and I wanted in. Fumbling around inside his large briefcase, he told us we needed the proper attitude first. Emerging with a small stack of books, he said, "Read these!" Then he flipped the books into my lap. I groaned at the thought of reading all those volumes. If this guy wanted me to develop a good attitude,

giving me books was having the opposite effect. However, I wanted to make some extra cash, so I assured him I would try.

13     I started reading the books each night. They were self-help, positive-mental-attitude manuals. Reading those books opened up my world; they put me in touch with a me I didn't know existed. The books told me I had potential, possibly even greatness. I took their message in like an old Chevrolet being pumped full of premium no-lead gasoline. It felt so good I started reading more. Not only did I read at night; I read in the morning before I went to work. I read during my breaks and lunch hour, waiting for signal lights to turn green, in between bites of food at supper, and while sitting on the toilet. One of the books I read said that there is no limit to the amount of information our brains will hold, so I began filling mine up.

14     The process of reading was slow at first, just as it had been when I was a kid, but it was just like playing the guitar. If I struck an unclear chord, I would try it again, and if I read something unclear, I would simply read it again. Something happened: the more I read, the better I got at it. It wasn't long before I could focus in and understand without reading things twice. I began feeling good about my reading skills, and because of the types of books I was reading, I started feeling good about myself at the same time.

15     The income from my day job blossomed while the selling and recruiting business grew demanding, disappointing, and fruitless. We stopped

working that soil and our business died, but I was hooked on reading. I now laid aside the self-help books and began reading whatever I wanted. I got my first library card, subscribed to *Sports Illustrated*. I found a book of short stories, and I dove into poetry, as well as countless newspaper articles, cereal boxes and oatmeal packages. Reading, which had been a problem for me, became a pleasure and then a passion.

16     Reading moved me. As I continued to read in a crowded lunch room, sometimes I stumbled across an especially moving short story or magazine article. For example, a young Romanian girl was saved from starvation and deprivation° by an adoptive couple from the U.S. I quickly jerked the reading material to my face to conceal tears when she entered her new home filled with toys and stuffed animals.

17     Not only did reading tug at my emotions; it inspired me to make a move. All those positive-mental-attitude books kept jabbing me in the ribs, so last fall, at age twenty-seven, I decided to give college another try. Now I am back in school, but it's a different road I travel than when I was a teenager. Mom and Dad paid the amount in the right-hand column of my tuition bill then, but now I am determined to pay for college myself, even though I must miss the sound of the pizza delivery man's tires on my blacktop driveway. I hope to work my way out of my blue collar by paying for school with blue-collar cash.

18     As a meat-cutter, I usually spend between 45 and 50 hours a week with a knife in my hand. Some weeks I have

spent 72 hours beneath a butcher's cap. In one two-week period I spent 141 hours with a bloody apron on, but in that time I managed to show up for all of my classes and get all of my homework done (except being short a few bibliography cards for my research paper).

19    Working full time and raising a family leaves me little free time. If I am not in class, I'm studying linking verbs or trying to figure out the difference between compound and complex sentences.

20    There are other obstacles and challenges staring me in the face. The tallest hurdle is a lack of time for meeting all my obligations. For instance, my wife works two nights a week, leaving me to care for my two daughters. A twelve-hour day at work can lead to an evening coma at home, so when Mom's punching little square buttons on a cash register, I hardly have the energy to pour corn flakes for my kids, let alone outline a research paper.

21    Going to college means making choices, some of which bring criticism. My neighbors, for example, hate my sickly, brown lawn sandwiched between their lush, green, spotless plots of earth, which would be the envy of any football field. Just walking to my mailbox can be an awful reminder of how pitiful my lawn looks when I receive an unforgiving scowl from one of the groundskeepers who live on either side of me. It is embarrassing to have such a colorless lawn, but it will have to wait because I want more out of life than a half-acre of green turf. Right now my time and money are tied up in college courses instead of fertilizer and weed killer.

22    But the toughest obstacle is having to take away time from those I love most. I am proud of the relationship I have with my wife and kids, so it tears my guts out when I have to look into my daughter's sad face and explain that I can't go to the Christmas program she's been practicing for weeks because I have a final exam. It's not easy to tell my three-year-old that I can't push her on the swings because I have a cause-and-effect paper to write, or tell my seven-year-old that I can't build a snowman because I have an argument essay to polish. As I tell my family that I can't go sledding with them, my wife lets out a big sigh, and my kids yell, "Pu-leeze, Daddy, can't you come with us?" At these times I wonder if my dream of a college education can withstand such an emotional battering°, or if it is even worth it. But I keep on keeping on because I must set a good example for the four little eyes that are keeping watch over their daddy's every move. I must succeed and pass on to them the right attitude toward school. This time when I graduate, because of the hurdles I've overcome, there will be a celebration—a proper one.

## First Impressions

Freewrite for ten minutes on one of the following.

1. Did you enjoy reading this selection? Why or why not?

2. What is the attitude in your family towards higher education? Is it similar to that of Berry's parents, or is it different? Explain.

3. Do you do any reading for pleasure? If not, what keeps you from enjoying reading?

## Vocabulary Check

_C_  1. In the excerpt below, the word *cliques* means
   A. grades.
   B. schools.
   C. groups.       *Synonym clue: classifications.*
   D. sports.

   "In every high school there are cliques and classifications. I worked just hard enough to stay above the bottom, but I did not want to work hard enough to get into the clique with the honor roll students." (Paragraph 5)

_D_  2. In the excerpt below, the word *mediocrity* means
   A. luxury.
   B. heavy drinking.       *Examples of low quality: worked just hard*
   C. unemployment.         *enough to keep from getting fired; paid*
   D. low quality.          *just enough to keep from quitting.*

   "After graduation I followed my father's example and went to work, plunging into the lukewarm waters of mediocrity. . . . I worked just hard enough to keep from getting fired, and I was paid just enough to keep from quitting." (Paragraph 10)

_C_  3. In the excerpt below, the word *fruitless* means
   A. easy.
   B. illegal.
   C. unsuccessful.     *If the business died, it must have been unsuccessful.*
   D. enjoyable.

   ". . . the selling and recruiting business grew demanding, disappointing, and fruitless. We stopped working that soil and our business died. . . ." (Paragraph 15)

# Reading Check

## Central Point and Main Ideas

_B_ 1. Which sentence best expresses the central point of the entire selection?

A. Berry was never encouraged to attend college or to challenge himself mentally on the job.

Answer A covers only paragraphs 1–2 and 10–12.
Answer C covers only paragraph 22.
Answer D covers only paragraphs 5–9.

B. After years of not caring about education, Berry changed his attitude and came to love reading, gain self-esteem, and attend college.

C. Berry's wife and children often do not understand why he is unable to take part in many family activities.

D. Berry was given a high-school diploma despite the fact that he did little work and rarely attended class.

_A_ 2. Which sentence best expresses the main idea of paragraph 13?

A. Influenced by self-help books, Berry developed a hunger for reading.

B. People who really care about improving themselves will find the time to do it and to simplify.

C. Self-help books send the message that everyone is full of potential and even greatness.

D. There is no limit to the amount of information the brain can hold.

Answer B is unsupported; answers C and D are too narrow.

## Supporting Details

_B_ 3. The author's reading skills

A. were strong even when he was a child.

B. improved as he read more.

See paragraph 14.

C. were strengthened considerably in high school.

D. were sharpened by jobs he held after high-school graduation.

_D_ 4. The first time the author attempted college, he

A. quit in order to spend more time with his children.

B. could not read well enough to understand the material.

C. did so well he immediately signed up for a second course.

D. often skipped class and rarely did his homework.

See paragraph 11.

## Inferences

_C_   5. In stating that his graduation night "was quite a fitting closure for the end of high school," Berry implies that

*See paragraph 13. Just as Berry wasted his high school years, he "got wasted" and crashed into a stop sign on graduation night.*

    A. he was sorry high school was finally over.

    B. car troubles were a common problem for him in high school.

    C. his behavior had ruined that night just as it had ruined his high-school education.

    D. despite the problems, the evening gave him good memories, just as high school had given him good memories.

_C_   6. We can infer from paragraph 21 that the author

    A. does not tend his lawn because he enjoys annoying his neighbors.

    B. receives a lot of mail.

    C. is willing to make sacrifices for his college education.

    D. has neighbors who care little about the appearance of their property.

*Berry has chosen to spend his time and money on a college education, rather than on lawn care.*

## The Writer's Craft

_B_   7. The first sentence of paragraph 4 indicates which kind of relationship to the material that came before it?

    A. Illustration (the author is giving an example of what he has just explained)

*Contrast transition: On the other hand.*

    B. Contrast (the author is showing that what follows is different from what has gone before)

    C. Addition (the author is adding a detail to a list of items)

    D. Time order (the author is telling the next part of the story)

_C_   8. When Berry refers to his dad, his tone is

    A. sentimental and reverent.

    B. angry and ashamed.

    C. loving and respectful but also critical.

    D. scornful and pessimistic.

*See paragraphs 2–3 and 10. Berry calls his father "a good man" whom he loves and respects for being "a responsible husband and father." But he also criticizes his father for prejudicing him against education and for setting an example of "mediocrity."*

Starting in
paragraph 13, Berry
relates the inspiring
story of his turnaround
and decision to return
to college. Answer A
covers only
paragraphs 18–22.
Answer B is not
supported. Answer C
covers only paragraphs 8–9 and 19–22.

___D___ 9. The main purpose of this essay is to

   A. inform readers that it is difficult to attend college while working full time.

   B. persuade readers that they should spend less time with their family and more time reading.

   C. entertain readers with amusing anecdotes about the author's high school misadventures and busy family life.

   D. inform readers of how Berry's attitude toward education changed after he began reading self-help books.

___B___ 10. In the conclusion of his essay (paragraphs 21–22), Berry mainly provides

   A. statistics about the value of earning a college degree.

   B. a series of examples that illustrate his commitment to earning a college degree.

   C. an anecdote about his daughter's Christmas program.

   D. a summary of his main ideas.

> Specific examples: Berry's neglect of his lawn; his choice to study for a final exam or write a paper, rather than spend time with his kids.

## Discussion Questions

1. As Berry read self-help books, his attitude toward learning improved. In fact, reading those books eventually led him to return to college. Have you ever read a book that influenced the way you thought, acted, or felt about yourself? What was it you read, and how did it affect you?

2. Although Berry's father did not encourage him to go to college, Berry sees many good things about his dad. In what ways was his father a positive role model for him? From Berry's own actions as an adult, what valuable lessons might he have learned from his father's example?

3. Berry discusses some of the difficulties he faces as a result of being in college—struggling to find time to meet his obligations, giving up lawn care, spending less time with his family. If you are in college now, what difficulties do you face as a result of fitting college into your life? If you plan to go to college someday, what do you think will be some of the obstacles you might face?

4. In closing his essay, Berry writes that at his college graduation, "there will be a celebration—a proper one." With what earlier event is he contrasting this graduation? Judging from how Berry describes himself and how he has changed, how do you think the two celebrations will be different?

## Paragraph Assignments

1. Write a paragraph about one memory of yours that concerns reading. That memory may be a positive or negative one. For example, you may remember the pleasure of having a parent read to you at bedtime. Or you may remember being humiliated when you made a mistake reading in front of the class. Describe in detail exactly what you remember. End your paragraph by explaining why you think that memory has stayed with you so strongly.

   Here are two students' responses to this assignment, one involving a negative memory and one involving a positive one.

> One of my most embarrassing memories is of reading aloud in class when I was in fourth grade. I was not a strong reader. I had to concentrate hard on each word, say it, and then move on to the next word. So I was very slow and didn't really think about the meaning of what I was reading. One day in religion class, the teacher was having us read out loud from our textbook. She called on me. I stood up and started where the last student had left off. The lesson was about Pope John Paul I. I struggled along and read like this. "In. August. 1978. He. Was. Elected. Poop." Because I was concentrating so hard, I didn't realize I'd said "poop" instead of "Pope" until I heard the class roar with laughter. My teacher shouted at the class to be quiet and then shouted at me for saying something so disrespectful. I was so confused and embarrassed I started to cry. That made the other kids laugh even more. From that day on, the thought of reading out loud made me feel sick to my stomach.

> I don't recall a lot about grade school, but I do remember one specific moment in the second grade when words were all very exciting and mysterious to me. My mother had read to me for years, however, so books weren't new to me. My very favorite books were the Babar series about an adventurous elephant. Because of the stories, my room was filled with stuffed elephants, pictures of elephants, and even an elephant-shaped chair. I was eager to learn how to read on my own, but I became very nervous when we had to read

*out loud in class. The worst was when we had to sound out a new word—sometimes kids laughed at the weird sounds we made trying to figure it out. One rainy morning, it happened. The biggest new word yet appeared when it was my turn to read. It was huge! I quickly turned to the surrounding pages for pictures that might give a clue, but it was a chapter without pictures. I was doomed. So I began sounding it out. The beginning wasn't hard, but then there was a combination of a "p" and "h" together. Somehow, I remembered the word "phone." So I made an "f" sound. Then the end of the word was easy—it was a small bug, a simple word we had learned months ago. I took a breath and pieced the word together: "Ell . . . e . . . f . . . ant." Elephant! Everyone stared at me in shocked admiration. I couldn't believe it. I had just discovered how to read the name of my very favorite animal. I'll never forget that moment.*

2. Berry's dad, who had disliked school, did not encourage him to get an education. Furthermore, Berry admits that as a child, he struggled with reading. Consequently, he did not actually learn to enjoy reading until he was an adult. Write a paragraph that supports the following point:

   ● Parents can encourage their children to enjoy reading by _____, _____, and _____.

   To support your point, be sure to describe in detail each step that parents can take to help their children enjoy reading. Use transitions to introduce each step. For example, you might write: "First of all, parents should make sure that their children see them reading. . . . A second step parents can take to encourage their children to read is . . . Finally, parents can . . ."

## Essay Assignments

1. Berry did not have a realistic idea of what he wanted to do after high school, although he did like to imagine himself in a good-looking suit and carrying a briefcase. What vision do you have of yourself in the future? Write an essay in which you state what you hope to be doing ten years from now. Then describe in your supporting paragraphs three different obstacles or challenges that you will face in pursuing your goal. Explain why those challenges are significant ones for you and just how you plan to overcome them.

2. Many people enter college immediately after high school. But an increasing number, like Berry, return to college after years, even decades, out of school. The two approaches are likely to produce very different college experiences. Write an essay in which you compare and contrast going to college directly from high school and going to college later in life. Your thesis statement might be something like this: "Going to college right after high school would be very different from going to college later in life." Then in each paragraph in the body of your essay, choose one aspect of the college experience and compare and contrast the two approaches. For example, you might write about how the two approaches would be differently socially, educationally, and financially.

## Check Your Performance                    A CHANGE OF ATTITUDE

| Activity | Number Right | Points | Score |
|---|---|---|---|
| **Vocabulary Check** (3 items) | _____ | x 10 = | _____ |
| **Reading Check** | | | |
| Central Point and Main Ideas (2 items) | _____ | x 7 = | _____ |
| Supporting Details (2 items) | _____ | x 7 = | _____ |
| Inferences (2 items) | _____ | x 7 = | _____ |
| The Writer's Craft (4 items) | _____ | x 7 = | _____ |
| | | TOTAL SCORE = | _____% |

Enter your total score into the **Performance Chart: Fifteen Reading Selections** on the inside back cover.

# 11 Abusive Relationships among the Young

## Miriam Hill

## Preview

It's shocking but true: by the time of high-school graduation, one in three girls will have been involved in an abusive relationship. What begins as a romantic relationship becomes characterized by physical violence, stalking, and emotional abuse. Why are young women so vulnerable to abuse? Why do they stay with and even defend their abusers? What drives young men to hurt and humiliate their girlfriends? And most importantly, how can a girl make the abuse stop? This selection explores a problem that is common but often hidden out of sight, due to the victims' tangled feelings of hurt, guilt, and fear.

## Words to Watch

*hovering* (1): hanging
*demographic* (4): social group
*primarily* (6): mainly
*intimidate* (22): persuade by frightening

1   When Sarah first set eyes on Joe at a back-to-school dance, she thought he was really cute. And when they started dating, he showered her with flowers, compliments, and tickets to the movies. But their relationship quickly went downhill, as Joe began to insult, make demands, and then physically abuse her. The final straw came when Joe kicked her, knocking her into a wall, where she hit her head and lost consciousness. "I woke up and he was hovering° over me," Sarah, now 18, recalls. "I just wanted to get away." Four months after their first date, Sarah stood in line at the family division of the Santa Clara County, California court clerk's office, waiting to pick up a copy of a restraining order.

2   Kayla Brown's story began much like Sarah's. At first, her high school boyfriend was highly respectful, even calling Kayla's mom to introduce himself. But then he began calling her every hour to see where she was and what she was doing. Finally, he slammed a chair

into a table and raised a fist to strike her during an argument in the school cafeteria. Kayla confided in her mother, who had also been involved with an abusive man. When her mother advised her to break off the relationship, Kayla did so. But the process took months. To make sure she was never alone with her ex-boyfriend, she had friends accompany her everywhere, even to the school lavatory.

3    Heather Norris wasn't so lucky. She was 17 when she met her boyfriend, Joshua Bean, and 20 when he stabbed her to death.

4    Why does "love" turn so ugly? What is behind what many are calling an "epidemic" of abusive relationships among the young? The statistics are alarming: one in three girls will have an abusive dating relationship by the time she graduates from high school, and females from the ages of 16 to 24 are the most likely demographic° to experience dating violence. And in today's world, social networking sites and texting are only making it easier for abusers to harass, humiliate, and stalk their victims. It's not only men who abuse women; however, when abuse turns physical, it is the women who wind up in the emergency room.

5    One factor that helps make abusive relationships common is the value our society places on being in a relationship. Whether it's on TV, in movies, in magazines, or on the Internet, the message is that being alone is for losers. Teenage girls, in particular, measure their self-worth by having a boyfriend. Think of it: from an early age, girls in our culture are taught that being a "princess" is the ideal state of femininity. Is it any wonder they long for a Prince Charming to come and sweep them off their feet?

6    Dr. Jill Murray, an expert in the field of abusive relationships, puts teenage girls' strong need for social acceptance in psychological terms: "Adolescents are primarily° concerned with the way they appear to their peers. That is one reason girls are often desperate for a boyfriend in high school. If their friends are dating, they feel out of place if they are not."

7    Ron Davis agrees. He runs a teen program at a middle school in Walnut Creek, California.

8    "Girls at 16 are looking for love, anybody who's going to show any affection at all," he says. "They fall in love so fast with anybody. That's when they get taken advantage of." Young people whose parents have neglected them emotionally are even more likely to become involved in abusive relationships.

9    Experts also agree that children who are exposed to violence at home often repeat it in their adult relationships. A girl who sees her father or another male abuse her mother learns to view abuse as a natural part of a relationship. Similarly, when a boy observes his father or another male dominate his mother and sister with emotional and physical abuse, he grows up believing that it is "normal" for him to control a woman by abusing her. Such abuse may include touching his girlfriend inappropriately in public in order to prove to others that she "belongs" to him. It may also include

calling her or texting her repeatedly in an attempt to monitor her behavior.

10 In addition, male abusers often hold a stereotyped idea of male and female relationships. In their view, women are inferior to men, so a girlfriend should "know her place." This macho attitude is reinforced by some religious groups, whose teachings emphasize that a man is the natural head of the household and should always be obeyed. Physical or emotional abuse of a female partner is thus viewed as "discipline."

11 Coming from a home where substance abuse takes place is another strong predictor of involvement in an abusive relationship. Abusers generally have a low tolerance for frustration and turn to alcohol or drugs to escape feelings of failure or powerlessness. Alcohol, in turn, lowers inhibitions and increases aggression. Likewise, chronic use of marijuana or crystal meth causes rage and paranoia. In many cases, children of substance abusers adopt their parents' dysfunctional pattern of behavior. Undergoing financial difficulties such as the loss of a job only makes it more likely that people will take out their feelings of frustration on those closest to them.

12 Complicating matters is the fact that young women who have very limited experience in relationships often confuse jealousy and possessiveness with love. At first they are flattered when a boy calls or texts them at all hours. "It shows he loves me," they tell themselves. Shockingly, in one recent study, some teens reported receiving 200 to 300 texts *a day* from boyfriends or girlfriends wanting to know where they were, who they were with, and why. And up to 82 percent of parents had no idea what was happening.

13 "Youths don't recognize that as stalking behavior," says Tatiana Colon, head of the Teen Dating Violence Task Force in Alameda County, California. In other words, it's not about love, it's about control. And control is at the core of abusive behavior.

14 Of course, few girls consciously choose to become involved with an abuser. As in the case of Sarah and Kayla, the relationship usually starts off tenderly. But then a pattern begins to emerge—with abusers emotionally or physically abusive one minute, sweetly apologetic the next.

15 "Honey, I didn't mean it—I'll never do it again," is a common refrain. Furthermore, abusers often have "Dr. Jekyll" and "Mr. Hyde" personalities. That is, they are careful to present only their good "Dr. Jekyll" side to outsiders. It's not unusual for them to be charming and popular—star athletes and good students. In cases such as these, girls are understandably reluctant to confide that they are being abused for fear of not being believed. When Sarah told school authorities that Joe was abusing her, they ordered him to attend a different school. But other girls told Sarah, "How could you do this to him? He's *so cute.*"

16 Another reason girls fail to tell others that they are being abused is that they feel it's their responsibility to fix whatever is wrong in the relationship.

17 "Think of articles in women's magazines," says Dr. Murray. "There is

always at least one in which the tone of the article is how to fix your relationship." As Murray points out, there are basically three types of relationship articles: how to catch a man, how to hold onto a man, and how you must fix whatever is wrong in a relationship.

18 Ever notice that men's magazines don't have similar articles?

19 Girls who come from homes where they have been expected to care for a depressed parent are especially likely to fall into this "caretaker" pattern of thinking. Having been trained as children to be "good little helpers," they hold the mistaken belief that they can rescue the abuser. And since few abusers are abusive all the time, they hold out hope that his good side will win out.

20 "He comes from a bad home. I'm all he's got. I can save him," they often think. Although an abuser may express remorse and swear that he will never do it again, experts warn that abuse involves a cycle that feeds itself. It *will not* stop unless drastic action is taken. In fact, 80% of abusers fail to stop their abuse *even with* therapy. According to Murray, an abused woman will typically go back to her abuser seven to nine times before she leaves for good—if she's still alive.

21 Abuse often begins with insults such as "You're fat, you're ugly and stupid. Nobody else would want you." Such hostility is a form of what psychologists term *projection*. In other words, whatever the abuser dislikes about himself, he will "project" onto his partner. By destroying her self-confidence, he feels his power increase. Of course, women can also be guilty of projection. For example, a young woman who cheats on her boyfriend may guiltily accuse him of cheating on her.

22 Emotional abuse generally escalates to physical abuse. At first, an abuser may punch a wall next to his victim or throw something or kick a chair. Such behavior is meant to threaten and intimidate°. An abuser will then graduate to pushing, slapping, pulling hair, kicking, or punching his victim. Sexual abuse is the most serious form of relationship abuse. In fact, date rape accounts for 67% of sexual assaults among teens. Sadly, some young women still believe that it is a male's right to demand sex from his partner whenever he feels like it. Experts disagree. They maintain that if sex is not completely consensual, it is rape.

23 Young women often downplay abuse. "He lost control. It was the alcohol talking, not him," they'll say. Perhaps saddest of all, some young women actually believe their abuser when he insists, "You made me do it."

24 "No one actually loses control," says Scott A. Johnson, author of *When 'I Love You' Turns Violent*. "Rather a conscious decision is made . . . to blame the victim." He adds, "If you are being abused, your significant other is telling you loudly and clearly, 'I do not love you!'"

## What To Do

25 If you know a young person who is in an abusive relationship, how do you advise him or her to get out? Experts agree that it is best *not* to confront the abuser. Such confrontations can

become violent, as the abuser seeks at all costs to reestablish control over his victim. "If I can't have you, no one will," is a classic threat, and one that should be taken at face value.

26      Instead of confronting an abuser, victims should confide in someone trustworthy, such as a teacher, guidance counselor, doctor, friend, or parent. Contact the National Teen Dating Abuse 24/7 Helpline at 1-866-331-9474, **www.loveisrespect.org** or the National Domestic Violence Hotline:

1-800-799-7233. Both organizations help victims of abuse design a personal safety plan to lower the risk of being hurt by an abuser.

Remember, there is nothing "loving"  27 about being treated as someone's possession. And no one should have to put up with abusive behavior. So don't be silent if you or someone you know is being abused. You can make it stop, but only if you let others know what's happening.

## First Impressions

Freewrite for ten minutes on one of the following.

1. Did you enjoy reading this selection? Why or why not?

2. Do you know anyone who is in an abusive relationship? What has been that person's response to the abuse?

3. Why do you think relationships like Sarah's, Kayla's, and Heather's are becoming more and more common? Or are we just hearing about them more often?

## Vocabulary Check

___A___  1. In the sentence below, the word *monitor* means
   A. keep track of.
   B. ignore.
   C. return.
   D. stop.

   What would repeated calling or texting enable a boyfriend to do to his girlfriend's behavior?

   "Such abuse may include touching his girlfriend inappropriately in public in order to prove to others that she "belongs" to him. It may also include calling her or texting her repeatedly in an attempt to monitor her behavior." (Paragraph 9)

_B_ 2. In the excerpt below, the word *escalates* means
    A. becomes less frequent.
    B. gets worse.
    C. disappears.
    D. explains.

> Pushing, slapping, pulling hair, kicking, or punching the victim is worse than punching a wall or kicking a chair.

"Emotional abuse generally escalates to physical abuse. At first, an abuser may punch a wall next to his victim or throw something or kick a chair.... An abuser will then graduate to pushing, slapping, pulling hair, kicking, or punching his victim." (Paragraph 22)

_B_ 3. In the excerpt below, the word *consensual* means
    A. enjoyable.
    B. agreed to by both parties.
    C. risk-free.
    D. within the bonds of marriage.

"Sadly, some young women still believe that it is a male's right to demand sex from his partner whenever he feels like it. Experts disagree. They maintain that if sex is not completely consensual, it is rape." (Paragraph 22)

> If sex is demanded by only the male, it is not agreed to by all involved.

## Reading Check

### Central Point and Main Ideas

_D_ 1. Which sentence best expresses the central point of the selection?

Answer A covers only part of paragraph 4 and paragraphs 12–13. Answer B covers only paragraphs 9 and 11. Answer C covers only part of paragraph 20.

    A. Today, modern technology is making it easier for abusers to harass, humiliate, and stalk their victims.
    B. Children who are exposed to violence and substance abuse at home often become involved in abusive relationships.
    C. Abuse involves a cycle that feeds itself and will not stop unless drastic action is taken.
    D. There are a number of factors that cause young people to become involved in abusive relationships.

_C_ 2. The implied main idea of paragraphs 5–8 is that

Paragraph 5 suggests this idea, and paragraphs 6–8 offer support. Answers A and D cover only part of paragraph 5. Answer B covers only paragraph 6.

    A. many girls in our culture long for a Prince Charming to come and sweep them off their feet.
    B. psychologists such as Dr. Jill Murray believe that adolescents are primarily concerned with the way they appear to their peers.
    C. because teenage girls in our culture place such a high value on being in a relationship, they are more likely to become involved in abusive relationships.
    D. TV, the movies, magazines, and the Internet all communicate the message that it's important to be in a relationship.

_____A___ 3. The main idea of paragraph 9 is stated in its
   A. first sentence.
   B. second sentence.
   C. third sentence.
   D. fourth sentence.

*Answers B and C illustrate the main idea. Answer D describes one kind of abuse that may result.*

## Supporting Details

_____C___ 4. According to the selection, which of the following statements would an abusive male *not* be likely to say?
   A. "She belongs to me."
   B. "Women should know their place."
   C. "It's up to me to fix whatever is wrong in this relationship."
   D. "You made me do it."

*Answer C is what an abused female (not an abusive male) might say. For answer A, see paragraph 9. For answer B, see paragraph 10. For answer D, see paragraph 23.*

_____D___ 5. According to the selection, a girl who sees her father or another male abuse her mother
   A. is more likely to stay single.
   B. is more likely to demand respectful treatment from her partner.
   C. is more likely to abuse her male partner.
   D. tends to view abuse as natural.

*See paragraph 9, second sentence.*

## Inferences

_____C___ 6. We can conclude from paragraphs 5–8 that
   A. most girls who once pretended to be princesses will become involved in abusive relationships.
   B. it is natural for boys to grow up to become "Prince Charming."
   C. it's not good for girls to base their self-worth on having a boyfriend.
   D. all of the above.

*The paragraphs point out that basing one's self-worth on having a boyfriend can lead to being taken advantage of. Answers A and B are not supported.*

_____C___ 7. On the basis of paragraphs 16–18, we can conclude that
   A. most of the men who read men's magazines aren't interested in women.
   B. men's magazines would be more popular if they carried stories about how men should fix romantic relationships.
   C. in general, men aren't interested in reading about how to fix romantic relationships.
   D. men's magazines deliberately encourage abuse in relationships.

*Answer C is supported by the fact that men's magazines do not contain articles about how to fix a relationship (while women's magazines almost always do). Answers A and D are not supported. Answer B is not supported and is also illogical.*

Answer B is supported by paragraphs 9–11, which suggest many teens don't see loving relationships at home. Answers A and D are not supported. Answer C is contradicted by paragraphs 12–13.

___B___ 8. We can infer from the selection that

A. only children who are exposed to violence at home become involved in abusive relationships.

B. many young people today don't know what a loving relationship looks like.

C. loving someone means wanting to know what he or she is doing at all times.

D. young men who are physically unattractive are more likely to become abusive toward women.

## The Writer's Craft

___A___ 9. The author begins her essay with

A. a brief story.

B. a series of questions.

C. shifting to the opposite.

D. going from broad to narrow.

Paragraph 1 tells the story of Sarah's abusive boyfriend, Joe, ending with Sarah getting a restraining order.

___D___ 10. To conclude her essay, the author uses

A. a brief story.

B. a summary.

C. a series of questions.

D. a final thought and recommendation.

The author tells readers not to put up with abusive behavior and urges them to let others know if they are being abused.

# Discussion Questions

1. Was there anything in this selection that surprised you? If so, what was it, and why did you find it surprising? Was there any information that you disagree with? Explain.

2. Think back to when you were in high school. Was it considered normal to be in a relationship? Were kids who weren't in relationships looked on as "losers"? If so, was dating violence ever discussed? Explain.

3. The selection focuses mainly on males who abuse females. Do you think that women abusing men is also a serious problem? Why or why not?

4. Experts believe that dating violence is on the rise. Whether it is or not, it's clearly a serious problem. In your view, is there anything that can be done to reduce the likelihood that young people will become involved in abusive relationships, either as an abuser or as a victim? If so, what?

# Paragraph Assignments

1. As the author explains, it is not wise for a concerned friend to confront an abuser. But if you had a friend in an abusive relationship, what would you *like* to say to the abuser? Write a paragraph that expresses your thoughts.

   Here is one student's response to this assignment:

   > If someone was abusing my friend, I would be so angry it would be hard to decide what I wanted to say. I would have to calm down and try to decide what actually might be helpful. Eventually, I think, I would say something like this: "Abuse is a cycle. Were you abused when you were a kid? Or did you see the men in your life abuse women? If so, I am really sorry that happened to you. I hope you'll see a counselor to talk about that and get the help you need. But you have to take responsibility now for stopping that cycle. Every time you abuse my friend, you're putting more and more ugliness out into the world. Younger boys see what you're doing and think, 'That's how a man is supposed to act.' If you ever have children, they're likely to become abusers or to be abused themselves, because this is the example you're setting them. You know what would really show you to be a strong man? If you looked at yourself in the mirror and said, 'I'm going to stop this cycle here.' Otherwise, you're just a weak bully who deserves the world's contempt."

2. The essay says that many girls' "strong need for social acceptance" is a reason they are likely to end up in abusive relationships. What other evidence have you seen that teen girls are influenced by the need for social acceptance? Write a paragraph in which you write about some aspect of girls' behavior that you think is driven by the need to be accepted.

## Essay Assignments

1. Abusive relationships are clearly bad relationships. But not all bad relationships are abusive. Write an essay about three relationships you have observed that you think were poor ones, although not necessarily abusive. Perhaps they were bad because the participants had such different personalities, or did not communicate well, or shared few common interests.

    Begin with a thesis statement something like this: "Three poor relationships I have observed involve my friend Pam and her boyfriend Rick, my sister and ex-brother-in-law, and my Aunt Frances and Uncle Steve."

    In each case, provide specific details about what (in your view) made the three relationships unsatisfying ones.

2. The essay makes it clear that obsessive attention and being treated as a possession are *not* signs of a healthy love. By contrast, what *are* some signs of a healthy, respectful relationship?

    Write an essay in which you identify three characteristics of a good relationship. Give examples of how people in a good relationship demonstrate these characteristics.

---

### Check Your Performance    ABUSIVE RELATIONSHIPS AMONG THE YOUNG

| Activity | Number Right | Points | Score |
|---|---|---|---|
| **Vocabulary Check**  (3 items) | _____ | x  10  = | _____ |
| **Reading Check** | | | |
| Central Point and Main Ideas  (3 items) | _____ | x   7  = | _____ |
| Supporting Details  (2 items) | _____ | x   7  = | _____ |
| Inferences  (3 items) | _____ | x   7  = | _____ |
| The Writer's Craft  (2 items) | _____ | x   7  = | _____ |
| | | TOTAL SCORE   = | _____% |

Enter your total score into the **Performance Chart: Fifteen Reading Selections** on the inside back cover.

# 12  A Door Swings Open

## Roxanne Black

## Preview

No one can stay a child forever. For some, the events that mark childhood's end are barely remembered. For others, a sudden, unforgettable occurrence forever marks the boundary between childish innocence and adult understanding. In "A Door Swings Open," author Roxanne Black describes such a moment.

## Words to Watch

*foreboding* (15): a feeling that something bad is going to happen
*chronic* (18): lasting for a long time; continuing to occur
*remission* (21): lessening of the symptoms of a disease
*terse* (30): brief and to the point
*intoned* (37): said something in a slow and serious way
*muster* (39): gather

1   I sat at my bedroom window in my wheelchair, watching my high-school rowing team pull away from the shore, eight friends smiling and waving as they moved into the choppy water. Not long ago, I'd been one of them.

2   I loved everything about rowing: the feeling of freedom, the teamwork, the sense of strength and accomplishment. When I rowed, I was at peace and forgot about my problems. Not that I'd had many then. In most ways, I was a typical New Jersey teenager, a shy high-school freshman who lived with her mother in a small row house that overlooked Lake's Bay. My mother and I didn't have two dimes to rub together, but with that view from our windows, we considered ourselves rich.

3   It was after rowing one afternoon that I had the first warning that something might be wrong with me—a sharp stab of back pain that took my breath away.

4   "What's the matter?" my mother asked when she saw me wincing.

5   "I don't know," I said, stretching. "I guess I strained a muscle."

6   By evening, the pain was almost too painful to bear. My mother filled a hot bath with Epsom salts, and later gave me a heating pad. I took a couple of Tylenol and decided I'd stay away from crew practice for a few days. In my young life, this had been the antidote for any ailment. Eventually everything passed, given time and a little rest.

7    But not this time. Instead of decreasing, the pain grew so intense that I could barely sit up in bed the next morning.

8    My mother took one look at me and said, "I'm taking you to the doctor."

9    But by the time we arrived at the office, the pain had subsided; and the doctor advised that we simply continue with the heating pad and baths.

10    Two days later, I developed chest pains that by evening were so acute I could barely breathe. Now I was beginning to worry.

11    This time the doctor prescribed antibiotics, thinking I might have an infection. The pains intensified over the next few days; then they too vanished.

12    This pattern of new symptoms that appeared, intensified, then vanished continued with an itchy red rash, which covered my body. After it mysteriously disappeared, my ankles swelled so severely that I was unable to fit into any of my shoes.

13    Although the doctor tracked my reports, took bloodwork, and examined me closely, he couldn't figure out what was wrong. My symptoms were elusive; it was hard to pin them down.

14    Finally he referred me to a specialist. By the day of my appointment, all my symptoms had subsided except for my swollen ankles. My mother and I arrived at his office, expecting this new doctor would prescribe another medication for what was probably an allergic reaction.

15    Although I'd never seen this doctor's face before, his cool, sober expression as we walked in gave me a sense of foreboding°.

16    After a routine examination, he studied my bloodwork, then touched my ankles, which were so full of fluid they could be molded like lumps of clay.

17    Then he looked up and a strange word floated from his mouth. Lupus. I saw it, like in a cartoon caption, odd and ominous, hanging in the air.

18    The word meant nothing to me, but my mother's reaction did; she covered her face with her hands. In her work as a nurse, she'd spent years caring for patients with chronic° illness. As I watched her sniff and take out a Kleenex, it hit me that this must be serious, something that Tylenol and bed rest weren't going to solve.

19    My health had always been part of my identity, something I was as certain of as my strong legs and pumping heart. Now I was being told baffling facts about kidney function, inflammation, and antibodies.

20    But when the doctor said I was to be admitted to a children's hospital in Philadelphia the following day for testing, I realized a chapter of my life was suddenly ending and a new one was about to start.

21    When I returned home, I looked up lupus in our medical dictionary: a chronic autoimmune disease, potentially weakening and sometimes fatal, that was first discovered in the Middle Ages. The illness follows an unpredictable course, with episodes of activity, called flares, alternating with periods of remission°. During a flare, the immune system attacks the body's cells and tissue, resulting in inflammation and tissue damage.

22    The words "sometimes fatal" stood out to me, as if they were written in blood. Just as alarming were the lists of possible signs: dermatological, musculoskeletal, hematological, renal, hepatic, pulmonary. What else was there?

23    How had this ancient disease—that only affected one in many hundreds in the United States—ended up in Atlantic City, residing in a teenager like me?

24    For that, there was no answer.

25    "There's always one moment in childhood when the door opens and lets the future in," Graham Greene wrote. I don't know if most people remember that moment, but I do.

26    At the children's hospital, I shared a room with a three-year-old girl with a charming face and shiny black hair cut in a bob. She was so energetic and lively, I assumed she was someone's daughter or sister, until I glimpsed a tiny hospital ID bracelet on her wrist.

27    Her name was Michelle, and we bonded from the moment we met. She brought a herd of plastic ponies to my bedside, and we brushed their manes and made up stories.

28    "Why's she here?" I asked when her parents arrived, looking drawn and worried.

29    "She has a hole in her heart," her mother told me. "She's having open-heart surgery tomorrow."

30    A steady stream of doctors arrived to talk to Michelle's parents. I heard the terse° murmur of their voices behind the curtain that separated our room. Through it all, Michelle dashed between the beds, oblivious to the drama around her. She was so vital and energetic, it was hard to believe that anything serious was wrong with her.

31    I'd never known a sick child before, and now I was in a hospital full of them. It seemed unnatural seeing toddlers on IV's, babies on ventilators, adolescents with leg braces, struggling to walk. A parade of pediatric malfunction passed my door, children smashed in motor accidents, suffering from muscular dystrophy and leukemia. This alternate world had existed all along, behind my formerly sunny, innocent life.

32    The next day I was to find out the results of my kidney biopsy, and Michelle was headed to surgery. Before she left, she walked over and hugged me so tightly that I could smell the baby shampoo in her hair. Then she solemnly handed me a drawing she'd made of a house, a girl, and a tree.

33    "This is you, isn't it?"

34    She nodded.

35    "Well it's beautiful, thanks. I'll see you later."

36    I waited all day for them to bring Michelle back, trying to distract myself by reading and crocheting, but it was no use. Breakfast came and went, then lunch, and still there was no sign of her.

37    Early in the evening, I was talking on the pay phone in the hallway when an alarm sounded, and doctors began running down the hall from all directions. A woman's voice intoned° a code over the loudspeakers, a foreign babble.

38    As I hung up, I saw two new figures running down the hallway. Their features grew terribly familiar as they

approached. It was Michelle's parents, their faces smeared with tears, heading in the same direction as the doctors.

39    My mother came out and hurried me back into the room. When she shut the door, I stood there, looking at Michelle's bed, at the picture on the table she had drawn for me. I took out a little prayer book I'd brought along and began a prayer, filling it with all the love and intention I could muster°. A long, terrible female scream pierced the silence.

A young floor nurse walked in 40 a short while later. Her sad face was statement enough, but then she told us. Michelle hadn't made it. She'd suffered a heart attack and died.

So there it was, and I had to face it: 41 Life wasn't fair. Prayers weren't always answered. The young and innocent could be lost. The door had swung open, and I had been pushed through to the other side.

# First Impressions

Freewrite for ten minutes on one of the following.

1. Did you enjoy reading this selection? Why or why not?

2. Had you heard of lupus before reading this piece? Are you familiar with it, or with any similar disease?

3. Do you know anyone who, like Roxanne, has a chronic illness? What are some ways it affects that person's life?

# Vocabulary Check

_A_  1. In the excerpt below, the word *subsided* means
   A. became less.
   B. gotten worse.
   C. returned.
   D. stayed the same.

   *If the doctor suggests continuing the same treatment, it must have had the desired result—the pain became less.*

   "My mother took one look at me and said, 'I'm taking you to the doctor.'
   "But by the time we arrived at the office, the pain had subsided; and the doctor advised that we simply continue with the heating pad and baths." (Paragraphs 8–9)

___D___ 2. In the excerpt below, the word *elusive* means
     A. difficult to treat.
     B. difficult to see.
     C. difficult to forget.
     D. difficult to define.

> The synonym-like clue *hard to pin . . . down* suggests that *elusive* means "difficult to define."

> "Although the doctor tracked my reports, took bloodwork, and examined me closely, he couldn't figure out what was wrong. My symptoms were elusive; it was hard to pin them down." (Paragraph 13)

___A___ 3. In the excerpt below, the words *oblivious to* mean
     A. unaware of.
     B. saddened by.
     C. confused by.
     D. conscious of.

> If Michelle is dashing back and forth in the room, she is unaware of the drama around her.

> "A steady stream of doctors arrived to talk to Michelle's parents. I heard the terse murmur of their voices behind the curtain that separated our room. Through it all, Michelle dashed between the beds, oblivious to the drama around her." (Paragraph 30)

# Reading Check

## Central Point and Main Ideas

___D___ 1. The central idea of the selection is that
     A. Black was shocked to learn that she had a chronic disease.
     B. Black was saddened when a little girl she met in the hospital died.
     C. before becoming ill with lupus, Black had been in excellent health.
     D. as the result of her own chronic illness and the death of a child, Black realized that life isn't fair.

> Answer A covers only paragraphs 19–24.
> Answer B is suggested by paragraphs 39–40.
> Answer C covers part of paragraph 19.
> Answer D, the central point, is suggested in the concluding paragraph.

___C___ 2. Which sentence best expresses the main idea of paragraph 2?
     A. When Black rowed, she forgot about her problems.
     B. Black lived with her mother in a small row house overlooking Lake's Bay.
     C. In most ways, Black, who loved rowing, was a typical teenager.
     D. Although Black and her mother didn't have much money, they considered themselves rich.

> Answers A, B, and D each cover only one sentence of the paragraph.

## Supporting Details

_D_ 3. Black first thought the intense pain she was experiencing was
   A. an insect bite.
   B. an allergic reaction.                     See paragraph 5.
   C. an infection.
   D. a muscle strain.

_C_ 4. When the doctor tells Black she has lupus, her mother
   A. tells the doctor he's wrong.
   B. screams and then breaks out into loud sobs.    See paragraph 18.
   C. covers her face with her hands and takes out a Kleenex.
   D. says she knew it all along.

_B_ 5. Michelle was in the hospital because she had
   A. leukemia.
   B. a hole in her heart.
   C. a brain tumor.                          See paragraph 29.
   D. been injured in an auto accident.

## Inferences

_A_ 6. It is reasonable to conclude that
   A. in most respects, Michelle was a typical little girl.
   B. Graham Greene had also known a child who died young.
   C. Black blames the doctors for not saving Michelle's life.
   D. all of the above.        Michelle is "energetic and lively," likes toy animals,
                          is friendly, and draws pictures—just like most little girls.

_C_ 7. The author implies that
   A. Michelle was terrified of having open-heart surgery.
   B. Michelle appeared sickly to most people.
   C. Black realized that Michelle had died even before hearing the news
      from the nurse.
   D. Black will never pray for anyone again.
                    See paragraphs 37–40. The alarm, the behavior of Michelle's
                          parents, and the nurse's sad face all reflect the terrible
## The Writer's Craft         fact that Michelle didn't make it through surgery.

_B_ 8. Black begins her story with the image of herself watching the rowers
      because
   A. the rowers remind her of Michelle, her hospital roommate.
   B. she wants to contrast her life before lupus with her life now.
   C. rowing is what caused her to develop lupus.
   D. she had always wanted to learn to row, but was never able to.
        Black was a normal teenager until she contracted lupus. Answers A and C are
                    unsupported.  Answer D is contradicted by paragraphs 1–2.

Black's <u>A</u> 9. In paragraphs 6–13, the details that Black provides
"elusive" symptoms
could also have been
due to a muscle strain,
an infection, or an
allergic reaction.

A. demonstrate why her illness was difficult to diagnose.
B. show that her doctor didn't really care about her condition.
C. make it clear she was unconcerned about her condition.
D. demonstrate that she complained a lot about her problems.

<u>D</u> 10. Black uses Michelle's death as a symbol of her realization that
A. she, too, would die.
B. she had no hope of ever being cured.
C. she needed religious faith.
D. life is not fair.     See paragraph 41. The "door" that has "swung open"
for Black refers to the realization that in the real world,
prayers are not always answered, and innocent people die.

## Discussion Questions

1. When Black enters the hospital, she becomes aware of an "alternate world" that "had existed all along, behind my formerly sunny, innocent life." What is this "alternate world"? What, in particular, does she find surprising about it?

2. Black quotes Graham Greene, who wrote, "There's always one moment in childhood when the door opens and lets the future in." What might this statement mean? According to Black's story, when did this experience happen to her? Why do you think she was so upset afterward?

3. Have you ever known anyone who, like Black, suffers from chronic illness? If so, how does it affect his or her life? What adjustments has the person made in order to live with this condition?

4. Do you remember a moment in *your* life when "the door opened and let the future in"? Describe the event, and explain what it made you realize.

## Paragraph Assignments

1. Even in the face of tragic events, such as the death of Michelle, some people will say, "Everything happens for a reason." Do you believe that "everything happens for a reason"? Write a paragraph in which you explain your answer.

2. When Black was diagnosed with lupus, she writes, "I realized a chapter of my life was suddenly ending and a new one was about to start." In your own life, when has there been a change that felt like a chapter ending and a new one starting? Write a paragraph about that change in your life.

Here is one student's response to this assignment:

> When I think of a chapter in my life ending and another beginning, I think about when my mom married my stepfather. I was 10, and Mom and I had been on our own since I was a baby. I think most life changes have good and bad aspects, and this one was no exception. I liked my stepdad, but it was strange having a third person living in our little family. My mom and I had been very close over the years, and I wasn't sure I liked the idea of sharing her with anybody. Also, it was a struggle for my stepdad and me to figure out our relationship. I tested him more than a few times, telling him "You're not my dad!" when he disciplined me. But thanks to his patience and kindness, as well as seeing how happy my mom was with him, we all moved ahead together into a happy new chapter of life. Today I know how lucky I am that Ted came into our lives, and I am grateful he hung in there with a not-always-so-wonderful stepdaughter!

## Essay Assignments

1. After developing lupus, Black looked back with new appreciation at the healthy body she had once taken for granted. What are some qualities of your own self that you appreciate? You might think of physical or mental abilities, or aspects of your personality. Write an essay about three things that you like about yourself. Provide details about how those abilities or qualities enhance your life.

2. In the course of "A Door Swings Open," Roxanne Black is faced not only with the onset of her own serious illness, but also with the tragic death of a little girl she had only recently befriended. Such unforeseen circumstances raise the question of how much responsibility we as a society have toward those whom life has treated unfairly. In your opinion, should government play a role in helping individuals overcome crisis situations, or should responsibility rest with the individual? Write an essay supporting your position. Your thesis might look like one of these:

● Government should play a leading role when life treats people unfairly.

● Whatever life brings, it is up to the individual to look after him- or herself.

To support your thesis statement, describe three specific situations in which people face serious challenges. These challenges may involve health care, natural disasters, education, housing, jobs, childcare, providing for the elderly, and so on. Explain in each case what role you envision the individual playing and what role (if any) you envision the government playing. You may discuss situations that have actually occurred or ones that might occur.

---

## Check Your Performance                    **A DOOR SWINGS OPEN**

| Activity | Number Right | Points | Score |
|---|---|---|---|
| **Vocabulary Check** (3 items) | _____ | x  10  = | _____ |
| **Reading Check** | | | |
| Central Point and Main Ideas (2 items) | _____ | x  7  = | _____ |
| Supporting Details (3 items) | _____ | x  7  = | _____ |
| Inferences (2 items) | _____ | x  7  = | _____ |
| The Writer's Craft (3 items) | _____ | x  7  = | _____ |
| | | TOTAL SCORE  = | _____ % |

Enter your total score into the **Performance Chart: Fifteen Reading Selections** on the inside back cover.

## 13 A Drunken Ride, a Tragic Aftermath

### Theresa Conroy and Christine M. Johnson

## Preview

It is a sequence of events that occurs all too often—high-school kids gather for a party that quickly turns drunken and raucous. The party spills out into the roadways, and an evening of alcohol-fueled celebration turns into a nightmare of twisted metal, mangled bodies, and anguished survivors. As this article makes clear, the horror of such a night does not end with the funerals of those who died.

## Words to Watch

*carnage* (19):  massive slaughter
*catharsis* (62):  refreshing release of emotional tension
*fathom* (64):  understand
*vicariously* (94):  by imagining someone else's experience
*peer-group* (97):  made up of people of a similar age, grade, etc.

1   When Tyson Baxter awoke after that drunken, tragic night—with a bloodied head, broken arm, and battered face—he knew that he had killed his friends.

2   "I knew everyone had died," Baxter, 18, recalled. "I knew it before anybody told me. Somehow, I knew."

3   Baxter was talking about the night of Friday, September 13, the night he and seven friends piled into his Chevrolet Blazer after a beer-drinking party. On Street Road in Upper Southampton, he lost control, rear-ended a car, and smashed into two telephone poles. The Blazer's cab top shattered, and the truck spun several times, ejecting all but one passenger.

4   Four young men were killed.

5   Tests would show that Baxter and the four youths who died were legally intoxicated.

6   Baxter says he thinks about his dead friends on many sleepless nights at the Abraxas Drug and Alcohol Rehabilitation Center near Pittsburgh, where, on December 20, he was sentenced to be held after being found delinquent on charges of vehicular homicide.

7    "I drove them where they wanted to go, and I was responsible for their lives," Baxter said recently from the center, where he is undergoing psychological treatment. "I had the keys in my hand, and I blew it."

8    The story of September 13 is a story about the kind of horrors that drinking and driving is spawning among high-school students almost everywhere, . . . about parents who lost their children in a flash and have filled the emptiness with hatred, . . . about a youth whose life is burdened with grief and guilt because he happened to be behind the wheel.

9    It is a story that the Baxter family and the dead boys' parents agreed to tell in the hope that it would inspire high-school students to remain sober during this week of graduation festivities—a week that customarily includes a ritual night of drunkenness.

10    It is a story of the times.

11    The evening of September 13 began in high spirits as Baxter, behind the wheel of his gold Blazer, picked up seven high-school chums for a drinking party for William Tennent High School students and graduates at the home of a classmate. Using false identification, according to police, the boys purchased one six-pack of beer each from a Warminster Township bar.

12    The unchaperoned party, attended by about fifty teenagers, ended about 10:30 p.m. when someone knocked over and broke a glass china cabinet. Baxter and his friends decided to head for a fast-food restaurant. As Baxter turned onto Street Road, he was trailed by a line of cars carrying other partygoers.

13    Baxter recalled that several passengers were swaying and rocking the high-suspension vehicle. Police were unable to determine the vehicle's exact speed, but, on the basis of the accounts of witnesses, they estimated it at fifty-five miles per hour—ten miles per hour over the limit.

14    "I thought I was in control," Baxter said. "I wasn't driving like a nut; I was just . . . driving. There was a bunch of noise, just a bunch of noise. The truck was really bouncing.

15    "I remember passing two [cars]. That's the last I remember. I remember a big flash, and that's it."

16    Killed in that flash were: Morris "Marty" Freedenberg, 16, who landed near a telephone pole about thirty feet from the truck, his face ripped from his skull; Robert Schweiss, 18, a Bucks County Community College student, whose internal organs were crushed when he hit the pavement about thirty feet from the truck; Brian Ball, 17, who landed near Schweiss, his six-foot-seven-inch frame stretched three inches when his spine was severed; and Christopher Avram, 17, a premedical student at Temple University, who landed near the curb about ten feet from the truck.

17    Michael Serratore, 18, was thrown fifteen feet from the truck and landed on the lawn of the CHI Institute with his right leg shattered. Baxter, who sailed about ten feet after crashing through the windshield of the Blazer, lost consciousness after hitting the street near the center lane. About five yards away, Paul Gee, Jr., 18, lapsed into a

coma from severe head injuries.

18    John Gahan, 17, the only passenger left in the Blazer, suffered a broken ankle.

19    Brett Walker, 17, one of several Tennent students who saw the carnage° after the accident, would recall later in a speech to fellow students: "I ran over [to the scene]. These were the kids I would go out with every weekend.

20    "My one friend [Freedenberg], I couldn't even tell it was him except for his eyes. He had real big, blue eyes. He was torn apart so bad. . . ."

21    Francis Schweiss was waiting up for his son, Robert, when he received a telephone call from his daughter, Lisa. She was already at Warminster General Hospital.

22    "She said Robbie and his friends were in a bad accident and Robbie was not here" at the hospital, Schweiss said. "I got in my car with my wife; we went to the scene of the accident."

23    There, police officers told Francis and Frances Schweiss that several boys had been killed and that the bodies, as well as survivors, had been taken to Warminster General Hospital.

24    "My head was frying by then," Francis Schweiss said. "I can't even describe it. I almost knew the worst was to be. I felt as though I were living a nightmare. I thought, 'I'll wake up. This just can't be.'"

25    In the emergency room, Francis Schweiss recalled, nurses and doctors were scrambling to aid the injured and identify the dead—a difficult task because some bodies were disfigured and because all the boys had been carrying fake driver's licenses.

26    A police officer from Upper Southampton was trying to question friends of the dead and injured—many of whom were sobbing and screaming—in an attempt to match clothing with identities.

27    When the phone rang in the Freedenberg home, Robert S. and his wife, Bobbi, had just gone upstairs to bed; their son Robert Jr. was downstairs watching a movie on television.

28    Bobbi Freedenberg and her son picked up the receiver at the same time. It was from Warminster General. . . . There had been a bad accident. . . . The family should get to the hospital quickly.

29    Outside the morgue about twenty minutes later, a deputy county coroner told Rob Jr., 22, that his brother was dead and severely disfigured; Rob decided to spare his parents additional grief by identifying the body himself.

30    Freedenberg was led into a cinderblock room containing large drawers resembling filing cabinets. In one of the drawers was his brother, Marty, identifiable only by his new high-top sneakers.

31    "It was kind of like being taken through a nightmare," Rob Jr. said. "That's something I think about every night before I go to sleep. That's hell. . . . That whole night is what hell is all about for me."

32    As was his custom, Morris Ball started calling the parents of his son's friends after Brian missed his 11:00 p.m. curfew.

33    The first call was to the Baxters' house, where the Baxters' sixteen-year-

old daughter, Amber, told him about the accident.

34    At the hospital, Morris Ball demanded that doctors and nurses take him to his son. The hospital staff had been unable to identify Brian—until Ball told them that his son wore size 14 shoes.

35    Brian Ball was in the morgue. Lower left drawer.

36    "He was six foot seven, but after the accident he measured six foot ten, because of what happened to him," Ball said. "He had a severed spinal cord at the neck. His buttocks were practically ripped off, but he was lying down and we couldn't see that. He was peaceful and asleep.

37    "He was my son and my baby. I just can't believe it sometimes. I still can't believe it. I still wait for him to come home."

38    Lynne Pancoast had just finished watching the 11:00 p.m. news and was curled up in her bed dozing with a book in her lap when the doorbell rang. She assumed that one of her sons had forgotten his key, and she went downstairs to let him in.

39    A police light was flashing through the window and reflecting against her living-room wall; Pancoast thought that there must be a fire in the neighborhood and that the police were evacuating homes.

40    Instead, police officers told her there had been a serious accident involving her son, Christopher Avram, and that she should go to the emergency room at Warminster General.

41    At the hospital she was taken to an empty room and told that her son was dead.

42    Patricia Baxter was asleep when a Warminster police officer came to the house and informed her that her son had been in an accident.

43    At the hospital, she could not immediately recognize her own son lying on a bed in the emergency room. His brown eyes were swollen shut, and his straight brown hair was matted with blood that had poured from a deep gash in his forehead.

44    While she was staring at his battered face, a police officer rushed into the room and pushed her onto the floor—protection against the hysterical father of a dead youth who was racing through the halls, proclaiming that he had a gun and shouting, "Where is she? I'm going to kill her. I'm going to kill him. I'm going to kill his mother."

45    The man, who did not have a gun, was subdued by a Warminster police officer and was not charged.

46    Amid the commotion, Robert Baxter, a Lower Southampton highway patrol officer, arrived at the hospital and found his wife and son.

47    "When he came into the room, he kept going like this," Patricia Baxter said, holding up four fingers. At first, she said, she did not understand that her husband was signaling that four boys had been killed in the accident.

48    After Tyson regained consciousness, his father told him about the deaths.

49    "All I can remember is just tensing up and just saying something," Tyson

Baxter said. "I can remember saying, 'I know.'

50    "I can remember going nuts."

51    In the days after the accident, as the dead were buried in services that Tyson Baxter was barred by the parents of the victims from attending, Baxter's parents waited for him to react to the tragedy and release his grief.

52    "In the hospital he was non-responsive," Patricia Baxter said. "He was home for a month, and he was nonresponsive.

53    "We never used to do this, but we would be upstairs and listen to see if Ty responded when his friends came to visit," she said. "But the boy would be silent. That's the grief that I felt. The other kids showed a reaction. My son didn't."

54    Baxter said, however, that he felt grief from the first, that he would cry in the quiet darkness of his hospital room and, later, alone in the darkness of his bedroom. During the day, he said, he blocked his emotions.

55    "It was just at night. I thought about it all the time. It's still like that."

56    At his parents' urging, Baxter returned to school on September 30.

57    "I don't remember a thing," he said of his return. "I just remember walking around. I didn't say anything to anybody. It didn't really sink in."

58    Lynne Pancoast, the mother of Chris Avram, thought it was wrong for Baxter to be in school, and wrong that her other son, Joel, a junior at William Tennent, had to walk through the school halls and pass the boy who "killed his brother."

59    Morris Ball said he was appalled that Baxter "went to a football game while my son lay buried in a grave."

60    Some William Tennent students said they were uncertain about how they should treat Baxter. Several said they went out of their way to treat him normally, others said they tried to avoid him, and others declined to be interviewed on the subject.

61    The tragedy unified the senior class, according to the school principal, Kenneth Kastle. He said that after the accident, many students who were friends of the victims joined the school's Students Against Driving Drunk chapter.

62    Matthew Weintraub, 17, a basketball player who witnessed the bloody accident scene, wrote to President Reagan and detailed the grief among the student body. He said, however, that he experienced a catharsis° after reading the letter at a student assembly and, as a result, did not mail it.

63    "And after we got over the initial shock of the news, we felt as though we owed somebody something," Weintraub wrote. "It could have been us and maybe we could have stopped it, and now it's too late. . . .

64    "We took these impressions with us as we then visited our friends who had been lucky enough to live. One of them was responsible for the accident; he was the driver. He would forever hold the deaths of four young men on his conscience. Compared with our own feelings of guilt, [we] could not begin to fathom° this boy's emotions. He looked as if he had a heavy weight upon his head and it would remain there forever."

65    About three weeks after the accident, Bucks County Senator H. Craig Lewis launched a series of public forums to formulate bills targeting underage drinking. Proposals developed through the meetings include outlawing alcohol ads on radio and television, requiring police to notify parents of underage drinkers, and creating a tamperproof driver's license.

66    The parents of players on William Tennent's boys' basketball team, which lost Ball and Baxter because of the accident, formed the Caring Parents of William Tennent High School Students to help dissuade students from drinking.

67    Several William Tennent students, interviewed on the condition that their names not be published, said that, because of the accident, they would not drive after drinking during senior week, which will be held in Wildwood, New Jersey, after graduation June 13.

68    But they scoffed at the suggestion that they curtail their drinking during the celebrations.

69    "We just walk [after driving to Wildwood]," said one youth. "Stagger is more like it."

70    "What else are we going to do, go out roller skating?" an eighteen-year-old student asked.

71    "You telling us we're not going to drink?" one boy asked. "We're going to drink very heavily. I want to come home retarded. That's senior week. I'm going to drink every day. Everybody's going to drink every day."

72    Tyson Baxter sat at the front table of the Bucks County courtroom on December 20, his arm in a sling, his head lowered and his eyes dry. He faced twenty counts of vehicular homicide, four counts of involuntary manslaughter, and two counts of driving under the influence of alcohol.

73    Patricia Ball said she told the closed hearing that "it was Tyson Baxter who killed our son. He used the car as a weapon. We know he killed our children as if it were a gun. He killed our son."

74    "I really could have felt justice [was served] if Tyson Baxter was the only one who died in that car," she said in an interview, "because he didn't take care of our boys."

75    Police officers testified before Bucks County President Judge Isaac S. Garb that tests revealed that the blood-alcohol levels of Baxter and the four dead boys were above the 0.10 percent limit used in Pennsylvania to establish intoxication.

76    Baxter's blood-alcohol level was 0.14 percent, Ball's 0.19 percent, Schweiss's 0.11 percent, Avram's 0.12 percent, and Freedenberg's 0.38 percent. Baxter's level indicated that he had had eight or nine drinks—enough to cause abnormal bodily functions such as exaggerated gestures and to impair his mental faculties, according to the police report.

77    After the case was presented, Garb invited family members of the dead teens to speak.

78    In a nine-page statement, Bobbi Freedenberg urged Garb to render a decision that would "punish, rehabilitate, and deter others from this act."

79    The parents asked Garb to give

Baxter the maximum sentence, to prohibit him from graduating, and to incarcerate him before Christmas day. (Although he will not attend formal ceremonies, Baxter will receive a diploma from William Tennent this week.)

80    After hearing from the parents, Garb called Baxter to the stand.

81    "I just said that all I could say was, 'I'm sorry; I know I'm totally responsible for what happened,'" Baxter recalled. "It wasn't long, but it was to the point."

82    Garb found Baxter delinquent and sentenced him to a stay at Abraxas Rehabilitation Center—for an unspecified period beginning December 23—and community service upon his return. Baxter's driver's license was suspended by the judge for an unspecified period, and he was placed under Garb's jurisdiction until age 21.

83    Baxter is one of fifty-two Pennsylvania youths found responsible for fatal drunken-driving accidents in the state in 1985.

84    Reflecting on the hearing, Morris Ball said there was no legal punishment that would have satisfied his longings.

85    "They can't bring my son back," he said, "and they can't kill Tyson Baxter."

86    Grief has forged friendships among the dead boys' parents, each of whom blames Tyson Baxter for their son's death. Every month they meet at each other's homes, but they seldom talk about the accident.

87    Several have joined support groups to help them deal with their losses. Some said they feel comfortable only with other parents whose children are dead.

88    Bobbi Freedenberg said her attitude had worsened with the passage of time. "It seems as if it just gets harder," she said. "It seems to get worse."

89    Freedenberg, Schweiss, and Pancoast said they talk publicly about their sons' deaths in hopes that the experience will help deter other teenagers from drunken driving.

90    Schweiss speaks each month to the Warminster Youth Aid Panel—a group of teenagers who, through drug use, alcohol abuse, or minor offenses, have run afoul of the law.

91    "When I talk to the teens, I bring a picture of Robbie and pass it along to everyone," Schweiss said, wiping the tears from his cheeks. "I say, 'He was with us last year.' I get emotional and I cry. . . .

92    "But I know that my son helps me. I firmly believe that every time I speak, he's right on my shoulder."

93    When Pancoast speaks to a group of area high-school students, she drapes her son's football jersey over the podium and displays his graduation picture.

94    "Every time I speak to a group, I make them go through the whole thing vicariously°," Pancoast said. "It's helpful to get out and talk to kids. It sort of helps keep Chris alive. . . . When you talk, you don't think."

95    At Abraxas, Baxter attended high-school classes until Friday. He is one of three youths there who supervise fellow residents, who keep track of residents' whereabouts, attendance at programs,

and adherence to the center's rules and regulations.

96    Established in Pittsburgh, the Abraxas Foundation provides an alternative to imprisonment for offenders between sixteen and twenty-five years old whose drug and alcohol use has led them to commit crimes.

97    Licensed and partially subsidized by the Pennsylvania Department of Health, the program includes work experience, high-school education, and prevocational training. Counselors conduct individual therapy sessions, and the residents engage in peer-group° confrontational therapy sessions.

98    Baxter said his personality had changed from an "egotistical, arrogant" teenager to someone who is "mellow" and mature.

99    "I don't have quite the chip on my shoulder. I don't really have a right to be cocky anymore," he said.

100    Baxter said not a day went by that he didn't remember his dead friends.

101    "I don't get sad. I just get thinking about them," he said. "Pictures pop into my mind. A tree or something reminds me of the time. . . . Sometimes I laugh. . . . Then I go to my room and reevaluate it like a nut," he said.

102    Baxter said his deepest longing was to stand beside the graves of his four friends.

103    More than anything, Baxter said, he wants to say good-bye.

104    "I just feel it's something I have to do, . . . just to talk," Baxter said, averting his eyes to hide welling tears. "Deep down I think I'll be hit with it when I see the graves. I know they're gone, but they're not gone."

## First Impressions

Freewrite for ten minutes on one of the following.

1.  Did you enjoy reading this selection? Why or why not?

2.  If you were the parent of one of the boys who were killed, would you have responded to Tyson Baxter in the same way the parents in the story did? Or would you have behaved differently? Explain.

3.  Do you know of alcohol-related accidents involving students? Did the accidents seem to have any effect on other students' attitudes toward drinking?

## Vocabulary Check

_A_  1.  In the sentence below, the word *spawning* means
    A.  producing.
    B.  preventing.        Since we know the dreadful accident
    C.  protecting.        happened as a result of drinking and
    D.  predicting.     driving, this activity must have produced it.

  "The story of September 13 is a story about the kind of horrors that
  drinking and driving is spawning among high-school students almost
  everywhere . . ." (Paragraph 8)

_B_  2.  In the sentence below, the word *appalled* means
    A.  relieved.
    B.  horrified.        How would a person who had just lost his child
    C.  pleased.       react when he learned the person responsible for
    D.  aware.                     his loss was having fun at a game?

  "Morris Ball said he was appalled that Baxter 'went to a football game
  while my son lay buried in a grave.'" (Paragraph 59)

_C_  3.  In the sentence below, the word *deter* means
    A.  punish.
    B.  pay.            What might learning about a horrific accident
    C.  prevent.         and multiple deaths do to teenagers' plans
    D.  hide.                        to drive while drunk?

  "Freedenberg, Schweiss, and Pancoast said they talk publicly about their
  sons' deaths in hopes that the experience will help deter other teenagers
  from drunken driving." (Paragraph 89)

## Reading Check

### Central Point and Main Ideas

_A_  1.  Which sentence best expresses the central point of the entire selection?
    A.  The experience of Tyson Baxter and his friends should serve as an
        example to teens of the dangers of drinking and driving.
    B.  The parents of the boys killed in the accident have never forgiven the
        driver, Tyson Baxter.
    C.  Drinking has become a routine part of life for many teenagers.
    D.  Because of a high-school student's drunk-driving accident, a state
        senator began work on a bill targeting underage drinking.

              See paragraphs 8–10. The details that follow graphically
              illustrate what can happen when people drink and drive.

_A_ 2. Which sentence best expresses the main idea of paragraph 8?
- A. Many people are affected by the consequences of high-school students' drinking and driving.
- B. Parents who lose their children may be consumed with hatred.
- C. The driver of the automobile feels a great deal of grief and guilt.
- D. High-school students across the country are drinking and driving more.

Answers B and C are too narrow; each applies to only part of the one-sentence paragraph. Answer D is not mentioned in the paragraph.

## Supporting Details

_A_ 3. Which of the following was *not* a consequence of the accident?
- A. Students pledged not to drink during senior week at Wildwood, New Jersey.
- B. A senator held a series of public forums to think up ways to fight underage drinking.
- C. Many William Tennent students joined a Students Against Driving Drunk chapter.
- D. The parents of the boys who died began to meet every month.

See paragraph 67. Note that the students pledged not to drive after drinking, but they still intended to drink.

_D_ 4. The task of identifying the bodies was made more difficult because
- A. the boys' friends were sobbing and screaming.
- B. the bodies were badly disfigured.
- C. the boys were carrying fake identification.
- D. of all of the above.

See paragraphs 25–26.

## Inferences

_A_ 5. From the comments made at court by the parents of the victims, we can infer that the parents
- A. did not blame their own sons for their underage drinking.
- B. believed Baxter had gotten false identification for their sons.
- C. felt all of the victims that survived should be punished.
- D. felt all of the above.

See paragraphs 73–74, 78–79, and 84–86, in which the parents place the entire blame on Baxter. Answers B and C are unsupported.

_C_ 6. We can infer from the statements made by seniors in paragraphs 67–71 that
- A. many students at Baxter's high school had not heard of his accident.
- B. graduation parties will be strictly chaperoned.
- C. some students do not take seriously the dangers of alcohol abuse.
- D. the drinking age is lower in Wildwood than in other places.

Despite what happened, the students still intend to drink heavily during graduation week. Answers A, B, and D are not supported.

_B_   7. We can assume that after being released from Abraxas, Tyson Baxter will
   A. never drive a car again.
   B. visit the graves of the four boys killed in the accident.
   C. become a role model in the fight against drunk driving.
   D. pretend that the accident never happened.

> See paragraphs 100–104. Answers A and C are unsupported; answer D is unsupported and unlikely.

## The Writer's Craft

_B_   8. The authors begin and end their article with
   A. remarks by the authors about the dangers of drunken driving.
   B. quotations from Tyson Baxter.
   C. quotations from the police who were first on the scene of the accident.
   D. quotations from parents of the boys who died.

> See paragraphs 1–2 and 98–104.

_C_   9. In general, this reading is organized according to which of the following patterns?
   A. Listing order: a list of the measures people took after the accident to prevent drunk driving.
   B. Cause-effect: explaining why so many teens get drunk during senior week.
   C. Time order: the sequence of events that took place on September 13 and afterward.
   D. Comparison-contrast: comparing and contrasting student attitudes toward drinking and driving before the accident and after the accident.

> Starting with paragraph 11, the events are related in the order in which they happened, including the reactions of others involved.

_C_ 10. The authors' primary purpose in this selection is to
   A. inform readers of ways that parents cope with the tragic deaths of their children.
   B. persuade readers that laws should be passed to make it more difficult for teenagers to purchase alcoholic beverages.
   C. persuade people in general, and particularly young people, not to drink and drive.
   D. entertain readers with a dramatic and horrifying true-crime story.

> See paragraphs 8–9. The authors have told this story, with the consent of the Baxters and the families of the victims, to serve as an object lesson for all of us.

## Discussion Questions

1. The authors write in paragraph 14: "'I thought I was in control,' Baxter said. 'I wasn't driving like a nut; I was just . . . driving.'" What does this tell us about the effects of alcohol on drivers?

2. To what extent do you think Tyson Baxter was responsible for the accident? Do you feel his passengers also were at fault in any way? If so, to what extent were they also responsible? Is there anyone else that you think is partly to blame for the accident?

3. What do you think would be an appropriate punishment for Tyson Baxter? If you were the judge in his case, what sentence would you give him? Why?

4. Why do you think that, even after knowing what had happened to Tyson Baxter and his friends, some of his classmates would brag about their plans to "drink very heavily" during senior week? What, if anything, do you think could change those students' attitudes about drinking?

## Paragraph Assignments

1. While drunk drivers can be any age, a large percentage of them are young. Write a paragraph explaining what you think would be a truly effective way of making young people understand the horrors of drunk driving. Keep in mind that the young are being cautioned all the time and that some of the warnings are so familiar that they probably have little impact. What approach would be so unusual, dramatic, or unexpected that it might really get young people's attention? Start your paragraph with a topic sentence such as the following: "Here is a way to truly convince the young of the horrors of drunk driving." Then, in the rest of your paragraph, develop your suggestion in great detail.

2. Tyson Baxter's friends might still be alive if he had not been drunk when he drove. But there is another way their deaths could have been avoided—they could have refused to get into his car. Such a refusal would not have been easy; after all, nobody likes to embarrass, anger, or offend a person who has offered him or her a ride. To help your readers prepare for such an occasion, write a paragraph in which you suggest several ways to turn down a ride with a driver who may be drunk.

## Essay Assignments

1. People have different views about how severely Tyson Baxter should be punished. Some believe that the intoxicated boys in his car share the blame for what happened. Others say that by offering to drive, Baxter assumed total responsibility for the accident. Write an essay about what you think would be an appropriate punishment for Tyson Baxter, and why. Your thesis statement should state the chosen punishment—for example:

   ● The most appropriate punishment for Tyson Baxter would be life imprisonment.

   ● For several reasons, Tyson Baxter should have received a one-year sentence to a minimum-security prison.

   Your supporting paragraphs should develop the various reasons why that punishment is appropriate.

2. Drinking and driving is one of the more tragic, unwise activities that young people get involved in. What are some other dangerous, unwise, or silly activities or behaviors that teenagers (and/or adults) often get caught up in? Write an essay describing three of these activities and people's involvement in them. Your essay may be serious or light-hearted. In either case, provide lots of specific examples of each behavior and how the people involved are affected by it.

   Here is one student's response to the assignment:

   > The other day I was in the store where I work and a young guy, probably about 17, asked me where he could find the door locks. I wasn't sure—I'm new on the job—but I looked around for a minute and found them. Then I went back to find the guy and tell him. The problem was, there were several guys about his age in the store, and at first I didn't know which one had asked me for help. They were all dressed almost alike, and I thought to myself, "Teenagers!" Teens are at the stage in their lives where the most important thing in the universe is being accepted by their peers. This need for acceptance leads them to make some ridiculous choices. At the high school my younger brother goes to, I've observed three such ridiculous behaviors.
   >     The first and silliest choice of all concerns how the guys dress. I'll start from the top down. First, there is the baseball cap. But it can't be worn in a normal way. No, it

either has to be backwards or perched at a ridiculous angle on the head. Then there's the required white t-shirt that is at least two sizes too large. Then comes the most special touch of all—the pants with a 42-inch waistline sagging below the butt of a kid who weighs maybe 130 pounds. Throw in a pair of untied shoelaces, and the guy can barely move. He just shuffles along as though he's 90 years old.

Then there's the girls, whose wardrobes are basically the opposite of the guys. Instead of being ten times too big, the girls' clothes are several sizes too small. Their tiny shirts become belly t's. Pair them with low-cut jeans that are so tight they look sprayed on, and you've got that muffin-top look around the middle that is so attractive (not!) Oh, and don't forget the view from the rear. The huge gap between the jeans and the shirt gives plenty of room for the viewer to read the below-the-waist tattoo that completes this oh-so-classy look.

The third silly teen behavior is the tendency to move and think as a pack, not as individuals. Going to the mall requires at least nine other friends to go with you. Moving down the sidewalk requires that you and your homies take up the entire space. You listen only to music that has been approved by the group; you see only movies that your friends like. You ignore people who aren't in your particular pack, and you hang out with people you might not like all that much, but who are accepted. And as mentioned above, you do it all wearing nearly identical clothing.

Hopefully, most young people eventually grow out of the stage where they have to look and act just like their peers. With any luck, they'll discover that it's really more interesting to be themselves.

- *Circle one answer:* Does the introduction (a) go from broad to narrow, (b) tell a story, (c) ask questions, or (d) shift to the opposite?

- Underline the thesis statement.

- Underline the topic sentences for the three supporting paragraphs.

- *Circle one answer:* Does the conclusion end with (a) a summary, (b) a final thought, or (c) both?

## Check Your Performance                    A DRUNKEN RIDE, A TRAGIC AFTERMATH

| Activity | Number Right | Points | | Score |
|---|---|---|---|---|
| **Vocabulary Check**  (3 items) | _____ | x   10 | = | _____ |
| **Reading Check** | | | | |
| Central Point and Main Ideas  (2 items) | _____ | x    7 | = | _____ |
| Supporting Details  (2 items) | _____ | x    7 | = | _____ |
| Inferences  (3 items) | _____ | x    7 | = | _____ |
| The Writer's Craft  (3 items) | _____ | x    7 | = | _____ |
| | | **TOTAL SCORE** | = | _____ % |

Enter your total score into the **Performance Chart: Fifteen Reading Selections** on the inside back cover.

## (14) Migrant Child to College Woman

### Maria Cardenas

## Preview

Maria Cardenas grew up in a family of migrant workers. As the family moved from state to state, following the fruit and vegetable harvest, Maria became used to backbreaking labor, poverty, and violence. The brutality she encountered, as well as her own lack of education, could have snuffed out her hopes for a better life. But, as this selection will show, Maria has found the courage both to dream and to make her dreams become reality.

## Words to Watch

*abducted* (18): taken away by force
*taunted* (22): cruelly teased
*briskly* (24): in a lively manner
*GED* (24): general equivalency diploma (equal to a high-school diploma)

1   As I walk into the classroom, the teacher gazes at me with her piercing green eyes. I feel myself shrinking and burning up with guilt. I go straight to her desk and hand her the excuse slip. Just like all the other times, I say, "I was sick." I hate lying, but I have to. I don't want my parents to get in trouble.

2   I'm not a very good liar. She makes me hold out my hands, inspecting my dirty fingernails and calluses. She knows exactly where I've been the past several days. When you pick tomatoes and don't wear gloves, your hands get rough and stained from the plant oils. Soap doesn't wash that out.

3   In the background, I can hear the students giggling as she asks her usual questions: "What was wrong? Was your brother sick, too? Do you feel better today?" Of course I don't feel better. My whole body aches from those endless hot days spent harvesting crops from dawn to dusk. I was never absent by choice.

4   That year, in that school, I think my name was "Patricia Rodriguez," but I'm not sure. My brother and I used whatever name our mother told us to use each time we went to a new school. We understood that we had to be registered as the children of parents

437

who were in the United States legally, in case Immigration ever checked up.

5     My parents had come to the States in the late '60s to work in the fields and earn money to feed their family. They paid eight hundred dollars to someone who smuggled them across the border, and they left us with our aunt and uncle in Mexico. My five-year-old brother, Joel, was the oldest. I was 4, and then came Teresa, age 3, and baby Bruno. The other kids in the neighborhood teased us, saying, "They won't come back for you." Three years later, our parents sent for us to join them in Texas. My little heart sang as we waved good-bye to those neighbor kids in Rio Verde. My father did love us!

6     My parents worked all the time in the fields. Few other options were open to them because they had little education. At first, our education was important to them. They were too scared to put us in school right away, but when I was 8 they did enroll us. I do remember that my first-grade report card said I was "Antonietta Gonzales." My father made sure we had everything we needed—tablets, crayons, ruler, and the little box to put your stuff in. He bragged to his friends about his children going to school. Now we could talk for our parents. We could translate their words for the grocer, the doctor, and the teachers. If Immigration came by, we could tell them we were citizens, and because we were speaking English, they wouldn't ask any more questions.

7     In the years to come, I often reminded myself that my father had not forgotten us like the fathers of so many

kids I knew. It became more important for me to remember that as it became harder to see that he loved us. He had hit my mother once in a while as I was growing up, but when his own mother died in Mexico in 1973, his behavior grew much worse. My uncles told me that my father, the youngest of the family, had often beaten his mother. Maybe it was the guilt he felt when she died, but for whatever reason, he started drinking heavily, abusing my mother emotionally and physically, and terrorizing us kids. The importance of our education faded away, and now my papa thought my brother and I should work more in the fields. We would work all the time—on school vacations, holidays, weekends, and every day after school. When there were lots of tomatoes to pick, I went to school only every other day.

8     If picking was slow, I stayed home after school and cooked for the family. I started as soon as I got home in the afternoon. I used the three large pots my mother owned: one for beans, one for rice or soup, and one for hot salsa. There were also the usual ten pounds of flour or *maseca*, ground corn meal, for the tortillas. I loved this cooking because I could eat as much as I wanted and see that the little kids got enough before the older family members finished everything. By this time there were three more children in our family, and we often went to bed hungry. (My best subject in school was lunch, and my plate was always clean.)

9     Other than lunchtime, my school life passed in a blur. I remember a little about teachers showing us how to

sound words out. I began to stumble through elementary readers. But then we'd move again, or I'd be sent to the fields.

10    Life was never easy in those days. Traveling with the harvest meant living wherever the bosses put us. We might be in little houses with one outdoor toilet for the whole camp. Other times the whole crew, all fifty or one hundred of us, were jammed into one big house. Working in the fields meant blistering sun, aching muscles, sliced fingers, bug bites, and my father yelling when we didn't pick fast enough to suit him.

11    But we were kids, so we found a way to have some fun. My brother and I would make a game of competing with each other and the other adults. I never did manage to pick more than Joel, but I came close. One time I picked 110 baskets of cucumbers to Joel's 115. We made thirty-five cents a basket.

12    Of course, we never saw any of that money. At the end of the week, whatever the whole family had earned was given to my father. Soon he stopped working altogether. He just watched us, chatted with the field bosses, and drank beer. He began to beat all of us kids as well as our mother. We didn't work fast enough for him. He wanted us to make more money. He called us names and threw stones and vegetables at us. The other workers did nothing to make him stop. I was always scared of my father, but I loved him even though he treated us so badly. I told myself that he loved us, but that alcohol ruled his life.

13    I knew what controlled my father's life, but I never thought about being in control of my own. I did as I was told, spoke in a whisper, and tried not to be noticed. Because we traveled with the harvest, my brothers and sisters and I attended three or four different schools in one year. When picking was good, I went to the fields instead of school. When the little kids got sick, I stayed home to watch them. When I did go to school, I didn't understand very much. We spoke only Spanish at home. I don't know how I got through elementary school, much less to high school, because I only knew how to add, subtract, and multiply. And let's just say I got "introduced" to English writing skills and grammar. School was a strange foreign place where I went when I could, sitting like a ghost in a corner alone. I could read enough to help my mother fill out forms in English. But enough to pick up a story and understand it? Never. When a teacher told the class, "Read this book, and write a report," I just didn't do it. I knew she wasn't talking to me.

14    In 1978, my mother ran away after two weeks of terrible beatings. Joel and I found the dime under the big suitcase, where she had told us it would be. We were supposed to use it to call the police, but we were too scared. We stayed in the upstairs closet with our brothers and sisters. In the morning, I felt guilty and terrified. I didn't know whether our mother was alive or dead. Not knowing what else to do, I got dressed and went to school. I told the counselor what had happened, and she called the police. My father was arrested. He believed the police when they said they were taking him to jail

for unpaid traffic tickets. Then the police located my mother and told her it was safe to come out of hiding. My father never lived with us again although he continued to stalk us. He would stand outside the house yelling at my mother, "You're gonna be a prostitute. Those kids are gonna be no-good drug addicts and criminals. They're gonna end up in jail."

15    My father's words enraged me. I had always had a hunger for knowledge, always dreamed of a fancy job where I would go to work wearing nice clothes and carrying a briefcase. How dare he try to kill my dream! True, the idea of that dream ever coming true seemed unlikely. In school, if I asked about material I didn't understand, most of the teachers seemed annoyed. My mother would warn me, "Please, don't ask so many questions."

16    But then, somehow, when I was 14, Mrs. Mercer noticed me. I don't remember how my conversations with this teacher started, but it led to her offering me a job in the Western clothing store she and her husband owned. I helped translate for the Spanish-speaking customers who shopped there. I worked only Saturdays, and I got paid a whole twenty-dollar bill. Proudly, I presented that money to my mother. The thought "I can actually do more than field work" began to make my dreams seem like possibilities. I began to believe I could be something more. The month of my sixteenth birthday, Mrs. Mercer recommended me for a cashier's job in the local supermarket. I worked there for six weeks, and on

Friday, January 16, 1981, I was promoted to head cashier. I was on top of the world! I could not believe such good things were happening to me. I had a good job, and I was on my way to becoming my school's first Spanish-speaking graduate. I thought nothing could go wrong, ever again.

17    But that very night, my dreams were shattered again—this time, I thought, permanently. The manager let me off at nine, two hours early. I didn't have a ride because my brother was not picking me up until 11:00 p.m. But I was in luck! I saw a man I knew, a friend of my brother's, someone I had worked with in the fields. He was a trusted family friend, so when he offered me a lift, I said, "Of course." Now I could go home and tell everybody about the promotion.

18    I never made it home or to my big promotion. The car doors were locked; I could not escape. I was abducted° and raped, and I found myself walking down the same abusive road as my mother. My dreams were crushed. I had failed. In my old-fashioned Mexican world, I was a "married woman," even if I wasn't. To go home again would have been to dishonor my family. When I found I was pregnant, there seemed to be only one path open to me. I married my abductor, dropped out of tenth grade, and moved with him to Oklahoma.

19    "My father was right," I thought. "I am a failure." But dreams die hard. My brother Joel was living in the same Oklahoma town as I was. He would see me around town, my face and body bruised from my husband's beatings. But unlike the workers in the fields who

had silently watched our father's abuse, Joel spoke up. "You've got to go," he would urge me. "You don't have to take this. Go on, you can make it."

20    "No!" I would tell him. I was embarrassed to have anyone know what my life had become. I imagined returning to my mother, only to have her reprimand me, saying, "What's the matter with you that you can't even stay married?"

21    But Joel wouldn't give up. Finally he told me, "I don't care what you say. I am going to tell Mother what is going on."

22    And he did. He explained to our mother that I had been forced to go with that man, that I was being abused, and that I was coming home. She accepted what he told her. I took my little girl and the clothes I could carry, threw everything into my car, and left Oklahoma for Florida. My husband taunted° me just as my father had my mother: "You'll be on food stamps! You can't amount to anything on your own!" But I proved him wrong. I worked days in the fields and nights as a cashier, getting off work at midnight and up early the next day to work again. I don't know how I did it, but I kept up the payments on my little car, I didn't go on food stamps, and I was happy.

23    But as Antonietta grew up and started school, I began to think my little triumphs were not enough. I was thrilled to see her learning to read, doing well in school. And when she would bring me her simple little books and trustingly say, "Read with me!" it filled me with joy. But I realized the day would come, and come soon, that I would be unable to read Antonietta's books. What would she think of me when I said, "I can't"? What would I think of myself?

24    Teaching myself to read became the most important goal in my life. I began with Antonietta's kindergarten books. I thought sometimes how people would laugh if they saw me, a grown woman, a mother, struggling through *The Cat in the Hat*. But with no one to watch me, I didn't care. Alone in my house, after my daughter was asleep, I read. I read everything we had in the house—Antonietta's books, cereal boxes, advertisements that came in the mail. I forced myself through them, stumbling again and again over unfamiliar words. Eventually I began to feel ready to try a real story, a grown-up story. But my fears nearly stopped me again. We lived near a library. Antonietta had asked again and again to go there. Finally I said "all right." We walked in, but panic overwhelmed me. All those people, walking around so briskly°, knowing where to find the books they wanted and how to check them out! What was someone like me doing there? What if someone asked me what I wanted? Too intimidated to even try, I insisted that we leave. I told Antonietta to use the library at her school. I struggled on in private, eventually earning my GED°.

25    The years passed, and I married a wonderful man who loved me and my daughter. He was proud that I had some real education, and he knew that I wanted more. But I couldn't imagine that going on in school was possible.

26    Then, in 1987, I was working for the Redlands Christian Migrant

Association. They provided services for migrant children. One day, in the office, I spotted something that made my heart jump. It was a book called *Dark Harvest*. It was filled with stories about migrant workers. Although my reading skills had improved, I had still never read a book. But this one was about people like me. I began reading it, slowly at first, then with more and more interest. Some of the people in it had gone back for a GED, just as I had! Even more—some had gone on to college and earned a degree in education. Now they were teaching. When I read that book, I realized that my dream wasn't crazy.

27      My husband and I took the steps to become legally admitted residents of the United States. Then, my husband found out about a federal program that helps seasonal farm workers go to college. I applied and found I was eligible. When I took my diagnostic tests, my reading, English, and math levels turned out to be seventh-grade level. Not as bad as I thought! The recruiter asked if I would mind attending Adult Basic Education classes to raise my scores to the twelfth-grade level. Mind? I was thrilled! I loved to study, and in spite of a serious illness that kept me out of classes for weeks, my teacher thought I was ready to try the ABE exams early. Her encouragement gave my confidence a boost, and I found my scores had zoomed up to a 12.9 level.

28      Then, in the fall of 1994, I took the greatest step of my academic life. Proud and excited, I started classes at Edison Community College in Florida.

Of course, I was also terrified, trembling inside almost like that scared little girl who used to tiptoe up to the teacher's desk with her phony absence excuses. But I wasn't a scared little kid anymore. My self-confidence was growing, even if it was growing slowly.

29      I laugh when I look back at that day I fled in terror from the library. My family and I might as well live there now. We walk in with me saying, "Now, we have other things to do today. Just half an hour." Three hours later, it's the kids saying to me, "Mom, are you ready yet?" But it's so exciting, knowing that I can learn about anything I want just by picking up a book! I've read dozens of how-to books, many of them about gardening, which has become my passion. I can't put down motivational books, like Ben Carson's *Gifted Hands* and *Think Big*. I love Barbara Kingsolver's novels. One of them, *The Bean Trees*, was about a young woman from a very poor area in Kentucky whose only goal, at first, was to finish school without having a child. I could understand her. But my favorite author is Maya Angelou. Right now, I'm re-reading her book *I Know Why the Caged Bird Sings*. She writes so honestly about the tragedy and poverty she's lived with. She was raped when she was little, and she had a child when she was very young. And now she's a leader, a wonderful writer and poet. When I see her—she read a poem at President Clinton's inauguration—I am very moved. And I can't talk about my life now without mentioning Kenneth and Mary Jo Walker, the president of Edison Community College and his

wife. They offered me a job in their home, but so much more than that: they have become my friends, my guardian angels. I am constantly borrowing books from them, and they give me so much encouragement that I tell them, "You have more faith in me than I do myself."

30    Sometimes I have to pinch myself to believe that my life today is real. I have a hard-working husband and three children, all of whom I love very much. My son Korak is 11. Whatever he studies in school—the Aztecs, the rainforest, Mozart—he wants to find more books in the library about it, to learn more deeply. Jasmine, my little girl, is 7, and is reading through the *Little House on the Prairie* books. Like me, the children have worked in the fields, but there is little resemblance between their lives and mine as a child. They are in one school the whole year long. They work at their own pace, learning the value of work and of money—and they keep what they earn. Antonietta, who inspired me to begin reading, is 17 now. Although she's only a junior in high school, she's taking college calculus classes and planning to study pre-med in college, even though her teachers have encouraged her to become a journalist because of her skill in writing.

31    And guess what! My teachers compliment my writing too. When I enrolled in my developmental English class at Edison, my teacher, Johanna Seth, asked the class to write a narrative paragraph. A narrative, she explained, tells a story. As I thought about what story I could write, a picture of a scared little girl in a schoolroom popped into my head. I began writing:

32    *As I walk into the classroom, the teacher gazes at me with her piercing green eyes. I feel myself shrinking and burning up with guilt. I go straight to her desk and hand her the excuse slip. Just like all the other times, I say, "I was sick." I hate lying, but I have to. I don't want my parents to get in trouble.*

33    I finish my narrative about giving my phony excuses to my grade-school teachers and hand it in. I watch Mrs. Seth read it and, to my horror, she begins to cry. I know it must be because she is so disappointed, that what I have written is so far from what the assignment was meant to be that she doesn't know where to begin to correct it.

34    "Did you write this?" she asks me. Of course, she knows I wrote it, but she seems disbelieving. "You wrote this?" she asks again. Eventually I realize that she is not disappointed. Instead, she is telling me something incredible and wonderful. She is saying that my work is good, and that she is very happy with what I've given her. She is telling me that I can succeed here.

## An Update

35    And she was right. I graduated from Edison as a member of Phi Theta Kappa, the national academic honors society for junior colleges. I went on to Florida Gulf Coast University, where I earned my bachelor's degree in elementary education. I've had the pleasure of seeing my children make their successful ways in the world: Antonietta

is a lawyer; Korak is a college student, and Jasmine is serving in the military. Most wonderfully of all, I am a third-grade teacher. My students are Hispanic, and many of them are the children of migrant workers, like me. But unlike me, they do not sit in the back of the classroom, scared and ignored. Unlike me, they do not hear that they will never do more than travel the country picking crops. They are growing up knowing that, like their teacher, they can achieve much in life. It is my great joy that I can help teach them that.

## First Impressions

Freewrite for ten minutes on one of the following.

1. Did you enjoy reading this selection? Why or why not?

2. Have you ever known anyone who frequently moved from one town (or school) to another? What effects did all that moving have on the person?

3. Why do you think Maria didn't immediately leave her first husband when he began to beat her? If you were in Maria's situation, what would you have done?

## Vocabulary Check

_D_ 1. In the excerpt below, the word *options* means
   A. opinions.
   B. pleasures.
   C. gifts.
   D. choices.

   *If Maria's parents had little education, they would have few choices other than working in the fields.*

   "My parents worked all the time in the fields. Few other options were open to them because they had little education." (Paragraph 6)

___A___  2.  In the sentence below, the word *reprimand* means
   A. scold.
   B. ignore.               The mother is scolding her daughter when she says,
   C. compliment.           "What's the matter with you that you can't even . . ."
   D. support.

   "I imagined returning to my mother, only to have her reprimand me,
   saying, 'What's the matter with you that you can't even stay married?'"
   (Paragraph 20)

___C___  3.  In the excerpt below, the word *intimidated* means
   A. thoughtful.
   B. bored.                If she is overcome by panic, she must be fearful.
   C. fearful.
   D. critical.

   "We walked in, but panic overwhelmed me....What was someone like me
   doing there? What if someone asked me what I wanted? Too intimidated
   to even try, I insisted that we leave." (Paragraph 24)

## Reading Check

### Central Point and Main Ideas

The other       ___B___  1.  Which sentence best expresses the central point of the entire selection?
choices are all too       A. Maria's goal was to graduate from college and teach migrant children
narrow. Sentence             to achieve their dreams.
A does not include        B. With hard work and courage, Maria was able to overcome great
her difficulties and         difficulties and achieve her dream of a better life.
how she overcame          C. Some books are filled with inspirational stories that can help us all.
them. Sentences C         D. Maria shows that certain skills, including writing and mathematical
and D cover only             abilities, are necessary if we want to succeed in college.
paragraphs 26 and 27,
respectively.

___A___  2.  The topic sentence of paragraph 10 is its
   A. first sentence.
   B. second sentence.      The second, third, and last sentences give details
   C. third sentence.       of what was hard about Maria's life in those days.
   D. last sentence.

___B___ 3. Which sentence best expresses the main idea of paragraph 26?

Answers A, C, and D are too narrow. Answer A covers only sentence 1. Answer C covers only the minor detail in sentence 2. Answer D ignores the last sentence of the paragraph, which describes how the book affected her.

A. In 1987, Maria worked for the Redlands Christian Migrant Association.

B. The book *Dark Harvest* convinced Maria that her dream for a better education wasn't crazy.

C. The Redlands Christian Migrant Association provided services for migrant children.

D. The book *Dark Harvest* contained stories about migrant workers, including some who had gone on to college and became teachers.

## Supporting Details

___D___ 4. To see if Maria had been working in the fields, her teacher inspected her
   A. clothing.
   B. homework.
   C. shoes.
   D. hands.

See paragraph 2. Maria's "dirty fingernails and calluses" prove she's been working in the fields.

___C___ 5. Maria was encouraged to leave her abusive husband by her
   A. mother.
   B. daughter.
   C. brother.
   D. employer.

See paragraph 19.

## Inferences

___C___ 6. We can infer from paragraph 14 that

The father's stalking and yelling at Maria's mother is evidence for answer C. Answers A, B, and D are unsupported.

A. Maria's father should have been given another chance to live with his wife and children.

B. Maria's mother didn't care about her children.

C. Maria's father was angry that he no longer had control over his wife and children.

D. Maria's father spent several years in jail.

We can assume that by sharing her story, Maria wants to give other people in similar situations the courage to take control of their lives. Answer A is unsupported. Answer C is contradicted by paragraph 24. Answer D is contradicted by paragraph 34.

___B___ 7. We can conclude from the selection that

A. most migrant workers prefer working in the fields to other types of employment.

B. Maria hopes that her story will inspire others, just as the book *Dark Harvest* inspired her.

C. it was easy for Maria to teach herself to read.

D. Maria's teacher, Mrs. Seth, suspected that Maria had paid someone to write her narrative for her.

### The Writer's Craft

_B_    8. The author introduces her article by

See paragraphs 1–3.
Maria tells a story
about one of the
times she returned
after an absence.

  A. making general statements about the life of a migrant worker.
  B. telling a story about her experience in school.
  C. asking questions about creating better schools for migrant children.
  D. presenting an opposite idea: imagining herself as a teacher.

_D_    9. In paragraph 29, the author's tone is mainly

  A. humorous and playful.
  B. warm and nostalgic.
  C. detached and instructive.
  D. enthusiastic and appreciative.

Maria shows enthusiasm and appreciation
for reading and for the Walkers, who gave
her a job and befriended her as well.

_B_    10. What audience did Maria Cardenas seem to have in mind when she wrote this essay?

Just as Maria
encourages her own
students, she is
encouraging other
students to persevere,
as she did.

  A. Teachers of developmental English
  B. Students who are struggling to get an education
  C. College administrators
  D. Women who are locked in abusive relationships

## Discussion Questions

1. Maria's children worked in the fields, as their mother did when she was younger. In what ways were those children's lives different from Maria's life when she was a child working in the fields?

2. Why might it have been so important to Maria to learn to read after her daughter began school? What do you think she imagined might happen if she did *not* learn to read?

3. Why do you think Mrs. Seth cried upon reading Maria's narrative about giving phony excuses to her grade-school teacher? Why might Maria have thought that Mrs. Seth was disappointed with what she had written?

4. What do you think Maria means when she says she encourages migrant children to "stand on their own two feet"? What do you think *all* children must learn in order to "stand on their own two feet"?

## Paragraph Assignments

1. All through her adult life, Maria Cardenas made herself do things that were very scary or difficult for her. For example, she left an abusive husband, despite not knowing how she would cope on her own. She made herself learn to read. She forced herself to begin college. She did all these things because she believed the long-term benefits would outweigh the short-term difficulties.

   When have you made yourself do something difficult, even though it would have been easier not to? Maybe it was one of these:

   ● Apologizing for something you did wrong

   ● Starting a new class or job

   ● Moving to a new town

   ● Speaking up for yourself to someone who was treating you badly

   Write a paragraph about what you did and why. In it, answer these questions:

   ● What did I do that was difficult?

   ● Why did I find doing it so hard or frightening?

   ● Why did I think doing it would be worthwhile?

   ● How did I feel about myself after I'd done it?

   You might begin with a topic sentence similar to one of the following:

   ● One of the hardest things I've ever had to do was to transfer to a new school halfway through my freshman year.

   ● Apologizing to my sister for playing a cruel trick on her was a difficult moment for me.

2. Many people would describe Maria as courageous. She is courageous not because she goes out and performs dramatic, heroic acts, but because she has faced her fears and made brave choices, not easy ones.

   Think of someone you know whom you would consider courageous. Write a paragraph in which you describe this person and explain why you see him or her as brave. Include specific examples that demonstrate this person's courage.

Here is one student's response to the assignment:

I think of my aunt Lizette as a courageous person. She isn't some big hero who does anything that makes headlines, but in my opinion she shows courage every day. Lizette is 30 and has multiple sclerosis, or MS. She found out she had it when she was only 22. What MS does is that it gives her odd symptoms at unpredictable times. Sometimes she's in pain. Other times she feels uncontrollable itching, or tingling as if her arms or legs are asleep. No one can tell how fast Lizette's MS will progress, but she knows she could end up totally disabled. I think if I were in Lizette's situation I would be very angry and depressed. But Lizette just deals with her illness without making a big deal about it. She works and travels and goes out dancing and lives her life to the fullest. When she has a bad flare-up of symptoms, she is very matter-of-fact about it, not complaining or getting down. Lizette doesn't have a choice about having MS, but she chooses to deal with it in a very brave way.

## Essay Assignments

1. Like Maria, many people reach adulthood without having learned to read well. Unlike Maria, many of those people live the rest of their lives as non-readers. Learning to read as an adult is challenging for a number of reasons. Some of those reasons are as follows:

   - Easy-to-read material is often written for small children, and such material may seem boring or insulting to adults.

   - Adults are often ashamed of being poor readers, and they may fear they will be further humiliated if they seek help.

   - Adults often have work and family commitments that make attending classes difficult.

   Keeping those challenges in mind, write an essay in which you describe a plan for teaching adults in your community to read. You could begin with a thesis statement something like this: "For our adult-literacy program to succeed, it will have to deal with several challenges." Then go on to organize your essay by addressing a specific challenge in each paragraph and explaining how you would overcome it.

2. Maria feels a strong drive to help migrant children learn to speak English and to "stand on their own two feet." If you were offered the chance to help three different groups of people, who would those groups be? (You might choose, for example, to help politicians, world leaders, salespeople, teachers, students, waiters or waitresses, bosses, gamblers, smokers, drinkers, professional athletes, slow or fast drivers, motorcycle riders, TV or Internet addicts, gang members, teenage girls or boys, senior citizens, city dwellers, suburbanites . . .) Write an essay in which you explain which groups you would help and why, and describe what you would do in each case to help those involved. Your essay can be either humorous or serious.

---

## Check Your Performance    MIGRANT CHILD TO COLLEGE WOMAN

| Activity | Number Right | Points | Score |
|---|---|---|---|
| **Vocabulary Check** (3 items) | _____ | x  10  = | _____ |
| **Reading Check** | | | |
| Central Point and Main Ideas (3 items) | _____ | x  7  = | _____ |
| Supporting Details (2 items) | _____ | x  7  = | _____ |
| Inferences (2 items) | _____ | x  7  = | _____ |
| The Writer's Craft (3 items) | _____ | x  7  = | _____ |
| | | TOTAL SCORE  = | _____ % |

Enter your total score into the **Performance Chart: Fifteen Reading Selections** on the inside back cover.

# 15 Students in Shock

## John Kellmayer and Alina Wyden

## Preview

Going to college has always been a significant transition, filled with change and challenges. But today, those challenges can threaten a student's well-being as never before.

## Words to Watch

*aptitude* (5): natural ability
*anorexia* (8): an abnormal lack of appetite which can result in serious illness or death
*bulimia* (8): an abnormal craving for food that leads to heavy eating and then intentional vomiting

1   For several generations, young people have heard the same promise: If they worked hard and went to college, the American dream would be theirs. A college degree would be the ticket to a satisfying career, an income that would allow them to buy a home and raise a family, and eventually, a comfortable retirement. And for previous generations, that promise has generally been true.

2   But for today's young people, the rosy promise of college is too often replaced by anxiety, disappointment, and crushing debt. The result is that many of today's college students are suffering from a form of shock. Going to college has always had its ups and downs, but today the "downs" of the college experience are more numerous and difficult than ever before.

3   Lisa is a good example of a student in shock. She is an attractive, intelligent twenty-year-old junior at a state university. Having been a straight-A student in high school and a member of the basketball and softball teams there, she remembers her high school days with fondness. Lisa was popular then and had a steady boyfriend for the last two years of school.

4   Now, only three years later, Lisa is miserable. She has changed her major four times already and is forced to hold down two part-time jobs in order to pay her tuition. She suffers from sleeping and eating disorders and believes she has no close friends. Sometimes

451

she bursts out crying for no apparent reason. On more than one occasion, she has considered taking her own life.

5      Dan, too, suffers from student shock. He is nineteen and a freshman at a local community college. He began college as an accounting major, but hated that field. So he switched to computer programming, because he heard job prospects were good in that area. Unfortunately, he discovered that he had little aptitude° for programming and changed majors again, this time to psychology. He likes psychology but has heard horror stories about the difficulty of finding a job in that field without a graduate degree. Now he is considering switching majors again, but is panicking at the idea that he has already invested money in courses that won't count toward his eventual degree. To help pay for school, Dan works nights and weekends as a sales clerk at Walmart. He doesn't get along with his boss, but as so many of his friends can't find any job at all, he doesn't dare quit to look for another one. A few months ago, his longtime girlfriend broke up with him.

6      Not surprisingly, Dan has started to suffer from depression and migraine headaches. He believes that in spite of all his hard work, he just isn't getting anywhere. He can't remember ever being this unhappy. He has considered talking to somebody in the college counseling center. He rejected that idea, though, because he doesn't want people to think there's something wrong with him.

7      What is happening to Lisa and Dan is happening to more college students every year. Increasing numbers of young people are suffering from "student shock." The evidence is disturbing. A national annual survey of college freshmen reports that by 2012 the emotional health of incoming students was at its lowest point since the survey began in 1985. "The American Freshman: National Norms" reported that the percentage of students who rated their emotional health as "above average" had fallen to 52 percent.

8      This kind of emotional distress means that large numbers of students will experience depression intense enough to warrant professional help. At schools across the country, psychological counselors are booked months in advance. Stress-related problems such as anxiety, migraine headaches, insomnia, anorexia°, and bulimia° are epidemic on college campuses.

9      Suicide rates and self-inflicted injuries such as deliberate cutting among college students are higher now than at any other time in history. There are approximately 1,100 college suicides per year, making suicide the second most common cause of death among college students.

10      College health officials believe that these reported problems represent only the tip of the iceberg. They fear that most students, like Lisa and Dan, suffer in silence, convinced that "everyone else" is doing just fine.

11      But many college students *aren't* doing just fine, and there are three significant reasons why—reasons that, in many cases, are intertwined.

12    The first reason that today's college students are suffering more than students of earlier generations is a weakening family support structure. The transition from high school to college has always been difficult. But in the past, students typically had firm family support to help them get through it. Today, with divorce rates at a historical high and many parents experiencing their own psychological and financial difficulties, that solid familial support and guidance may not be available. And when students who do not find stability at home are bombarded with numerous new and stressful experiences, the results can be devastating.

13    Another problem college students face is the large and bewildering selection of majors available. Because of the magnitude and difficulty of choosing a major, and thereby prepare for a career, many students are wracked by indecision. Students often switch majors, many more than once. As a result, it is becoming commonplace to take five or six years to earn a bachelor's degree. Students who have changed majors are often depressed to realize the courses they have completed will not count towards the new major. They feel they have wasted not only time, but precious tuition dollars. Rather than accumulate more debt, many students drop out. Forty-three percent of all four-year college students start college but never complete it.

14    The related, and final, major cause of "student shock" is the ugly reality of today's economy. At the same time that a college degree is considered the minimum qualification for most American jobs, today's college graduates are facing a job market that is the worst since World War II. The current U.S. unemployment rate is about 7.9 percent, but for 20- to 24-year-olds, it is closer to 14 percent. Just as alarming, only half of recent college graduates who *are* working are in jobs that require a college degree. Most are waiting tables, foaming lattes, and doing other low-wage work. There are 80,000 bartenders in America with bachelor's degrees.

15    Even while college degrees are worth less in the job market, their price is skyrocketing. In the last thirty years, the cost of tuition and fees has tripled for all colleges—public, private, and community. At the same time, student financial aid has been slashed to the bone. Students are graduating with more debt than ever before—an average of $25,000. Without a well-paying job to move into, and in many cases without health insurance, many new graduates will carry that ever-increasing debt with them for decades, making it difficult for them to move ahead with plans to marry, buy a house or a car, or make other traditional inroads into adult life.

16    It's not a pretty picture. And while there is no magic cure-all, students can—and should—take steps to insure against falling into student shock. If you are a college student, or soon to be one, here is some serious advice:

17    First, you should never hesitate to make use of any helpful services offered by your college. You are paying for those services, and you deserve them. Just a few sessions of psychological

counseling can be tremendously helpful when you're feeling depressed, panicky, or paralyzed with indecision. Campus stress-management workshops may be available; and these, too, can be helpful and also make it clear that you're not the only one to experience college stress.

18    But more importantly, students today, more than at any time previously, must take a coldly realistic look at their plans for college and a career. When you are considering a college and a major, you must realize that you are making what amounts to a business decision that will significantly impact your life for years to come. It is essential to shop around for the school that will offer the best possible combination of affordability and the courses that you want. It is imperative that as you choose a major, you research the job possibilities in that field and how you can best position

yourself to land one of those jobs. You can do that by going to your school's vocational counseling office to ask what fields are expected to be hiring in the near future; by interviewing people in the line of work you are considering; and by looking at the "Fastest Growing" occupations in the online *Occupational Outlook Handbook*, a publication of the Bureau of Labor Statistics that provides information about hiring trends for hundreds of careers (**http://www.bls.gov/ooh/**).

It's a tough time to be a college    19 student or new graduate. But "student shock" does not have to defeat you. If you go into college with a realistic perspective about why you are there and what you want to get out of your degree, you will lessen any "shocks" that might lie ahead.

## First Impressions

Freewrite for ten minutes on one of the following.

1. Did you enjoy reading this selection? Why or why not?

2. Do you agree that this is a particularly difficult time for college students? Why or why not?

3. Have you decided what you will major in in college? How did you arrive at that decision?

## Vocabulary Check

___B___  1. In the sentence below, the word *prospects* means
- A. failures.
- B. possibilities.
- C. candidates.
- D. limitations.

> If he switched into the field, it must have been because of the possibilities of getting a good job.

"So he switched to computer programming because he heard the job prospects were good in that area." (Paragraph 5)

___D___  2. In the excerpt below, the word *warrant* means
- A. fight.
- B. have no need for.
- C. get degrees in.
- D. justify.

> If the depressions are intense, they would justify seeking professional help.

"This kind of emotional distress means that large numbers of students will experience depression intense enough to warrant professional help. At schools across the country, psychological counselors are booked months in advance." (Paragraph 8)

___A___  3. In the excerpt below, the word *imperative* means
- A. extremely important.
- B. unusual.
- C. easy to explain.
- D. highly probable.

> Synonym clue: *essential.*

"It is essential to shop around for the school that will offer the best possible combination of affordability and the courses you want. It is imperative that as you choose a major, you research the job possibilities in that field and how you can best position yourself to land one of those jobs." (Paragraph 18)

## Reading Check

### Central Point and Main Ideas

___B___  1. Which sentence best expresses the central point of the selection?
- A. Going to college is a depressing experience for many students.
- B. To lessen student shock, students need to be realistic about why they are in college and what they can get out of their degree.
- C. Lisa and Dan have experienced too much stress at school to enjoy college life.
- D. Unlike previous generations, today's college graduates are not assured an income that will allow them to live the American Dream.

Answer A ignores paragraphs 16–18. Answer C covers only paragraphs 3–6. Answer D covers only paragraphs 1–2 and 14.

_A_ 2. At times, a main idea may cover more than one paragraph. The main idea of paragraphs 3 and 4 is stated in the

Answers B, C, and D
are supporting details
showing that Lisa is
in shock.

A. first sentence of paragraph 3.
B. second sentence of paragraph 3.
C. first sentence of paragraph 4.
D. last sentence of paragraph 4.

_A_ 3. The main idea of paragraph 14 is stated in the
A. first sentence.
B. second sentence.
C. third sentence.
D. last sentence.

Answer B is a major detail supporting the main idea. Answers C and D are minor details.

## Supporting Details

_B_ 4. According to the authors, students are graduating with more debt than ever before because
A. lenders have made it too easy for students to obtain credit cards.
B. college costs have risen steeply while financial aid has been slashed.
C. most students no longer work while they attend college.
D. parents can no longer afford to contribute to the cost of their children's education.

See paragraph 15.

## Inferences

_B_ 5. We can infer from paragraphs 5 and 6 that
A. it was a mistake for Dan to have switched from computer programming to psychology.
B. Dan should visit the college counseling center.
C. Dan needs to work harder to achieve his goals.
D. Dan's girlfriend broke up with him because he is depressed.

_C_ 6. We can conclude from paragraph 14 that
A. becoming a bartender requires a bachelor's degree.
B. it is possible to earn a good living without graduating from college.
C. these days, it is very difficult for college graduates to break into the job market.
D. half of all recent college graduates will never get a job that requires a college degree.

**Item 5:** Dan has real problems: his choice of major, his job, and his personal life. Counseling, as indicated in paragraph 17, would help him cope.

**Item 6:** Paragraph 14 presents "the ugly reality of today's economy," which is the reason that today's college graduates have such trouble getting their first job. Answer A is untrue. Answer B is not discussed in the paragraph. Answer D is unsupported.

## The Writer's Craft

_C_ 7. Which method of introduction do the authors use in this selection?
- A. Telling a brief story
- B. Asking one or more questions
- C. Shifting to the opposite
- D. Going from the broad to the narrow

*Paragraph 1 describes the "rosy" future that college students in the past could expect—an outcome no longer possible in today's world.*

_C_ 8. In paragraphs 11–14, the authors mainly

*List words: three significant reasons. Paragraphs 12, 13, and 14 each explain one of the reasons.*

- A. contrast today's college students with college students of earlier generations.
- B. describe the process of switching college majors.
- C. list reasons why so many of today's college students are suffering from student shock.
- D. illustrate how the majority of students go about paying for their college education.

_D_ 9. The main purpose of this article, as suggested in the closing paragraphs, is to

*Expressions in paragraphs 16–18 such as "students can—and should— take steps," "students must take a coldly realistic look," "you must realize," and "it is essential" indicate the article's persuasive purpose.*

- A. inform people of the existence of the phenomenon called "student shock."
- B. inform readers that a college education is no longer a ticket to a rosy future.
- C. entertain readers with dramatic stories of how college students struggle to overcome anxiety and depression.
- D. persuade students to be coldly realistic about their plans for college and a career.

_D_ 10. The authors' tone as they describe problems facing college students and the current job market for college graduates is
- A. matter-of-fact.
- B. scornful.
- C. distressed.
- D. concerned.

*See, especially, paragraphs 16–18. By detailing two cases of student shock and by then urging students to use mental-health services and be "coldly realistic" about their plans, the authors reveal their concern.*

## Discussion Questions

1. Dan, one of the students described in this selection, was reluctant to use the college counseling services because he didn't want people to think there was something wrong with him. Is it your experience that people see talking to a counselor as a weird, negative thing? Or are people open to seeking a counselor's help?

2. Do you think most people enter college with a realistic idea of what they want to accomplish there? Explain your answer.

3. Do you have a clear idea of what career you want for yourself? If you're not yet sure, how do you imagine you will eventually make that decision? If you do have a clear idea, what steps are you taking to make yourself an attractive job candidate?

4. Do you know how much money you will have to borrow in order to go to college? Do you know when you will have to begin repaying that money? How might you become better informed about those questions?

## Paragraph Assignments

1. What is your biggest concern about attending college? Is it about the money? Making friends? Choosing a major? Doing well in your courses? Write a paragraph explaining your biggest concern, why it worries you, and how you are trying to deal with it.

   Here is one student's response to this assignment:

   > The biggest concern I have about attending college is definitely how I can balance my time. Going to classes and keeping up with assignments is hard enough, but I have several other significant demands in my life. I work 20 hours a week as an order picker at a local warehouse. I need the money badly, and when I can get extra hours, I have to grab them. Furthermore, I have a three-year-old son to take care of. Fortunately, we live with my parents, who are both more than willing to watch Jayden when I'm at school or work, but when I'm home, he is definitely my responsibility. Trying to study and work on papers with a very active toddler around is not easy. I'm determined to get my degree, but trying to find ways to fit in school, work, and parenthood often worries me. Giving up sleep and a social life is the only way I'm able to make it all work.

2. How can a person still in high school benefit from the information presented in this selection? Write a one-paragraph letter to a class of high-school seniors. In it, give them advice on how to best prepare themselves for further schooling and a career.

# Essay Assignments

1. The authors cite three areas that are big sources of stress for students today: lack of family support, the number of majors available, and problems connected to today's economy. Write an essay in which you explain how each of those areas has or has not been a source of stress for you as you attempt to complete your education.

2. According to the authors of "Students in Shock," 43 percent of all four-year college students start college but never complete it. Review the reasons that students don't graduate, as indicated in the selection. Then write an essay in which you identify and discuss three steps that can be taken to increase the number of college students who complete college. Your thesis, for example, might look like the following:

   ● The percentage of college students who graduate from college would increase if we _____, _____, and _____.

   Explain why each of these steps would make it easier for students to graduate. (Note: You may wish to research this topic on the Internet by Googling "increase college completion rates" or "increase college graduation rates.")

---

## Check Your Performance                    STUDENTS IN SHOCK

| Activity | Number Right | Points | Score |
|---|---|---|---|
| **Vocabulary Check** (3 items) | _____ | x  10  = | _____ |
| **Reading Check** | | | |
| Central Point and Main Ideas (3 items) | _____ | x  7  = | _____ |
| Supporting Details (1 item) | _____ | x  7  = | _____ |
| Inferences (2 items) | _____ | x  7  = | _____ |
| The Writer's Craft (4 items) | _____ | x  7  = | _____ |
| | | TOTAL SCORE  = | _____ % |

Enter your total score into the **Performance Chart: Fifteen Reading Selections** on the inside back cover.

# Limited Answer Key

*An important note:* To strengthen your reading skills, you must do more than simply find out which of your answers are right and which are wrong. You also need to figure out (with the help of this book, the teacher, or other students) *why* you missed the questions you did. By using each of your wrong answers as a learning opportunity, you will strengthen your understanding of the skills. You will also prepare yourself for the mastery tests in Part One and the vocabulary and reading comprehension questions in Part Two, for which answers are not given here.

## Answers to the Practices in Part One

### 1 Vocabulary Development for Reading and Writing

#### Practice 1: Examples

1. Examples: *numerous paper cups, ticket stubs, sandwich wrappings, cigarette butts;* C
2. Examples: *white bread, rice, mashed potatoes;* C
3. Examples: *New York, Boston, Philadelphia;* B
4. Examples: *extra calcium, large doses of vitamin C;* A
5. Examples: *backing his car into the side of his boss's Cadillac, trying to walk through a glass door;* B
6. Examples: *the death of a child, the death of a spouse;* B
7. Examples: *buying or selling a product;* C
8. Examples: *baptisms, church weddings, funeral services;* B
9. Examples: *"adware," "clickthrough rate," "spambot";* A
10. Examples: *car dealerships, department stores, frozen-yogurt stands, online drugstores;* B

#### Practice 2: Synonyms

1. self-important
2. powerful
3. cloudy
4. secret
5. believable
6. discussion
7. force
8. rich
9. prove
10. variety

#### Practice 3: Antonyms

1. Antonym: *in-depth;* A
2. Antonym: *temporary;* A
3. Antonym: *allowed;* C
4. Antonym: *old;* A
5. Antonym: *order;* B
6. Antonym: *planned;* B
7. Antonym: *expert;* C
8. Antonym: *making progress;* C
9. Antonym: *concerned;* C
10. Antonym: *carefully thought-out;* B

#### Practice 4: General Sense

1. C
2. A
3. A
4. C
5. A
6. B
7. C
8. B
9. A
10. C

# 2 Main Ideas in Reading

## Practice 1

| | | | |
|---|---|---|---|
| 1. | S<br>S<br>G<br>S | 6. | S<br>S<br>S<br>G |
| 2. | S<br>S<br>S<br>G | 7. | S<br>G<br>S<br>S |
| 3. | S<br>G<br>S<br>S | 8. | G<br>S<br>S<br>S |
| 4. | G<br>S<br>S<br>S | 9. | S<br>S<br>G<br>S |
| 5. | S<br>S<br>S<br>G | 10. | S<br>S<br>S<br>G |

## Practice 2

*Answers will vary. Here are some possibilities:*

1. milk, coffee
2. football, basketball
3. father, nephew
4. tuna, egg salad
5. newspaper, magazine
6. shrimp, crabmeat
7. angry, pleading
8. selfishness, dishonesty
9. loyalty, honesty
10. "Hi there," "Good morning"

## Practice 3

| | | | |
|---|---|---|---|
| 1. | S<br>S<br>P<br>S | 3. | S<br>S<br>S<br>P |
| 2. | S<br>S<br>S<br>P | 4. | P<br>S<br>S<br>S |

## Practice 4

| | | | |
|---|---|---|---|
| 1. | S<br>S<br>S<br>P | 3. | S<br>P<br>S<br>S |
| 2. | S<br>S<br>P<br>S | 4. | P<br>S<br>S<br>S |

## Practice 5

| Group 2 | Group 4 |
|---|---|
| A. SD | A. SD |
| B. MI | B. SD |
| C. T | C. MI |
| D. SD | D. T |

**Group 3**
A. MI
B. T
C. SD
D. SD

## Practice 6

**Paragraph 1**
1. *Topic:* B
2. *Main idea:* Sentence 1

**Paragraph 2**
1. *Topic:* A
2. *Main idea:* Sentence 1

**Paragraph 3**
1. *Topic:* C
2. *Main idea:* Sentence 1

**Paragraph 4**
1. *Topic:* A
2. *Main idea:* Sentence 2

## Practice 7

1. a number of advantages
2. several ways
3. three major inventions
4. A series of mistakes
5. two important steps
6. some alarming facts
7. First of all
8. In addition
9. Also
10. Finally

# 3   Supporting Details in Reading

## Practice 1 *(Wording of answers may vary.)*

### Passage 1

1. Serious money problems
   a. Checks that bounce
   b. Minimal monthly payment on credit card cannot be made
2. Distinct mood pattern
   a. Tension before shopping
3. Shoplifting
4. Other addictive behaviors

*Words that introduce a list:* signs of addiction to shopping

*Words that introduce:*
   *First major detail:* One
   *Second major detail:* second
   *Third major detail:* Another
   *Fourth major detail:* Last of all

### Passage 2

1. Cheaper
   b. Another $30 for drinks and snacks
2. More comfortable
   a. No bumper-to-bumper traffic
3. More informative
   a. Close-ups and instant replays
   b. Detailed explanations by commentators

*Words that introduce a list:* several advantages

*Words that introduce:*
   *First major detail:* One
   *Second major detail:* Moreover
   *Third major detail:* Finally

## Practice 2 *(Wording of answers may vary.)*

### Passage 1

Be specific.      Stick to the present.
Don't use insults.   Complain privately.

*Words that introduce a list:*
   several sensible guidelines

*Words that introduce:*
   *First major detail:* First
   *Second major detail:* Second
   *Third major detail:* In addition
   *Fourth major detail:* last

### Passage 2

Chest discomfort
Pain or discomfort in upper body
Shortness of breath
Lightheadedness, nausea, or cold sweat

*Words that introduce a list:*
   various signs

*Words that introduce:*
   *First major detail:* For one thing
   *Second major detail:* Next
   *Third major detail:* Also
   *Fourth major detail:* Finally

# 4   Main Ideas and Supporting Details in Writing

## Practice 1 *(Wording of answers may vary.)*

1. *Point:* Being a celebrity is often difficult.
   *Supporting details:*
   1. Celebrities have to look almost perfect all the time.
   2. Celebrities sacrifice their private lives.
   3. Celebrities are in constant danger of the wrong kind of attention.

2. *Point:* People lie for different reasons.
   *Supporting details:*
   1. To avoid hurting someone's feelings
   2. To avoid a fight
   3. To fit in
   4. To avoid spending more time with someone

3. *Point:* There are several positive ways to encourage your family to exercise more often.
   *Supporting details:*
   1. Emphasize how good they'll feel and look if they work out regularly.
   2. Set an example.
   3. Make exercise a family activity.

4. *Point:* Serious depression has definite warning signs.
   *Supporting details:*
   1. A change in sleep patterns
   2. Abnormal eating patterns
   3. Trouble in thinking or concentrating
   4. A general feeling of hopelessness

5. *Point:* Several factors can interfere with having a good memory.
*Supporting details:*
1. Lack of motivation
2. Lack of practice
3. Self-doubt
4. Distraction

## Practice 2

*Answers will vary.*

## Practice 3

| | |
|---|---|
| 1. A, C, E | 6. A, C, E |
| 2. B, C, D | 7. A, D, F |
| 3. B, D, E | 8. A, D, E |
| 4. B, C, D | 9. A, B, D |
| 5. A, B, E | 10. B, D, F |

## Practice 4

| | |
|---|---|
| 1. C | 6. C |
| 2. A | 7. C |
| 3. A | 8. A |
| 4. B | 9. A |
| 5. C | 10. B |

## Practice 5

| | |
|---|---|
| 1. B | 6. B |
| 2. A | 7. A |
| 3. B | 8. B |
| 4. B | 9. B |
| 5. B | 10. A |

# 5    Understanding the Writing Process

*There are no correct answers to the practice exercises in this chapter.*

# 6    Relationships in Reading

## Practice 1

1. B  Another
2. A  also
3. D  In addition
4. C  For one thing
5. E  second

## Practice 2  *(Answers may vary.)*

1. A  After
2. E  When
3. D  Then
4. B  Before
5. C  during

## Practice 3  *(Wording of answers may vary.)*

**A. Main idea:** Research has revealed three different types of kindness.
1. Natural
2. Rule-guided
3. Imitative

**B. Main idea:** Opossums cope with danger by using a few defense methods.

| | |
|---|---|
| Play | Scare off |
| dead | enemies |

## Practice 4  *(Wording of answers may vary.)*

**Main idea:** All of us have certain fears at different points in our lives.
1. Young children worry about something bad happening to their parents.
2. Teenagers fear social rejection.
3. Parents fear that their children will be harmed.
4. Elderly people are afraid of poor health and death.

## Practice 5  *(Wording of answers may vary.)*

**Main idea:** To study a textbook effectively, follow a few helpful steps.
Read and mark the selection.
Write study notes.
Study the notes.

## Practice 6

| | |
|---|---|
| 1. B | 6. B |
| 2. A | 7. A |
| 3. A | 8. B |
| 4. B | 9. A |
| 5. A | 10. B |

# 7 Relationships in Writing

*There are no correct answers to the practice exercises in this chapter.*

# 8 More Relationships in Reading

## Practice 1 *(Answers may vary.)*

1. For example
2. Once
3. such as
4. For instance
5. example

## Practice 2

A. Term being defined: *stimulant*;
   *Definition*—3; *Example 1*—4;
   *Example 2*—5

B. Term being defined: *jargon;*
   *Definition*—1; *Example 1*—3;
   *Example 2*—4

## Practice 3 *(Answers may vary.)*

1. just as
2. Similarly
3. as
4. similar
5. just like

## Practice 4 *(Answers may vary.)*

1. but
2. Although
3. on the other hand
4. Despite
5. however

## Practice 5 *(Wording of answers may vary.)*

A. Comparison: Abraham Lincoln and John
   F. Kennedy
B. Contrast: High school and College

## Practice 6 *(Answers may vary.)*

1. Because
2. Therefore
3. resulted in
4. As a result
5. reason

## Practice 7 *(Wording of answers may vary.)*

A. *Main idea (the effect):* Two reasons
   explain weight gain among the Japanese.
   *Cause 1:* Less active lifestyles
   *Cause 2:* High-fat diet

B. *Main idea (the cause):* Increases in the
   numbers of elderly people will have a
   major impact in Europe, Canada, and the
   United States.
   *Major supporting details (the effects):*
   1. Fewer people available to fill jobs
   2. Bigger demand on pension systems
   3. Great strain on national medical
      services

## Practice 8

| | |
|---|---|
| 1. B | 6. A |
| 2. A | 7. C |
| 3. C | 8. B |
| 4. B | 9. A |
| 5. C | 10. C |

# 9 More Relationships in Writing

*There are no correct answers to the practice exercises in this chapter.*

# 10 Inferences in Reading and Writing

## Practice 1

A. 1. C
   2. A
   3. B

B. 4. B
   5. C
   6. C

## Practice 2

A. 2, 3
B. 2, 4

## Practice 3

A. 1
B. 3, 5
C. 3, 4

## Practice 4

1. C; simile
2. B; simile
3. A; metaphor
4. C; simile
5. B; metaphor

## Practice 5

1. B
2. C
3. B
4. A
5. C

# 11 Longer Selections in Reading and Writing

## Practice

2

# Acknowledgments

Berry, Grant. "A Change of Attitude." Reprinted by permission.

Black, Roxanne. "A Door Swings Open." Originally published as "In the Beginning." From *Unexpected Blessings* by Roxanne Black, copyright © 2008 by Roxanne Black. Used by permission of Avery Publishing, an imprint of Penguin Group (USA) Inc.

Cardenas, Maria. "Migrant Child to College Woman." Reprinted by permission.

Conroy, Theresa, and Christine M. Johnson. "A Drunken Ride, A Tragic Aftermath." Originally published in *The Philadelphia Inquirer*. Reprinted by permission of the authors.

Davidson, Anne. "Taming the Anger Monster." Reprinted by permission.

Davies, Alice M. "'Extra Large, Please.'" Used with the permission of Alice M. Davies.

Gregory, Dick. "Shame," from *Nigger: An Autobiography*. Copyright © 1964 by Dick Gregory Enterprises, Inc. Used by permission of Dutton, a division of Penguin Putnam Inc.

Hamill, Pete. "The Yellow Ribbon." Copyright by Pete Hamill. Used by permission. All rights reserved.

Hansen, Sara. "All Washed Up?" Reprinted by permission of the author.

Hill, Miriam. "Abusive Relationships among the Young." Reprinted by permission of the author.

Hughes, Langston. "Early Autumn." From *Short Stories* by Langston Hughes. Copyright © 1996 by Ramona Bass and Arnold Rampersad. Reprinted by permission of Hill and Wang, a division of Farrar, Straus, and Giroux, LLC.

Kellmayer, John, and Alina Wyden. "Students in Shock." Reprinted by permission.

Logan, Paul. "Rowing the Bus." Reprinted by permission.

Mack, Marilyn. "Adult Children at Home." Reprinted by permission.

Mrosla, Sister Helen P. "All the Good Things." Originally published in *Proteus*, Spring 1991. Reprinted by permission as edited and published by *Reader's Digest*.

# Index